REDEMPTION REDEEMED:

A Puritan Defense of Unlimited Atonement

Expanded Edition

BY JOHN GOODWIN, M.A.
Fellow of Queens College, Cambridge

Edited by John D. Wagner

Wipf & Stock
PUBLISHERS
Eugene, Oregon

Redemption Redeemed:
A Puritan Defense of Unlimited Atonement
Expanded Edition
by John Goodwin
Edited by John D. Wagner
Copyright © 2001, 2004 by John D. Wagner
ISBN: 1-59244-730-9
Wipf and Stock Publishers
199 West 8th Ave, Suite 3
Eugene, Oregon 97401
www.wipfandstock.com
Previously published by:
The Wesleyan Office, London, 1846.
Thomas Tegg, London, 1840.
John Macock, London, 1651.

FOREWORD

John Goodwin (1593-1665), the eminent English pastor and Puritan divine, was a man ahead of his time.

Educated at Cambridge University, he was raised and indoctrinated in Calvinistic absolute predestination, the dominant Christian perspective of his day. In the 1640s he began preparing for a series of lectures to refute the doctrines of Arminianism, and entered a thorough investigation of the controversy and its many aspects. The ultimate result was his rejection of Calvinism and adoption of Arminian theology.

He completed *Redemption Redeemed* in 1650 and published it the following year. The original version was a multi-issue polemic against Calvinism. This edition, replacing a shorter 2001 version, offers the fuller text of the chapters devoted to a comprehensive refutation of the limited atonement doctrine. Goodwin's writing remains to this day a superb and eloquent defense of the Biblical position of unlimited atonement that Jesus Christ "by the grace of God tasted death for every man." Considering the heavy writing style so typical of Puritans, I have included some moderate editing to enhance clarity and readability, correct typographical errors in some scriptural references, and translate Greek words into the English-alphabet equivalent.

Goodwin represented an Arminian strand of Puritanism and was a major figure in the decline of Calvinist influence in England. In the contemporary period as Christians enter the 21st Century and Calvinism with its disturbing implications is making a resurgence, Goodwin's master work is a welcome and much needed contribution to those seeking to understand the truths of God's word.

John D. Wagner
Editor

CONTENTS

CONTENTS

CHAPTER VI

CHAPTER VII

CHAPTER VIII

CHAPTER IX

INTRODUCTION

THE following work, which is humbly presented to the public, on the most important subject of the redemption of the world by Jesus Christ, was written, or rather completed, in the year 1650; and dedicated to the reverend Dr. BENJAMIN WHICHCOTE, Provost of King's College, and Vice-Chancellor of the University of Cambridge, together with the rest of the heads of colleges, and students in divinity, in that famous university. It is not my design to enter into any panegyrics, either on the author or his work; the work will speak for itself, and the public must be their own judges of its merit; truth, I believe, was the object he had in view, and this he prosecutes and supports by almost every possible argument.

He appears to have been well acquainted with the weak reasoning used by those of the contrary judgment to himself to support the doctrines of absolute and unconditional election and reprobation, and a limited atonement; and therefore he presents his arguments against those pernicious errors in a masterly manner. Well may those of the Calvinistic persuasion ridicule him and his work in the manner they have frequently done, because he hath so clearly exposed their errors, and made their babel to totter, and I expect no better treatment, for attempting to revive and spread his most valuable work. But let this be as it may, if I can be any ways useful to my fellow creatures, in enlarging their views of the redemption of Jesus Christ, and liberating them from that contractedness of mind which is inseparably connected with a belief of the Calvinistic decrees, my end will be answered.

It is a question that has been frequently proposed, If there be no such doctrine as absolute and unconditional *predestination* and *election*, why did *all* the ancient writers teach it? To this I answer; 1. I will venture to affirm that not one in a hundred of those who propose and insist on this question, ever read any, much less all the ancient writers. What they mean by ancient writers is, such as wrote before and after the synod of Dort. But those are rather late than ancient writers. 2. All, even of those writers, do not teach such a predestination and election as are contended for by the rigid Calvinists. 3. None of those that are justly entitled to the character of the ancient writers, and who lived in the three first centuries after our

Saviour's days, ever taught any such, as is sufficiently manifest in the quotations from them in the course of this work. St. Augustine indeed did teach it afterwards, and his followers; yet not without frequently contradicting themselves.

But then, it is further asked, How come the doctrines of absolute election, &c., and the limited extent of our Saviour's death is taught and so generally received in our own country? They were first introduced into the world by St. Augustine, Bishop of Hippo, in Africa, about 400 years after our Saviour's days. But they made their appearance in a very crude, indigested, and inconsistent form, and so continued for a number of years: till Calvin, who was contemporary with Luther, attempted to reduce them into a system and from hence it is, that the maintainers of these doctrines have obtained the name of Calvinists. But neither did Calvin himself give the system its finishing stroke: for it would be easy to produce quotations from his works, wherein he asserts both ways, viz. that Christ died for *all*, and that he only died for the *elect*. After this, in the year 1618, the synod of Dort gave a kind of finishing stroke to this system of Calvin, and brought it into the form we find it in most of the puritanical writers. Though indeed among these, there is hardly one, but who has here and there a sentence tending to establish the doctrine of an unlimited atonement, which they at other times, when they are guided by the synod's leading strings, condemn as error and heterodoxy.

But in reference to the prevalency of these doctrines in our own country, it must be observed, that in the reign of Queen Elizabeth there were two men of great note for their learning and parts in the University of Cambridge; the one Dr. Whitaker, who was Regius Professor of Divinity; and the other Peter Baro, a Lady Margaret Professor of Divinity there. Whitaker, who had married into a family much attached to the Geneva Masters, gave himself up to their opinions; and among other points, which chiefly rested in the authority of Calvin and Beza, he began to urge the opinion of absolute predestination, which entirely excludes the greatest part of mankind from the redemption of Christ and sufficient grace; and that according to the design of God and of Christ, he maintained that reprobation is not a negative, but a positive act in God, with respect to man considered in the mass not yet corrupted; and that by means of this decree, and the will of God, many men rush into eternal destruction.

Peter Baro being of the contrary judgment to Whitaker, the disputes between these two celebrated professors ran very high, and for a considerable time drew the youth of the University into two parties; Whitaker at length went to London, and going to Dr. Whitgift, Archbishop of Canterbury, informed him, that the University was disturbed with the Pelagian opinions, to remedy which, he desired that nine articles (afterwards known by the name of the Lambeth Articles) which he had drawn out, might be sent to Cambridge, with the approbation of some of the Bishops. These Articles were so artfully framed, that they might be approved of even by those who differed not a little from his opinion, and yet might afterwards be used by himself for the confirmation of it.

A convention of a few Bishops and other ministers was held in November, 1595, in which the articles received their approbation.

And Whitgift, although he approved not of Whitaker's opinions, yet through easiness of temper, and fear of discord, he submitted. These articles were transmitted to Cambridge. Whitaker boasts that he had gotten the victory. And meeting with the Chancellor of Cambridge, who was also one of the Queen's Privy Council, he acquainted him with what he had done, and showed him the articles. That great man, easily perceiving how dangerous it was to determine in points so much contested, heartily disapproved of all that was done, saying, that he would make the authors of this business repent of it. Accordingly he laid the matter before the Queen, informing her what had been decreed by a few divines about the most weighty questions, in which men of the greatest learning could never agree: adding that it was plain what those aimed at who had done this: for they thought and taught, that whatsoever was done in human affairs, whether it were good or bad, it was all *necessitated* by the ruling force of an *immutable decree:* and that this necessity was laid upon the very wills of men also, that they could not will otherwise than they did will. "Which things," says he, "if true, most sovereign Lady, in vain do I, and others of your Majesty's faithful servants, hold long councils about what is needful to be done in any affairs, and what may be of use to yourself and your kingdom, seeing that all consultation about things that necessarily come to pass, is downright folly."

The Queen was moved, and ordered Archbishop Whitgift to be sent for. He came, and the subject of the Lambeth Articles was brought forwards: the Queen's counselors being present, pressed very hard upon him by urging the illegality of the convention; and proceeding to the question concerning *fate*, "they determined, that this opinion was opposed to good morals and the commonwealth." The event was, that the Lambeth Articles were suppressed.

Whitaker died in a short time after the Lambeth convention, and was succeeded in the Regius professorship by Dr. John Overall, afterwards Bishop of Norwich, a man of most excellent learning. He taught in this manner, That sufficient grace is offered to every man; that Christ died for every man; that grace leads the way in everything that is good, and free will informed by grace follows after; that grace operates in such ways as cannot be explained, not however by determining to every particular act in a natural manner, and that justifying grace cannot consist with mortal sins before they are repented of.

After this King James I, having ascended to the throne, a conference was held at Hampton-Court, in 1603; and although King James did not think proper to establish absolute predestination at this time, according to the wish of Dr. Reynolds and his party, yet he did much towards it afterwards, by countenancing the proceedings of the synod of Dort, and causing the Bible to be newly translated, which translation, as well as the former, being made mostly by such as were staunch friends to the doctrine of Calvin, no wonder that many texts appear to favour it.

As we are come down to the time of the synod of Dort, I will here give my readers a brief account of that assembly. The universal doctrines were generally taught in the *Belgic* churches, before Arminius either wrote or spoke in their defense; and as Dr. Heylin has proved, were the national persuasion before Calvinism was heard of. However, in time, Calvinism spread, and just before the synod of Dort, the Calvinists persecuted the *Remonstrants*, as those were termed who held the general doctrines. The Remonstrants put themselves under the protection of one Barnevelt, a man of great power, in the council of state for the United Provinces; by whose means they obtained an edict from the states of Holland and of West Friezland in 1613, requiring and enjoining a mutual toleration of opinions.

But this indulgence, though very advantageous to the Remonstrants, cost them dearly in the end. For Barnevelt having some suspicion that Maurice of Nassau, Prince of Orange, Commander General of the forces of the United Provinces, had a design to make himself absolute master of those countries, made use of them for the encouraging of such patriots as durst appear in maintenance of the common liberty. This service they undertook rather because they found that the Prince had passionately espoused the quarrel with the Calvinists. From this time the breach was so widened that it could not be closed again, without either weakening the power of the

Prince, or the death of Barnevelt.

This last they easily accomplished, for he was put to death contrary to the fundamental laws of the country and the rules of the union. The Calvinists having gained their end, thought it a high point of wisdom to keep their adversaries under, and to effect that by a National Council, which they could not by their own authority. To this end, the States General being importuned by the Prince of Orange, a national synod was appointed, to be held at Dort, in 1618—To which the different churches sent their delegates, and some eminent divines were commissioned by King James to attend the synod for the Realm of Britain. A synod, says my author, is much like that of Trent, in the *motives* to it, as also in the *managing* and *conduct* of it. For as neither of them was assembled till the sword was drawn, the terror whereof was able to effect more than all other arguments; so neither of them was concerned to *confute*, but *condemn* their opponents.

Though most of the British Divines were brought over to subscribe the Calvinistical and tyrannical decrees of the synod, yet not all. Mr. John Hales did not: a man never mentioned without the epithet of the ever-memorable, on account of his very extensive learning and knowledge. He went into Holland, chaplain to Sir Dudley Carlton, ambassador to King James I, to the United Provinces, at the time of the synod of Dort: and became acquainted with the most secret deliberations of that synod. He was, says Bishop Pearson, who was long and intimately acquainted with him, a man of so great sharpness, quickness, and subtlety of wit, as ever this or perhaps any nation bred. His industry strove, if it were possible, to equal the largeness of his capacity, whereby be became as great a master of polite, various, and universal learning as ever yet conversed with books. He went to the synod of Dort a rigid Calvinist; but on hearing Episcopius's reasons against those doctrines, he from that time renounced John Calvin.

Dr. Goad was another of those Divines deputed by King James to go to the synod. He was, says my author, a person every way eminent in his time, having the repute of a great and general scholar, exact critic and historian, a poet, orator, schoolman and divine. He went to the synod in the room of Dr. Hall, who came back indisposed, where he acquitted himself with applause in defence of Calvin's doctrines. But the force of truth, and an impartial consideration of the reasons offered in its defence, at length prevailed with him to alter his judgment; and he then stood forth an advocate for the other side of the question. Dr. Womaek, bishop of St. David's, is said to have been convinced by the powerful reasoning of Arminius, and to come over to the Remonstrants.

But notwithstanding some few deserted the good old cause of rigid Calvinism, it was known to be too useful a state-engine to be given up by the managers of the synod. Accordingly by their decree it was established as orthodoxy. And had they stopped here, there had been no great harm done. But they decreed moreover that no one should he admitted to the ministry, nor suffered to preach, nor teach a school, that was not in their sense orthodox. Nay, to such a length did they proceed in some places, that they would not suffer a man to be a parish clerk or sexton, who was not approved of for his orthodoxy. But they did not stop here. They imprisoned, banished, confiscated the goods, and ruined all those worthy ministers, whose consciences would not suffer them to subscribe to the horrible decree. Thus we see the spirit of Calvinism, and how it came to he honoured with the name of orthodoxy, and to be so prevalent in this nation.

I shall say no more of the national mischiefs that have arisen in this land by means of Calvinism being pronounced orthodoxy; nor how great a hand the Jesuits had in the time of the civil war, in artfully and secretly pushing on predestination amid the Geneva customs, under a pretence of reforming the doctrine and discipline of the church, when their grand aim was to destroy both. But I have seen much of the mischief arising from it, with regard to particular persons. How many have been heard to curse and blaspheme the God of love, in a manner shocking to think of, on account of his supposed horrible decree? We have known other serious Christians, of a timorous disposition, walk for years together on the very brink of despair, always in fear lest they should not be of the number of the elect, and so finally perish. Others, who for many years were happy in God, and walked as became the gospel, who afterwards fell; and then rocking themselves in the cradle of perseverance, have vainly fancied that they never could fall so as to perish, and therefore have given themselves up to take their full swing of sin. Who can tell the mischief that these unscriptural doctrines leave done and are capable of doing in the world? In short, the doctrine of absolute election, like the Pharisees with their *key of knowledge*, hinders many from entering into the Kingdom of Heaven, who were entering in, as also many who were entering it turns out again. For who would strive to enter in at the strait gate, if they were fully persuaded that by virtue of an absolute and eternal decree, such and such persons should never be able to enter in and by virtue of such a decree, such and such other persons should be thrust in head and shoulders.

The mischievous consequences of such doctrine the Bishop of London was well aware of: for at the Hampton Court conference, when Dr. Reynolds and others of his party insisted on the Lambeth Articles being added to the thirty-nine articles of the Church of England, the good Bishop observed to King James I: "that very many in those days neglected holiness of life, presuming too much on persisting in grace; laying all their religion on predestination, saying, *if I shall be saved, I shall be saved*," which he termed a *desperate doctrine*, and showed it to be contrary to good divinity and the true doctrine of predestination. By such arguments the King was persuaded, and the Lambeth Articles were wisely and justly rejected.

It hath been frequently intimated that the extent of the death of Christ, which is the leading subject of this work, is of no great importance, and that we need not trouble our heads about it; namely, whether he died for *all*, or only for a *few*, provided we believe in him for ourselves I must confess that I have been in danger of falling into the same sentiment myself, and thereby in some measure eclipsing the glory of the blessed gospel of Jesus Christ. But the subject, if duly considered, will appear to be of greater importance than many are ready to imagine; and our author must have been deeply convinced of this, or he would not have taken so many pains to set it in a true point of light.

1. Its importance will appear, if we only consider it as a part of divine revelation. The great and blessed God, in compassion to our ignorance, hath been graciously pleased to favour us with a revelation of his mind and will, which bears the stamp of divinity in every part of it. There is nothing unimportant, or trifling in this book; every part of it undoubtedly ought to he carefully attended to, and firmly believed by us. In it we are particularly informed for whom the Son of God laid down his life. It contains a revelation of the mind of the Deity, so far as it was proper for him to make it known. It was given by the inspiration of God; designed in a peculiar manner for the information and instruction of men; and to treat it with any degree of slight or indifference, is in effect, so far, to slight and disregard that glorious Being who is the author of it.

2. The importance of the extent of our Saviour's death will farther appear, by considering how deeply mankind are interested in it. The whole human race is concerned in the death of the Lord Jesus Christ. It respects our everlasting felicity and happiness, in comparison of which, all time concerns of this present world, however important, are mere trifles. It is in a peculiar manner connected with our hope of glory, and the only way to

come to the enjoyment of it. For if there should be any among the sons of men for whom the Lord Jesus Christ did not die, these are unavoidably, and without any fault of their own, excluded from all possibility of happiness. For Christ is the only Redeemer; the only way to glory; and "there is not salvation in any other."

As all appear to be so deeply interested in the death of Christ, it ought to be remembered within all seriousness; and being a manifestation of the greatest love and regard for us, it therefore very justly demands suitable and grateful returns. Under this consideration, it should influence the temper and conduct of all mankind, wherever this transaction of divine love is known by a preached gospel. If Christ died for all, it ought in the plainest and most unequivocal language be made known to all who hear the gospel. All ought cordially to believe it, and earnestly to seek for the salvation which he has procured for them; and to love, praise, and serve him for it. All who do not thus gratefully remember such a wonderful instance of love, will be justly condemned.

On the other hand, if Jesus Christ did not die for all, it is evident that no one is under any obligation to pay this grateful regard for him, until he comes to know that Jesus Christ died for him in particular. It is in the very nature of things impossible, nor can it in justice be required, that any one should acknowledge favours which he never received; or make returns of love and obedience in the consideration of a fact which he does not know to have ever existed. That "Jesus Christ died for our sins" is the leading fact recorded in the gospel, 1 Cor. 15:3, and without the belief of this truth we cannot be real Christians. But if Jesus Christ died for all men, and this be recorded in the gospel, (which our author clearly proves) it evidently follows that all men which hear the gospel, ought to believe it with that faith which worketh by love, both to God and man; and all who do not thus believe, experience, and act, fall under righteous condemnation.

3. The extent of the death of Jesus Christ, will appear still of greater importance, when we consider that it will affect our views of the day of judgment, and the manner in which we shall be dealt with at the great day. If no evidence can he produced from scripture that Christ died for us, we cannot rationally suppose that we are in danger of being condemned because we have not believed in him, and loved him, and served him as our Saviour. But if we believe that Jesus died for all, and that those which are condemned, are condemned "because they have not believed in the name of the only begotten Son of God ;" it naturally follows that we may be

accepted through him at the great day, unless we neglect the great salvation he hath procured for us, in which case we cannot be accepted. When St. Paul says, "If any man love not the Lord Jesus Christ, let him be Anathema Maranatha," 1 Cor. 16:22, *let him be accursed when the Lord cometh*; he evidently teaches us that our love to Christ shall be brought into question. We are now called upon to love him, and are under the greatest obligation so to do, because of his great love to us. Thus it appears that the extent of our Saviour's death will affect the proceedings of the judgment day, and ought to affect us in the prospect of those proceedings.

4. As a further proof of the importance of the extent of the death of Christ, our views of it essentially affect the character of Almighty God. Now, if the blessed God, who was under no obligation to give his Son to die for any, did, of his own free and sovereign pleasure, give him to die for *all*; this was undeniably a more glorious and striking instance of love, than if he had only given him to die for a part of mankind. As the subject before us so materially affects the character of the blessed God, especially his darling attribute of love, we cannot but consider it of very considerable importance, and most worthy of our serious consideration. Let it be our business to follow the example of our much esteemed author, endeavouring to investigate this important subject, with a due deference and entire submission to what the scripture says of it.

The extent of our blessed Saviour's death, whether universal or limited, is a matter of pure revelation. We should never have known that God had pitied poor sinners, or that he had given his Son to die for any, had not the inspired volume informed us of it. It is the gospel of the blessed God, the good news sent from heaven to earth, by which we understand that the Lord Jesus did "his own self bear our sins in his own body on the tree." Neither could we have known the character nor number of those for whom the Redeemer laid down his life, but by the same precious gospel. We are therefore under the necessity of submitting, in the most implicit manner, to that testimony, as the only and the complete source of information on this subject. The gospel, on this much controverted subject, tells us that which could otherwise never have been known by mortals, at least in the present world. As this is the subject of pure revelation, concerning which we should otherwise be entirely ignorant, we may naturally expect the revelation of it is clear and express, calculated, if we attend with seriousness, to give us all the information which is necessary.

To suppose that such an important matter as the extent of our Saviour's death were left doubtful, or not clearly revealed in the scripture, would be a reflection on the perfection of divine revelation and the goodness of God. If Jesus Christ died for a part of mankind only, we may certainly very reasonably expect, from the goodness of God, and the perfection of revelation, to find this related in clear and express terms, as all other peculiar doctrines of the gospel are. On the other hand, if he died for all mankind, this is undoubtedly expressed in clear language, especially when the importance of the doctrine is duly considered. In this case we cannot suppose that we should be left to mere inference; much less could we expect to find expressions, when the subject is professedly treated of, which naturally convey ideas quite contrary to what the Holy Ghost intended to convey; this would reflect on the plainness and perspicuity of the word of God, and confound common sense. It would indeed be very unreasonable and absurd to expect any thing of this kind; and I hope, through the blessing of God, that the work before us will make it sufficiently appear to every unprejudiced mind, that we have the clearest instructions in the word of God on this very interesting subject. It is a matter of real gratitude, that we are not left to grope in the dark, or wander in the wild mazes of uncertainty, or to follow the fancies and opinions of men; but we have a most sure word of prophecy, to which we shall do well always to take heed, as to a light shining in a dark place. Therefore, my dear readers, let us never arrogantly and proudly set up our own opinions unsupported by the word of the Lord, as an article of faith; but ever implicitly submit in all matters of religion to what divine revelation teacheth.

Lest I should weary my readers with a tedious introduction, I would conclude, by observing, that our reverend author tells us in his original dedicatory epistle to this work, that the prize that he ran for was to make the best of every opportunity, to excite, provoke, and engage those whom he judged best qualified among his brethren to bless the world, labouring and harassing itself under its own vanity and folly; by bringing forth the glorious Creator, and ever blessed Redeemer, out of their pavilions of darkness into a clear and perfect light, to be beheld, reverenced, and adored in all their glory: to be possessed, enjoyed, and delighted in, in all their beauty and desirableness, by the inhabitants of the earth.

In this same epistle, after apologizing for its uncommon length, and the uneasiness on that account which he supposes it might give those to whom the work was dedicated; he concludes it in the following words: "I shall discharge you from any sufferings from my pen at present, only with my soul poured out before the great God and Father of lights in prayer for you, that he would make his face to shine upon you; quickening your apprehensions, enlarging your understandings, ballasting your judgments, and strengthening your memories; giving you ability of body and willingness of mind to labour in those rich mines of truth (the scriptures) breaking up before you the fountains of these great depths of spiritual light, and heavenly understanding; assisting you mightily by his Spirit in the course of your studies; lifting you up in the spirit of your minds above the faces, fears, and respects of men; drawing out your hearts and souls to relieve the spiritual necessities and extremities of the world around you; making you so many burning and shining lights in his house and temple, the joy, glory, and delight of your nation; vouchsafing to you as much of all that is desirable in the things of this world as your spiritual interests will bear, and the reward of prophets respectively in the glory and great things of the world to come." He subscribes himself their poor brother in Christ, always ready in love to serve the meanest of them. I am well aware, that though some will be pleased at the revival and spread of this work, others will be offended: yea, are already offended. One person I met with, expressed himself as being sorry for me, on having seen the advertisement, that I had not a better subject than to oppose the redemption of Christ. I appeal to the public; it is not the design of this work to oppose the redemption of Christ, but to establish it, and enlarge our views of its fulness, extent, and glory, in the ample provision that is made for all poor sinners. The spread of truth is the object I have in view; and may the great God of truth give his blessing to the feeble efforts of one of the weakest and most unworthy of his servants towards the accomplishing of this invaluable end, and to his name shall be all the glory for evermore, Amen.

The Rev. John Bates

CHAPTER I
Four several veins or correspondences of Scriptures propounded, holding forth the death of Christ for all men, without exception of any. The first of these argued.

THE premise considered, is one of the strangest and most troublesome sayings that, to my remembrance, I have ever met from the pen of a learned and considerate man. I find it in the writings of a late opposer of universal atonement. "I know," saith he, "no article of the gospel which this new and wicked religion of universal atonement doth not contradict." That which he called a "new and wicked religion," the doctrine of universal atonement, I shall, God assisting and granting life and health for the finishing of this present discourse, evince both from the main and clear current of the Scriptures themselves, as likewise by many impregnable and undeniable demonstrations and grounds of reason, to be a most ancient and divine truth. Yea, it is none other but the heart and soul, the spirit and life, the strength and substance, and very sum of the glorious gospel itself.

Yea, I shall make it appear from ancient records of best credit, and from the confessions of modern divines themselves, of best account, adversaries in the point, that universal atonement by Christ was a doctrine generally taught and held in the churches of Christ for three hundred years together after the apostles. And if I conceived it worth the undertaking, or were minded to turn the stream of my discourse that way, I question not but I could make it as clear as the sun shining in his might, that there is "no article of the gospel," as this man's dialect is, I mean, no great or weighty point of the Christian faith, that can stand with a rational consistency *unless* the doctrine of universal atonement be admitted for a truth.

Yea, upon a diligent and strict inquiry it will be found, that if any man holds such a limited redemption as is commonly taught and believed amongst us, and yet withal lives holily and like a Christian, he acts in full contradiction to such a principle, and happily denies that in practice which erroneously he holds in judgment. God, in such cases as these, makes grapes to grow on thorns, and figs on thistles: nor doth there want anything by sense and visibility of the disproportion between the cause and the effect, to make the lives and ways of such persons miraculous. Neither doth anything nor all things that I could ever yet meet with, either from the tongues or pens of the greatest patrons of particular redemption, deliver me from under much admiration, that conscientious and learned men, professing subjection of judgment to the Scriptures, should either deny universal or assert particular redemption; considering that the Scriptures, in particularly, plainness and expressness of words and phase, do more that ten times over deliver the former.

Whereas the latter is no where asserted by them, but only stands upon certain venturous consequences and deductions, which the weak judgments of men, so much accustomed to error and mistake, presume to levy from them; together with such arguments and grounds, which, upon examination, will be found either to have no consistency with the sound principles either of reason or religion, or else no legitimate coherence with the cause which they pretend unto.

Let us first hearken unto the Scriptures lifting up their voices together for the redemption of all men by Christ without exception. We shall afterwards, in due process of discourse, give a fair consideration to those inferences and consequences of men wherein the strength of their Scripture proofs standeth for the support of the contrary opinion.

And first it is considerable, that the Scriptures not only speak to the heart of the doctrine asserted in great variety of texts and places, but also in great veins and correspondences, or consorts of texts, each consort consisting of several particulars of like notion and phrase. I shall recommend only four of these companies unto the reader; which when we shall have pondered in some or all the particulars respectively relating unto them, we shall add, to make full measure, the contributions of some single texts besides.

The first division or squadron of Scriptures which speak aloud the universality of redemption by Christ, are such which present the gift and sacrifice of Christ as relating indifferently unto the world. The name of this kind of Scriptures, for the number of them, may be Legion for they are many. Some of the principal and best known of them are these: "God so loved *the world*, that he gave his only-begotten," &c., John iii. 16; "that *the world* through him might be saved," ver. 17. "Behold the Lamb of God which taketh away the sin of *the world*," John i. 29. "My flesh, which I will give for the life of *the world*," John vi. 51. "And he is the propitiation for our sins; and not for ours only, but also for the sins of *the whole world*, 1

John ii. 2. "And we have seen and do testify that the Father sent the Son to be the Saviour of *the world*, 1 John iv. 14. "For I came not to judge *the world*, but to save *the world*," John xii. 48. "For God was in Christ reconciling *the world* unto himself," &c., 2 Cor. v. 19. To omit many others.

The second post of Scriptures standing up to maintain the same doctrine with uniformity of expressions amongst themselves, are such which insure the ransom of Christ, and the will or desire of God for matters of salvation, unto *all men* and *every man*. Some of these are – "Who gave himself a ransom *for all*," 1 Tim. ii. 6. "Because we thus judge, that if one died *for all*, then were all dead; and that he died *for all*, that they who live," &c. 2 Cor. v. 14, 15. "That he, by the grace of God, should taste of death *for every man*," Heb. ii. 9; "who will have *all men* to be saved," &c., 1 Tim. ii. 4; "not willing that *any* should perish, but that *all* should come to repentance," 2 Pet. iii. 9. "Therefore, as by the offence of one the judgment came upon all men to condemnation; even so by the righteousness of one, the free gift came upon *all men* to the justification of life," Rom. v. 18; with some others.

A third sort of party of Scriptures, confederate with the former, (for substance of import, between themselves for matter of expression) are such which hold forth and promise salvation indifferently to him, and to whosoever will or shall believe. Of this sort are these, with their fellows: "And *him* that cometh unto me, I will in no wise case out," John vi. 37; "He that believeth in me shall never thirst," ver. 35; "*He* that believeth, and is baptized, shall be saved," Mark xvi. 16; "That *whosoever* believeth in him should not perish," John iii. 16; "That through his name, *whosoever* believeth in him shall receive remission of sins," Acts x. 43; "Even the righteousness of God, which is by faith of Jesus Christ *unto all*, and upon *all* that believe:... for all have sinned," Rom. iii. 22, 23. It were easy to make this pile also much greater.

A fourth association of Scriptures, all pregnant with the doctrine we assert, consists of such places where Christ is said to have died for those who yet may perish, yea, and actually do perish: and again, where such men are said to have been bought by him, and to have been "sanctified by his blood," who yet through their own negligence and wilfulness in sinning, bring destruction upon themselves, and perish everlastingly. Places of this kind are famously known. "Destroy not him with thy meat, *for whom Christ died*," Rom. xiv. 15; "And through thy knowledge shall the weak *brother perish, for whom Christ died?*" 1 Cor. viii. 11; "Even denying the Lord that *bought* them, and bring upon themselves swift *destruction*," 2 Pet. ii. 1; "For if after they have escaped the pollutions of the world, through the knowledge of the Lord and Saviour Jesus Christ, they are again entangled therein, and overcome, the latter end is worse with them than the beginning," 2 Pet. ii. 20; "Of how much sorer punishment, supposed ye, shall he be thought worthy, who hath trodden under foot the Son of God, and hath counted the blood of the covenant, wherewith he was sanctified, an unholy thing, and hath done despite unto the Spirit of Grace?" Heb. x. 29; "Then his lord, after he had called him, said unto him, O thou wicked servant, I forgave thee all that debt because thou desiredst me. Shouldest not thou also have had compassion on thy fellow-servant? And his lord was wroth, and delivered him to the tormentors, till he should pay all that was due to him. So likewise shall my heavenly Father do also unto you, if ye from your heart forgive not every one his brother their trespasses?" Matt. xviii. 32, 33 &c.

Let us begin with the texts of the first of the four orders mentioned, where the death of Christ is presented as relating unto the world. From the tenor and import of all the Scriptures of this denomination and tribe, it will be made evident that Christ died for all men, without exception of any, the word *world* in these places being necessarily to be understood in the proper and comprehensive signification of it, (I mean for all men and women in the world, in and according to their successive generation) and not for those that shall believe, or the like. We shall, for brevity's sake, argue only some of these places, and leave the light of their interpretations for a discovery of the sense and meaning of the rest.

The first proposed of these, was that place of renown, "God so loved the world, that he gave," &c. John iii. 16. Evident it is from hence, that Christ was given, viz. unto death for them, or for their sakes, whoever they be that are here meant by the world. There are but three significations of the world, that to my remembrance I ever heard of as competitors in this place. First, some by the world, here understand the elect dispersed up and down the world. By the elect, they mean all those, and those only, who shall in time actually be saved, whom they call the elect, because they judge them to have been chosen by God from eternity out of the generality of mankind, with an intent by him in time, with a strong hand and power irresistible, to be: 1. Brought to believe; 2. Caused, or made to persevere, believing unto the end; and, 3. Hereupon eternally saved, the residue of men being absolutely rejected and left to that unavoidable and heavy doom of perishing everlastingly. But that this is not the sense of the word *world* in the Scripture in hand, will appear by the light of these considerations.

1. The word *kosmos*, here translated *world*, was never known to have any such sense or signification in the Greek tongue; nor was it, nor is it to be found in any author who wrote in this language, before, or about the time, when John wrote his gospel, in such a signification, nor yet in anywhere near to it. Now the gospel, as is generally acknowledged, and that upon sufficient grounds, was written in the Greek tongue chiefly for the gentiles' sake, amongst whom this language was known and understood far and near, that they might be brought to believe, and so be saved by it. It is no way likely that the evangelist should use words, especially in such master veins and main passages of it, as this is, in an uncouth, unknown, and unheard of signification.

2. Nor can it be proved, that it is to be taken in the sense now opposed, in any other place of the Scriptures themselves; but in very many places it signifies the universal system, body, or generality of men in the world, (we shall not need to instance for the proof of this, places being so frequent and obvious) as also for that part of the generality of men which is opposite, and contra-distinguished to the saints, *i.e.* to the elect, in their sense of the word elect, who yet would have these signified by the world. This latter signification of the word *world*, is evident in these Scriptures: - "We know that we are born of God, and that the whole *world* lieth in wickedness," 1 John v. 19. "Even the Spirit of Truth, whom *the world* cannot receive, " &c. John xiv. 17; "If ye were of *the world*, the *world* would love her own: but because ye are not of *the world*, but I have chosen you out of *the world*, therefore the *world* hateth you," John xv. 19; to omit many others.

3. If by *the world* in the Scripture in hand be meant the elect, in the sense of the assertors of this signification, then it will follow, that God out of his great love gave Christ unto those, or for those, who stood in no need of him, at least either to preserve them from perishing, or to invest them with a right or title to eternal life, which yet are here laid down as the two only, or at least as two main ends of that great gift. For if exemption from perishing, or salvation, be absolutely, and without all consideration, awarded or decreed by God unto men before, or from eternity, they have a full right and title unto them, or unto the possession and enjoyment of them, by virtue of this award or decree, without the intervening of anything else whatsoever. For what better right or title can there be to the enjoyment of anything than a decree of heaven? Or the award of him who hath an

unquestionable right and power to dispose of all enjoyments whatsoever, as, and to whom he pleaseth? But more of this consequence hereafter.

4. The structure itself of the sentence, and tenor of these words, riseth up against this sense of the word in question. For (a.) If by the word *world* we understand the elect, we destroy the very grammar of the place, and make it an uncouth and harsh sentence, such, doubtless, as cannot be paralleled in any author, nor yet in the Scriptures themselves. Read we then the place thus, "So God loved his elect, that he gave his only begotten Son, that whosoever..." – I demand how, or in what regular sense, that universal distributive particle, whosoever, *pas ho*, everyone that, shall be understood? It is a thing generally known to those that understand anything in the rules of grammar, yea, the vulgar dialect of those that speak reason or common sense confirmeth it, that partitive or distributive particles of speech always suppose a difference, at least in possibility, between the things parted or distributed, and this in reference to what occasioneth the distribution. As for example, suppose a great king having many sons, should express himself thus: "I so love my children, that whosoever of them shall be dutiful unto me; I will bestow principalities, dukedoms, or other great matters upon them." Should he not plainly imply a possibility, at least, that some of them might not prove dutiful unto him? In like manner, if the word *world*, in the Scripture in hand, should signify the elect, the distributive, whosoever, must needs imply that some of these elect might possibly not believe, and so perish; because believing, and not perishing thereupon, occasions the distribution here made.

(b.) Though our Saviour, in this period of Scripture, mentioneth only the benefit intended by God in the gift of his Son, to those that shall believe, viz., non-perishing and the obtaining of everlasting life; yet he plainly implies, and supposeth withal, the misery and loss which they should certainly suffer who shall not believe. Except this be supposed, we shall altogether misfigure our Saviour's mind and scope in the place, and make him speak more like a man void of understanding than himself. For then the taste and savour of his words would be this: "God so loved the world, that he gave his only begotten Son, that whosoever believeth or not believeth in him should not perish but," &c. Therefore, certain it is, that he in the place in hand insinuates that condemnation or perishing of those who shall not believe, as he asserts the salvation or nonperishing of those who shall believe. And besides, it is contrary to reason, especially in seriousness of discourse, in a positive and strict manner to suspend that upon the performance of such or such a condition which may be had without any such performance. This then being granted, that our Saviour here supposeth the certain perishing of those who shall not believe, the place, according to their sense, who by the world will need understand the elect, must run thus: "So God loved the elect, that whosoever of them believed should not perish;" but on the contrary, that whosoever of them should not believe, should perish. Which, according to their principles, against whom we now argue, is as if a man should say, whichsoever of my sheep is no sheep, but a goat, shall have no pasture with his fellows.

(c.) They who by the world here understand the elect, must, if they will not baulk with their principles, suppose that Christ speaks at no better rate of wisdom or sense in this Scripture than thus: "So God loved the world, that he gave his only begotten Son, that whosoever did that which was not possible for them to decline or not to do, should not perish, but," &c. Whoever, being serious and in his wits, required that in the nature of a condition from any man, especially in order to the obtaining of some great important thing which he, of whom it was required upon such terms, was necessitated or had no liberty or power but to perform? What father ever promised his son his estate, either in whole or in part upon condition that whilst he rode upon a horse he should not go on foot? Or upon condition that he would do that, which a force greater than he was able to resist should necessitate him to do? So that the whole tenor and carriage of the verse renders the interpretation of the word *world*, hitherto encountered, a mere nullity in sense, reason, and truth.

5. The context and words immediately preceding, will at no hand endure that sense of the word *world*, against which we have declared hitherto. This little word for, "For God so loved," &c., being casual, importeth not only a connexion of these words with what went before, but such a connexion or relation as that which intercedes between the cause and the effect. So that the words in hand must be looked upon as assigning or exhibiting the cause or reason of that effect, which was immediately before mentioned. This being granted, as without breach of conscience it can hardly be denied, it will appear as clear as the light of the sun, that by *world*, in the place under contest, cannot be meant the elect only. The tenor of the two next foregoing verses, for together they make but one entire sentence, is this: "And as Moses lifted up the serpent in the wilderness, even so must the Son of man be lifted up, that whosoever believeth in him, or every one believing in him, should not perish, but have everlasting life." John iii. 14,

15. So that the effect here mentioned and expressed is the salvation and everlasting happiness of what person or persons soever of men, or of mankind, shall believe in Christ. The reason or cause hereof our Saviour discovers and asserts in the words in hand: "For God so loved the world, that he gave," &c. If now by the world we shall understand only the elect, the reason or cause here assigned of the pre-mentioned effect will be found inadequate to it, and insufficient to produce it. For God's love to the elect, and his giving his Son for their salvation only, is no sufficient cause to procure or produce the salvation of *whosoever* shall or should believe on him. For certain it is, that there is salvation in Christ for no more than for whom God intended there should be salvation in him. If there be salvation in him for none but the elect only, then is it not true that whosoever believes in him shall be saved. For certain it is, that no man's believing puts any salvation into Christ for him; therefore if it were not there for him before he believed, yea, or, whether he believed or not, neither would it be there for him, though or in case he should believe.

6. Lastly, by the word *world*, in the Scripture in hand, is not meant the elect, nor any thing equivalent hereunto, is evident also from the context in the verse and words immediately following, where our Saviour goeth forward in his doctrine, thus: "For God sent not his Son into the world to condemn the world, but that the world through him might be saved." John iii. 17. This particle, *for*, being, as we lately noted, casual or ratiocinative, plainly showeth that he useth the *world*, or speaks of the world in this verse, where he speaks of the condemnation of it, in the same sense, wherein he spake of it in the former, and the means of the salvation of it; otherwise he should not argue ad idem, *i.e.* to the point in hand. Now then to make him here to say, that God sent not his Son into the world, *i.e.* to take the nature or to live in the condition of the elect, to condemn the elect, but that the elect &c. is to make him speak as no man, I suppose spake, but not for excellency of wisdom or gracefulness of expression, but for weakness in both. To say that God sent not his son into the world to condemn his elect, were but to beat the air, or to fight against a shadow; I mean, solemnly to deny that, which no man was ever likely to imagine of affirm. For how, or by what way of apprehension, should it ever enter into any man's thought that God should send his Son into the world to condemn those, whom out of his infinite love he had from eternity decreed to save with strong hand, out-stretched arm, and power omnipotent and invincible? Or are not these the elect, in their notion of election, with whom we have now

to do? Therefore cerntainly, the world, in the Scripture before us, doth not signify the elect.

A second interpretation of this word asserted by some, is, that by *the world* is meant genus humanum, for mankind indefinitely considered. If I rightly understand the mind of those who thus interpret, as neither importing all, nor any of the individuums or persons contained in or under this species or kind, but only the specifical nature of man common to them all; as when the Jews said of the Centurion, that he loved their nation, Luke vii. 5, their meaning was not either that he loved all that were Jews without exception of any; nor yet that he loved any particular person of them more than another; but only that he was lovingly disposed towards them as they were such a particular nation, as viz., Jews. But that this interpretation either falls in, in substance, with the former, and so is already condemned with the condemnation thereof; or else, with the third and last, which, as we shall hear presently, findeth in this Scripture a love in God towards all the individual persons of mankind, without exception of any; or else, that it vanisheth into nothing, and hath no substance at all in it, may be thus demonstrated.

If by mankind, indefinitely considered, be neither meant a special or determinate number of the persons of men (which the former interpretation asserteth) nor yet the universality, or entire body of men, consisting of all particular persons of men which either have been, now are, and shall be hereafter (which the third interpretation avoucheth) then is it only the nature of man abstractively considered, which we may with the schoolmen, call humanitas, humanity, or the specifical nature of man, not the persons of men, some, or all, which God precisely love with that love, out of which he gave his only begotten Son. If so, then it undeniably follows, that Christ was given out of as much love to one person of mankind as to another, or, which is the same, not out of any love to any at all. For certain it is, that humanitas, or the specifical nature of man, is not the person of any man. And so, according to this interpretation, God should love the reprobates as much as the elect, and consequently give his only begotten Son to death, as well for the one as the other.

Besides, if it were the human nature, indefinitely considered, (in the sense pre-declared) which God is here said to have loved with that love, out of which he gave his only begotten Son, from hence also it must needs follow, inasmuch as the reprobate (so called) partakes every whit as much in this nature as the elect, that Christ was given as much for the one as for the other. Again, if by the world, be meant the human nature, in the sense distinguished, the distributive particle, *whosoever*, with the following words, will be found incongruous, and no ways answering the former part of these verse, either in sense or regularity of construction. For the human nature is but simply one and the same nature or thing, nor doth it contain any plurality of species, or individual human natures under it; whereas a distribution cannot be but of some general, which containeth many particulars under it. And upon the supposal of such sense of the word *world*, to make the construction regular in the latter part of the verse, the tenor of the whole must run thus: For God loved the human nature, that he gave his only begotten Son, that what human nature soever believed in him should not perish, &c. If this construction be ridiculous, so must that interpretation needs be which produceth it. Lastly, (to answer the illustration of this interpretation of this interpretation from Luke vii.) the Jews, who said the Centurion loved their nation, did not suppose that he loved only a handful or small number of their nation, and hated all the rest with an irreconcilable hatred; nor did they say, that he so loved their nation, that whosoever of this nation should trust him, he would be a signal benefactor unto them, or the like: nor did they, by their nation, understand the Jewish race, lineage, or descent, abstractively considered, and without reference to any person or persons whatsoever of this nation (for their nation, in this sense, was wholly incapable of any fruit or expression of his love, or having a synagogue built to it or for it.)

So that this instance no way parallels or fits the interpretation of the word *world*, for the illustration or confirmation whereof it is brought. But the plain meaning of the Jews saying that the Centurion loved their nation, was this, that he was ready and willing to do any office or service of love to any person or persons of their nation, because of their national relation, rather than to any other, upon such a consideration, when he had opportunity. The two pretenders being nonsuited , a sufficient way, I presume, is made for the admission of the right heir. Therefore,

The third, and last interpretation of *the world*, in the Scripture under debate, is, that by it is signified universum genus humanum. The whole compass of mankind, or all and every individual person subsisting at any time in the human nature, without exception of any. This exposition stands with the ordinary and best known signification of the words, and withal gives smoothness and regularity of construction unto the period or sentence, which both the former (as upon examination hath been found) take from it, is of perfect accord with the context, and besides magnifies the love of God in the freeness, fullness, and extent of it incomparably above and beyond either of them; for,

1. The word world, *kosmos,* very frequently and familiarly both in the Scriptures themselves, and in other authors, signifieth the generality of mankind, or of men: in the Scriptures especially, when it relates unto persons, it seldom or never signifieth any thing else, but either the generality or men simply and absolutely, or else that generality of men which comparatively comprehendeth all men. I mean the whole number of wicked and unregenerate men, who, in respect of their vast multitudes, and inconsiderable number of the godly (in comparison of them) are by John termed the whole world, "And we know that we are of God, and *the whole world* lieth in wickedness." 1 John v. 19. Or, lastly the promiscuous generality or persons, good and bad together, be they fewer or more, where a man converseth, or hath opportunity to come amongst, or speak unto. Several instances were lately given of the second signification of the word, from the Scriptures. Instances of the first signification, also, there any many. "Ye are the light of the world," Matt. v.14. "And the world knew him not," John i. 10. "And I speak to the world those things which I have heard of him," John viii. 26. "But I have chosen you out of the world," John xv. 19. "Which thou gavest me out of the world," John xvii. 6. "God forbid: for then how shall God judge the world?" Rom. iii. 6. "As by one man sin entered into the world," Rom v. 12. "But God hath chosen the foolish things of the world" and "the weak things of the world," 1 Cor. i. 27. "There are, it may be, so many kinds of voices in the world," 1 Cor. xiv. 10.

The world is never used in Scripture for the elect or godly party in the world, considered by themselves, or apart by others. It is used either for the wicked of the world alone, or apart by themselves, or else for both godly and wicked taken together, and as mixed one with another. It would be very strange that our Saviour should use it in that by-sense, and unheard of elsewhere, in so eminent a place and passage of the gospel as that in hand, and not in the familiar and best known signification of it.

2. This interpretation of the word accommodates the whole verse or sentence with clearness of sense and regularity of construction, as is evident unto those who understand what the one and what the other of these mean. For by it the genuine and proper use and import of the distributive particle, whosoever, is fully salved, which is destroyed by either of the former, and such a distribution of a general made by it, which supposeth a possibility

of a difference between the particulars contained under it, and into which the said general is distributed, according to the exigency of those things, in reference whereunto the distribution is made. As for example: here is a distribution made of this general, the world, *i.e.* of all mankind, by this distributive pronoun, *whosoever*. The occasion of this distribution is to show who, or what particulars contained under this general, *i.e.* what particular persons of mankind shall not perish, but have everlasting life; and withal, by a tacit antithesis or in consequential way, as hath been already noted, to show what other particulars contained under the same general shall perish, and not to have everlasting life. The former are said to be such as shall believe on the only begotten Son of God; the latter are clearly implied to be such who shall not so believe. Now, if it should be supposed that there was, or is, not possibility that any such difference should be found between the particulars, into which the general is here distributed, as believing, and not believing, the distribution would be altogether needless and vain; yea, and would dissense the whole sentence. These things are plain and sensible to every understanding that knows what belongs to common sense or regularity of syntaxis.

3. This exposition of the word *world*, makes a clean joint, a rational and pleasant coherence, between this verse and that which follows; as also between this and the two verses immediately precedent. The words of the two preceding verses are these, "And as Moses lifted up the serpent in the wilderness, even so must the Son of man be lifted up; that whosoever believeth in Him should not perish, but have everlasting life." Now, certain it is, that Moses did not lift up the serpent with an intent of healing to be conferred by it upon such or such a definite or determinate number of persons; nor with an intent, either on his part or on God's part, that none should look upon it but only such a parcel or determinate number of men; but with an intent, not only that whosoever in the event did look upon it, and could not but look upon it, might look upon it; but that whosoever would, might look up unto it, and that whosoever, being stung with the fiery serpents, did look up unto it, should be healed thereby.

This is evident from the story. "Make thee," saith God to Moses, "a fiery serpent, and set it upon a pole; and it shall come to pass, that *every one that is bitten*, when He looketh upon it, shall live," Numb. xxi. 8. Now, then, all men without exception being stung with that fiery serpent, sin, unless Christ should be lifted up upon the cross, with an intent on God's part and in himself; (a.) That every man, without exception, might believe in him;

and (b.) That every man that should believe in him, should be saved by him. He could not be said to be lifted up, as (*i.e.* upon the same terms of a universal accommodation on which) Moses lifted up the serpent in the wilderness. Therefore, our Saviour, to give the world a satisfying account how it comes to pass that the Son of man, meaning himself, should be lifted up upon such terms, viz. for the universal benefit of salvation unto all mankind, he assigns the love of God to the world, as the reason or productive cause of it. For God so loved the world that, &c. Therefore, by the world, he must needs mean all mankind, or the generality of men, that were bitten or stung with sin, unless we will say, that God gave his son for the salvation of those whom he loved not.

The tenor of the following verses is this, "For God sent not his Son into the world to condemn the world, but," &c. In these words our Saviour confirms his former assertion, touching the love of God to the world, in giving his Son for the salvation of it, by rejecting that reason or motive of his sending him into the world, which men might imagine did occasion this his sending by God, and besides which, there could none other well be imagined, but only that which he had asserted, viz. an intent or purpose in Him, in God, of condemning the world by Him. Now to make Christ to say, that God sent not his Son into the world to condemn mankind, or the generality of men, as having sinned against him, is to make him say that which is savoury and comfortable, and that which opposeth, or is apt to prevent such a sad imagination, as was very incident to the minds of men through a consciousness of the guilt of sin, viz. That if God ever did, or should, send his Son amongst them, it would be to judge or condemn them.

But to make him say, that God sent not his Son into the world to condemn the elect, *i.e.* those few whom he infinitely loved, and to whom he had peremptorily, and without all possibility of reverse, decreed non-condemnation before this sending of him, is to make him speak at an extreme low rate of sense or reason, and to labour, as the proverb is, in lifting a feather. Inasmuch as no such thought or imagination as this was ever like to bear upon or trouble any man's spirit; inasmuch then as no other interpretation of *the world*, in the former verse, but only that which hereby understandeth the generality of men-sinners, will accommodate this verse, in respect of the connexion between them, with any tolerable sense, evident it is, that that must needs be the true interpretation thereof.

By the way, when Christ saith, "For judgment I am come into the world," &c. John ix. 39, He no ways opposeth what he here saith, viz. "That God sent him not into the world to condemn the world." For in the former place, he speaks not of the intent, but of the event; in this, not of the event, but of the intent of his sending or coming into the world. Christ was not sent into the world with any intent on God's part, nor came with any intention of his own, to make those which see to become blind, meaning either to augment or to discover to their shame the spiritual blindness and ignorance in such men, who being ignorant, presume of their knowledge by one means or other; but with an intent to heal the blindness of all, to their comfort, peace, and glory. Therefore, if any man through a foolish and proud conceit of his own knowledge and wisdom, shall stumble at, or reject the gospel and doctrine of Christ as foolishness, and so discover himself to be blind, ignorant, and foolish in the end; this is merely adventitious and accidental, in respect of the antecedent, primary, and direct intention of God in sending Christ into the world, as Calvin himself affirmeth.[1]

If it be demanded, but did not God intend that whosoever should stumble at or reject Christ, should in such a sense, be made blind? I answer, Yes, doubtless: God did intend to punish all manner of sins with judgments suitable to them. But his intention of making those blind, in the sense declared, who should reject Christ or his doctrine, was not that intent or purpose, out of which he sent Christ into the world, which was the genuine and natural product of his love, but such an intent which his perfect hatred of sin, especially of sin committed against the law of grace, formed in him.

4. The interpretation of the word *world*, now under assertion, magnifies that divine attribute, the love of God, incomparably more and above either of the former. They, who by the world understand the elect only, (which is the substance, also, of the second interpretation, unless it chooseth rather to resolve itself into this third, as was lately proved) allow a very small, narrow, and inconsiderable sphere, for so noble, active and diffusive a principle, as the love of God is, in comparison of those who extend it to the whole circumference of mankind. The whole element, and vast body of the air, in all the dimensions of it, height, depth, length, and breadth, make but a proportionable sphere for the sun, wherein to display the fulness of the glory, and to express the activity of his abundant light. Nor will the whole universe of creatures, take the whole number and entire host of them, a *prima ad ultimam, et ab ultima ad primam*, make a theatre any whit too large, capacious, or extensive, for the abundant riches and fullness of the love of God to act like themselves upon. They who present the love of God in the gift of his son Jesus Christ, as contracted to the narrow compass of

---

1. Calv. in Joh. iii. 17. (Unless indicated otherwise, quotes from Calvin are from his multi-volume commentary series on the Bible.—Editor)

the elect, *i.e.* of those only who shall in the end be saved, and preach this for the gospel unto the world, do by men, in respect of their spiritual accommodation, as God should do by the world in their temporal, in case he should keep his sun in a continual eclipse, suffer ten parts of the light of it to be perpetually obscured.

5. This interpretation, we now plead is of fair and dull consistency teach and affirm, concerning the nature of God, his mercy, sweetness, love, goodness towards all his creatures, his equal and impartial administration of rewards and punishments in the world, his non-exception of persons, his ardent, serious, and compassionate desires that none should perish. It means that even the vilest and wickedest of men should return from the evil of their ways, and be saved, his not delighting in the death of those who do perish, with much more of like consideration and import. There is an obvious and manifest agreement between the exposition we contend for, and all such veins of Scripture expression, as these: whereas the other interpretations are at an absolute and manifest defiance with them.

And, lastly, the sense now argued for is attested by Calvin himself upon the place, with several other Protestant divines. "Both," saith he, "are here distinctly delivered unto us; namely, the faith in Christ is of saving nature *unto all*; and that Christ therefore brought life because his heavenly Father would not have *mankind* to perish, *which he loveth.*" And more plainly afterwards: "He useth a note of universality, both that he may invite all to the participation of life, and that he may cut off matter of excuse from unbelievers. The word world, which he useth before likewise, importeth as much. For though there will be nothing found in the world worthy the favour of God, yet he showeth himself *propitious*, or favourable, *unto the whole world*, in that he calls all men without exception to believe in Christ, which is nothing else but an entrance into life."[2] In the former of these passages, the interpretation we stand for, is largely enough asserted; but in the latter, we have it with measure heaped up, pressed down, and running over. For here, he doth not only say that God showeth himself propitious, or favourable unto the *whole world*, but further, that he calls all men to faith in Christ, and invites all men to participation of life.

Therefore, doubtless, his judgment was, at least whilst he had this Scripture before him for his steerage, that there was life and salvation in Christ for all men, and that upon such terms that all might partake of it. There was also one another: and, consequently, that he died for all men: inasmuch as there can be no life in him for those to partake, for whom he

2 Calv. in Joh. iii. 15, 16.

died not, no more than there is for the devils. Gualter, another Protestant author of approved learning and worth, avoucheth the same sense. "And this," saith he, "he more clearly expresseth, when being to name those whom God so loved, he doth not mention Abraham, Isaac, or Jacob, Moses, David, the prophets, the Virgin Mary, the apostles, or holy martyrs, but the world, which our evangelist in his epistle affirmeth to lie wholly in wickedness, and of which Christ himself more than once affirmeth the devil to be the prince."[3]

So that this writer, by *the world*, doth not understand the elect only, or the world of the elect, whereof the devil is no where affirmeth by Christ to be the prince, nor which is any where affirmed by John to lie wholly in wickedness, but the world at large, and which comprehendeth reprobates as well as the elect. But of all our reformed divines, there is none speaks more expressly and professedly to the mind of the interpretation held forth, that learned Musculus. "By the world," saith he, speaking of the Scripture in hand, "he understands the universe of mankind: so that here his love of the world, and his love of men, is the same." And elsewhere, thus: "After the same manner it is in this redemption of mankind whereof we speak. That reprobates and desperately wicked men partake not of it, *is not through any defect of the grace of God*: nor is it meet that, for the sons of perdition' sake, it should lose the glory and title of a *universal redemption*, since *it is prepared* (or procured) *for all*, and all are called to it."[4]

Nor were there men wanting in the Synod of Dort itself, who, though anti-remonstrants by profession, yet frequently by expression did plainly close with that doctrine which they would be thought to oppose concerning the particular in hand. Our English divines lay down this thesis: "God, out of compassion to mankind being fallen, sent his Son, who gave himself a price of redemption for the sins of the *whole world*." In the explication of this thesis they say, "That price which was paid for all, and which shall certainly benefit all that believe, yet shall not benefit all men." And presently after, "So then Christ died for all men, that all and *every one*, by the mediation of faith, may through the virtue of this ransom, obtain remission of sins and eternal life."[5]

Evident is that these men, by God's love to the world, understand his love of compassion to all mankind, inasmuch as not a part or some, but the whole and all particulars of mankind, were fallen. Besides, saying, "that all and everyone" may "through the mediation of faith obtain forgiveness of sins and eternal life through the virtue of Christ's ransom," they clearly

3. Gualter. Homil. 20, in Johan.
4. Musc. loc. de Philanthropia Dei; Idem. Loc., de Redempt. Gen. Humani.
5. Syn. Dord. Sentent. Theol. Mag. Brit. de artic.ii thes. 3.

imply that remission of sins and salvation are purchased by Christ for all and every man upon the same terms and after the same manner, and with the same intention on God's part, inasmuch as he intends the donation of remission of sins unto no man, not withstanding the virtue of the ransom of Christ, but through the mediation of faith. And through the mediation he intends, yea, promiseth, it unto all men without exception; yea, so say our countrymen, that all and everyone many through the said mediation obtain it. Nor were these men altogether without company in that Synod in such expressions. Immediately after the suffrage and sentence of the ministers of Geneva upon the second article, I find one (I suppose of those who were sent from Geneva) delivering himself thus: "There is certain common love of God towards all men, wherewith he loved all mankind, being fallen, and seriously willeth or desireth the salvation of all." Afterwards, speaking of condemnation of unbelievers, "such an event as this," saith he, "is not of itself intended by God, but accidentally follows through the fault of men." Yet again, "If this redemption be not supposed as common benefit bestowed upon all men, that indifferent and promiscuous preaching of the gospel which was committed to the apostles to be performed in all nations will have no true foundation." Doubtless, that which is bestowed upon all men by God, was by him intended for all men in the purchase of procurement of it, and this out of love to all those on whom it is bestowed and for whom it was purchased. It were easy to multiply quotations of like import with these from many convened in that Synod, who are supposed to have condemned that doctrine which holds forth universal redemption by Christ as error. But the certain truth is, that if this was their intention or attempt, the truth was at many turns too hard for them, and prevented them, and gained many a testimony from her adversaries.

For the fathers, they who shall please to peruse and ponder the commentaries or exposition of Augustine, the chief of the Latin fathers, and of Chrysostom, the chief of the Greek, upon the place, will easily perceive that their sense of the word *world* was the same with that which hath been avouched. "Is not Christ life?" saith the former, "and yet Christ died; but death died in the death of Christ, because life, being dead, slew death: the fulness of life devoured death: death was swallowed up in the body of Christ." In all these passages evident it is that the Father speaks of that death which had equally seized upon all men, or whereunto all men, without exception of any, were alike obnoxious: therefore, affirming this death to be dead by the death of Christ, to be devoured by the fullness of life,

&c., he supposeth it equally dead, devoured, removed or taken away in respect of all men. Awhile, after, having rehearsed these words, "For God sent not his Son to judge the world, but that the world might be saved by him," he infers thus: "Therefore, as much as lieth in the physician, he came to save or heal the sick. He slayeth himself who will not observe the precepts of the physician. He came a Saviour unto the *world*. Why is he called the Saviour of the world, but that he should save the world?"[6] Doubtless, he that speaketh these things had not yet dreamt of any signification of *the world* in the Scripture in hand, but only that which we have asserted; nor did he imagine that Christ was given or sent into the world upon any other terms than those which equally and indifferently respected the healing of all that were sick, or the saving of all that were lost. Otherwise why should he insert this provisional cause, "as much as in the physician lieth," meaning Christ? This plainly importeth that he came to heal such sick ones, who notwithstanding slew themselves by neglecting his precepts; yea, and that he could do no more than he did in or by his death to save those from perishing who do perish, and consequently that he died as much for these as for those who are saved.

Nor, doubtless, had the other (I mean Chrysostom) any other notion of *the world* in the said Scripture than the former. For, describing those whom God is here said to have loved, he gives no other description of them than which agreeth as well to the reprobate as elect, affirming them to be such "who come from the earth and ashes, who are full of an infinite number of sins, who injured or offended him without ceasing, very wicked," or deserving nor pardon. And afterwards, "but we neglect" or despise "him, being naked and a stranger, who died for us. And who then shall deliver us from punishment" or judgment "which is to come?"[7] clearly implying, that those for whom Christ died may notwithstanding suffer and undergo the wrath and punishment "which is to come."

It were easy to levy many more quotations, both from the authors already mentioned, and from many others as well ancient as modern, of a full and clear concurrence with the interpretation given. But I take no pleasure in quotations from men, nor do I know any great use of them, unless it be to heal the offence which truth is always apt to give to prepossessed and prejudicated minds. The use which more commonly is made of them is grand abuse, being nothing else but the interposing or thrusting of the credits and authorities of men between the judgment of men and the truth, that so the one should not easily come at the other. However, we have, I trust, made it

6. Aug. in Johan. tractat. 12.
7. Chrys. Homil. xxvii in Johan.

fully evident by many demonstrations, in full conjunction with the judgments of learned men, that the Scripture in hand casteth the light of that love of God, out of which he gave his only begotten Son to death, with an equal brightness upon all mankind; and consequently, that this death of his faceth the whole posterity of Adam with the same sweetness and graciousness of aspect.

The Scripture last opened, speaking so plainly and fully (as we have heard) the point in hand, might well be accepted as a sufficient security, that all its fellows mentioned with it, as in effect they speak, so likewise they intend and mean the same thing. Yet because prejudice is not easily controlled, and hard of satisfaction, let us impartially examine one or two more of the company. We shall find universal atonement as well at the bottom as at the top, as well in the heart as in the face of them. The former of the two shall be that of the apostle Paul, "To wit, that God was in Christ reconciling the world unto himself, not imputing their trespasses unto them, and hath committed unto us the word of reconciliation," 2 Cor. v. 19. That by the world, which God is here said to have "been in Christ reconciling unto himself," cannot be meant the elect only, but the universality of men, is clear upon this account: First, it is not here said, that God in Christ did actually, or in facto esse, reconcile the world unto himself, but that "he was reconciling the world," &c. *i.e.* God was, and is, and ever will be (for the unchangeable perpetuation of the acts of God are usually expressed in the Scriptures by verbs signifying the time past, for the reason specified in the last chapter) in, *i.e.* by, or through Christ, following and prosecuting his great and gracious design of "reconciling the world unto himself."

Participles of the present tense active, import the currency or carrying on, the consummation, or ending of an action, on endeavor. Secondly, by the "reconciling the world unto himself," in, or through Christ, which is here ascribed unto God, must of necessity be meant, either such an act or endeavour in him, by which he gains, or rather seeks and attempts to gain the love and friendship of the world, which was and is full of hatred and enmity against him; or else such an act, by which he went about to reconcile himself, *i.e.* to render and make himself propitious and benevolous unto the world. Now, take either of these senses, it is impossible that by the word "world" should be signified only the elect, or indeed any thing by the generally of men.

If we take the act of God, he termed the "reconciling the world unto himself," in the former sense (which doubtless is the true sense of it, as clearly appears from the next verse, and subsequent clause in this) by the world cannot be meant only the elect, because God doth not by Christ, or in Christ, held forth and preached in the ministry of the gospel, see to bring over these only unto him in love, or to make only these his friends. Neither doth he send the word of reconciliation (as the apostle calleth it) *i.e.* the gracious message of the gospel, by which this reconciliation is to be actually made only unto them, but promiscuously to the generality, or universality of men, without exception of any: "Go and preach the gospel to very creature under heaven," Mark xvi. 15; and therefore, Paul did but keep to his commission, when, as he saith, he "preached Christ, warning *every* man, and teaching *every* man in all wisdom, that he might present *every* man perfect in Christ Jesus." Coloss. i. 28. Evident it is, that in the ministry and preaching of this word, God doth as well and as much, and after the same manner, persuade the obstinate and many of those who never come to believe, as he doth those who are overcome and persuaded hereunto. It is said concerning the ancient Jews, that "the Lord God of their fathers sent to them by his messengers, rising up betimes and sending, because he had compassion on his people, and on his dwelling place;" and yet it follows, "But they mocked the messengers of God, and despised his words, and misused his prophets, until the wrath of the Lord arose against his people, til there was no remedy." 2 Chron. xxxvi. 15, 16.

So that God is very whit as serious, as urgent and pressing in the ministry of his world and gospel, upon those who remain obdurate and impenitent to the last, as he is upon those who in time come to repent and to believe on him. And Paul (Acts xvii.) preached the same sermon, used the same addressment and application of the word to those who mocked which he did to those who believe, Acts xvii. 30-33. Evident therefore it is, that God as well seeks and attempts the reconciling of such unto himself by Christ, who in time perish, as he doth those who are saved; and that he doth vouchsafe as well the same inward as outward means, at least remotely unto both, shall be proved in due place.

If we shall take the latter sense of the phrase, wherein God is said to be "reconciling the world unto himself," and understand hereby such an act, whereby he renders or seeks to render himself loving, gracious, and propitious unto the world, neither yet can the word "world" signify anything by the generality of universality of men, or howsoever, not the elect in particular. The reason is, because God cannot, in any tolerable sense or construction of words, be said to reconcile himself unto those with whom he is not angry or offended, or to render himself loving and propitious unto those to whom his love is so great already, that by reason of it he peremptorily resolves to give unto them absolutely the greatest and most desirable of all good things, even no less than eternal life itself, which includes in it the richest and fullest enjoyment of God himself, whereof the creature is capable. Now we know this is the posture, or relation, wherein the elect stand before and unto God (at least as is generally held and maintained by those that are contrary minded in the present controversy) viz. as persons with whom God is so far from being angry or displeased, that he is pleased by absolute purpose or decree to confer eternal life upon them. Therefore certainly God cannot be said by any act whatsoever to reconcile himself, or render himself propitious unto these.

But now, by the *world*, we understand the great bulk or body of men in the world, with whom God is, and may truly and properly enough be said to be displeased for their sins. So he may be said to reconcile himself unto them; at least if by a reconciling, we mean such an act, by which he takes a course, or useth means, to bring himself into a complacency, or love of friendship with them, as when a father useth means to recover his son of the phrensy, or plague. It is true, a father loves his son with a benevolous affection, or with a love of pity, as we commonly call it, even whilst he is under a phrensy, and hath the plague upon him.

But he takes no pleasure in his company, doth not delight to converse with him as with a friend, bestows nothing upon him at the present, but only in order to his recovery; and in the case by all that he doth for him in this kind, he cannot recover him, he never proceeds to settle his inheritance upon him. But when and whilst he doth that which is proper to recover him, out of such distempers, he may be said, in this sense, to do an act whereby to reconcile himself to his son, viz. to make way for himself to take pleasure in his company, and to converse with him and to deal further by him as a friend.

In like manner it is as true that God cannot properly or according to the usual sense or signification of the word, be said to do any act whereby to reconcile himself to the world in general, much less to his elect in particular, because he always bears a benevolous affection to it, as appears, John iii. 16, the Scripture lately opened. So again, Tit. iii. 4, and elsewhere, he was never so far angry or offended with the world, but that he seriously and affectionately sought the good of it; yet in such a sense or consideration wherein, notwithstanding his affection or benevolence or commiseration towards it, he is said to be angry with men for their sins, and to hate them for their wickedness, and to resolve to destroy them everlastingly if they repent not, he may be said to do such an act, whereby to reconcile himself unto it, as, viz., when he doth that by which he is like to take men off from their sins, and to bring them to repentance; and consequently to cause his own anger and hatred towards them for their sins to cease.

But however, this is not the primary or direct sense of the phrase in the Scripture in hand, as was formerly intimated, but only that which follows upon it. For God by seeking to reconcile the world unto himself, in the former sense, takes a course likewise to reconcile himself unto it, in the latter. But take either the one interpretation or the other, there is no colour or pretence, by the "world," to understand the elect only.

If it be objected and said: Yea, but God is here said to be "in Christ, reconciling the world unto himself, not imputing the trespasses unto them." Doth not this imply that God reconciles none unto himself but those only, to whom he doth not impute their trespasses or sins? Now it is certain that God doth impute their sins unto all men, his elect only excepted; therefore he reconciles none unto himself in Christ but these only. To this I answer.

1. By concession, it is true, God doth actually, and in the event reconciles none unto himself by Christ, *i.e.* he brings no man to faith and repentance, but withal he forgives him his sins; or, which is the same, he imputes not his trespasses unto him. But,

By way of exception, I answer further, that it was no part of the apostle's intent in this place to speak of any spiritual or inward act of God, by which particular men are actually, and de facto converted or reconciled unto him, and consequently obtain forgiveness, or a non-imputation of their sins; but only concerning that great and gracious dispensation or act of grace, together with his counsel or project therein, in which or whereby he did, as it were, posture himself, and take a standing with the best advantage to save the world. For this end and purpose, I mean for the saving of the world or of men, upon such terms as he was willing, and as only became him to save them, it was necessary, (a.) That he should reconcile them unto himself. It was no ways convenient for God, as neither consisting with his wisdom nor holiness, to take those into part and fellowship with himself in his own blessedness and glory, who should hate him and be full of enmity and hard thoughts against him, and would not admit of terms of reconciliation with him. (b.) To effect this reconciliation, and to bring men over unto him in love, who generally through a consciousness of guilt, contracted by their evil works, and because of that contrariety between his holy laws, and their lusts and vile dispositions, hated him, it was necessary that he should take a course, and have a means suitable and proper, and which every ways honored a God of infinite wisdom. Now this course or means the apostle here expesseth to be, the non-imputation of their sins unto them, *i.e.* the tender, offer, or promise of the forgiveness of all their sins, upon the reconcilement.

God, by the proposal and tender of such and incomparable grace, favour, and blessing as this unto men, upon such sweet and gracious terms, makes account to reconcile the world unto himself, to bring off his creature, man, from hatred and hard thoughts, to a love and honourable esteem of him. (c.) and lastly, to put himself into a way of capacity of making so rich and glorious a proposal as this of forgiveness of sins unto the world, he put himself, as it were, into his Christ; or, as our apostle's expression is, he was in Christ; meaning, that that which God did, or intended to do, by his being in Christ, as mediator, was immediately and in reference unto a further end, that by means of his death he might offer free pardon and forgiveness of sins unto the world; mediately, and as more principally intended, that he might, by means of this offer, reconcile the world unto himself, *i.e.* prevail with men to repent of their sins, and turn in faith and love unto him.

Evident it is from the very letter of the context, that the apostle's intent in this Scripture was only to express and declare the tenor or purport of the gospel, or, as he calls it, of that word of reconciliation, the ministry whereof, he saith, in the end of the verse, was committed unto him. Do but read in the former verse to this, and you will clearly see it: "And all things are of *God,* who hath reconciled us to himself by Jesus Christ, and hath given unto us the ministry of the reconciliation; to wit, that God was in Christ reconciling," &c. As if he should say, he hath given unto us the ministry of that reconciliation, the tenor, substance, or purport whereof is this, viz., or to wit, "that *God* was in Christ reconciling," &c. So that here is nothing at all affirmed, or intended to be spoken concerning men actually or effectually reconciled or brought home unto God, or what their privileges are, in one kind or other; but only to show how or by what means God hath projected or contrived the reconciling of men to himself, which is expressed to be, as hath been said, by the message or doctrine of forgiveness of sins, sent and preached unto them by Christ.

Nor are the best and most confessedly orthodox of our reformed divine, dissenters from the interpretation given of the Scripture in hand, especially as concerning the sense and import of the word *world.* "God," saith

Musculus upon the place, "inhabiting his Son Christ, and directing him in all things, reconciled unto himself not us only, but even *the world, i.e., all mankind,* which was, is, or shall be from the beginning of *the world* to the end thereof, by giving his Son unto death for all men." And soon after: "It is most true which the apostle saith, that *God* reconciled the world unto himself in Christ, not imputing their sins unto them as concerning the work itself of reconciliation, being prepared or made ready for all mankind, and sufficient for them." Calvin also, though altogether so expressly as the former, yet with clearness enough, secondeth the same interpretation, writing on the place thus: "But the fuller and richer sense is, that God was in Christ, and then, that he reconciled the world unto himself." And a little after, "To what purpose then did God appear in Christ unto men? For reconciliation, that they who were strangers might be adopted for sons." If this were the end of the reconciliation for which God appeared in Christ unto men, that they who were strangers might be adopted for sons, it must needs follow, that the end which God propounded unto himself in this reconciliation, was the adoption of all men without exception, inasmuch as all men were strangers unto him. Among the ancients, Chrysostom expounds the word *kosmos,* world, in the text in hand, by the word *oikoumenēn,* which properly signifies the inhabited part of the world, or the persons of men wheresoever inhabiting in all the world; in which sense it is used, Acts xvii. 31, and in very many places besides in the Scriptures.

A third text of that squadron of Scriptures yet in hand, and the last of this character that we shall insist upon, is that mentioned from 1 John ii. 2, "And he is the propitiation for our sins: and not for ours only, but also for the sins of the whole world." Some, to keep the light of that truth which we have now under assertion, from shining out of this Scripture in their eyes, and in the eyes of others, have essayed, amongst them, a three-fold deprivation of the sense and import of these words, "the whole world." By the whole world, say some, John means the elect living in all parts of the world; others, men of all sorts and conditions; others, Jews and Gentiles. Some, to avoid the like danger, I mean of being convinced of the truth, and suspecting, as they have caused enough, the security of those interpretations, take sanctuary under the wing of this distinction. Christ, say they, is a propitiation for the sins of the whole world, *i.e.* of all men in the world in point of sufficiency, but not by way of intention on God's part. Yet let us afford the honour of a trial to the three interpretations mentioned.

For the first, which, by the whole world, understands only the elect, this hath been resolved into smoke already, in this chapter; where, if the reader please to look back, he may see it smoking still. The other two being confederate with it, for both the one and the other are the same in substance of matter with it, and differ only in terms of explication, must needs fall with it. For both they, who by the whole world, in the Scripture in hand, understand men of all sorts and conditions, by these men of all sorts and conditions understand the elect only; and they also, who interpret Jews and Gentiles, understand no other, either Jews of Gentiles, but the elect only. So that all the three interpretations are interpretatively but one and the same. And, therefore, as in case Abraham's son by Sarah had been sacrificed, Isaac could not have escaped; no more can any one of the three interpretations mentioned stand, if any one of them fall, there being but one and the same faint spirit of life in them all.

That which their respective assertors plead for their legitimacy, is of no value at all. For their plea is, that the word "world," and "the whole world," do in several other places signify sometimes the elect only; sometimes, men of all sorts, ranks, and conditions; sometimes likewise, Jews and Gentiles; and hereupon they conclude, that they may admit of the same sense and signification, both in the Scripture in hand, and in all the other Scriptures usually brought upon the theatre of discourse, for the same end and purpose with it. But the mouth of this plea is easily stopped. For

1. The determinate signification of a world in one place, is no argument of the same sense or signification of it in another place. Elohim, Gen. i. 1, signifieth him who is by nature *alēthinon theon*, John xvii, 3, a true God subsisting in three persons; but this is a weak proof that it is to be taken, or that it may be taken in the same sense, Psal. lxxxii. 6, where the prophet introduceth God speaking thus to, and concerning the rulers of the earth: I have said, "Ye are Elohim," or gods. That the word *kosmos* signifieth, 1 Peter iii, 3 as it is translated, "adorning," is no argument at all that it so signifieth John iii. 16, or in twenty places besides where it is used. Nay, in one and the same period or sentence, where the same word is twice used, it does not follow that because it is used, and must necessarily be taken in such or such a sense, determinately, in one of the places, therefore it must be taken in the same sense likewise in the other. As for example; where Christ saith to the scribe, "Let the dead bury their dead," Matt. viii. 22, because in the first place, by dead, are meant persons spiritually dead, or dead in sins and trespasses; it no ways follows from hence, that therefore it signifieth such as are spiritually dead in the latter place.

So likewise in that passage of our Saviour, "Whosoever drinketh of this water, shall thirst again; but whosoever drinketh of the water that I shall give him, shall never thirst," &c. John iv. 13, 14; by water, in the first place, he clearly meaneth that common and material element commonly known by the name of water. But in the latter, water analogically only, and spiritually so called, viz. the gift of the Spirit, as himself interpreteth, John vii. 39; iv. 14, compared. Therefore, to heap up a multitude of quotations from the Scriptures, wherein the word "world," or "the whole world," doth or may signify either a certain species, or determinate kind of persons living up and down the world, or men of all sorts and conditions, or Jews and Gentiles; and from either and evidence, or possibility of any, or all of these significations in these places, to infer either a necessity or possibility of a like signification of the words, either in the Scripture in hand, or in those other places argued in this chapter, is but to beat the air, or build upon the sand.

2. If the said words, either may be taken, or necessarily must be taken, in the places so multiplied, in any of the said significations, it is a sign that there is a sufficient ground of reason in the context respectively, to enforce either the necessity or possibility of such significations. Now then to infer or suppose, either a like necessity of the same signification, where there is no sufficient ground in the context to enforce either, which is the case in hand, but many sufficient grounds to overthrow such significations, as hath been in part already, and shall, God assisting, be out of hand further manifested, as concerning the texts insisted upon in this and the following chapter, is as if I should prove that such or such a man must needs be a prisoner at London, because he is a prisoner in York; or that he hath the liberty of the Tower of London, because he may walk where he pleaseth within the liberties of York Castle. The signification of words in one place, is not to be adjudged by their signification in another, unless both the contexts stand uniformly, and impartially affected towards this signification.

3. That neither of the two texts already opened, will at any hand endure any of the three significations of the world "world," (mentioned on the previous page) as pretended unto, hath been argued into the clearest evidence. That the text in hand no whit better comports with any of them than they, appeareth thus:

(a.) If any of the said three significations of "the whole world," should be here admitted, the apostle (or rather the Holy Ghost by the apostle) must be supposed to speak after no better rate of reason than this, "Christ is the propitiation not for our sins only, but also for the sins" of some few particular men besides, whom you know not, or of some few persons, as well of the Gentiles as of the Jews. For none of the three interpretations amounts to anything more than this, as is evident. They who interpret, that Christ is the propitiation for the sins of Jews and Gentiles, by Jews and Gentiles do not mean the two great divisions of men in the world commonly distinguished by these names, in all the particulars of either division, (for this is the sense and interpretation which we contend for) but that small and comparatively inconsiderable remnant of both, who in conclusion come to be actually saved. There is the same consideration of the two other interpretations. Now what weight, or worth of notion, or savour of sense there should be, in informing the Christians here written unto, that Christ was the propitiation for some few men's sins besides theirs, or as well as theirs, I yet understand not.

(b.) The natural and plain inclination of the context, leads to the interpretation and sense of "the whole world" contended for. For the apostle doth not simply say, that "Christ is the propitiation for the sins of the whole world," but he saith it by way of an emphatical antithesis, or addition to this saying, that he was "the propitiation for their sins." "And he is the propitiation for our sins: and not for ours only, but also for the sins of the whole world." This last clause, "but also for the sins of the whole world," is clearly added by way of augmentation or further strengthening to the ground of their faith and comfort. Now evident it is, that there will be little or nothing found in it tending to any such end, as the further enlargement of their comfort, or strengthening to their faith, above what the former clause presented, but rather that which will be prejudicial and ensnaring unto both, unless these words, "of the whole world," be taken in their comprehensive signification, I mean for all men in the world without exception. For to say thus unto a believer, or to a professor of the faith of Christ, who is doubtful about the grounds of his faith, and but weak in the comfort of it, (which was apparently the condition of those to whom John writes this epistle, and in consideration whereof that very clause we now speak of was added to the former) "Christ is the propitiation for the sins" of the elect, or of some few particular men, must needs rather add to their doubtings than their faith, and augment their fears rather than their comforts; yea, and would take from rather than add to that ground of consolidation, which he had administered in the former clause, "and he is the propitiation for our sins." For when I am in suspense, and doubtful in my spirit whether Christ died for me, or be a "propitiation for my sins," or no, how should it any ways tend or conduce to my establishment, for me to know or consider, that Christ died for his elect, or for some particular men, both of Jews and Gentiles, and for some only? Hath not such a doctrine, or consideration as this, fuel in it to increase the burnings of my fears within me, instead of water to quench or allay them? Or can I be ever a whit the more strengthened to believe that Christ died for me, by believing that he died for some particular men? Or must not my fears in this kind, I mean, whether Christ died for me, or no, needs be the more provoked and enraged within me, by considering, that Christ died for some particular men only?

Or doth such an assertion as this, that Christ died for some particular men, though never so substantially proved, though never so effectually believed, any ways enable, or dispose me to believe, that I am one of those particular men for whom he died? Nay, rather must not rumination or feeding upon such a notion, or conception as that, falling in conjunction with the weakness and doubtfulness of my faith, together with the sense and conscience of my many corruptions and infirmities otherwise, of necessity involve and perplex me with so much the more grievous and inextricable fears, that I am none of those particular men, none of those few for whom alone Christ died? Therefore any of those restrained interpretations of "the whole world," which we have opposed, do most manifestly oppose the plain scope and drift of the Holy Ghost, which was, as hath been proved, the strengthening or encouragement of their faith upon rich and excellent terms; whereas the true interpretation of the words, and that which we plead, hath the fairest and fullest consistence with such an intent, which can lightly be imagined. For the consideration, that Christ by his death became a propitiation, or made a full atonement for the sins of men, without exception, as it tends to magnify "the unsearchable riches" of the grace "of Christ," on the one hand, and so is proper to strengthen the hand of every man's faith; so, on the other hand, it throws down every mountain, and fills every valley, removes all obstructions, takes away all impediments, clears all scruples, and so prepares a plain and smooth way for every man to come unto Christ by believing, yea, and cuts off all occasions of relapses, or faintings in faith afterwards.

How it comes to pass, and how it may well stand with the justice of God, that notwithstanding the death of Christ for the sins of all men, yet all men are not saved, shall be taken unto consideration in due time and place.

Concerning the distinction mentioned, of Christ's dying sufficiently for all men, but not efficaciously or intentionally, on God's part, as it was first hammered out by workmen of no great credit with us for spiritual building, (the schoolmen, I mean) so is it built upon a false foundation or supposition, as viz. the intentions are attributable unto God upon the same terms in every respect wherein they are competible unto men. The contrary position is that God is, and very properly may be, said to intend, whatsoever he vouchsafeth proper and sufficient means to effect especially with a command to improve or use them accordingly, whether the thing be effected or no.

So that to affirm and grant, that Christ died sufficiently for all men, and yet deny that he died intentionally for all men, is to speak contradictions, and to pull down with the left hand what a man hath built up with his right. Certainly he that levyeth and employeth a proportion of means sufficient and proper for the bringing of any thing to pass, must needs, in one sense or other, in one degree or other; be supposed to intend the bringing to pass such a thing. Nor is it any dishonour at all unto God, nor in the least unworthy of him, that he doth not always attain his ends, or things intended by him, no more than it is that sin should be committed in the world, notwithstanding his opposing it by his authority, law, and threatenings, though in strictness and propriety of speech it is most true, that God never fails of his intentions or ends, if by intentions and ends we mean only such things which are absolutely and positively intended by him.

But in this sense the actual salvation of particular men, under any other consideration than as believers, is none of his intentions. "God so loved the world, that he gave his only begotten Son," (not simply or absolutely that the world, *i.e.* every man, no nor yet that any man should be saved, or "have everlasting life,") but that "whosoever believeth" should have it. So that the absolute and positive intentions of God concerning the salvation of men, are not concerning the salvation simply of men, or of any man as such, but of believers; and of such intentions as these he never faileth, of suffers disappointment.

Besides, if Christ died sufficiently for all men, either God intended this sufficiency of his death for or unto all men or not. If not, then was the glory or sovereign worth of this death of his, besides the intentions of God. God did not intend any such completeness of merit or satisfaction in his death as were in it. But this, I presume, tempteth no man's thoughts or belief. If, then, God did intend the sufficiency of his death for or unto all men, why may it not be said, that he intended his death itself accordingly? And so, that Christ died intentionally, on God's part, for all men? The word sufficiently is not *terminus diminuens*, no term of diminution. Therefore the argument follows roundly: if God intended the sufficiency of Christ's death for all men, then he intended his death itself for all men; and, consequently, Christ died not sufficiently only, but intentionally also for all men. And so the distinction vanisheth.

1. How can he, who payeth nothing at all for a man, nor intends to pay anything, be notwithstanding said to pay that which is sufficient for him? Suppose a man be in debt, and in danger of imprisonment for it, can a sufficient payment be said to be maid for him, whether any thing at all be paid for him, or in order to the keeping of him from imprisonment or not? When nothing at all is paid for that man that is a great debtor, but that remains as much a debtor and in as great danger as before, can that which is sufficient or enough for him, or for his discharge, be said to be paid for him, unless, haply, it be in a sense very delusory and deriding, in which sense, doubtless, Christ did not pay any ransom for any man? Suppose a man should pay a great sum of money only for the redeeming of John and Peter, being captives, by which money he might if he had pleased have ransomed me also, and a thousand more, being in the same condition of captivity with them. Can this man, by reason of the payment of such a sum as this upon the terms specified, be said to have paid that which is sufficient to ransom me? Or is that sufficient to ransom me, which was only paid for the ransom of another?

2. If there were a sufficiency in the death of Christ for all men, or for the salvation of all men, and God did not intend it for all men, but for a few, a number inconsiderably only, then will the death of Christ be found rather a matter of dishonour or disparagement unto him, than of honour? Suppose a man were possessed of a very great estate in gold, silver, and other the good things of this life, whereby he is able to relieve the necessities of all his neighbours round about him, who are generally poor, and that to such an extremity that without relief from him they must inevitably perish; in case this man should resolve to relieve only two or three of these indigent persons with this his abundance, and rather throw the rest of it into the midst of the sea, than minister unto any more of them, though they be many thousands, and these every whit as necessitous and as well deserving as the other; would not this great estate, in such a case and upon such terms as these, be a blot rather, and reproach, than an honour or matter of repute to this man, and declare him to be of a very unnatural, ignoble, and inhuman spirit?

In like manner, if God shall have satisfaction, merit, and atonement before him, abundantly sufficient to save the whole world from perishing everlastingly, and shall purpose rather to let it be "like water spilt upon the ground, which cannot be gathered up," than dispose of it towards the salvation of any more than only a small handful of men, comparatively, leaving innumerable souls to perish irrecoverably, and without mercy; would not this abundance of merit and satisfaction, upon such an account as this, be, in the eyes of all considerate men, an obscuring veil over the mercy, love, goodness, and bounty of God, and occasion the creature to judge of him, as a God rather envying than desiring the peace and welfare of men?

And if God so deeply abhorred the fact of Onan, "in spilling the seed upon the ground, lest he should give seed unto his (deceased) brother," that he slew him for it, Gen. xxxviii. 9, 10, how dare men present him so near unto communion in such a fact, as the spilling, interverting, or non-consigning of the far greater part of the merit of the death of Christ unto men, lest they should be saved, would render him?

3. If Christ died sufficiently for all men, and not intentionally, as, viz. not for reprobates, so called, then he died as much for the devils themselves as he did for the greatest part of men. Because his death, in respect of the intrinsical value and worth of it, was sufficient to have redeemed the devils as well as men. Yea, if the sufficiency of the price paid by Christ, be a sufficient ground to bear such a saying as this, that he died sufficiently for all men, he may be said to have died, not only for reprobates as reprobates, and so for unbelievers as unbelievers, (viz. sufficiently) but for the devils also, quatenus devils: inasmuch as there is no defect imaginable in the price we speak of, in respect of the absolute and inherent dignity, value, or worth of it, but that all these, even under the considerations mentioned, might have been redeemed by it as well as the elect. But that Christ died for reprobates as reprobates, and for devils as devils, in one sense or other, were never yet, I conceive, the sayings or thoughts of any man, nor, I suppose, ever will be; certain I am, cannot reasonable be.

4. Lastly, as yet there hath no sufficient ground been shown, either from the Scriptures, or from principles of reason, for the distinction under contest, nor I believe, ever will be, or can be. Therefore they who distinguish between Christ's dying for all men, sufficiently and intentionally, opposing the one to the other, affirming the former, and denying the latter, do not only go about to set lambs together by the ears, which will not fight, but also speak things most unworthy of God, and which render him a far greater deluder or derider of his poor creature, man, than a benefactor or

well-willer to him, in all his declarations and professions of love unto him, in the gift of his Son Jesus Christ to make his atonement, and procure redemption for him.

Upon consultation had with the premises, with other considerations, haply, of like import, some of the greatest and most learned opposers of universal redemption, Piscator and Beza by name, have stigmatized the aforesaid distinction, (at least that member of it wherein Christ is said to have died sufficiently for all men) as harsh, barbarous, homonymous; yea, the former of the two as absolutely false. "That expression," saith Beza, "Christ died for the sins of all men, sufficiently, but not efficaciously, though in a rectified sense it be true, yet is it extremely harsh, and no less ambiguous than barbarous. For the particle *for* imports either the counsel of the Father, according to which Christ suffered, or else the effect itself of his sufferings, or rather both; whereas neither of them belong to any but the elect."[8] Piscator to his antagonist, thus: "The proposition laid down is false, viz. that Christ died sufficiently for every particular or single man; this is thy assertion. For Christ died most sufficiently for the elect, paying the price of their redemption, I mean his precious blood, that blood of the Son of God. But for reprobates Christ died neither in one kind nor other, neither sufficiently nor efficaciously."[9]

8. Beza ad Acta Coloq. Monpelg. part ii. p. 217.
9. Pisc. contra Schaffman, p. 123.

CHAPTER II
Wherein several texts of the second sort of Scriptures propounded in Chap. I, as holding forth the Universality of Redemption by Christ, are discussed.

THE first of these Scriptures there mentioned was this: "Who gave himself ransom for all," or for all men, "to be testified in due time," 1 Tim. ii. 6. Let the context adjoining to this Scripture be narrowly sifted, and then, if we shall but grant that the apostle speaks either sap, sense, savour, or anything congruous to the judgments or understandings of men, we shall not be able to deny but that it carries the doctrine asserted with a high hand of evidence in it.

Evident it is, that the apostle in this verse goes on with the confirmation or further proof of that reason of his, laid down in verse 4, for the making good what he had said in verse 3: "For this is good and acceptable in the sight of God our Saviour." This is good, meaning the performance of that duty whereunto he had exhorted verses 1 and 2, viz. that "Supplications, prayers, intercessions, giving of thanks, should be made for *all men*, for kings, and for all that are in authority," &c. Now then, most evident it is, that by *all* men, in this first verse, for whom prayers, &c. are to be made unto God, is not meant some of *all* sorts of men, nor yet *all* the elect or the like, but *all* of *all* sorts of men whatsoever, except haply those who have barred up the way of our prayers for them, by that unpardonable sin against the Holy Ghost, as John intimates, 1 John v. 16.

For that which followeth verse 2 clearly evinceth it; "For kings, and for all in authority." Certainly if this be good and acceptable in the sight of *God*, that we should pray for *all* of one sort or degree of men in the world, especially for all in authority, (in which sort or rank of men there are many as unworthy and incapable of our prayers as in any other) it is good and acceptable in his sight likewise, that we should pray for *all* in *all* other ranks or sorts of men whatsoever. For there is nothing imaginable to cause a difference in this point. So then, to prove that it is "good and acceptable in the sight of *God* to pray for all men," without exception, the apostle layeth down this ground, verse 4: "That God will have all men to be saved."

If now by *all* men in this reason we shall understand only some of *all* sorts of men, or *all* the elect only, as our opponents assert, we shall shorten the arm of the apostle's argument so far that it will not reach half way towards that conclusion. For the proof shall make him reason very weakly, and, indeed, ridiculously, as viz., after this manner: "It is good and acceptable in the sight of God that we should pray universally for all men, without exception of any, because God will have all his elect to be saved, or some out of every sort of men." There is little savour of an argument in this; whereas the rationality and strength of the apostle's arguing rightly understood, is pregnant and full of conviction.

"It is good and acceptable in the sight of God" that we should pray for *all* men, without exception, because his will is to have *all* men, without exception, saved. The strength of this argument lieth in this ground, or clear principle in reason, viz., that a conformity unto his own will, in the will and endeavours of men, is, and must needs be, "good and acceptable in the sight of God." Now then to prove that God's will is, that *all* men without exception, should be saved, the apostle brings this reason, in the words in hand, viz., that "Christ Jesus gave himself a ransom for all men." So that (in the Greek) *pantōn, all* men here, in this reason, must of necessity be of the same extent, with the same word in the doctrine or conclusion which was to be proved; otherwise we shall make the apostle stumble at that stone in arguing, at which only novices, or liars-in-wait to deceive, are wont to stumble, as viz., when there is more put into the conclusion than into the premises. That which here lay upon the apostle's hand to prove, was, as hath been undeniably evicted, that God's will is to have all men, without exception, saved.

Now, to prove this by such an argument or assertion as this, that Christ gave himself a ransom either for *all* his elect, or for some of all sorts of men, or for some as well Gentiles as Jews, and for no others, is as if I should undertake to prove the bountifulness of a prince towards all his subjects, being many, by such an argument as this, that he sent by a special servant of his very great rewards to two or three of them, but resolved to do nothing at all for any more of them. Therefore, universality of redemption by Christ is the most unquestionable doctrine of the apostle in this Scripture.

The next specified in the said catalogue or inventory, was, "Because we thus judge, that if one died for *all*, then were *all* dead; and that he died for *all*, that they who live should not henceforth live unto themselves, but unto him who died for them, and rose again." 2 Cor. v. 14, 15. We see the apostle's judgment here is very clear, that Christ died for *all*. He once clearly supposeth that "if one died for all," *i.e.* since one died for *all*, the particle *if*, being ratiocinantis, not dubitantis, as in twenty places besides, meaning Christ; and once plainly asserteth it, "and that he died for all," *i.e.* we also judge that he died for *all*.

That which is commonly given by way of answer to this and other Scriptures, both of the former and latter import, by those who look another way in the controversy in hand, is not much considerable. They pretend that both the word "world" and such terms of universality as "all," "all men," "every man," &c., in many places of Scripture used, and accordingly are to be understood in a restrained signification, as sometimes for many or greater numbers of men; sometimes for some of all sorts; sometimes for Jews and Gentiles, or the like. From whence they would infer, that therefore such terms and expressions as these are in the Scripture in hand, and in the others formerly cited for our purpose, to be taken in some of these limited significations; and not in the rigour or extent of what they properly signify, as viz., for an absolute and unlimited universality of men. For to this we answer,

1. By way of concession, most true it is, that these notes or terms of universality, "all," "all men," "every man," &c., are in many places of Scripture necessarily to be taken in some such limited and restrained signification as is affirmed. But then,

2. I answer further, by way of exception, four things:

(a.) That neither the terms we speak of, nor any other words or expressions in Scripture, are in any other case, or upon any other pretence whatsoever, to be taken out of their proper and best-known significations, but only when the tenor of the context or some circumstance of the place doth necessitate and enforce such a construction of them. Now, evident it is, by what hath been formerly argued upon the Scriptures alleged, that there is no necessity at all in respect of any the respective contexts, nor of any circumstance in any of them, to understand the said terms of universality any otherwise than in their most proper, *i.e.* in their most extensive and comprehensive significations.

(b.) That which is more than this, we have evidently proved that the very tenor of the several contexts wherein the aforesaid places are found, doth absolutely enforce and necessitate us unto such a proper and comprehensive signification of the said terms of universality, as hath been contended for. So there can be no reasonable, regular, or grammatical sense or construction made of those places, unless such a sense of these terms be admitted.

(c.) To reason thus, that these words or terms, are to be taken in this or in that sense in such and such places of Scripture; therefore they must or they may be taken in the same sense in such and such *other* places of Scripture, is to reason ourselves into a thousand errors and absurdities. For example, evident it is, that in the Scripture, John xviii. 16, where it is said that Peter stood at the door, by the word *door* is meant a door of wood or some such material; but it would be ridiculously erroneous to infer from hence that therefore it is to be taken, and may be taken, in the same sense in John x. 9, where Christ saith, "I am the door." So again, when Paul saith that Christ sent him "to the gentiles to open their eyes," Acts xxvi. 18, evident it is, that by the word *eyes* he means their inward eyes, their minds, judgments, and understandings. But from hence to conclude that therefore when David saith about idols, "eyes have they..." Psal. cxv. 5, the word *eyes* is to be understood in the same sense, is to conclude that which common sense itself abhorreth.

So that the weakness of all such arguings or pleadings as this, that "all," "all men," "every man," are in various places of Scripture to be taken in a limited sense, for some of all sorts of men, for Jews and Gentiles, or the like, and therefore are to be taken in the same sense in all others where they are found – is notorious and most unworthy of considering men. Though, whilst a man is a prisoner, he cannot go whither he desires, but must be content with the narrow bounds of this prison; it doth not follow from hence, that therefore, when he is discharged and set at liberty, he must needs continue in his prison still, especially when his necessary occasions call him to another place, whither also he hath desire otherwise to go.[1]

We have, as concerning the former Scripture, evidently proved that the terms "all" and "all men" must be of necessity taken in their most proper, free, and unlimited significations; and shall, God assisting, demonstrate the same in those yet remaining. Let us at present, because the place in hand is pregnant and full to our purpose, evince, above all contradiction, that the words "*all*," or "*all* men," in it cannot, with the honour of Paul's intellectuals, be understood otherwise. "Because we thus judge," saith he, "that if one died for *all*, then were *all* dead: and that he died for *all*, that they who live," &c. Observe that clause of distribution, "that they who live." "We judge that Christ died for *all*, that they who live," *i.e.* that all they, without

---

1. See more about this in Chap. I.

exception, who recover, and are, or shall be delivered from his death by Chris for them, "should not live unto themselves," &c. So then, if by the word "all" or "all men," for whom the apostle here judgeth or concludeth that Christ died, we shall understand the universality of the elect only, "for *all* men," *i.e.* for all the elect, and for these only, we shall grievously misfigure the fair face a worthy sentence, and render it incongruous and inconsistent with all rules and principles of discourse.

For then the tenor of it must rise and run thus: We judge that Christ died for all the elect, that all the elect who shall live and be recovered from death by Christ, should not live, &c. Doth not the ears of every man's reason, yea, of common sense itself, taste an uncouthness and unsavouriness of sound in such a texture of words as this? Yea, doth not such a carriage of the place clearly imply that there are or may be some of the elect themselves who shall not live or be restored from dead by Christ, and consequently shall not be bound upon any such engagement to live unto him? Doubtless, if by the word *all,* the apostle had meant all the elect, and these only, he would not have added, "that they who live," but rather, that they or these might live: for these words, "that they who live," clearly import a possibility at least, yea, a futurity also, *i.e.* that it would so come to pass, that some of those all, for whom Christ died, would not live, and consequently would be in no capacity of living from themselves to live unto him.

The uncouthness and senselessness of such interpretations as these was somewhat more at large argued in the next preceding chapter; but now let us take the word *pantōn, all,* in the proper and due signification of it, viz. for the generality or universality of men, the sense will run clear, and have a savoury and sweet relish with it: "Because we thus judge," *i.e.* upon clear grounds and principles of reason, argue and conclude, "that if one died for all men, then were all men dead;" *i.e.* obnoxious unto death, dead in law, as good as dead, otherwise they should not have had any need that another should die for their preservation; "and that he died for all men," *i.e.* we further also judge and conclude that he died for all men, with this intent or for this end amongst others, "that they who live," *i.e.* that whosoever of those, for whom he thus died, shall be saved by this death of his for them, "should," in consideration of, and by way of signal thankfulness for such a salvation, "not live unto themselves," *i.e.* only and chiefly mind themselves whilst they live in the world, in their carnal and worldly interests, "but unto him who died for them and rose again," *i.e.* promote his interest and affairs in the world, who so notably engaged them hereunto by dying for them, and, by resuming his life and being after his death, is capable of their love and service to him in this kind.

In such a carriage of the place as this, there is spirit and life, evidence of reason, commodiousness of sense, regularity of construction, no forcing or straining of words or phrases, or the like. Whereas, in any such expositions which contract the signification of the word *pantōn* (all) men, either to the elect, or to any lesser number of men than all, there will be found a universal disturbance in the sentence, nothing orderly, smooth, or clear.

By the way, the apostle in saying that Christ died for all men, that they who live should not live unto themselves, &c. doth not intend to confine the duty of thankfulness for Chris's death only unto the saints, or those that are put into an estate of salvation by it, as if wicked men and unbelievers owed him no service at all upon that account. Paul only shows, that Christ expects or looks for no such denial of themselves for his sake at the hands of any, but of theirs only who come actually to taste and partake of the great benefit and blessing of his death. Thus then we see, that the word "all," and "all men," though in some place or places it may, yea, of necessity must signify only some men, or some parts of all men, yet in those two lately insisted upon, it must with the like necessity signify all men without exception.

(d.). And lastly, for the word "world," which was the term of contention in the former head of Scriptures, though I deny not, but that in some places it signifies only some part of men in the world, and not the entire universality of men, as Luke ii. 1; Acts xiv. 27, and frequently elsewhere. Yet I do deny that it anywhere signifies precisely that part of the world which the Scripture call the elect, I absolutely deny, neither hath it yet been, nor, I believe, ever will be proved; and the rather, because the Holy Ghost delights still, as some instances have been given in Chap. I, and more might be added without number, to express that part or party of men in the world, which is contrary unto the saints, and which are strangers and enemies unto God, by "the world." This by way of answer to that exception of pretence against the exposition given of the Scriptures alleged, viz. that the word "world," and those general terms "all" and "every man," are sometimes used in a restrained signification.

Concerning the exposition given of the Scripture last argued, were it not clear and pregnant enough by the light wherein it hath been presented, further countenance might be given unto it, by showing what friends it hath amongst our best and most approved authors. Among the ancients,

Chrysostom is generally esteemed, and that worthily, the best interpreter of the Scriptures. His sense of the place under debate is plainly enough the same with ours. "For," saith he, writing upon the place, "He (meaning Christ) had not died, or would not have died, for all, had not all died or been dead." In which words he clearly supposeth, that Christ died for as many as were dead, and consequently for *all*, without exception, inasmuch as *all*, without exception or difference, were dead. A little after, thus: "for it argueth an excess of much love, both to die for *so great a world*, and to die for it being so affected or disposed as it was."

Amongst our later divines, Musculus is not the least, if not equal to the greatest. Yet he also gives the right hand of fellowship to the interpretation given upon the place. "But Christ," saith he, "died not only for his friends, but for his enemies also; *not for some men only, but for all*, without exception. This is the unmeasurable or vast extent of the love of God." But the cause we plead needs no such advocates as these, being potent enough with its own evidence and equity, and therefore we shall retain no more of them.

A third text of Scripture presented upon the same account with the former, was, "that he by the grace of God should taste death *huper pantos* for every man." Heb. ii. 9. This clause importeth that universality of atonement made by the death of Christ, which we maintain more significantly, if more may be, and with less liableness to any evasion or shift, than any of the former places engaged in the warfare. To show that the Lord Christ, though clothed with a body of flesh, wherein he was capable of dying as well as other men, yet did not suffer death simply through the malice or power of his enemies, but upon an account far superior to these. The inspired writer attributes his death to the grace of God, *i.e.* the love and gracious affections of God, not towards some, or a few, no, nor yet towards all men collectively taken or in the lump, but towards all men distributively taken, *i.e.* towards every particular and individual man. "*Huper pantos,*" saith the Holy Ghost, "for every man;" *i. e.* to procure eternal redemption and salvation for every man, without the exclusion of any. I cannot apprehend what can reasonably be said to alienate the mind or import of this Scripture from our present cause.

Evident it is, and you shall find our best interpreters of the place affirming the same, that the author in these words, "that through the grace of God he might taste death," &c., assigns a reason, or two rather, of what he had said a little before concerning the incarnation and humiliation of Jesus Christ, whom he had in the former chapter asserted to be the Son of God, to prevent or heal any scandal or offence that either had already, or might afterwards arise in the minds of these Hebrews, through the unlikelihood, strangeness, or incredibleness of such a thing. It is a saying among philosophers, and many men have experienced the truth in it that knowledge of reasons or causes of things causeth admiration, and prompts all troublesomeness of thoughts about them to cease.

So then, the author's drift and intent in these words mentioned, being to satisfy the Hebrews concerning such a strange, wonderful, and unheard of thing, as, 1. That the Son of God should be made man; and, 2. That being made man, he should suffer death; it is no ways credible but that he should, (a.) Assign such a cause as would carry the greatest weight of satisfaction in it; and (b.) Express himself in such perspicuity and plainness of words, that they might not lightly mistake his meaning, lest if by occasion of his words they should first apprehend the reason or cause assigned by him, to be more weighty or considerable than he intended it, and afterwards should come to understand that it was far lighter and less considerable. Their scandal and offence, instead of being healed or prevented, would be more strengthened and increased, as usually it comes to pass in such cases.

Now, evident it is, 1. That the author's words in this place, "That He, through the grace of God, should taste death for every man," in the plainest, the most obvious and direct sense and signification of them, hold forth the doctrine which we maintain for truth, here being no restraint at all, nor the least whispering of any limitation to be put upon that term of universality, *pantos*, every man; and 2. As evident it is, that the death of Christ for all men, without the exception of any, which is the doctrine we assert, and the grace of God so intending it, amount to a far more weighty consideration and satisfaction, touching those great dispensations spoken of, (the incarnation and humiliation of the Son of God) than his dying only for a few, or for a select number of men, and the grace of God commensurable hereunto.

Therefore there is not the least question to be made, but that the large, and not the limited sense, was the author's sense in the words now under debate. And when the Holy Ghost expresseth himself, as we have heard, "That he, through the grace of God, should taste death for *every man;*" for any man to come and interpret thus, *for every man, i. e.* for some men, or for a few men, which, if not for form, yet for matter and substance must be their interpretation who oppose the exposition given, is not to interpret, but to correct, and to exercise a magisterial authority over the Scriptures.

Nor had Pareus himself the heart to decline the interpretation asserted, though he seems somewhat desirous by some expressions, to hide this his ingenuity from his fellows, to avoid their offence, "Whereas," saith he, the author "saith, for every man, it respects the amplification, or extent, of the death of Christ. *He died not for some few*; the efficacy, or virtue, of it appertains unto ALL. Therefore there is life prepared," (or made ready) "in the death of Christ, for ALL afflicted consciences," &c. The truth is, that there can he no solid ground of peace or comfort to any afflicted conscience whatsoever, without the supposal of Christ's death for every man, without exception, as hath been argued in part in Chapter 1, and might be further evicted above all contradiction.

Amongst the orthodox fathers, Chrysostom, who, as we heard, avouched the exposition given of the former Scripture, stands by his own judgment and mine, in his explication of this. "That he, through the grace of God, should taste death for every man; not only," saith he, "for the faithful, or those that believe, but for *all the world*. He indeed died for ALL men. For what if all men do not believe? yet he hath done his part," or fully performed that which was proper for him to do.

The Scripture next advancing in the fore-mentioned troop was, "Who will have *all men* to be saved," (speaking of God) " and to come unto the knowledge of the truth," 1 Tim. ii. 4. Whereunto (for conformity in import) we shall join the last there specified, which is this: "The Lord is not slack concerning his promise as some men count slackness; but is long suffering to us-ward, not willing that any should perish, but that *all* should come to repentance." 2 Pet. iii. 9. Concerning the former of these places, we clearly evinced, earlier in this chapter, from the unquestionable tenor and carriage of the whole context, that by "*all* men," cannot possibly be understood, either some of all sorts of men, or Jews and Gentiles, or all the elect, or the like; but of necessity, *all* of all sorts of men, simply and universally, without the exception of any, whether Jews or Gentiles. Any other interpretation or sense of the words, *pantas anthrōpous*, all men (1 Tim. 2:4), but this, renders the apostle palpably impertinent and weak (that I say not ridiculous) in his arguing in this place.

This I plainly demonstrate in the place above cited: I now add, that if it be said that God will have all men to be saved, because he will have some of all sorts of men to he saved; it may more properly and truly be said of him, that he will have all men to be destroyed, at least in their sense, who hold an irreversible reprobation of persons personally considered, from eternity, because not simply some, but a very great part of all sorts of men, now extant in the world, will in time perish, and that according to the decree or will of God; the tenor whereof is, that all persons dying in impenitency and unbelief shall perish. Yet the Scriptures do no where say upon any such account as this, either in terminis, or in substance, that God will have all men to perish, and not to come to the knowledge of the truth. Which is somewhat more than a topic argument, that God is not therefore said to will that all men should be saved, and come to the knowledge of the truth, only because he will have some, some few of all sorts of men to be saved, and come to this knowledge: but simply because his will is to have all men, without exception, (viz., as they are men, and whilst they are yet capable of repentance) to be saved, and in order thereunto to come to the knowledge of the saving truth, *i.e.* the gospel.

Nor doth it follow, that the will of God is changeable, in case he should will the same man as this day to be saved, and so on the morrow to perish, but only that such a man is changeable, as we shall further show, God willing, in due time. Now then, if it be the will of God to have all men, without exception, saved, &c., most certain it is that Christ died, and intentionally on God's part, for all men, without exception. That because it is not imaginable that God should be willing to have those saved for whom he was unwilling that salvation should be procured.

The latter of the two Scriptures lately brought upon the theatre of our present discourse, acts the same part with the former. There it is said of the Lord (Christ) that he is not "willing that any should perish, but that *all* should come to repentance." If so, then certainly there neither was, nor is, nor ever shall be any, for whom Christ was not willing, did not intend, to die, and to purchase repentance. So that his death was intentionally for all men, as well in respect of himself, as of God the Father. Besides those slimy evasions and shifts of making bondmen of Christ's freemen, I mean of an arbitrary and importunate confining the expressions importing a simple and absolute universality, in such Scriptures as these, to petty universalities, as of the elect, of species, sorts, or kinds of men, &c., (the nakedness whereof hath been detected over and over) our adversaries in the cause in hand are wont to take sanctuary from such Scriptures as the two now in debate, under the wing of this distinction. "It is true," say they, "God wills that all men should be saved, and so that all should come to repentance, voluntate signi, with his signified or revealed will; but this doth not prove but that voluntate beneplaciti, with the will of his pleasure, or purpose, he may be willing that many, even far the greatest part of men, should perish." But to show the vanity, or at least the impertinency of this distinction to the business in hand:

1. I would demand of those who lean upon the broken reed of this distinction, in opposition to the clear and distinct sense given of the two Scriptures last mentioned, what they mean by their voluntas signi, the signified or revealed will of God. And wherein doth the opposition or difference lieth between this and that other will of God, which they term the will of his good pleasure or purpose? If by his signified or revealed will, they mean only the precepts or commandments of God concerning such and such duties, which God would have practised and done by men, (which is all the account that some of the greatest opposers in the point in hand give of it) I do not understand how, or in what respect, God can be said to will the salvation of all men, and that none should perish. For,

(a.) Salvation actively taken, is an act of God himself, not of men; and consequently cannot be said to be a duty enjoined by him unto men, and therefore not to be willed neither by him, by way of precept or command.

(b.) Salvation, passively taken, is not an act, but a state or condition; and consequently is no matter of duty; and so cannot be said to be willed by God in such a sense.

If by the signified or revealed will of God, in the distinction now under canvass, be meant the declaration which he hath made in his word concerning the final or eventual salvation or condemnation of men, evident it is, that neither in this sense can be said to will the salvation of all men; because he hath declared and signified unto the world that few comparatively will or shall in time be saved.

If it be pleaded, that in this sense God may be said to will the salvation of all men with his signified or revealed will, because he enjoins faith and repentance unto all men, which are the means of salvation; and he that enjoins the means, may, in a consequential way, be said to enjoin the end in the same injunction, I answer,

If God enjoins faith and repentance unto all men, it argues that he preacheth the gospel unto all men; and consequently, that they who have not the letter of the gospel preached unto them by books or men, as many heathen nations have not at this day, yet have the spirit, substance, and effect of the gospel preached to them otherwise, as, viz. by God's creation and gracious government of the world, which is, as I have shown elsewhere,[2] purely evangelical and corresponding with the Scriptures. But how this will stand

2. Divine Authority of the Scriptures, p. 184, 185, 332, 333.

with our adversaries' judgment in the case depending, I understand not.

2. It is the sense of one of the greatest patrons of the adverse cause, that "the precept or injunction of God[3] is not properly the will of God because," saith be, "he doth not hereby so much signify what himself willeth to be done, as what is our duty to do." I confess that no signification whatsoever, whether of what a man willeth or decreeth to be done, or of what is the duty of another to do, can properly be said to be the will of the signifier; but yet that will, wherewith or out of which God willeth or commandeth us to do that which is our duty to do, is as properly his will as that whereby he willeth or decreeth things to be done.

My will or desire that my child should obey me, or that he should prosper in the world, is as properly my will as that whereby I will or purpose to show the respects of a father unto him in providing for him; being as proper, natural, and direct an act of that principle or faculty of willing within me whereby I will the former, as that act itself of this faculty wherein I will the latter is. For the principle or faculty within me of willing, how numerous or different soever the acts of willing which I exert by virtue of this faculty may be, is but one and the same; and this faculty being natural, there can be no such difference between the acts proceeding from it which should make some to be more proper and others less, though some may be better and others worse.

But this difference can have no place in the acts of the will of God; therefore, if the precept or preceptive will of God be not properly his will, neither can any other will of his, or any other act of his will, be properly such. If so, then that will of God, or act of will in God, whereby he willeth or enjoineth faith and repentance, and consequently salvation, unto all men, is as properly his will as that whereby he willeth the salvation of any man. Therefore, if there be any secret or unrevealed will in God, whereby he willeth the destruction of any man at the same time when he willeth the salvation of all men, (be it with what kind of will soever) these two wills must needs interfere and contradict the one the other.

Nor will that distinction of the late-mentioned author salve a consistency between them, wherein he distinguisheth between the decree of God and the thing decreed by him, affirming that "the thing which God decreeth may be repugnant to or inconsistent with the thing which he commandeth, though the decree itself cannot be repugnant to the command."[4] The vanity of this distinction clearly appeareth upon this common ground, viz. that acts are differenced and distinguished by their objects: therefore, if the

3. Dr. Twisse, Vindicia Gratie, &c. p. 171.
4. Twissus, ubi supra.

object of God's decreeing will, or the thing decreed by him, be contrary to the thing preceptively willed or commanded by him, impossible it is but that the two acts of his will, by the one of which he is supposed to will the one, and by the other the other, should digladiate and one fight against the other. Therefore, certainly, there is no such pair or combination of wills in God as the distinction of voluntas signi and beneplaciti (as applied in the question in hand) doth suppose. It is impossible that I should inwardly and seriously will or desire the death of my child, and yet at the same time seriously also will and enjoin the physician to do his best to recover him.

Again, if God enjoin faith and repentance unto all men, with a declaration that he enjoineth them in order to their salvation, or with a promise that, upon their obedience to this injunction of his, they shall be actually saved, then can he not at the same time will with a secret will the condemnation of any? But most evident it is, that unto whomsoever he enjoineth faith or repentance, he enjoineth them in order to their salvation, and with promise of actual salvation upon their obedience to this injunction, Mark 1. 15; Acts iii. 19; John xx. 31, &c. Therefore, impossible it is, that he should secretly intend, will, or purpose the destruction of any to whom he enjoins faith and repentance.

The consequence in this argument is so rich in evidence, that it needs no proof. If a prince should inwardly and resolvedly determine to put such or such a malefactor to death, and yet by proclamation or otherwise promise him his life or a pardon upon condition he would reform his course, would this be a strain of divine perfection, or like unto one of the ways of God?

There is a sense, I confess, wherein the distinction now in consideration may be admitted. If by the signified or revealed will of God be meant nothing else but such declarations or manifestations made by God, which, when made by men, are signs of a will, purpose, or desire in them, suitable to their respective tenors and imports, (which is clearly their sense of this member of the distinction who were the first coiners of it, I mean the schoolmen)[5] there is no inconvenience in granting a revealed will in God distinguished from or opposed unto a will of good pleasure or of purpose in him. This sense makes no opposition of wills in God, nor yet between things willed or purposed by him. It only showeth or supposeth that the will and good pleasure in God extendeth not to the actual procurement of obedience from men unto all those laws or commands which he judgeth meet to impose upon them; or, which is the same, that God hath not positively decreed that all men shall, or shall be necessitated by him to live in

5. Aqu. Sum. part I, qu. 19, Art. 12. in Cor.

subjection to all those laws which he hath appointed unto them.

This sense is orthodox, and blameable, but holds no intelligence with that opinion which supposeth one will in God, according unto which he willeth all men to be saved; and another, according unto which he willeth the far greatest part of men to be damned, and both antecedent. For otherwise, two such wills as these are fairly and clearly enough consistent in him. God, according to the distinction of the will of God into antecedent and consequent, first set on foot by some of the fathers, Chrysostom, and Damascen by name, and since made use of by the schoolmen, may, with the former, be said to will the salvation of all men. Yet with the latter be said also, in a sense, to will the condemnation of far the greatest part of them.

His antecedent will, the distinction being admitted as it ought to be, having so clear a foundation in Scripture, respecteth men simply as men; his consequent will relateth to them as considerable under the two opposite qualifications, or immediate capacities of life and death, or of salvation and condemnation; the one of these being faith persevered in unto death, the other, final impenitency or unbelief. According to the former of these wills, God is said to will the salvation of all men, partly because he vouchsafeth a sufficiency of means unto all men whereby to be saved; partly also, because he hath passed no decree against any man which either formally, or consequentially, or in any consideration whatsoever excludeth any man, personally considered, from salvation before he voluntarily excludeth himself by such sinful miscarriages and deportments, which, according to the revealed will of God, render him utterly incapable thereof.

According to the latter of these wills, as he peremptorily willeth the salvation of all those who are faithful unto death; so doth he as peremptorily will the condemnation of all those who shall not be found in the faith of Jesus Christ at their end. The latter, through their own deplorable and voluntary carelessness and negligence, proving to be in number far the greater part of men, God, upon this supposition, and in a consequential way, may be said to will the condemnation of the greatest part of men, and the salvation only of a few, comparatively. But of these things more hereafter.

In the meantime, evident it is from the Scriptures argued, that Christ died intentionally for all men, without exception, considered as men; and that there was nothing more procured, nor intended to be procured, thereby for one man than another, personally considered, or simply as men. Only this was intended in this death of Christ, in the general, that whosoever, whether few or whether many, should with a true and persevering faith believe in him, should actually partake of the benefit and blessing of this his death in the great reward of salvation; and on the other hand, that whosoever, whether few or whether many, should not believe in him with such a faith, should, upon this account, be excluded from all participation in the great blessing of salvation purchased by his death. This notwithstanding the purchase that was made, and intended to be made for them as for those who come actually to inherit; even as the marriage feast in the parable was as much provided, prepared, and intended for those, who upon their invitation came not, as it was for those who came and actually partook of it; unless we shall say that the king who made this feast intended it not for those whom, notwithstanding, he solemnly invited to it, and with whom he was highly displeased for their refusal to come, being invited, Matt. xxii. 3, 4, &c.

And that the death of Christ, and the gracious intentions of God therein, did, and do equally and uniformly respect all men, is abundantly manifest from that declaration made by the Lord Christ himself on this behalf, formerly opened; "For God so loved the world, that he gave his only begotten Son, that whosoever believeth in him should not perish, but have everlasting life." John iii. 16. Those words, "that whosoever believeth on him should not perish," &c., evidently import indifferenced and impartial intentions on God's part towards men in the gift of his Son.

The last Scripture of the division yet in hand was this, "Therefore as by the offence of one, the judgment came upon all men to condemnation; even so by the righteousness of one, the free gift came upon all men unto the justification of life," Rom. v. 18. Evident it is, that the apostle in this passage compareth the extent of the condemnation which came by the sin of Adam, with the extent of the grace of justification which came by Christ, in respect of the numbers of persons unto whom they extended respectively, and finds them in this point commensurable the one unto the other.

The persons upon whom the gift of justification cometh by Christ, are made equal in number unto those upon whom the judgment of condemnation came by Adam. For as the offence of Adam is here said to have come upon *all men* unto condemnation, so also is the gift of justification of life, *i.e.* of such a justification upon which, and *by means* whereof, men are saved, which comes by Jesus Christ and said to come *upon all men* likewise. Now to say, that *all men* in the former clause is to be taken properly and signifies *all men*, indeed, without exception of any, which all expositors grant without exception of any, but in the latter improperly and with limitation, yea, with such a limitation, which comparatively, and a few only excepted, excludes *all men*, there being not the least ground or reason in the context to vary the signification of the words, or to make them to signify more in the one clause and fewer in the other, is to exercise an arbitrary dominion over the expressions of the Holy Ghost, and to invent and set up significations and senses of words at pleasure.

Nor doth it at all ease the matter, to say or prove, that in other places of Scripture this phrase *pantas anthrōpous*, all men, signifies not all without exception, but only a great number, or all of one particular sort or kind of persons; because,

1. If it can be proved that in other places of Scripture it so signifies, I mean not all without exception, but only some greater number or numbers of men, it seems then there is a reason why it should or must so signify in these places; otherwise, it could not be proved that there it so signifies. But here is no reason at all to be given why it should be taken out of the proper and native signification, or signify any lesser number than all men simply. Now to refuse the proper signification of a word, where there is no other reason why it should be refused, but only because it is to be refused where there is a reason, and so a necessity, to refuse it, is as if one should persuade a man that is hungry to forbear meat whilst he may have it, because he must forbear it when he cannot get it. When the context or subject matter doth require a by, less proper or limited signification of a word or phrase, this signification is put upon them by God. But when there is no occasion or necessity, either in respect of the one or of the other, why such a signification should be put upon them, now if it be done, the doing of it is arbitrary, and from the lawless presumption of men. How much more when men shall do it, not only without any sufficient ground or reason, but against reason? That is the case of those, who by all men in the latter clause of the verse in hand, will needs understand only some men, and these but few comparatively. For,

2. Though one and the same word or phrase, is sometimes to be taken in a different signification in one and the same period or sentence, as elsewhere is observed, yet this is nowhere to be done, but where there is manifest and pregnant reason for the doing of it, as in these and the like eases. "Let the *dead* bury their *dead*," Mat. viii. 22. So again, "Whosoever drinketh of this *water* shall thirst again; but whosoever shall drink of the *water* that I shall give him, shall never thirst more..." John iv. 13, 14. There is a

plain reason why by the "dead," in the end of the former of these places, should be meant such as were naturally or corporally dead, viz. because such only are to be buried with that kind of burial, whereof our Saviour had occasion to speak, as appears from the former verse. Again, why by "the dead" in the beginning of the said passage, should be meant those that are spiritually dead, and not those that are corporally dead, there is this reason, every whit as plain as the former, viz. because those that are naturally or corporally dead, are not capable of burying those that are dead, either with one kind of burial or other. So why the word "water," in the latter of the passages mentioned, should in the first place signify material or elementary water; in the latter, spiritual water or the Holy Ghost, reasons are obvious and near at hand; we shall not need to name them. But why the words, *pantas anthrōpous*, all men, in the place of the apostle under debate, being twice used, should be conceived so far to vary in their significations as in the former clause, to signify all men without exception; in the latter, very few men, no like reason, nor indeed any competent, can be given.

3. Though "all men" doth in some places signify only a greater number of men, not all men simply or universally, yet it never signifieth a small number of men, either in opposition to or in comparison with a greater, least of all with the greatest number that is, as they must make it signify in the Scripture in hand, who will have no more signified by it, in the latter of the two clauses where it is used, than only those who come in time to be actually saved by Christ. For these are a very small number, "Few there be," saith Christ, "that find it," speaking of the strait gate which leadeth unto life, in comparison of those upon whom condemnation came by Adam.

4. If condemnation should come upon all men simply by the offence of Adam, and righteousness only upon some men, and these but a few neither, comparatively, by the obedience and gift of Christ, then where sin abounded, grace should not much more abound, as the apostle saith it did; nay, sin should much more abound, and grace be confined to a narrow compass, comparatively. To say that the superabounding of grace above sin here spoken of, is to be considered in the intensiveness of it, *i.e.* in its prevalency over sin where it is vouchsafed, not in the extensiveness of it, as if it extended to more persons, is thus far acknowledged for a saying of truth. Grace doth not extend to more persons than sin, at least not to more persons of men, because sin extendeth unto all, and grace cannot extend to more than all. But if we shall straiten and limit grace in respect of the

extent of it, to a small number of persons, the glory of the greater abounding of grace above sin in respect of the prevalency of it, where it is in such a sense given, will be fully matched or rather overcome and swallowed up by the prevailing extensiveness of sin above grace. We must searcheth for a better interpretation.

5. The apostle, both before and after, Romans 5: 15 and 19, speaks of the condemned ones of Adam and the justified ones of Christ, by one and the same numerical expression. He tells us in both places of many dead by Adam, and of no fewer than many justified and redeemed by Christ. Now what the Holy Ghost makes equal for men to disequalize, especially to such a proportion or degree that the one number shall be inconsiderable, and as nothing in comparison of the other, is to lift up themselves above their line, and so take hold of vanity instead of truth. The apostle's expression, verse 15, is somewhat more emphatical, "For if through the offence of one many be dead, much more the grace of God and the gift by grace, which is by one man Jesus Christ, hath abounded unto many."

If it shall be supposed that many more millions of men are dead through the offence of Adam, than are justified or made alive by the grace of God in Christ, Paul's glorying over the grace of God in Christ, as much more abounding to the justification of many, must fall to the ground. For, if by the offence of Adam all became dead, and a few only be made alive by the gift of the grace of God in Christ, who will not judge but that the offence of one much more abounded to the death of many, than the grace of *God* to the justification or life of many? The apostle is therefore referring to something more; an objective justification for all men (and a full justification for those who receive it) that broke the power of the devil and of Adam's sin.

6. And lastly, the apostle having said, verse 20, that "Where sin abounded, grace did much more abound;" he adds, verse 21, "that as sin hath reigned unto death, so did grace reign through righteousness unto eternal life, through Jesus Christ our Lord." Now, evident it is from verses 12 and 14, that sin reigned over all men, without exception, unto death; therefore, grace must have a proportionable reign unto life, *i. e.* must by a strong and overruling hand put all men into a capacity for life and salvation. If so, it undeniably follows that Christ died for all men, without exception for any, because otherwise all men could not be put into an estate of grace or salvation by Him.

Nor was this interpretation counted either heretical or erroneous by the most orthodox expositors of old. Chrysostom himself commenting upon the place, makes the apostle to speak thus, "If all men were punished through the offence," (or his offence, meaning Adam's) "they" (*i. e.* these all men) "may doubtless be justified from hence;" (*i. e.* by that overabundance of grace and righteousness as he there speaketh, which is given in Christ.) The former part of his commentary is more full and pregnant to this purpose, but because the transcription would be somewhat long, I leave it to be read in the author himself. Nor are there wanting amongst our late reformed divines, surnamed orthodox, men of eminent learning, piety and worth, who subscribe the said interpretation. "That our reparation," (restauration) saith Mr. Bucer upon the place, "is made by Christ, and that it is more efficacious than the sin of Adam, and that it is of *larger extent,* is that which the apostle argueth in this and the following section."

Again, upon those words, "Sed non ut *paraptōma,*" and thus: "The apostle here meaneth, that the grace of Christ did more profit mankind, than the sin of Adam damnified it." Doubtless, if all men, without exception, were brought into a condition of misery by the sin of Adam, and but a handful only, in comparison, made happy by the grace of Christ; the grace of Christ cannot be said to have profited mankind more than the sin of Adam damnified it. Yet again, upon verse 16, "For whereas the world was lost" (or undone) "by the one sin of Adam, the grace of Christ did not only abolish this sin, and that death which it brought," (upon the world) "but likewise took away an infinite number of other sins, which we, the rest of men, added to that first sin."

The commensurableness of the grace of Christ with the sin of Adam, in respect of the number of persons gratified by the one, and damnified by the other, cannot lightly be asserted in terms more significant. Nor do the words following import anything contrary hereunto, wherein the author addeth, "that the said grace of Christ bringeth all that are of Christ into a full or plenary justification." For by a full or plenary justification, it is evident that he means an actual justification, yea, (as he explains himself a little after) that justification which shall be awarded unto the saints at the great day of the resurrection; to the obtaining of which, it is acknowledged, that men must receive a new being from Christ by faith. In what sense Christ abolished the sin of Adam, together with that death which it brought into the world; and so in what sense he is said to have brought righteousness, justification, and salvation unto all men, remains to be unfolded in due place. Upon the 17th verse the aforesaid author yet more clearly attests the substance of our interpretation, where he gives an account how the grace of Christ may be said to be of larger extent than the sin of Adam, notwithstanding it be true that this grace took away nothing but what, in a sense, was the fruit and effect of sin.

"If we consider," saith he, "that every particular man by his transgressions increaseth the misery of mankind, and that whosoever sinneth, doth no less hurt his posterity than Adam did all men; it is a plain case, that the grace of Christ hath removed more evils from men than the sins of Adam brought upon them. For though there be no sin committed in all the world which hath not its original from that first sin of Adam, yet all particular men who sin, as they sin voluntarily and freely, so do they make an addition of their own proper guilt and misery. *All which evils*, since the alone *benefit of Christ hath taken away*, it must needs be that it hath taken away the sins of many, and not of one only. Manifest, therefore, is it, that more evils have been removed by Christ, than were brought in by Adam."

And yet more plainly and expressly to the point in hand (if more may be) upon verse 18, the sense whereof he gives thus: "As by the fall of one, sin prevailed over all, so as to make all liable unto condemnation: so likewise the righteousness of one so far took place on the behalf of all men, that *all men may obtain the justification of life* thereby." By this time I suppose Bucer hath said enough, both to assert the interpretation of the Scripture in hand, that hath been given, as also the universality of redemption by Christ.

The said Scripture calls for the sense and exposition asserted, with such a loud and distinct voice, that Gualter also (another divine of the same rank and quality with the former) could not but hearken to it. "As by the offence of one," saith he, completing the apostle's sentence, and rendering his sense therein, "condemnation was propagated unto all men; so also, by the righteousness of one, justification of life was propagated...unto all men." Again thus, "As by the offence of one Adam, the judgment or guilt came upon all men to condemnation; so also by the righteousness of one Jesus Christ, the gift or benefit of God, abounded unto all men to justification of life."

Any man that shall read with a single eye what Calvin himself hath written upon the said contexture of Scriptures, cannot judge him an adversary to the premised exposition. "Paul," saith he, upon verse 15, "simply teacheth that the amplitude," or compass, "of the grace purchased by Christ, is greater than of the condemnnation contracted by the first man." Not long after, "The sum of all comes to this, that Christ overcomes Adam: the righteousness of Christ vanquisheth Adam's sin: Adam's malediction," or curse, "is overwhelmed with Christ's grace: the death which proceeded from Adam is swallowed up by that life which comes from Christ."

Doubtless if the curse brought upon men by Adam prevails and remains still untaken off upon far the greatest part of men, it is not overwhelmed within the grace of Christ: nor is the death which proceeded from him swallowed up by the life of Christ, if still it reigns and magnifies itself over and against far greater numbers of men than the life itself of Christ preserves or delivers from it. Upon verse 18, he presenteth his thoughts in these words, "He," Paul, "makes grace *common unto all men*, because it is exposed unto," or laid within the reach of, "all men: not because it is in the reality of it extended unto all men," *i. e.* not because it is accepted or received by all men, as the words following plainly show: "For," saith he, "though *Christ suffered for the sins of the whole world*, and through the goodness or bounty of God be offered unto all men, yet all men do no take, or lay hold on him." So that if Calvin would but quit himself like a man, and stand his own ground, he would remonstrate as stoutly as Corvine, or Arminius himself.

CHAPTER III
The third sort, or consort of Scriptures, mentioned in Chap. I, as clearly asserting the Doctrine hitherto maintained, argued, and managed to the same point.

WE shall not need, I conceive, to insist upon a particular examination of these Scriptures, one by one, (the method observed by us in handling the two former parts) because they are more apparently uniform and consenting in their respective importances than the previous passages examined. In which respect, a clear and thorough discussion of any one of them, or a diligent poising of the common tendency and import of them all, will be sufficient to evince their respective compliances with the cause in hand. The prospect of these texts is this. "And him that cometh to me, I will in no wise cast out." John vi. 37; "He that believeth on me, shall never thirst." ver. 35; "He that believeth, and is baptized, shall be saved." Mark xvi. 16; "That *whosoever* believeth in him should not perish..." &c. John iii. 16; "That through his name, *whosoever* believeth in him, shall receive remission of sins." Acts x. 43; "Even the righteousness of God, which is by faith of Jesus Christ, *unto all*, and *upon all* them that believe: for there is no difference: for all have sinned..." &c. Rom. iii. 22, 23; to omit very many others of like tenor and import.

In all these Scriptures, with their fellows, evident it is that salvation is held forth and promised by God unto all, without exception, that shall believe; yea, that it is offered and promised unto all men, upon the condition of believing, whether they believe or no. So that, upon such declarations of the gracious and good pleasure of God towards the universality of men as these, the ministers of the gospel, or any other men, may with truth, and ought of duty upon occasion, say to every particular soul of man under heaven, "If thou believest thou shalt be saved," even as Paul saith that he preached Christ, "warning *every man*, and teaching *every man* in all wisdom, that we might present *every man* perfect in Christ Jesus." Colos. i. 28. Yea, this apostle, saith, that God "now commandeth all men every where to repent," Acts xvii. 30. Now if the gospel, or God in the gospel, offereth salvation unto all men, without exception, and insureth it accordingly upon their believing, certainly he hath it to bestow upon them, in case they do believe. Otherwise he should offer or promise that unto them which he hath not for them, nor is able to confer upon them, though they should believe.

If he hath salvation for them, or to bestow upon them upon their believing, he must have it in Christ: because he hath no other treasury or storehouse of salvation, but only Christ.[1] "Neither is there salvation in any other," &c. Acts iv. 12. If God hath salvation in Christ for all men, Christ must needs have bought and purchased it for them with his blood, inasmuch as there is no salvation, no not in Christ himself, without or otherwise than by remission of sins; nor any remission of sins in or by him, without shedding of blood. Therefore all those Scriptures, wherein God promiseth and ascertaineth salvation unto all men, without exception, upon their believing, are pregnant with this truth, that Christ laid down his life for the salvation of all and every man.

If it be here replied and said, but though God in the gospel offers salvation unto all men, and promiseth salvation unto all men upon condition of their believing respectively, yet knowing certainly beforehand that none will believe, but only such and such by name, as viz. those for whom there is salvation purchased by Christ, he may upon a sufficient ground, and with security enough, promise salvation unto all men upon condition they will believe, I answer,

Though God, by means of the certainty of such his knowledge, may, without danger of failing in point of promise-keeping, or of being taken at his word to his dishonour, promise salvation unto all men, without exception, upon the terms specified, though it should be supposed that Christ hath not purchased salvation for all men; yet upon such a supposition as this, he cannot, either with honour or otherwise, or within truth make any such offer or promise. Not with honour; because for a man generally and certainly known to be worth but only one thousand pounds in estate, to offer or promise a hundred thousand pounds to any man that shall be willing to serve him, or to do such or such a courtesy for him, though he knew certainly that no man would accept his offer in either of these kinds, yet would such an offer or promise be a disparagement to him in the sight of wise and understanding men, yea, render him little other than ridiculous?

In like manner, it being supposed by our antagonists in the cause now under plea, that God hath declared it unto all the world in his gospel, that Christ hath died but for a few men, in comparison, and, consequently, that

1. See more of this, Chap. IV

himself hath salvation only for a few, in case he should promise salvation unto all men without exception, upon what account, service, or condition soever, must needs turn to dishonour in the highest unto him, and represent him unto his creature extremely unlike to himself. Suppose the devil had certainly known, as very possibly he might, that the Lord Christ would not have fallen down and worshipped him, upon any terms or conditions whatsoever. Would this have excused him from vanity, in promising him all the kingdoms of the world upon such a condition, when, as all the world knew, that not one of these kingdoms were at his disposal?

Again, neither can God, nor any minister of the gospel, say with truth to every particular man, if thou believest thou shalt be saved, unless it be supposed that there is salvation purchased or in being for them all. Because the truth of such an assertion cannot be salved by this, that all men or every particular man will not believe. The truth of a connex, or hypothetical proposition, of which kind this is, if thou Peter, or thou John believest, thou shalt be saved, doth not depend upon anything that is contingent, no, nor yet upon anything that is extra-essential to the terms of the proposition itself, (such as is, as well the non-believing as the believing of particular men) but upon the essential and necessary connexion between the two parts of the proposition, the antecedent and consequent. If this connexion be contingent, loose, or false, the proposition itself is false, though in every other respect it should be accommodated to the best. As, for example, in this proposition: If Isaac were Abraham's son, then was he truly godly; both the parts considered apart, are true; for true it is, 1. That Isaac was Abraham's son: and 2. That he was truly godly; yet the proposition is absolutely false; because there is no necessary or essential connexion between being Abraham's son and true godliness: therefore the one cannot be truly inferred or concluded from the other. In like manner, when I shall say thus unto a man, If thou believest thou shalt be saved, it is neither his non-believing, nor the certainty of my knowledge that he will not believe, that either maketh or evinceth such a proposition to be true. Because neither of these relates to the connexion of the parts thereof, nor contains the least reason or ground why the latter should follow upon the former. The man's not believing is no reason at all why, upon his believing, he should certainly be saved: no more is my knowledge, how certain soever it be, that he will not believe. But to verify such a proposition or saying, there must be a certain and indissolvable connexion between such a man's salvation and believing, in case he should believe.

Such a connexion as this there cannot be, unless there were salvation for him, which he might have and enjoy in case he should believe. Now certain it is, that if Christ died not for him, there is no more salvation for him in case he should believe, than there would be in case he should not believe: there being no salvation for any man, upon any terms or condition whatsoever, unless Christ hath purchased it for him by his death. Nor doth Christ's purchasing salvation for any man, depend upon such a man's believing; no more doth his non-purchasing salvation for him upon his not believing. So that, unless it be supposed that Christ hath purchased salvation for a man, whilst he remains yet an unbeliever, and though he should always remain an unbeliever, it cannot be supposed that Christ purchased salvation for him, though he should believe. And consequently, there can be no truth in this proposition or assertion, spoken to a man who should not believe: If thou believest thou shalt be saved; it being certain, upon the aforesaid supposition of Christ's non-dying for him, that he should not, could not be saved, no not though he should believe.

If it be replied, Yea, but the truth of this saying to any man whatsoever, "If thou believest thou shalt be saved," is sufficiently salved upon this account, that Christ died sufficiently for all men, though not intentionally so that in case any man whatsoever shall or should believe, there is salvation ready for him in Christ.

I answer, that the vanity, or mere nullity rather in respect of the coincidence of the members of this distinction, wherein Christ is affirmed to have died sufficiently for all men, but denied to have died intentionally for all men, hath been demonstratively and at large evinced formerly. I here only add, that if there be salvation ready in Christ for all and every man in case they should believe, then must this salvation be found in him, either naturally and in respect of his mere person, or by way of purchase and procurement, *i. e.* by means of his death. No man, I presume will affirm the former, as, viz. that there is salvation in Christ for any man, in respect of his mere nature or person; or howsoever, himself plainly denies it: "Verily, verily, I say unto you, Except a corn of wheat fall into the ground and die, it abideth alone: but if it die, it bringeth forth much fruit." John xii. 24. If there be no salvation in him for men but by purchase, and this with his blood, then hath he no more salvation in him than what he thus purchased; no man hath anything more by purchase than what he hath bought or purchased. Therefore, if Christ hath salvation in him for all men without exception, he must have purchased or bought it for them with his blood. If so, he must either purchase more than he intended, or else intended to purchase salvation for all and every man. And what is this, without any parable, but to die intentionally for all men? Therefore the distinction of Christ dying sufficiently for all men, but not intentionally, is ridiculous, and unworthy from first to last of any intelligent or considering man.

Nor is that distinction, because it relates to the subject-matter of our present chapter, so emphatically insisted upon by Mr. Rutherford, of much better import. "That eternal life," saith he, "should be offered unto all and every individual man, upon condition of faith; and that life should be offered unto all and every individual man, out of an intent on God's part to give life unto them in case they believe, are two sayings widely different."[2] For, doubtless, the latter hath every whit as much truth in it, yea, every whit as much clear and pregnant truth in it as the former, yea, hath in effect one and the same truth. For when God offers eternal life unto all and every individual man, upon condition of faith, is it not his intention that they should have eternal life upon their faith, or in case they should believe? If not, then in such an offer he should offer and promise that which he intends not to give or perform, no not according to the tenor of his promise. If it be said, in favour of the distinction: Though God intends to give eternal life to all and every individual man, upon condition they believe, this being the express tenor of his offer or promise, yet it follows not that such an intention in him should be his reason or ground of tendering such an offer or promise unto them.

Unto this I answer, that if this were the intent of the author, I mean to differentiate the latter proposition from the former in point of error or falsehood, upon this account, because the latter supposeth such an intention, as that mentioned, in God, to be the adequate reason or motive why he tenders such an offer or promise unto them, I should not much gainsay, because, I suppose, that God hath indeed other reasons, and these of greater weight, why he makes a tender of salvation unto all men upon condition of faith, than his intention of giving salvation unto them in case they shall believe. Yea, I do not conceive that either God or men do anything which they intend, simply out of their intentions thereof, or because they intend it, but out of a desire to effect, or to procure the effecting of it, or because they desire it.

But that the author's meaning in pleading the said latter proposition of error was far differing from this, appears sufficiently by the account which himself gives hereof in the sequel of his discourse. From this account it

2. Sam. Rhetorfortis. Exercit. Apolog. p. 309.

clearly appears, that in framing the said latter proposition, he useth those words, "ex Dei intentione," for "cum Dei intentione," and placeth the error of the proposition in this, viz. that it supposeth an intention to be in God of giving life unto all men upon their faith, when he makes the offer mentioned unto them. To prove this to be an error, he argues to this effect, from John xvii. 2: "God the Father gave power unto the Son to give eternal life to those *only* who were given unto him by the Father. But reprobates," saith he, "are not given unto the Son by the Father; therefore the Father gave no power unto the Son to give eternal life unto reprobates. Consequently the Son cannot, either according to his own, or to his Father's intention, offer remission of sins or eternal life unto reprobates." To this I answer, that the whole proceed of the argument ariseth from a mistaken ground, or a plain misunderstanding of the Scripture upon which it is built. For by a "power given unto the Son to give eternal life," &c. is not meant a power of dying for men, one or other, but a power of an actual and real investing men with eternal life, or a power to confer eternal life actually upon men, as appears from the former clause of the verse: "As thou hast given him power over all flesh, that he should give eternal life," &c. From whence it is evident, that the power here spoken of as given unto the Son to give eternal life, &c., is a consequent branch or effect of that power or sovereignty which the Father hath given him over all mankind, as, viz. to dispose of them, especially in respect of their eternal estates and conditions, according to such rules of righteousness and equity as the Father, with the Son, have judged meet and accordingly agreed upon, for the regulating of such high and important dispensations.

Now, a power of conferring eternal life upon men, may very well be conceived to be a branch or part of that sovereignty or larger power, which the Father hath given unto the Son over all flesh. But an injunction or command, or a free leave or liberty, notion it how you please, given unto Him to die for a few men, cannot reasonably be looked upon as any part or branch, especially as any such considerable or high-importing branch as this here expressed must needs be conceived to be, of that most transcendent and majestic power. Or,

By eternal life may very well be meant, not eternal life properly and formally so called, as, viz. the blessedness and glory of the world to come, but such a discovery or manifestation of God and His counsels, which is an effectual means to bring men in time to the possession and enjoyment of this life. It is a frequent dialect of Scripture to call the means and cause, yea, and sometimes an opportunity only, which are proper and effectual for the compassing, effecting, or obtaining a thing, by the name of the thing itself; which is to be, or may be, procured or effected by them. Thus Numb. xxii. 7, the wages or rewards by which time elders of Moab sent from Balak the king, to Balaam the wizard, expected to procure divinations, or some imprecatory and devilish practices against the people of God from him, are termed divinations. "And the elders of Moab," saith the text, " and the elders of Midian departed with the rewards of divination in their hand," &c. Thus, good tidings is put for the reward which good tidings usually procure unto them who bring them, 2 Sam. iv. 10. In this phrase of speech, the Scriptures, or the saving knowledge of God therein revealed, are, according to the general sense of our best interpreters, termed salvation, John iv. 22. So again, Heb. ii. 2,3. Thus wisdom is called a man's life, "Keep her, for she is thy life," Prov. iv. 13, because she is the means of life, *i.e.* of peace and well-being unto men. In this sense also, to forbear further instances which are in great numbers at hand, the gospel, and sometimes the preaching or ministry of it, is frequently termed the kingdom of heaven.

According to this manner of speaking, so familiar in the Scriptures, by eternal life, which the Son had power given him over all flesh, that he might give to as many as the Father had given him, may well be meant the words of eternal life, as Peter calls them, John vi. 68; or that manifestation of the name of God, as himself speaketh soon after, John xvii. 6, by which they might be effectually brought to the fruition and enjoyment of eternal life. And that this indeed is the very meaning of our Saviour, is abundantly evident by the sequel of the context all along, for several verses together. For having said that the Father had given him power over all flesh, that he should give eternal life to as many as he had given him, xvii. 2, he immediately declares, verse 3, what he means by eternal life, "And this is life eternal, that they might know thee the only true God, and Jesus Christ, whom thou hast sent." This notion he still carrieth on, saying, verse 6. " I have manifested thy name unto the men which thou gavest me out of the world: thine they were, and thou gavest them me," &c. So again, directly still to the same point, verse 8, "For I have given unto them the words which thou gavest me," &c.; yet again, upon the same account, verse 14, "I have given them thy word," &c. That which, verse 2, he had called eternal life, here he calls his Father's word, as before, the declaration or manifestation of his name, as we heard.

From the carriage of the context, that further is abundantly evident, that by those words, verse 2, "As many as thou hast given him," are not meant the elect, or the entire number of the elect, or of those for whom Christ died, (in Mr. Rutherford's sense) but precisely and particularly his apostles, of whom alone he speaks, and for whom alone, and apart from the rest of the elect, he prayeth all along the chapter, until verse 20, when he enlargeth his prayer thus, "Neither pray I for these alone, but for them also which shall believe on me through their word." From this passage, it is as clear as the sun at noon-day, that from the beginning of the chapter until now, he had managed his prayer and heavenly conference with the Father, with particular reference to his apostles, and had not mentioned anything about the residue of the elect. That he speaks of the apostles only verse 2, under those words, "As many as thou hast given me," is most apparent from verse 6, "I have manifested thy name unto the men which thou gavest me out of the world: thine they were, and thou gavest them me, and they have kept thy word." First, Christ had not yet manifested his Father's name to all the elect, meaning all the elect at this time in being in the world. Second, neither could he say to his Father concerning all the elect, that they had kept his word, many of them having not as yet received it.

Again, to pass by several things by the way making out the same truth, verse 12, thus, "While I was with them in the world," (meaning those of whom he had spoken from the beginning of the chapter) "I kept them in thy name," *i.e.* I preserved them from the exorbitances of the world by the knowledge of thy name, which still I have been communicating unto them; "Those that thou gavest me I have kept; and none of them is lost but the son of perdition," &c. Evident it is, that this son of perdition was one of that number of men which the Father had given him out of the world, and which he had kept entirely without the miscarriage of any one, this son of perdition only excepted. I presume, that neither Mr. Rutherford, nor any of his judgment will say that this "son of perdition" was one of the number of the elect; but certain it is, that he was one of that number of men which the Father had given unto Christ out of the world. The words are too express to bear a denial of this, "Those that thou gavest me I have kept; and none *of them* is lost but the son of perdition," &c. Therefore, by as many as the Father had given unto him, with an intent that he should give eternal life unto them, verse 2, are meant the apostles, and these only.

These may be said to have been given unto Christ by the Father, not because they were the Father's by election from eternity, for doubtless the son of perdition, as hath been said, was none of His in such a relation. Nor was it simply because they were by any peremptory designation appointed and set out by him from amongst other men, to make apostles for his Son, as if Christ had been necessitated to take these, and had no liberty or right of power to have taken any others into that relation. For how could then Christ say unto them that he had chosen them, viz. to the office and dignity of apostles, John vi. 70; xiii. 18; xv. 16-19 but because God the Father by a work appropriable unto him, of which I conceive we shall have occasion to speak more at large hereafter, had qualified, fitted and prepared them for Christ's hand and nurture, and so to make apostles of them in time; in respect of which work of God the Father, in and upon them, Christ, out of that wisdom wherein he excelled, and that knowledge which he had of the several frames and tempers of the hearts of men, made a prudent and deliberate choice of them from amongst other men for that service.

"Thine they were, and thou gavest them unto me." They are said to have been the Father's *i.e.* as it were, the Father's disciples, or persons "taught by the Father," John vi. 45, and so, after a sort, appropriable unto the Father, (as those that believe and are taught of Christ are said to be Christ's, or to belong to Christ) before they became Christ's apostles, or were chosen by him upon this account; and are said to have been given unto him out of the world by the Father, because they were peculiarly qualified, and as it were, characterized and marked out by the Father to be formed into apostles by his Son.

The word "give" is frequently found in such a signification as this in the Scriptures, and to import the preparing, furnishing, or fitting, whether of things or persons, for such and such ends and purposes, in reference to the accommodations of men. In this sense Christ is said to have "given some apostles, and some prophets, and some evangelists, and some pastors and teachers, for the perfecting of the saints, for time work of the ministry," &c.; *i. e.* to have every ways prepared, qualified, endowed, fitted, furnished persons for all these offices and services in his church, for the benefit of the saints, &c. Thus Acts xiii. 20, "he gave unto them judges," &c.; *i. e.* he qualified and furnished men amongst them from time to time, with public spirits and with gifts fit for government, &c. So Neh. ix. 27, "Thou *gavest* them saviours;" *i. e.* thou furnishedst men with hearts, and courage and wisdom, &c., to save them. See Eph. i. 22, God "*gave* him (Christ) to be the head over all things to the church;" *i.e.* he furnished him with sovereignty of power, wisdom, majesty, and with all manner of endowments otherwise requisite for such a head. Thus Psal. xliv. 11, "Thou hast *given* us like sheep appointed for meat," &c; i. e. by withdrawing thy presence, help, and protection from us, thou hast prepared and fitted us to become a prey and spoil to our enemies. In this sense also God saith to Jeremiah (i. 5), that he had given him (for so it is in the original) "a prophet unto the nations;" *i. e.* that he had furnished him, and meant to furnish him yet further, with prophetical gifts and endowments for the benefit of nations, if they would hearken to him. So Psal. xxi. 6, "Thou hast given him to be blessings," (so it is in the original, and in your marginal translation;) *i. e.* thou hast so furnished, qualified, and disposed of him, (meaning Christ,) that whosoever will apply themselves unto him, may be made happy and blessed by him. See also Ezek. xi. 15; Isa. xliii. 28, in the original, with other like. Our Saviour himself useth the word in the sense now instanced from the Scriptures, when he expresseth himself thus: "All that the Father giveth me, shall," or rather, will "come unto me," &c., John vi. 37; of which place more in due time.

Nor ought it to seem any hard, uncouth, or unpleasant expression unto us, wherein that which is prepared or any ways made fit for us, and withal so disposed of or set in our way that we may readily and lawfully serve ourselves with it, is said to be given unto us by him or them who thus prepare and dispose of it. He that shall prepare wholesome and savoury meat, such as a man loveth, and shall set it before him, and give him free leave to take it or eat of it, may in sufficient propriety of speech be said to give this meat unto him, yea, whether he takes or eats of it upon such terms or no. So God the Father, having wrought and fitted the men whom Christ chose for apostles, to serve and honour him in this capacity, and withal disposed of them in their times, residences, and conditions in the world, so that Christ might both readily and lawfully call them to his service, he may very well in these respects be said to have given them unto him.

Thus, by a diligent and narrow inquiry into Mr. Rutherford's Scripture, it evidently appears that there is nec vola muec vestigium, not the least mutter or peep, of any such notion in it as he imagineth, viz. that if Christ should offer eternal life unto any more than only unto the elect, (so called by him,) he must needs do it besides his own and his Father's intention. Here is not the least word, syllable, letter or apex concerning either the Father's or the Son's intentions about the offer of salvation unto men.

By the brief discussions of this chapter, it fully appears that all those texts of Scripture which offer either forgiveness of sins or salvation unto all men without exception, and which promise either or both these unto all men upon, or upon condition of, their believing, which are very frequently numerous, do with the clearest light and evidence of truth hold forth the universality of redemption by Christ. It therefore follows, in regular and due process of reason and discourse, that all they "make God a liar" in such Scriptures, who restrain the salvation or redemption purchased by Christ to any lesser number of men than all.

CHAPTER IV:
Wherein the Scriptures of the fourth and last association, propounded in Chap. I, as pregnant also with that great truth hitherto maintained, are impartially weighed and considered.

WE shall, God assisting, examine every of these Scriptures particularly, and so shall have occasion to exhibit the purport and tenor of them respectively as they shall be produced to act their several parts in order. We shall not here transcribe them, especially considering the reader may with very little pain see them in their muster, Chap. I; but shall only point at their several dwellings or situations in the Book of God, which are these: Rom. xiv. 15; 1 Cor. viii. 11; 2 Pet. ii. 1; 2 Pet. ii. 20; Heb. x. 29; Matt. xxiii. 32, 33; &c. We make these Scriptures of one and the same combination, and associate them by themselves because their import is in effect one and the same, they all supposing that Christ hath died for those who may perish notwithstanding, yea, for those who will perish. And, certainly, if he died for those who, not withstanding his dying for them, may perish, yea, and for those who will actually perish, as well as for those who shall be saved, he died for all men without exception.

As for that opinion of the Valentine Council, in France, mentioned by Estius[1] and adopted by him, as it seems, for his own, which supposeth some reprobates, as he calleth them, to have been redeemed by Christ, but not all,—this opinion, I say, is not like, as far as I conceive, to make many proselytes. Nor will it attract the judgments of considering men. For if the dying of Christ for men is to be esteemed a matter of love to them, as without all controversy and question it ought, what reason can there be imagined why he should die for apostate reprobates, (who yet are that kind of reprobate for which only Christ died, according to that opinion), rather than for those who, though living and dying in unbelief, yet never contracted the guilt of so desperate and provoking a sin? But this by the way.

The tenor of the Scripture first in view, amongst those lately appearing, is this: "Destroy not him with thy meat, for whom Christ died," Rom. xiv. 15.

1. The Greek word accurately translated "destroy" is *apollymi*. That the

---

1. In 2 Pet. ii. 1; see also Jo. Ball, Covenant of Grace, pg. 238.

destruction here spoken of, whereunto the strong Christian is so earnestly admonished and dehorted by the apostle from exposing the weak, is not any temporal destruction, but that which is of body and soul forever, is more clear than to require proof. It is not easily imaginable how or that a strong Christian, or any other man, by eating meat sacrificed unto idols, should expose a weak Christian unto the danger of any other destruction, but of that only which is decreed by God against those who shall depart from the faith, or finally apostatise from the profession of Christ. Besides, it is every man's notion, that this is that destruction, that first-born of things formidable and dreadful unto the precious souls of men, with which this great apostle had so much to do, and from which the great prize that he runs for with all his might in all his epistles, was to deliver them.

2. Whereas he chargeth men not to destroy those "for whom Christ died," though he doth not indeed suppose that all those shall be actually destroyed or perish, whom another may be said to destroy, *i. e.*, to do things tending to their destruction, which is the sense of the word in this place. Yet this he clearly supposeth, that such men "for whom Christ died" are obnoxious to destruction, may be destroyed, and perish everlastingly. Otherwise we shall quench the spirit of his zealous tenderness over the precious souls of weak Christians, expressed in this serious item or charge unto others, not to destroy them; yea, and make him speak very weakly, and, indeed, ridiculously. To admonish men in a serious and solemn manner, to take heed of destroying those who are out of all possibility of being destroyed, especially this being known to the men that are thus admonished, is as if a man should seriously and affectionately entreat an archer with his bow and arrows about him, to take heed of shooting too high for fear of hurting the sun, and causing it to fall down out of the firmament of heaven.

If it be said; Yea, but though it be supposed, that the persons admonished in this case do know in the general that they, for whom Christ died, are not under a possibility of perishing, yet they may be ignorant in particular, whether those men whose destruction they are like to procure or promote by the abuse of their Christian liberty, be of the number of those men for whom Christ died or no. And consequently the apostle may upon a good account admonish them to take heed of destroying such.

I answer, it can at no hand be supposed that the persons here admonished should be ignorant, whether the men about whose destruction they are so deeply cautioned by the apostle, be of the number of those "for whom Christ died," because the apostle himself so plainly and positively asserteth it: "For whom," saith he, "Christ died." Besides, the main strength and stress of the argument or motive by which he enforceth the dehortation standeth in this, that those persons, whosoever they be, whose salvation they shall endanger by eating things sacrificed to idols, are of those for whom Christ died. Now, to press an exhortation or dehortation upon the consciences of men by such a motive, wherein these men shall be supposed ignorant whether there be any truth or no, is to fight with a wooden sword; especially when it shall be yet further supposed, that such men are under an absolute incapacity of ever knowing whether there be any truth or no in this motive, which must needs be the case here, if we shall suppose there be any number of men for whom Christ died not. For, impossible it is, and so generally confessed to be, for one man certainly to know the truth of grace or faith in another; and much more to know the certainty of his perseverance unto the end; and consequently, according to the principles of anti-universalism, for any man to know whether Christ died for any man in particular and by name but himself.

Therefore most certain it is, that there is a possibility for those to perish and be destroyed for whom Christ died, or notwithstanding Christ's dying for them. And if so, then Christ's dying for men doth not suppose a necessity of their salvation. And if so, then Christ died as well for those who may not be saved, and shall not be saved, as for those who may, and shall; and consequently, for all men. For they who may, and shall be saved, and they who may not, neither shall be saved, together comprehend all men whatsoever.

The exposition of the Scripture in hand, as importing the death of Christ for those who yet may be destroyed and perish, is so pregnant with evidence and truth, that it hath subdued the judgments off all expositors I meet with unto it. "And Christ verily," saith Chrysostom upon the place, "refused not, neither to be made a servant, nor to die for him; and wilt not thou so much as neglect thy belly to save him? For although Christ was not like to (win, or) gain all men, yet did he die for all men, so fulfilling that which appertained to him." (in order to the procuring of their salvation.) Our late Protestant expositors follow in the same path. "Another consideration," saith Calvin, "wherein the offence of the brethren renders the use of things, in themselves good, vicious (or faulty) is, that in wounding a weak conscience, the price of the blood of Christ is dissipated (or dissolved); for even the most contemptible brother, or member of a Christian society, is redeemed by the blood of Christ; therefore a (very) unworthy thing it is, that he should be destroyed for the satisfaction of any man's belly." I trust that from henceforth, no man that shall read these passages from his pen will say but that Calvin clearly held a possibility of the destruction of such men for whom Christ died, and consequently, that Christ died for more than shall be saved: and if so, for all, as we formerly argued.

"He," meaning Christ, saith Peter Martyr, "hath *redeemed* him; wilt thou *destroy* him, (speaking of he apostle's weak brother). He hath shed his life, soul, and blood for thy brother; canst not thou for his sake abstain from a poor piece of meat?" Therefore the clear sense of this orthodox man is, that the redeemed of Christ may perish and be destroyed.

"If the salvation of our brethren," saith M. Bucer on the place, "be to be procured by us by the laying down of our lives, and nothing be to be respected in comparison thereof; how impious and accursed a thing is it, that any man should destroy a brother for meat." He had said immediately before: "If we follow Christ, he for the rescuing, or saving, our brethren, suffered death; therefore we also ought to lay down our lives for the salvation of the brethren, and to abhor the destroying of a brother more than death." Therefore he also plainly supposeth, that even such a brother may be destroyed, and that for meat, for whom Christ died.

Musculus speaks by the same spirit with the former. "To this grieving of the brethren, the apostle aptly subjoins the destruction of those who are offended at the unadvised liberty of those that are strong. For the mind being thus grieved, as being weak, easily falls to this point, viz., to begin by little and little, being shaken through a sinister suspicion, to fall away from Christianity and, *from true faith*." In which words, the author clearly avoucheth the opinion of those, not only who hold that those may be destroyed for whom Christ died, but theirs also, whose judgment stands for a possibility of falling away, and that to destruction, from true faith. But as to the former point, he speaks more significantly, a little after the former words. "It is all one, as if the apostle should say, Christ would have him saved, and sought it by his death; but thou dost not only despise thy brother, but opposest Christ also, and makest void," or of none effect, "through thy rashness, and that for the sake of meat, that *death* of his, which he underwent *for his sake*, and by which thou thyself also art saved."

Nor doth B. Aretius break rank, but marcheth in close order with his fellows. "The apostle's argument," saith he, "is from the effects: thou destroyest him with the use of things indifferent, whom Christ redeemed by his death. What madness is that?" And soon after, "Meat haply preserves thy life: but Christ died for him whom thou slayest, not by dying, but by living: what cruelty is this?"

Let R. Gualter bring up the rear, for saying, "The apostle in this teacheth that Christ himself is sinned against, yea, and that the merit of his death is overthrown when we destroy him whom he, by his death and blood, hath vindicated," or restored "unto life."

Here are many witnesses, though many more might readily be summoned in with the same evidence, and those of the first-born qualification for authority and credit in such cases, (I mean men orthodox and sound in the judgment of those, who assume the same honour unto themselves, and who are the high opposers of the doctrine under protection in the present discourse) speaking the same things plainly, expressly, and without parable, with the assertors of this doctrine. Neither, indeed, could they, or any other man, having such Scriptures before them as that last insisted upon, with the former, to order their judgments and thoughts conceive, or speak otherwise, with any tolerable ingenuity, or without some such winking with the eyes, which is unworthy men pretending friendship to the truth. But let us hear what the Spirit of God saith further in the point.

The next Scripture lately directed unto was 1 Cor. viii. 11: "And through thy knowledge," or through thy meat, as Chrysostom reads the place, "shall the weak brother perish, for whom Christ died." Some copies read the words with an interrogation, and thus, either our English translators or printers or both, deliver them unto us; others assertively. This difference in the pointing makes none in the matter or substance of the doctrine contained in the words. Only the interrogative is more piercing and provoking to the consideration of the truth imported. The tenor of the place is the same, in effect, with the last opened; and clearly supposeth, upon the account given in the traverse of that Scripture, that such a person may miscarry in the great business of salvation, notwithstanding Christ's laying down his life for him. The reader is desired to revise our debate upon the former place for his satisfaction herein; unless, haply, the consent of the best interpreters in that behalf will balance that accommodation.

"Thy Lord and Master," saith Chrysostom on the place, "refused not to die for him: but thou makest no reckoning of him, no not so much as to abstain from a polluted table for his sake; but sufferest him to *perish after salvation procured for him* upon such terms." And soon after, "So that here are four accusations," or matters of charge, "and these exceeding high; 1. That he is a brother. 2. That he is weak. 3. That he is one *whom Christ so highly prized as even to die for him.* 4. That after all this he perisheth for meat."

The expressness of the words overruled even Calvin's pen also to an assertion of the same truth. "He is indeed weak whom thou despisest, but yet a brother: for God hath adopted him. Therefore, cruel art thou who hast no care of thy brother. But that which follows is yet more pressing; viz., that even those that are rude or weak, are redeemed by the blood of Christ. For there is nothing of greater unworthiness than that Christ should not scruple to die, that the weak might not perish; and we in the meantime lightly esteem the salvation of those who have been redeemed at so great a price. A memorable saying, whereby we are taught how highly we ought to value the salvation or our brethren; and of these, not only, as considered in the lump, or in the general, but of every one of them in particular, inasmuch as *Christ's blood was shed for every one of them.*" Nor can it reasonably be pretended that by the brethren, for "every of which," he saith, "the blood of Christ was shed," he means only the elect. For evident it is, that he speaks of the generality of professors who were joined in external communion with the churches of Christ, many of whom he could not but know, were not elect, at least in the sense of such pretenders.

Aretius worketh the place thus: "Here is another fruit" (or effect) "of that licentious liberty, greater than the former. For the former only was, that by means of such an example men were strengthened in an evil error; but here he showeth, that he that is weak is even destroyed." And presently after: "In conclusion, this practice mightily differs from the example of Christ, for he died for the weak sinner," &c. So that this expositor also clearly supposeth, that men may destroy him for whom Christ died.

Nor doth learned Musculus vary a hair's-breadth from the import of these things, upon the place demanding thus: "How, I pray, can he be excused, who for meat's sake destroyeth him whom Christ redeemed with his blood?" And not long after: "What greater sin can be committed against Christ, than to slay" (or destroy) "him for whom he himself died?"

I finish the account with Mr. I. Diodati's gloss upon the words. "Perish," *i. e.* saith he, "shall be in danger of wounding his conscience mortally; and whereas before, though tenderness of conscience, he abhorred anything that drew near to idolatry, he may peradventure use himself to it to the shipwreck of salvation."

These expositors do not mince the words, as Piscator and some few others do, who destroying hereby the best of the nourishment in them gloss them thus: "Thy weak brother should perish," viz. "as to thee, or as much as lieth in thee."[2] I confess such a bridle as this doth well in the lips of some

---

2. See also the Annotations of the English Ministers upon 1 Cor. viii. 11.

other Scripture expressions, which will not be ruled by the truth without it, but it encumbers the Scripture in hand, and abridgeth the serviceableness of it. For if it shall be supposed, that that kind of offender against the weak Christian, of whom the apostle here spoketh, knoweth certainly beforehand that his act in eating meat sacrificed unto idols can have no such sad effect or sequel upon it, as the destruction of a weak brother, must he not need be tempted hereby to despise the apostle's charge on that behalf, being grounded mainly upon such an assertion or supposal, and so be comforted or encourage in his sinful practice? To put restrictions upon Scripture phrases or assertions, without necessity, and this demonstrable, either from other Scriptures, or unquestionable grounds of reason, is not to interpret the Scriptures now in being, but upon the matter to make new.

If it be replied in favour of the said limitation or explication of Piscator, that there will be great weight and force enough to command the consciences of men in the apostle's argument, and to take them off from abuse of their liberty, though it should be supposed that there is only a tendency in such a practice towards the destruction of weak believers, whether it be supposed that such persons may actually perish and be destroyed or not.

I answer, there can be no tendency supposed, in any action or means towards an impossibility. For that which is simply impossible, or which is the same in effect, impossible, upon a condition that is immutable and cannot fail, is never the more possible, nor any whit nearer unto being upon any other account, or for anything whatsoever that can be done. Therefore there is nothing can be done with any tendency towards the effecting of such thing. Besides, were it granted, that there is a tendency in such a practice, the forbearance whereof the apostle urgeth towards the destruction of a weak brother, yea, and further, that this practice in respect of such a tendency in it were sinful, yet would there be very little in either, or both these, to deter men from such a practice unless it be withal supposed that that sad effect, whereunto the said tendency is acknowledged to relate, may possibly be effected or produced by it.

For the more secure a sinner may be that his sinful practice will not be so sadly consequenced, as the nature and property of it only considered, it might very possibly be, the greater temptation lieth upon him to adventure upon it. The confidence which Judas had, that his act in betraying his Master would not have been accompanied with his death, but that he would now, as several times before he had done, find some way or other to make an escape from those into whose hands he was betrayed, was one main thing which betrayed him into the deadly snare of that most abominable fact. For it is said, that "When he (Judas) saw that he was condemned" (which implies, that this was more than he feared or expected, notwithstanding his act in betraying him) "(he) repented himself...and cast down the pieces of silver in the temple, and departed, and went and hanged himself." Matt. xxvii. 3-5.

Thirdly, and lastly, the mention and tender of an impossible effect by way of motive, to overule the consciences of men against a practice in one kind or other whereunto they are inclined, is little less than ridiculous. This is especially true when the said impossibility is presumed to be known beforehand to him, the overruling of whose conscience is attempted thereby. Suppose I be full of this persuasion, 1. That I am a true believer. 2. That being such, I am under an impossibility ever to fall away so as to perish, and under this double persuasion were very much addicted to such a sinful course; the consideration of my falling away and perishing were the most improper and impertinent argument that lightly could be pressed upon me, to persuade me out of the way and practice of my sin.

But some as willing to break loose from the Scripture in hand as the former, yet being not satisfied with their projection for an escape, try the same conclusion another way, and by another device. The apostle, say they, calls a weak professor of the gospel by the name of a brother, not as if it could be demonstratively know that he is a brother indeed, but because others stand bound by the law of charity to judge him such: after the same manner he saith that Christ died for him, not as if he would have men to believe this according to the judgment or with the certainty of faith, but only with the judgment of charity. Upon this supposal they draw up the apostle's argument for him, thus, "Thy brother shall perish for whom," &c. *i.e.* by the abuse of thy knowledge, thou mayest be the destruction of him whom thou art bound in charity to look upon as thy brother in Christ, and one of those for whom Christ died. But,

1. Why stand we not bound to believe, only with the judgment of charity, and not with the certainty of faith, that Christ is the Son of God, or Saviour of the world, &c. as well as to believe only after this manner, that he may "perish, for whom Christ died?" this latter being as positively, as clearly, as roundly and fully asserted by the Holy Ghost, as either of the former? Or what is such a liberty of interpreting Scriptures, as this, being interpreted, but an effectual door opened for the reducing of all things whatsoever in matters of religion, yea, the truth and authority of the

Scriptures themselves, to the judgment of charity, and consequently to the casting the judgment of faith out of doors? But,

2. To enjoin me a belief, only according to the judgment of charity, where a belief, according to the judgment of faith, would be ten times more beneficial and serviceable unto me for the preserving of me from sin, especially when the ground-work of Divine Revelation before me will better, and with less descant upon the words, admit the latter belief than the former, which is the case in the Scripture in hand, is very contrary to the rule of charity, which restraineth me from doing my neighbour any prejudice or harm, as well in his spiritual, as outward estate: yea, and much more in the former, than in the latter.

3. If I stand bound to believe with the judgment of faith, that it is impossible for any man to perish for whom Christ died, what will such a consideration as this (whether believed according to the one judgment of the other) viz. that Christ died for such or such a man, advantage me by way of preserving me from such a practice, which is apt to destroy him? For if it be a truth, that Christ did die for him, I need not, according to the supposition mentioned, be at all tender about doing anything, or forbearing anything, out of any apprehension of danger, lest by the one or the other I should occasion his destruction. If it be a truth, that Christ did not die for him, upon what account should the apostle suggest unto me that he did die for him, or that it may be that he did die for him, by way of argument, to deter me from doing that which may tend to his destruction? Suppose one part of the men in the world were impenetrable and invulnerable, the other part, as now they are, exposed unto the danger of death upon wounds received. Were it a congruous motive or ground of persuasion, whereby to caution me from wounding or smiting such or such a man with a sword, dagger, or the like, to inform me that this man is or may be invulnerable? Or that I ought to presume or judge this man to be invulnerable? Would not such an argument as this rather strengthen my hand to a smiting of him, than any ways occasion me to forbear? They clearly make the Holy Ghost himself to reason at no better rate of understanding than this, in the Scripture in hand, who make it only a matter of charity to believe that Christ died for a weak brother; and that in case he did die for him he is upon this account undestroyable.

And lastly, most evident it is that the scope of the apostle in 1 Cor. viii and in Rom. xiv to deter Christians from an unseasonable and undue use of their liberty and knowledge: and this by an argument or motive drawn, not so much from what is unseemly, uncomely, or dangerous, in respect of themselves, but from the consideration of what danger or damage may very possibly accrue thereby unto others. The whole tenor and carriage of both contexts proclaim this aloud: so that there needs no more proof of it than only the perusal of the chapters themselves. Now the danger or damage which a Christian, by such an abuse of his liberty, as is here expressed, may very possibly create or occasion to another, the apostle affirms to be the destroying of his brother, for whom Christ died, *i.e.* the depriving of him of that great salvation and blessedness, which Christ by his death purchased for him. Now if this strong Christian stands bound to believe, according to the judgment of charity, that this person is a true brother, and one for whom Christ died, he stands bound to believe, according to the same judgment at least, if not according to the judgment of faith itself, that he may perish through the abuse of his liberty.

Otherwise the apostle's argument for the dissuading of him from such abuse, cannot be supposed to take any place in him, nor work at all upon him, in order to such an end. For no consideration or saying whatsoever, unless believed with one kind of faith or other, can have any influence or operation upon men, either to persuade them to or from any practice. If, then, the strong Christian stands bound to believe, be it only according to the judgment of charity, that the weak professor is a brother indeed, and one for whom Christ died, he stands bound, also, to believe, according to the one judgment or the other, that he may perish though his unchristian misdemeanor in the use of his liberty. If so, then he, and consequently every other Christian, stands bound in conscience to believe that such a man may perish, for whom he stands bound in conscience likewise to believe that Christ died. For a belief, according to the judgment of charity, where it is required, is a matter of duty and conscience, as well as according to the judgment of faith, in cases appropriate hereunto.

Neither is it true, according to the principles of that opinion that we now plead, that a Christian stands bound in conscience to believe, no not according to the judgment of charity, that all that profess the faith of Christ are true brethren or persons for whom Christ died. For the patrons of this opinion generally hold, 1. That many who make such a profession, are hypocrites, and not true brethren. 2. That many of this number will perish at last in their hypocrisy and unbelief. And thus far they hold nothing but truth. Lastly, they hold yet further, which they should do better to let go, that Christ died for none of those professors, who perish in the end. These things they hold and believe, not with a belief according to the judgment of charity, but dogmatically, and according to the judgment or certainty of faith.

Now certain it is, that no man stands bound in conscience to believe that according to the judgment of charity, which is contrary to what he believeth, or what he truly judgeth himself bound in conscience to believe according to the judgment of faith. Because no law or rule of charity bindeth him to believe, with any kind of belief whatsoever that God is a liar or untrue in his word, which is the foundation and rule of what I stand bound to believe, according to the judgment of faith. Such men, therefore, who believe according to the judgment of faith, that all professors of Christianity shall not at last be saved, cannot with the safety of their own principles, say they stand bound in conscience to believe, with the belief of charity, that Christ died for them all. This is because in their notion and according to their grounds, these two propositions are inconsistent in truth viz. that Christ should die for all, and yet some perish. But thus it still happeneth to those who are engaged in the defence of an error: I mean, to entangle themselves, and to nonsensify such passages of Scripture which manifestly oppose their error, by such evasions, such unnatural and forced interpretations, which for the keeping alive of such a tenet, which were better dead, they are necessitated unto.

Nor will it avail them here to reply that they do not judge themselves bound in conscience to believe in a way of charity that all and every professor of the Christian faith are true brethren, or persons for whom Christ died, but only that there is no particular or single person in this heap concerning whom they stand not bound by the law of charity thus to believe, at least until they have ministered grounds of suspicion that indeed they are hypocrites. To this I answer,

1. In such an explication of themselves as this, they clearly grant that for a time, viz. until professors administer grounds of jealousy that their faith is not sound, they stand bound to conceive of them all, one or other, without exception, (I mean, according to the judgment of charity) that Christ died for them. But such a belief as this is contrary to what they believe dogmatically, as hath been said, and according to the judgment of faith. Therefore, they still interfere; for to believe that Christ died for every individual professor, and to believe that he died for all professors without exception, is but one and the same belief, nor can any difference be shown between them.

2. Neither is a symptom of hypocrisy, seen or observed in a professor, any sufficient ground for the reversal of such a judgment of charity con-

cerning him, according to which we judge him a person for whom Christ died; because, (a.) There may be many symptoms or signs of hypocrisy which are not demonstrative or of any essential eviction: and, (b.) If a man were an evicted hypocrite yet may he recover from this condemnation. Therefore, hypocrisy, though certainly known by a man, is no sufficient or reasonable ground, no, not according to the grounds of the doctrine now challenged, why I may not or ought not, in a way of charity, to judge that Christ died for him notwithstanding. Thus, then, we see at last that no colour, plea, or pretence, no turning, shifting, or winding about this way or that will salve the impertinency, that I say not importunate absurdity, of any interpretation whatsoever of the Scripture in hand, which doth not in a clear comportance with the words, scope, and drift of the apostle therein, suppose a possibility of their perishing for whom Christ died, and that in order to their non-perishing, as we shall have occasion to show further before the end of this chapter, in asserting another passage of Scripture to the same point.

The next in the order propounded is 2 Pet. ii. 1: "But there were false prophets also among the people, even as there shall be false teachers among you, who privily shall bring in damnable heresies, even denying the Lord that bought them, and bring upon themselves swift destruction." Here it is clearly supposed, and as good as in plain terms affirmed, that men bought by the Lord, viz. Christ, as all interpreters expound, may, yea, and that some will, "bring upon themselves destruction." If so, then evident it is that the Lord Christ bought with the price of his blood as well those who perish, and are destroyed by their own wickedness, as those that are saved; and consequently all men without exception.

That which is excepted against this interpretation and inference from the place, is very faint and weak. If you desire it, as it is, I shall impart it. First, say some, the Lord Christ is not here said to buy those here spoken of, and who are said to bring destruction upon themselves, after the same manner or upon the like terms on which he is or may be said to buy those that are saved. These he buys for one end or with one intent, as viz. to adopt for sons; those, with another, as viz. for slaves and vassals only. I suppose the world never heard of such a purchase as this made by Jesus Christ till these latter days. I mean, of men only to make slaves and vassals of them. Certain I am that the Scripture makes Christ's freemen and Christ's servants or bondmen all one: "For he that is called in the Lord," saith the apostle, "being a servant, is the Lord's freeman: likewise also he that is called, being free, is Christ's servant." (or bondman), 1 Cor. vii. 22. And, indeed, it is the blessed liberty and freedom which we obtain by Christ that makes us his servants or bondmen, *i.e.* which engageth us to be such unto him. But if Christ buys men with the price of his blood only for slaves and vassals, I would know whether they come to the actual enjoyment of this privilege (for such it must needs be supposed, as by the context itself will appear presently), by faith, or without faith. It cannot be said that they come to the possession of it by faith, for by faith men are put into the blessed relation of sons: "For ye are all the children of God," saith the apostle, "by faith in Jesus Christ," Gal. iii. 26. If they should come to it without faith, then Christ should show more favour, at least in this respect, to his vassals than to his sons. His sons come not to the actual enjoyment of their privilege but by faith; but his slaves, it seems, may attain the actual enjoyment of theirs without the performance of this or any other condition whatsoever.

Again, if Christ bought wicked men, and such as perish, for slaves and vassals, I would know whether they act the parts of slaves and vassals, and so serve him in that capacity which he aimed at in his purchase of them, or whether they act contrary to the nature and laws of slavery or vassalage. If they act as slaves and vassals, then they answer and fulfill their Lord's intentions and desires in his purchase, and so are not to be blamed, but commended rather. If it be said that they act otherwise, I mean, than as becometh slaves and vassals, this must be either by acting righteously or unrighteously. If it be by acting righteously that they transgress the law of slavery, then it follows that men may prove better, and live more holily, than Christ ever intended or desired they should. If it be by acting unrighteously, then Christ did not intend that those whom he bought for slaves should live unrighteously, but holily. If so, then were his intentions towards those whom he bought for slaves altogether as gracious as towards those whom he purchased for sons; his intentions towards and concerning these in his purchase of them, being clearly this, that they should "might serve him without fear in holiness and righteousness." Luke i. 74, 75.

Again, if Christ should buy some men for slaves and vassals, then, in case any of these, bought for such an end or with such an intention as this, should repent and believe, Christ should be not only disappointed in his bargain, but this by the righteousness of the persons bought or bargained for by him. To allege here, that it is impossible that any person who is bought for a slave should repent or believe, 1. Is absolutely untrue, there being no man but only he who hath sinned the sin against the Holy Ghost who is not in a capacity or possibility of repentance. 2. Though it were true, yet it hinders not at all the truth, or the force of the consequence in the proposition mentioned, viz. that in case any of those should repent whom Christ hath bought for slaves, then he should be disappointed in his bargain, and that by the righteousness of those bought by him. Reason teacheth us that a connex proposition may be demonstratively true and pregnant, though both the parts of it be never so false; as, for example, if Ishmael had been the natural son of Lot, he could not have been the natural son of Abraham. This is a proposition of a manifest and clear truth, yet both parts of it are false: for, (a). Ishmael was not the natural son of Lot. (b). He was the natural son of Abraham. Yet,

Again, if Christ bought some for slaves, then hath he some base, servile, hard or drudgery work to do, such as is not meet for sons to put their hand unto, for they have no need of slaves that have no servile our slavish work to do. But Christ hath no work to do but that which is honourable and worthy the most ingenuous of all his sons to do. "For all thy (God's) commandments," David saith, "are righteousness," Psal. cxix. 172. And a little before, "All thy commandments are truth," ver. 151. Now Christ hath no more work to be done by men in the world than God hath, neither hath God anymore than what is expressed and set forth in his commandments, and all these, as we heard from David, "are righteousness," *i. e.* requiring nothing but what is righteous and just for men to do, and consequently meet for sons, yea, chiefly for sons, or righteous ones, to do. Yea, God hath no need of any man's lie, or of any man's sin whatsoever. Therefore neither did Christ buy any for slaves.

Once more, if the persons here said to be bought by Christ, were bought by him for slaves, then must the apostle be conceived to extenuate their sin in denying him, by saying that he bought them. Whereas, by the emphatical carriage of the context it is evident, that his intent was by this consideration to aggravate their sin, and set forth the heinousness, the high demerit, and provocation of it. He that buys men being slaves, to make them freemen, and set them at liberty, may well expect thanks and free service from them; and if they should not own such a person as their great benefactor, they deserve not only to be divested of that liberty, which this benefactor of theirs hath purchased for them, but to be subjected to a bondage seven times more grievous than that from which they were delivered. But if a man shall buy those that were slaves before, only to put them into a condition of worse slavery than that wherein they were, they are not to be blamed if they deny him to be any great benefactor to them. In like manner, if Christ shall be here said to buy the men spoken of for slaves only, he should buy them out of a more easy slavery, from under a lighter condemnation, only to put them into a harder bondage, and subject them to a greater condemnation. Consequently, their not owning him, or their denying him as any benefactor unto them, were no just matter of provocation to him, nor of displeasure from God. What is that state of bondage or misery, in any kind, out of which Christ may be said to buy those whom he is suppose to buy for slaves? And what is the estate of slavery unto which he subjecteth them, or into which he putteth them, by this purchase, or buying of them, that so we may compare them together?

Doubtless that bondage and misery out of which these men can be supposed to be bought by Christ, is, in the utmost line and pitch of it, but an obnoxiousness or liableness to have been cast into hell-fire for their sin, committed in or contracted from Adam as soon as they were conceived or born, or the like. But that estate of slavery, whereinto (according to that interpretation of the place which we now oppose) they are bought, by being bought by Christ, is seven times more grievous than so. For, 1. Under this they are as liable to be thrown into hell-fire as in the other. Nay, 2. They are sure to be cast into hell-fire with much more guilt of sin upon them, than in their former condition they were capable of, and consequently to be so much the more grievously tormented forever. Therefore their sin of denying Christ is so far from being aggravated by their being bought by him for slaves, that indeed it is extenuated, and brought to nothing by it; and consequently, such an interpretation is diametrically opposite to the apostle's intent in the place.

Lastly, for this, if Christ bought the false teachers here spoken of, with other wicked men who in time perish for slaves, in what respect or with what intentions may he be supposed to have bought such infants, who dying in their infancy, and before the committing of actual sin, are supposed through the want of the privilege of election to perish? Must we have another device or notion whereby to form the intentions of Christ in his purchase of these? For it can at no hand of reason be said or thought that he bought these for slaves, inasmuch as he never intended that these should live so much as to the capacity of doing any work at all in one kind or other for him. If the assertors of the interpretation now ready to fall, shall think to relieve themselves at this point, by saying, it is not necessary that Christ should at all mind such children in his purchase, so as to buy them in one kind or other, but may well be conceived only to leave them as he found them, I would demand of them only this: How then, or upon what account such children should enjoy the benefit of life, though but for a short season, as for a month or two, &c., together with the comforts of life appropriate to their age as, as nourishment, nursing, looking to, &c. If no consideration at all was had of such in the death and purchase of Christ, I would gladly understand what other friend they had to mediate with God for such things on their behalf: or whether God be so far well pleased with them without all mediation, as to indulge such mercies and comforts unto them.

Nor can it with any colour of reason be said, that Christ bought the persons here spoken of for slaves, or servants unto the saints, because, 1. As the sphere of the affairs of this world moves, the saints are rather servants unto the wicked than these to them. "Thy seed," said God to Abraham, "shall be a stranger in a land that is not theirs, and they shall serve them; and they shall afflict them four hundred years," Gen. xv. 13. And, 2. Though there be a sense, wherein all things are said to be theirs (the saints') "All (things) are yours," &c. 1 Cor. iii. 22, &c. yet wicked men are in no other sense here said to be theirs, than that wherein Paul, Apollos, and Cephas, are said to be theirs. Therefore as it doth no way argue, that Paul, Apollos, and Cephas, were bought by Christ for slaves, because they are here said to be the saints', *i.e.* for their service and benefit, so neither doth it prove that wicked or impenitent men were bought for slaves by him, because they are here said to be theirs also, or because in some sense they are or may be serviceable to them.

Some seem to grant upon the account of the Scripture in hand, that Christ did buy some reprobates; (viz. such as are spoken of herein, and afterwards more fully described in the chapter;) but, say they, this concludes not the question in hand, unless it can be shown, that there is the same reason for all reprobates. "For," they say on, "the thing to be proved is, that Christ died equally for all and every man: and it is one thing to die for the reprobate in some sense, and to die for them with an intention and purpose to save them: and if Christ died for some, and but some, that perish in a manner not common to all and every man, it is manifest he died not equally for all men."[3] How unlike himself is the author in these passages? Or what pen ever dropped such divinity as this, with that which follows in the same contexture of discourse besides? For, 1. Is it reasonable to demand a proof, that there is the same reason for all reprobates (viz. in all circumstances, or in

3. Mr. J. Ball, Covenant of Grace, pp. 233-239.

every respect) to evince this, that Christ died equally for them all? Suppose that some of them be greater sinners, and some lesser, and sufficient proof can be made, that Christ died for the greater sinners amongst them (which the author of the said passages plainly grants). Is it reasonable ground of denial that he died for the rest that are lesser sinners than they? Or suppose there can be ten thousand differences shown between reprobates and reprobates, yet if there be none of them competent to evince a difference in the intentions of Christ, in or about his dying for them, they are all of them put together of no consideration at all, to prove that Christ died not equally for them, nor yet to infringe their assertion who affirm he did. As suppose some of them be tailors, others carpenters, a third part mariners, or the like, such differences as these, though never so many, are no ground whereon to conclude that Christ died not equally for them all.

Secondly, whereas he makes this the state of the question between him and his antagonists, whether Christ died equally for all and every man or no; confident I am that this is very palpable mistake, especially if by equally he means, as mean he must, if he means to speak congruously to the interest of his own discourse, intentions of procuring them by his death the actual enjoyment of equal conveniences, equal opportunities, equal accommodations in every kind for their respective salvations. For certainly no remonstrant was ever dissensed to such a degree, as to hold that Christ intended in or by his death, to purchase any such uniformity of divine dispensations in the government of the world at the hand of God, that all and every man, for example, should enjoy a ministry of the same efficacy and power for conversions, edification, establishment, &c. or that all and every man should be disposed of unto callings equally free from, and equally subject unto, temptations, occasions, opportunities of sinning, &c., with twenty and ten particulars more of like consideration which might readily be instanced. Nor was ever any contra-remonstrant engaged, or occasioned by any adversary to remonstrate against any such opinion as this.

But the question between them touching the intentions of God and of Christ in his death was, whether God did not as truly, as really, as cordially intend the salvation of one man as another, considered as men, in or by Christ's death. That God, in his providential dispensations, putteth a difference between one man's spiritual opportunities and another's, doth at no hand argue any different intentions in Him towards the one and the other in Christ's death, but may flow from several other principles or causes, as either from a different use and improvement in men of their original stocks of grace, or from different applications that have been made unto God by others, as in prayer, intercession, &c. in the behalf of some, in respect of others; or from different respects borne by God to the parents of the fore-fathers of some, in regard of their signal piety and serviceableness to his great name in their generations above others. Or lastly, from the wisdom of God in conjunction with his goodness in and about the government of the world, according unto which he judgeth it most expedient, as well for this own glory as for the comfort and equitable consideration of his saints, and such as walk before him with upright and perfect hearts, to make or to per-mit all that variety and disparity which is now seen in the world, in the spir-itual conveniences or accommodations of men, some men's proportion and allowance in this kind of being but the omer (a Hebrew unit of dry meas-ure), and other men's the ephah, which the Scriptures makes ten times larg-er than the other unit, Exod. xvi. 36. From some, or all of these considera-tions, and possibly from some others besides these, that inequality men-tioned between men and men in the enjoyment of the means of grace may very probably arise, so that there is not the least colour of a necessity to resolve it into any difference of intentions in God in the death of Christ.

And if difference of means vouchsafed unto men would argue different intentions in God touching their respective salvation in the atonement made by Christ's death, it will be found every whit as true that Christ died not equally for the elect themselves, as that he died not equally for all reprobates. Nay, if an estimate be made of the intentions by God in the death of Christ, concerning the salvations of men, by this rule it will be found that he bare more gracious intentions in the death of Christ towards many reprobates and their salvation, than towards many of the elect, or of those who in the end come to be saved. For nothing is more evident, than that many perish under greater and more excellent means of salvation than are vouchsafed unto many others, who yet are saved thereby. So that it is reasoning of no value which concludeth that "Christ died not equally for all and every man, because all and every man have not the same means of salvation granted unto them." See Matt. viii. 10-11; xv. 28; compared with xi. 20, 21, &c. Yet in what sense it is, at least, very probable, that all and every man have the same means of salvation vouchsafed unto them, shall be taken into consideration in due place.

Thirdly, whereas, the same author saith, "that it is one thing to die for the reprobate in some sense, and" (another, I suppose he means) "to die for them with an intention and purpose to save them;" I verily believe that neither he nor any of his persuasion in the present controversy, are able to credit such a distinction, unless captiously and altogether irrelatively to the business in hand, understood either by the Scriptures or any solid reason. For I confess I am yet to learn where, in the Scriptures, Christ is said to die for any, for whose salvation he died not. It is true Christ died not so precisely or adequately for the salvation of any man, as not to die for the obtaining of many other good things also for them, which are not comprehended in salvation formally taken; and in this sense the distinction may be admitted, inasmuch as upon this account it amounts to no more but this, it is one thing to say that Christ died for the reprobate in some sense, *i.e.* for the obtaining of lesser mercies for them; and another, to say that he died for their salvation, I confess that these two assertions are not formally, and every ways the same, as lesser things and greater things, compared only between themselves, are not the same. But such a sense as this no ways accommodates the author's discourse. Therefore, his meaning to make him speak like a man, must be, that to say that Christ died for the obtaining of some good things for reprobates, may, according to Scripture principles and grounds, stand and be justified; but to say that he died for the salvation of such men, cannot by that author's principles and grounds be evinced. But in this sense the said distinction hath not yet been, nor I believe, ever will be, in the latter member of it made orthodox or sound upon such terms.

The said author, in process of the same discourse, to save his bottle of hay or stubble from being burnt in the fire of the Scripture in hand, advanceth another distinction, every whit as helpless that way as the former. "We confess," saith he, speaking of the false teacher in the text before us, who bring swift destruction upon themselves, "that they were bought by the blood of Christ, because all these were fruits of Christ's death, whereof they were made partakers." But, a few lines after, he retracts upon the matter of substance of this his confession, by mincing it thus: "To these men their sins were remitted *in a sort*, in this world, and *in a sort* they were bought with the blood of Christ, but *inchoately* only, as they tasted the word of life."[4] Such shifting, intricate, and winding expressions as these, falling from the pens of grave and learned men, are the constant symptoms of a judgment distempered with some error, labouring and toiling in the service of it. First, who ever heard of sins remitted in a sort? Or who is able to notion such an expression? What is that remission which is in sort? If by remission of sins in a sort, he means remission of sins to degree, or with some imperfection, this contradicts the generally received opinion of

4. Mr. J. Ball, Covenant of Grace, p. 240.

Protestant divines, who admit no degrees, no magis and minus, in justification, still assigning this for one difference between justification and sanctification.

If by remission in a sort, he means a conditional remission (which seems to be his meaning by an expression used a few lines before) I know no other sense can be made of the expression, but only this, or of this import, viz., that God forgiveth some men their sins upon such terms as to reserve a liberty unto himself of reversing or recalling that grant, in case of such or such an unworthiness in them afterwards. This I judge to be most orthodox and true, though not in relation to some men only, but with reference unto all without exception, to whom God at any time granteth remission of sins in this world, (of which more before the close of this chapter). Yet this sense, I presume, no ways befriends the author's judgment in the controversy depending; so that the truth is, I know not what sense to make of his remission of sins upon condition, and in a sort.

Secondly, every whit as mysterious and uncouth to me as the former is that expression also of these men being bought with the blood of Christ in a sort. I wish that either some of the publishers of the discourse, or some other friend, either of the person or cause, or both would explain it. For as for his own explication (so intended, I suppose) in the words following; "But inchoately only, and as they tasted the word of life," is to me rather a further obscuration than explication. Were they bought with the blood of Christ inchoately only, and not perfectly? How then can this author say, in the passage next following, "That by promise he," God, "assured them of salvation if they did believe" and again, that "if they had unfeignedly believed in him, without question they should have been saved"? Would their believing have altered the intentions of God concerning them in the death of Christ? Or cause them to have been bought by the blood of Christ, though they were not bought before? Or did God assure them of such a salvation, which never was, nor ever so much as intended to be purchased or procured for them? Doubtless, if they should without question have been saved, in case they had unfeignedly believed, they were bought as perfectly and completely with the blood of Christ as any of the elect themselves, their unbelief notwithstanding; because their believing could not have procured or bought any other salvation to them, but only that which was fully and completely purchased and bought for them with the blood of Christ, without any dependence at all upon their faith. Therefore, unless we suppose that salvation was completely purchased for them by Christ in his death, we cannot say or suppose with truth, that in case they had believed, they should without question, have been saved.[5]

That which is behind, "And as they tasted of the word of life," is yet more inaccessible to my understanding than anything that went before. For how, or in what sense, with what congruity to a rational apprehension, can men be said to have been bought with the blood of Christ, as they tasted of the word of life? Surely the meaning is not that when or whilst they tasted of the word of life, they were so bought, (I mean with the blood of Christ) nor that their tasting of the word of life, was the formal or precise consideration under which Christ bought them, though the particle "as" frequently imports this consideration. As well the one as the other of these senses, are the abhorrings of common sense itself. Besides, they are at enmity with the principles of the author relating to the business in hand. Nor am I conscious of anything at all intended in the clause, unless, haply, this may be it; viz., that inasmuch as they tasted of the word of life, it is an argument that they were bought with Christ's blood, *i. e.* that they were partakers in the fruit and benefit of Christ's death, or that the intentions of God in the death of Christ extended thus far, or in this consideration, unto them. But can it enter into any reasonable man's thoughts to imagine, that if this had been all which the Holy Ghost intended to say, viz., that God intended by the virtue or means of Christ's death, to cause these men to taste of the word of life (especially with exclusion of all intentions in him to save them) that he would have expressed it by saying, that Christ bought them? Suppose a man should buy or procure such a quantity of meat and drink for a poor captive, as were sufficient to nourish him well and with good satisfaction two or three days, but should intend no such thing as to purchase his liberty, or redemption from captivity. Will any man call this a buying or redeeming of the person of this man?

It is a very strange thing to observe with what importunate bold, and broad-faced absurdities, error sometimes, though in company and conjunction with modesty and soberness of judgment, men will attempt an escape out of an exigency or strait. But further, to the point in hand, evident it is, as hath been already observed, that the apostle Peter, in these words, "who bought them," intends an emphatical aggravation of the sin of such teachers who should deny their Lord. Now, if there were nothing more intended in the said words, but only this, that their Lord procured this for them, that they should taste of the word of life, but intended nothing further or better than this to them, this would be so far from aggravating the sin mentioned,

5. See more of this, Chap. III.

that it would rather ease and qualify it. For if there was nothing purchased for them by the Lord Christ, but only this tasting of the word of life, impossible it was for them to have obtained anything more; weak and sinful man being in no capacity of obtaining more good in any kind than what a way hath been opened for him, in and by the death of Christ, to compass. Now, for a man to taste only of the word of life, and to be in no capacity of making any further progress in the way of salvation, nay, to be in no capacity of doing that by which he might be actually saved, no whit bettereth or sweeteneth any man's condition, but makes it much worse and much more grievous than otherwise it would have been.

"For it had been better," saith our apostle, "for them not to have known the way of righteousness," *i. e.* to taste of the word of life, "than, after they have known it, to turn from the holy commandment delivered unto them;" 2 Pet. ii. 21, which yet they must of necessity do, if they were in no capacity, under no possibility, of going forward, or of being saved. Now for a servant to deny or disclaim his Lord, in cause he never intended to make his condition any whit better, but in many respects worse, is a far lesser and lighter sin (if any at all) than it would be to deny him, upon a supposition that he had never done anything at all in relation to him, neither good nor bad. Therefore, this author is inextricably entangled with his exposition of the place in hand, and makes no earnings of it at all. He gives no tolerable account how those teachers, who brought swift destruction upon themselves, should be bought by Christ inchoately only, and in a sort, and not simply and absolutely, after the same manner, and upon the same terms that all other men, yea, the elect themselves, are bought by him.

Our English annotators, taking no notice of the former exposition of the place, as being, it seems, to them inconsiderable give us, instead thereof, our choice of two others; but both of them calculated likewise to serve the turn, not the truth. "The Lord that bought them," *i. e.* say they, "that gave a price sufficient for them, or by whom they professed that they were redeemed, and therefore they should not have denied him." But, for the former, we have once and again razed to the ground the polluted sanctuary of that distinction, which asserteth Christ's dying sufficiently for men, and yet denieth his dying intentionally for them.[6] Besides, here to interpret that Christ died sufficiently for the persons spoken of, without supposing that he died intentionally also for them, is clearly to overthrow the apostle's intention in the words, and to turn his aggravation of the sin he speaks of, rather into an extenuation than otherwise.

6. See Chap. I and III.

For he that shall pay that for the ease and benefit only of another, which was sufficient to have pleasured and eased me also as well as him, and yet shall neglect me in such a payment, and leave me in misery when he might, without the least trouble or charge to himself, above what he underwent upon another account, have relieved me, hath no cause to expect service or thanks from me, for such a payment. But I am the more excuseable if I neglect him, or refuse to own him as a friend, because he neglected me in my greatest extremity, and that when he had such a fair opportunity to have made me a happy man, and might have done it without the least inconvenience to himself, more than what he voluntarily put himself upon for the sake of others, to whom he was no whit more beholden or engaged than unto me. It is a palpably importunate and senseless conceit, to think that men are engaged in any bands of thankfulness or service unto Christ for dying sufficiently for them, unless he died intentionally also.

The latter exposition of the last-named authors was, that the Lord Christ is said to have bought these false teachers, because they *professed* themselves to have been bought by him. But, 1. Why do they not put such a gloss as this upon other places, where there is every whit as much reason to do it, as here? As when Paul saith, "For God hath not appointed us to wrath, but to obtain salvation by our Lord Jesus Christ," 1 Thess. v. 9, &c. why do they not interpret here; "For God hath not appointed us," &c. *i.e. we profess* that God hath not appointed us, &c. So, when the same apostle mentions "the church of God, which he hath purchased with his own blood," Acts xx. 28, why do they not gloss here: "God hath purchased the church with, &c. *i.e.* the church *professeth* herself thus purchased," &c. Partiality in interpretation of Scripture is every whit as bad and unchristian, as in civil judicatures.

Secondly, the great sin by which these false teachers are said to bring swift damnation upon themselves, is said to be, their denying the Lord that bought them. If, then, they denied this Lord that bought them, how can these expositors say, that they professed themselves bought by him? If it be replied, they might formerly profess themselves bought by him, though afterwards they denied him, and the apostle may charge them with sin in their present denial of him, upon the account of their former profession; I answer, that if formerly they professed themselves bought by him, but were not indeed so bought, and afterwards coming to understand or apprehend the truth, viz. that they were not so bought, they are not at all to be blamed for denying themselves to have been bought by him, or for denying that he bought them. To deny that to be so which is not so, especially when a man verily believes and apprehends it not to be, is no man's sin. Or if it be fur-' ther pleaded, in favour of the said gloss, that these false teachers might at the same time, when they professed themselves bought by Christ, deny him, viz. in a consequential way, as either by teaching such heretical doctrines, which overthrew his Godhead, manhood, &c. or else by an impious conversation; I answer, 1. That if they professed themselves bought by him, they could not lightly teach or hold forth any doctrine wherein they should deny, either his Godhead, manhood, satisfaction, or any other thing relating to him, without which he could not, in a rational way, have made such a purchase of them. Or, 2. If they did teach any such doctrine, it must be supposed that they did it unwittingly, and because they apprehended nothing in it of any inconsistency with their profession of being bought by Christ. For it is not to be thought that men will willingly and knowingly teach contradictions, or teach any opinion which they apprehend contradictory to what they daily profess to believe.

Now, for man unwittingly, and contrary to his intention and desire, to teach such a doctrine, which consequently involves, or leads unto an opinion that is dangerous and damnable, is nothing but what is incident to the best and most approved teachers, (as I could readily demonstrate by many instances) and therefore not like to be a sin of such high provocation, as to bring swift damnation upon them. But, 3, and lastly, that the apostle doth not speak of any such denial of the Lord Christ by these false teachers, which is by works or by wickedness of life and conversation, but of doctrine that is evident enough by the express tenor and carriage of the words themselves. "But there were false prophets also among the people, even as there shall be false teachers among you, who privily shall bring in damnable heresies, even denying," &c., 2 Pet. ii. 1, which clearly showeth that the denial of the Lord, here charged upon false teachers, stood not in works but in words, in false, heretical and damnable teachings. Therefore they are not, they cannot be here said to have been bought by Christ, because they professed themselves to have been redeemed by him.

Some, to evade that mortal stroke, which the Scripture in hand reacheth to that opinion, which denieth a possibility of perishing in those who are truly bought and redeemed by Christ, not being satisfied with any of the former come-offs, have devised this. The Lord, say they, is said to have bought these false teachers, not because he really indeed and in truth, bought them, but because in the opinion of judgment of men he had bought them. They were looked upon as persons redeemed and bought by him. And to credit this interpretation, they allege several texts where things or persons are said to be so or so, such or such, not because they were really that which they are said to be, but only because they were this in appearance, or according to the common estimate of men. As Matt. ix. 13; John ix. 39; Matt. xiii. 12; compared with Luke viii. 18. But this colour is as faint as any of the former, and as easily washed off. And,

1. It is very questionable whether in any of these places, either things or persons receive any denomination merely from appearance or opinion of men. Many things might be argued, and that with much probability, oppositum. But concerning the first of the places, most certain it is that there is no such notion to be found there. For that by the righteous, whom Christ saith that he came not to call to repentance, should be meant righteous only in show, or in the opinion of men, whether themselves or others, and not righteous truly and properly so called contradicts the manifest and declared intentions of Christ's coming into the world, which are frequently avouched and found to be the calling of sinners of all sorts, kinds, and degrees unto repentance; and therefore or hypocrites also, as well as others, and of persons conceited in the highest of their own righteousness. See Matt. iii. 7, &c.; 1 Tim, i. 12-15, compared with Phil. iii. 6, &c. (to omit many other places of like import). Besides, the occasion and tendency of our Saviour's words are of pregnant eviction, that by righteous he means persons truly such, and not in conceit or opinion only. He was charged as with matter of undue deportment in eating with publicans and sinners.

For his justification he pleads, that the whole have no need of physician, but the sick; meaning, that as the calling of the physician is no ways necessary, in respect of those that are strong, healthful, and sound, but only of the sick. So neither had his coming into the world been of any such necessity, as now it was, but for sinners; and that had men been righteous and spiritually sound, there had been no need for his coming unto them. And therefore as a physician is not to be blamed for conversing with the sick, inasmuch as the nature and end of his calling requires his presence with them, and not with those that are sound; so neither was he to be blamed for being in the company of sinners, seeing the great end and intent of his calling to the office of a Saviour was not to save or to be helpful unto such as were righteous, who upon such an account stood in no need of him, but to administer comfort and help unto sinners, who without help from him must needs perish. Now certain it is, that the righteous whom Christ compares unto the whole, who in that respect need no physician, are not men right-eous in show or in opinion only, for these stand in as much or more need of the physician than others; but those that are truly and sincerely right-eous. Therefore this Scripture holds no intelligence with that interpretation of the other, which is now under censure. But,

2. Be it granted for truth, that things and persons sometimes receive appellations only from an appearance of what they are called, or from the opinion of men judging them such. Yet such a line of interpretation as this is not to be stretched over what Scriptures we please, nor indeed over any but where the manifest exigency of the context calls for it. Otherwise we shall entitle men to a liberty of substituting shadows and appearances only, instead of realities, and substances of truth, where and when they please; and so to turn the mind and counsels of God in the Scriptures upside down. The contest of old between Jerome and Augustine about Paul's reproving Peter, Gal. ii., is of notable consideration to the business in hand. Jerome pleaded, that when Paul reproved Peter at Antioch, he did it not seriously or in good earnest; but affirmed, that these two apostles out of a kind of prudent charity agreed to make a show of a contest between them, when as indeed there was none. But how gravely and copiously doth Augustine declare against and argue down such a licentiousness of interpreting?

"The Scripture," saith he, "plainly saith, that Peter was worthy of reproof, or to be condemned. If then we are to take this liberty, or boldness, to say that indeed and in truth he did not amiss, but only dissembled for the sake of those that were weak, then the apostle Paul lies, in saying that he was worthy of blame or reproof. Admit this," saith this learned father, "and down falls all the authority and certainty of the Scriptures. For if they speak that which is false in one place, who can make it good that they speak truth in another?"[7] This is the brief of that famous dissertation between those two worthies in the Christian church. From whence it may appear of what dangerous consequence it is to expound that which the Scripture simply and plainly delivers as a truth, as spoken by way of appearance of human opinion only, when there is no apparent necessity enforcing such an exposition. And if there be some places which will bear or which call for such a figurative and catachrestical interpretation as this, they are but few; and those which are, must be discerned and distinguished from others by the manifest exigency of their respective scopes and imports, the least jot or tittle of which character is not to be found in the place in hand. For,

---

7. Aug. Epist. viii. vid. et Epist. ix. et xiv. et praecipue, Epist. xix.

3. Lastly, most evident it is, as hath been formerly also observed, and as many expositors, more than enough addicted to the contra-remonstrant opinion, themselves acknowledge, that the apostle's intent here is, to set forth the most heinous and horrid indignity of the sin of these false teachers in denying their Lord, by this aggravating consideration, that they deny such a Lord who bought them. Now, if it be supposed that this Lord really, and of love and good will to them, and out of a desire to free them from misery, bought or redeemed them, the consideration is of great pregnancy and force to demonstrate horrible ingratitude and impiety in them to deny him. But if on the contrary it be supposed, that he did not buy them with any intent to free them from their misery, but only make a show of such a thing, or only do that which might occasion men to think or to believe that he did so, this manifestly easeth and qualifies the guilt of their sin in denying him; and so is manifestly repugnant to the apostle's scope. For to make a show of love only, or to do that by which other men may be invited to think that a real kindness is done for such or such a man, when as indeed there is nothing done of any such consideration, nor ever intended to be done, doth no ways oblige this man in thankfulness unto him who accommodates him upon no better terms, but is rather a just ground of a harder and worse opinion of him.

If it be replied; Yea, but these false teachers knew nothing but that they were truly and really bought by Christ, and that out of a desire of saving them; nor had they any sufficient reason to judge otherwise. Therefore their sin in denying him is no way eased upon this account, that he did not indeed buy them with any such intent or desire, because, 1. Men are bound to judge, as they have reason to judge; and, 2. Are bound to act or practise according to their judgments; I answer,

There can be no sufficient ground for any man to believe that which is false, nor ought such a thing to be believed; at least with confidence of belief, or with any such belief, upon which he shall stand bound to engage in any material and weighty action or practice. Therefore if Christ did not really buy these false teachers, they could have no sufficient ground to believe that he did; at least to believe at any such rate of confidence, as rather to suffer the loss of any considerable good than deny it. If it be again replied that a man may stand bound to venture much upon probabilities, in many cases, though there be no certainty or truth in that which upon such probabilities he doth believe, I answer, possibly a man may indeed stand bound, in point of wisdom or prudence, in some cases to adventure much, in a simple consideration, upon probabilities only; but not in point of conscience.

As for example, a merchant or other man may stand bound in point of wisdom to adventure some considerable part of his state in a way of trade beyond the seas, upon probabilities only of a gainful return. Even in this case, upon a more exact consideration, it will appear that such a man doth not make this adventure upon any mere probability, one or more, but upon that which is certain. For the probability of a good return in this case is a certainty to him; he knows certainly, and beyond all doubt or question, that it is a thing probable or likely that he shall receive such a return, though he knows not certainly, but only probably, that he shall indeed receive it. Now the true ground upon which the merchant adventures is not the knowledge that he shall, or will gain by his adventure; for it is impossible for him to know this. But the knowledge and consideration of the likelihood of his gaining, which, as hath been said, he may, and doth know, and that certainly.

You will upon this say, it is like, the false teachers, in the Scripture in hand, had, or might have had, such a certainty as this, that the Lord Christ did really buy them. For it was very probable that he had so bought them, in regard of that illumination, external sanctification, and other gifts, whereof they were partakers; and consequently their sin in denying him was never the less upon any such account as this, that he had not indeed bought them: inasmuch as they were bound to believe that he had so bought them, and to behave themselves towards him accordingly. I answer, 1. Upon this supposition, that Christ did not indeed buy, or had not bought them, they could have no probability, no not upon their illumination, or outward gifts whatsoever, that he had, or should have so bought them; especially taking in the opinion of those against whom we manage our present discourse, viz., that Christ truly bought no more than come to be actually saved. For, (a.) If those truly bought by Christ be but very few in number, comparatively with those who were passed by, and not so bought by him, then no particular man, thus far, (I mean, as he is a member of mankind, or one of the generality of men) can have so much as a probable ground that he is one of those so bought by him. As when there are twenty, or forty blanks in a lottery, and only one prize, it is not probable or likely that he that draweth but once shall draw the prize. For it is twenty or forty to one that he shall not draw it. (b.) Neither doth the receiving of illumination, or any other common gift, upon the former supposals, make it probable unto any man, that Christ truly bought him, because very many receive illumination, at least in the sense of our opposers, &c., who live wickedly; and many also who fall away from that external sanctity, wherein they walked for a season. And our Saviour himself saith that "For many are called, but few are chosen," Matt. xx. 16; and again, that "iniquity shall abound," viz., in fierce and bloody persecutors, "the love of many shall wax cold," Matt. xxiv. 12; and yet again, that "many that are first, shall be last," Matt. xix. 30; to omit many others passages of like import. Therefore, no external or common gifts whatsoever, make it so much as probable unto any man, that he was truly bought by Christ, there being very many thus gifted, who will not in the end be saved. But,

Suppose our false teachers had probable grounds, from their illumination, &c., to believe that Christ had truly bought them, yet this probability, upon the premises last argued, could be but very faint, and mingled with much jealousy and fear of the contrary; and consequently nothing so binding upon them to own and honour Christ in the world as a certain knowledge, free from the pain and torment of fear of the contrary, that he had so bought them, would have been. So that though it should he yielded, which yet there is no sufficient reason to do, that the interpretation which we now oppose, doth not turn up by the very roots the drift and scope of the apostle in the place and words, yet it shakes them terribly, and leaves little spirit, strength, or force in them. If the merchant judged it forty-, twenty-, yea, or but ten-[8] to-one odds, that in case he should venture, he should never have any return of what he ventures, he would have but slender encouragement, and so little list to follow his sea trade with his whole estate upon such terms. Whereas certainty of returns with considerable gain, would the providence of God and condition of human affairs bear it, would multiply merchants without end; and withal render those very weak and unlike men, who, having means and opportunity to follow such an employment, should either be slothful and sit still, or else dispose of their estates in any other way, wherein little or no improvement could be expected.

In like manner, a certainty of knowledge that Christ truly bought a man with his blood, is a high and sacred engagement upon this man to acknowledge, own, and honour him as his great and blessed Lord and benefactor, in the sight of the world. This consequently renders him the reproach and abomination of men, in case he shall be ashamed of him, or deny him. Whereas a faint apprehension only of such a thing done for him, entangled and encumbered with a thousand questions, fears, and doubtings, hardly extricable, whether it was indeed done or no, makes the denial or disown-

8. Calvin. in 2 Pet. ii. 2.

ing of him, if not pardonable, yet much more excusable, and of far lighter provocation and demerit, than in the other case it would be.

Thus then at last we see, that no interpretation will sit with any tolerable closeness or congruity to the words and scope of the Scripture in hand, but only that which acknowledgeth the false teachers mentioned therein, are truly, really, absolutely, and completely bought by Christ. I mean after the same manner, and upon the same terms of love on God's part, after, and upon which those bought by him, who in the issue and event come to be saved. As for that objection, which lies in many men's thoughts against such an interpretation as this, as viz., that if Christ truly bought any man, he must of necessity at last be saved; we shall, God assisting, give a fair, clear, and satisfactory answer unto it, when we come to answer the arguments insisted upon, for the proof of the contrary doctrine to that which is maintained in the present discourse. But for that which some plead against the interpretation asserted, from Revel. xiv. 4, where those that are said to be redeemed or bought *apo tōn anthrōpōn*, from men, are termed the first fruits unto God, and to the Lamb, and are said to follow the Lamb wheresoever he goeth, which implieth their actual salvation.

The answer unto it is easy. For evident it is, from the description of the persons here spoken of, that they are such, not simply who were redeemed and bought by Christ, but who also truly believed in him, and persevered in faith and love unto the end; and consequently such, in whom the work of redemption performed by Christ obtained its ultimate and plenary efficiency and end. In which respect they are said, in a kind of emphatical manner, to be *ēgorasthēsan apo tōn anthrōpōn*, to have been redeemed, or bought, from men, or from amongst men, *i. e.* persons in whom the common redemption vouchsafed by Christ took place, and wrought to that great and signal differencing and distinguishing of them from other men, that whereas the grace of this redemption was buried under other men's wickedness and unbelief, and at last, in their destruction, it prevailed and magnified itself in the constant faith and holiness of these, and at last triumphed gloriously in their salvation. Whereby it came to pass, that these only seemed to have been redeemed amongst men, all others miscarrying, as if they had not been redeemed. So that there is nothing at all, scarce so much as an appearance of any thing, in this Scripture, against that interpretation of the other, for the establishing of which way hath been made through the fall of many others.

And doubtless he that shall attentively and with consideration read what

Calvin himself hath commented upon time place, must needs judge him very complaint with the said interpretation. "Although," saith he about 2 Pet. ii. 1, "Christ may be denied several ways, yet, in my judgment, Peter means that which is expressed in Jude, viz., when the grace of God is turned into wantonness. For Christ hath redeemed us, that he might have a people separated from all the defilements of the world, addicting itself unto holiness and innocency. *Wherefore they who, shaking off the bridle, cast themselves forward into all manner of licentiousness, are not without cause said to deny Christ, by whom they were redeemed.* So then, that the doctrine of the gospel may abide with us safe and sound, let this be always fixed in our minds, that we are redeemed by Christ, that he may be the Lord both of our lives and deaths." In this piece of commentary there are several passages which plainly declare the author's judgment to have been, at least when he wrote these things, that those are, and may be said to be redeemed by Christ, and that after the same manner that the saints themselves are redeemed, who yet may in the end perish. For, 1. In saying Christ hath redeemed us, questionless he (Calvin) includes himself, and all the godly, at least, that heard him or shall read these things. Now if he should mean that either himself or other godly ones were redeemed with any other kind of redemption than that spoken of in the text before him, viz., wherewith the false teachers, there mentioned, were redeemed, his commentaries should be quite besides the text.

2. He saith expressly, that "they who, shaking off the bridle, cast themselves forward, or headlong, into all manner of licentiousness, are not without cause said to deny Christ, by whom they were redeemed." Now, who are they that bring swift destruction upon themselves, but such as he here describes, and whom he supposeth to have been redeemed by Christ, and that with the same redemption whereof he had spoken immediately before, viz., wherewith himself and other godly ones had been redeemed? For to make him speak of two or several kinds of redemption specifically distinct, in one and the same passage, without giving the least notice of any distinction or difference at all between them, is to suppose him to equivocate, and to make him a transgressor of the known principles and rules of writing.

3. Lastly, when he exhorts, "let this always be fixed in our minds, that we are redeemed by Christ, that he may be the Lord of," &c. He cannot be supposed to address or speak only to those that were, or are truly godly, but to all those, at least, who judge themselves such; yea, clear it is, that he speaks to all persons genuinely professing Christianity, without exception.

Nor can he be supposed to invite or persuade any man to fix that in his mind, which is every whit as likely, if not much more likely, to be false than true, but only that which is most certainly and unquestionably true. Therefore he clearly supposeth, that all persons, who genuinely judge themselves godly, yea, that all real professors of Christianity, without exception, are redeemed by Christ; and consequently, that as well those apostates who perish as those that are saved, were redeemed by him. There being nothing more certain than that many who profess Christianity, yea, and who call themselves godly, will perish.

From henceforth then let no man put the doctrine maintained in this discourse to any such rebuke as this, that it was never held or countenanced by any divine of the order surnamed orthodox. We find the principal of this order, Calvin himself I mean, besides many others of name and note amongst them, once and again, yea, seven times over, very freely giving the right hand of fellowship unto it. We have been somewhat long in our vindication of the Scripture last argued; but the restless and endless importunity of men in persuading the Scriptures to entreat their darling error kindly, together with the difficulty of the Scriptures to be so persuaded, hath compelled us. But it is very incident to men to do by the Scriptures as they do by themselves. "God," saith Solomon, "hath made man upright; but they have sought out many inventions," Eccles. vii. 29. So may it be truly said, that God hath made many Scriptures upright, plain, clear, obvious for sense and meaning; but men are wont to seek out many inventions to perplex or misfigure this meaning. It is therefore necessary to oppose their fond conceits and imaginations.

The next Scripture of the consort designed for this chapter was 2 Pet. ii. 20, 21: "For if after they have escaped the pollutions of the world through the knowledge of the Lord and Saviour Jesus Christ, they are entangled therein, and overcome, the latter end is worse with them than the beginning. For it had been better for them not to have known the way of righteousness, than, after they have known it, to turn from the holy commandment delivered unto them." Here likewise it is most irrefutably and clearly supposed, that men who have been truly sanctified and regenerated, and consequently redeemed by Christ, may yet decline so as to perish in the end. For to deny that this expression of escaping the pollution of the world, through the knowledge of the Lord and Saviour Jesus Christ, doth import true sanctification, or regeneration, is to deny that the sun is up at noonday. For if the persons here said to have "escaped the pollutions of the world, through," &c., shall not be supposed truly and inwardly sanctified, &c., but only superficially and externally, they must be supposed withal, 1. To have been all this while in the midst of that greatest "pollution of the world," unbelief, which pollutes all other things unto men. Tit. i. 15. 2. To have been in the inward bent and frame of their minds and wills as much addicted to all other the pollutions hereof as at any time formerly. 3. Lastly, to have been all this while most damnable hypocrites and dissemblers. Now that the Holy Ghost should say, that unbelievers, persons inwardly full of all wickedness and filthiness, most vile hypocrites and dissemblers, have "escaped the pollutions of the world," especially "through the knowledge" (or rather acknowledgment), *en epignōsei* "of the Lord and Saviour Jesus Christ," is to me, and I think to all other impartially considering men, the first-born of incredibilities. Can a man be said to have escaped his enemies when he still remains under their power, and is in greater danger of suffering mischiefs from them than ever before? Or is not he, who being enlightened, retains the truth in unrighteousness, remains inwardly full of malice and wickedness, only garbing himself with a hypocritical outside, or mere profession of holiness, as much or more under the power and command of sin, as likely to perish everlastingly for sin, as ever he was, or could be before his illumination?

For if, during that condition of escape of which the Holy Ghost here speaks, *from first to last,* the men spoken of were inwardly full of all filthiness and wickedness, and consequently were vile hypocrites and dissemblers, our adversaries themselves confess in their managing this Scripture, though as they suppose to their advantage. Evident it is, say they, that all the while they were free from the pollutions of the world, they were still dogs and swine, and if so, as inwardly vile and wicked as ever, because it is said of them, ver. 22, "But it is happened unto them according to the true proverb, The dog is turned to his own vomit again; and the sow that was washed to her wallowing in the mire." But of this more anon.

1. That which is here expressed to be the cause or means of their escape or deliverance from the pollutions of the world, their knowledge (or acknowledgment rather, which is somewhat more) of the Lord and Saviour Jesus Christ, plainly evinceth it to have been such an escape, which is inward, cordial, and real, in conjunction with true sanctification, and not external, formal, or in show and pretence only. There is scarce anything more frequent or familiar in the Scriptures than the ascribing of justification, sanctification, yea, and salvation itself to the knowledge, some-

times of God, sometimes of Christ, sometimes of both. "By his knowledge shall my righteous servant" (saith Isaiah, speaking of Christ) "justify many." Isa. liii. 11. "By his *knowledge*," *i. e.*, as interpreters generally say means him (Christ) being known. "He calls that," saith Musculus, "the knowledge of Christ, not wherewith he himself knoweth, but whereby he is known by us."

The apostle Paul speaks of the knowledge of the Son of God, as one of the principal ends of that evangelical ministry which was by special grace given unto and is continued in his church, and joins it with the "perfecting of the saints," Eph. iv. 12, 13; and afterwards in the same chapter, ver. 22, 23, &c., ascribes "ye put off...the old man," and "be renewed in the spirit of your mind" unto it. The apostle John makes no scruple to pronounce him a liar, who shall say that he *knoweth Christ*, and yet "keepeth not his commandments." 1 John ii. 4. And again, that "whosoever sinneth" (*i. e.* lives wickedly) "hath not seen him, neither *known* him." 1 John iii. 6. That of our Saviour himself to this purpose is well known, "And this is life eternal, that they know thee the only true God, and Jesus Christ, who thou hast sent." John xvii. 8. It would be easy to multiply places of like import. Therefore certainly that obedience, that sanctification, that conformity in life and conversation to the word and will of God, which is begotten and raised in men by the knowledge, much more by the acknowledgment, or thorough knowledge (which the word *epignōseōs* seems to import) of "the Lord and Saviour Jesus Christ," is cordial obedience, true and real sanctification, and conformity to the will of God.

2. And lastly, if the escape and deliverance from "the pollutions of the world" here spoken of, was not inward, real, and accompanied with true sanctification, &c., how could the persons be in danger of an after-entanglement therewith, especially of an inward entanglement, and wherewith the heart should be ensnared? The Holy Ghost evidently implieth they were, 2 Pet. ii. 14, in ascribing unto them a "a heart they have exercised with covetous practices," or of being overcome? At least, how should their conditions be rendered so much more grievous and dreadful by any such entanglement than they were under the escape, as the Holy Ghost here clearly supposeth? If the escape here mentioned, importeth not true and real sanctification, the persons escaping must of necessity be supposed, all the time of this their escape, to have been "in the gall of bitterness and bonds of iniquity," and particularly to have been both hypocrites and unbelievers.

Now our Saviour himself supposeth hypocrites and unbelievers to be the first-born children of hell, and of "the lake that burneth with fire and brimstone for ever," in those two sayings of his, compared, viz. Matt. xxiv. 50,51, with Luke xii. 46. The tenor of the former is this: "The lord of that servant shall come in a day when he looketh not for him, and in an hour that he is not aware of, and shall cut him asunder, and appoint him his portion with *hypocrites*: there shall be weeping and gnashing of teeth." Of the latter, this: "The lord of that servant......will cut him in sunder, and appoint him his portion with the *unbelievers*." If hypocrites and unbelievers be of the first and primary designation for hell and eternal destruction (which the said passages clearly import), they cannot lightly through any apostasy whatsoever contract any worse or more grievous condition than their present condition is. The truth is, that I know no apostasy, of which a hypocrite or unbeliever is properly capable, but only that which is from Belial or from Satan.

All that the adversaries of the interpretation given, (and who will not acknowledge the escape here mentioned to imply anything more than a mere formal and outside sanctification) are able to plead from the words or context for themselves, is only that which hath been already touched, ver. 22, "The dog is turned to his own vomit again, and the sow," &c. From hence they conclude, that a dog is a dog and retains the same nature whilst his vomit and he are parted which he had before: and so a sow or a swine is the self-same creature inwardly, washed and unwashed. So were the persons resembled to these creatures, the same men in the inward frame and constitution of their hearts, even whilst they had made the escape here spoken of from the "pollutions of the world," which they were before; therefore they are not truly sanctified or regenerate.

But how weak this allegation is, sufficiently appears by the foundation on which it is built, which is that parables or similitudes run upon all fours, or that all things whatsoever found in the things resembling, are applicable also to the things resembled. God, in hearing the importunate and restless cries of his saints, is compared to an unrighteous judge, who though neither fearing God nor regarding man, was notwithstanding, overcome with the widow's importunity to do her justice. Now, to infer from hence, that because this unjust judge remained still unjust, even whilst he did justice to the poor widow, therefore God also, being compared to him, was unjust whilst he heard the prayers of his saints, would be an inference blasphemously ridiculous. Of no whit better calculation is that collection mentioned, wherein, because men are sometimes clean, and afterwards polluted, are compared in respect of such a change, to a dog returning to his vomit, and a washed sow to her wallowing in the mire; it is argued, that therefore during their cleanness, they must needs be, inwardly and in disposition, like unto these creatures. Besides, supposing the persons here spoken of to have been dogs and swine, I mean inwardly unclean and impure before the alteration here ascribed to them, the proverb of the dog returning to his vomit, &c. may in sufficient propriety of speech be applied unto them, without any supposal that under that alteration they should be dogs also. Suppose a dog should by casting up his gorge or vomit be turned into a sheep, and afterwards should by a contrary means, viz. by resuming it, become a dog again. Might it not truly and properly enough be said, that this dog, though lately a sheep, is now become a dog again? But the impertinency of the plea now impleaded, may be any man's vision that will but narrowly and impartially look upon it. Yea,

Calvin himself, it seems, was so far unsatisfied with it, that he could not own the interpretation attempted by it, but crosseth over the way to the other interpretation. "This," saith he upon verse 22, "is that in brief that Peter would say, that the Gospel is medicine which purgeth us with a wholesome vomit, but withal that there are many dogs, who to their destruction, resorb or resume what they have vomited up. And again, that the Gospel is a wash basin, which washeth away all our uncleannesses; but there are many swine, who soon after their washing tumble themselves in the mire. In the meantime, the godly are admonished to take heed of both, unless they mean to be reckoned amongst dogs and swine." If men, like dogs, may resume that to their destruction, which they have vomited or cast up, certainly when they had thus vomited, and till such a resorbition, they were sound and in a condition of salvation.

A man cannot reasonably be said to take anything to his destruction who had that in him before, which was a greater and more certain means to destroy him. Nor need godly men be admonished of anything, as like or possible to bring them into the account of dogs or swine, if such a transition be supposed to be impossible to them. Therefore, doubtless, Calvin resents much better that exposition of the place in hand, which supposeth the escape specified therein to include an inward and real sanctification, than that which resolves it into smoke and wind, I mean an external, formal, hypocritical sanctification.

Another Scripture ranged in the same division with the former, is of much the same consideration with them. "Of how much sorer punishment," said the sacred writer, "suppose ye, shall he be thought worthy, who hath trodden under foot the Son of God, and hath counted the blood of the covenant, wherewith he was sanctified, an unholy thing, and hath done despite unto the Spirit of grace?" Heb. x. 29. To say that this Scripture, with the former, doth not speak of a true and real sanctification, but of that only which is outwardly, seemingly, and hypocritically such, is to claim a mere arbitrary power for interpreting the Scriptures.

For, 1. The word here translated, "sanctification," is the same with that which our Saviour useth, John xvii. 17, where in the behalf of his disciples he prayed thus unto his Father, "Sanctify them through thy truth: thy word is the truth." If neither reason nor religion suffereth us here to interpret that Christ prayed unto the Father to sanctify his disciples outwardly, formally, seemingly only, but really and in truth, I would gladly know which of the two, or whether both, lead us to understand any other sanctification in the place in hand.

2. No one instance, I verily believe, can be brought throughout all the Scripture, where men are said to be sanctified by Christ, by the blood of Christ, by the knowledge of Christ or the like—but that the place is to be understood of a true, sound, and saving sanctification. But places of this interpretation are many, 1 Cor. i. 2; vi. 11; Eph. v. 25, 26; Heb. xiii. 12, &c.

3. There is this reason evincing with a high hand that the Scripture before us speaketh of an inward, real, and soul sanctification, viz. that the sin of the person here said to have been sanctified, in counting the blood of the covenant an unholy thing, i. e. in despising or profaning it, is aggravated by this consideration, that he was sanctified by it. The carriage of the verse clearly, and above all contradiction, evinceth this. Now, then, if we shall suppose that this person had received no more good, no greater benefit by this blood of the covenant, but only to be made an hypocrite or a dissembler by it, which must be affirmed, if the sanctification here attributed unto him be only a feigned or formal sanctification. This is so far from aggravating that sin of his in despising it, that it doth very much, if not altogether, extenuate and excuse it.

Nor can it be here pretended, with reason, that it was not the fault, nor any defect in the blood of the covenant, that he was not truly and really sanctified, but his own negligence and falseness of heart. For though it be true, that the reason why any man, especially enjoying the Gospel, proves a hypocrite, is not any deficiency in the blood there presented unto him by way of antidote, and for his cleansing, but his own negligence and unfaithfulness to his own soul, yet the sanctification spoken of in the Scripture in hand, is not attributed to the looseness or hollow-heartedness of the person in whom it was found, but to the blood of the covenant itself. Now that which is the proper and genuine effect of this blood, cannot be any hypocritical or mere outside thing; and, however, were this sanctification an hypocritical or mere outside thing, and so an occasional effect only of the blood of the covenant, yet would the consideration hereof be no just or fitting matter, whereby to aggravate the sin of him that should despise this blood.

Though I may be guilty, and an offender in a high degree to remain a hypocrite or a false-hearted man, under means so efficacious and proper to make me sound and upright-hearted, as the Gospel and the blood of the covenant held forth therein are, yet the consideration of my remaining a hypocrite in this case, is no ground why I should be judged, either by myself or others, the greater sinner for despising these means. It is rather an extenuation, as hath been said, of my sin in this kind than otherwise, to consider that though this blood of the covenant be a very efficacious and proper means to make me sound-hearted and sincere, yet it is not so efficacious and powerful in this kind as actually to subdue and overcome the hypocrisy and wickedness of my soul, without mine own endeavours in concurrence with it. Therefore, certainly the author of Hebrews would never instance in a counterfeit, unsound, or imperfect sanctification, wrought or occasioned by the blood of the covenant, to aggravate the sin of such a person who should despise it, by apostatising from the profession of it. But,

4. Lastly, suppose the Scripture in hand should be conceived to speak of an outward, formal sanctification, which consists in a civil or moral reformation of the outer man, (which yet the scope of the place will at no hand, as hath been argued, admit) yet it sufficiently reacheth, in point of proof, that which is intended from it, viz. that Christ died for those that perish. For this sanctification, of what kind soever it be – be it shadow, or be it substance – is ascribed to "the blood of the covenant," (*i. e.* the blood of Christ, wherein God covenanteth life and salvation unto the world upon their believing) as the efficient cause or means of it. Therefore this blood, howsoever, was shed for those that may and do perish.

If it be said, it is true it was shed for such men with such an intent on God's part as this, that they should be externally cleansed by it, and outwardly sanctified, but not that they should be really and internally sanctified, or, in time, saved by it; I answer, 1. That the strength of this objection hath been already trodden down in this chapter. 2. I here add, that if God intended an external sanctification only, by the death of Christ, for the persons mentioned in the objection, then were his intentions in Christ's death, in reference to these men, rather grievous than gracious; bent upon the aggravation and increase of their condemnation, not upon the advance of their salvation; and Christ himself should come unto them, not that they "might have life more abundantly," but that they might have hell and death more abundantly. Whereas most certain it is that "God sent not his Son into the world to condemn the world," much less to increase the condemnation of the world, "but that the world," that is, (as we formerly made good the interpretation, Chap. I) the generality of men, "might be saved." 3. And lastly, if Christ died for these men to invest them with an external sanctification, to make them outwardly holy, I would know whether, together with this outward sanctification, he did intend to procure for them by his death an inward principle answerable to it, out of which it should flow. If so, if he did intend to procure by his death an inward suitable principle for these men, out of which that outward sanctification should flow, then certainly he did intend to procure them a true and real sanctification. For what can we imagine a true and real sanctification should be more than a righteous, blameless, innocent, Christian conversation, issuing from an inward principle suitable to it?

If it be said, No, Christ did not intend by his death to procure for these men any such inward principle as you speak of; but only that outward conformity to the ways and laws of Christian religion, then it will follow that Christ died with an intention to make men hypocrites, or to procure hypocrisy for men. Because a fair show in outward practices and religious deportments, without an inward principle and frame of heart answerable to them, and which ariseth out of a hollow and unsanctified heart, is hypocrisy, and that in the plainest and most obvious signification of the word. Therefore, certainly, Christ did not shed his blood to purchase any such sanctification for men which some conceive to be meant in the Scripture in hand. Christ, in dying for men, intended nothing for men but that which is true, real, and saving in the nature and proper tendency of it. Intentions of making men hypocrites or Christians by halves, in one kind or other, are more fitting for Satan than for Christ.

In the meantime I desire the reader will please to understand this, that the interpretation asserted, and which understands the Scripture in hand of a true and real sanctification, is no slip of remonstrantism, but attested by very orthodox men, as the word now ruleth. Calvin himself writeth nothing upon the place but of good accord with it. "By a comparison of the benefits," saith he, speaking of what men received by Moses under the law, and what Christians now under the gospel receive by Christ, "he aggravates the ingratitude of men. It is a very unworthy thing to profane the blood of Christ, which is the matter" (he means, the principal or most material cause) "of our sanctification. Yet this they do who apostatise from faith." A little after: "But he," the author of Hebrews, "takes notice of the manner how the covenant is confirmed unto us, when he saith, 'We are sanctified;' because the blood shed would profit us nothing unless we were watered" or sprinkled "therewith by the Holy Ghost. From hence cometh expiation and holiness;" with much more to the like purpose in this commentary. Whereby evident it is, that this author, by the sanctification mentioned in the text, understands no other than that which was in himself. This is a *positional* sanctification wrought by the Spirit of God in the saints by watering or sprinkling them with the blood of Christ.

"By which he was sanctified," *i. e.,* say our English divines, in their annotations upon the place, "by which their sins were pardoned in regard of that meritorious sufficient sanctification purchased by it;" sending us back to their note on verse 10 of this chapter in Hebrews, where they interpret the word "sanctified" as signifying "our being freed from the guilt of our sin, and consecrated to God's service." So that there is little question but that these also understand the place to speak of a true sanctification indeed, and which either is, or flows from justification itself. And, long before them both, Chrysostom interpreted the place as speaking of such a sanctification which appertains to a son or child of God. "God," saith he, "hath made thee a son; and wilt thou be willing to be made a servant?"

The last of the Scriptures produced, to prove that Christ died even for those also who perish, as well as others, is Matt. xviii. 32-35. The tenor and carriage of this is of like consideration with the three last opened: excepting only, that whereas those speak of sanctification, this speaks of justification. The passages now to be insisted on lie in the body of a parable, which is somewhat large: the reader may please to peruse the whole, himself. The particulars in it for our purpose are contained in these words. "Then his lord, after that he had called him, said unto him, O thou wicked servant, I forgave thee all that debt, because thou desiredst me: shouldest not thou also have had compassion on thy fellow servant, even as I had pity on thee? And his lord was wroth, and delivered him to the tormentors, till he should pay all that was due to him. So, likewise, shall my heavenly Father do also unto you, if ye from your hearts forgive not every one his brother their trespasses." In these words we hear of a servant to whom his lord and master had freely forgiven all that debt which he owed unto him, which, as we find in the former part of the parable, was a vast sum of ten thousand talents, fit to typify or represent that great debt of eternal sufferings, which every man owes for sins and trespasses, unto God.

And yet we hear, also, that this same servant, by provoking this gracious lord and master of his by unmercifulness and cruelty to one of his fellow-servants, forfeited his former grace and mercy, which he had received from him in the forgiveness of his great debt, and that this forfeiture was taken by his lord, and he delivered by him to the tormentors, or prison-keepers, until he should pay the whole debt, *i. e.* forever, inasmuch as be had not, nor was ever able to procure, wherewith to make such a payment. What was intended and signified by all this is clearly expressed by our Saviour, in those last words which contain the application, and are the close of the parable: "So, likewise, shall my heavenly Father," &c. From which words the clear and direct scope and intent of the parable showeth itself to be this, viz. to give the world to know and understand, that if men, who have obtained forgiveness of sins by the means and grace of Jesus Christ, shall so far sin against the excellency and richness of this grace, as to deal cruelly and unmercifully by men, this act of grace towards them shall be cancelled and revoked, and the debt of their sins shall return and recoil again upon them.

Yea, he plainly tells his disciples themselves, (for this parable was in special manner directed unto them, as appears from the beginning of the chapter) that they themselves must not look to be exempted from this law of the righteousness and equity of God. "So likewise shall my heavenly Father do also unto you," or even unto you, notwithstanding any privilege you may seem to have above other men, by being disciples; he will neither deal better nor worse with you, but just as this lord did by that wretched and most unthankful servant of his, if you provoke him after the same manner, *i. e.* "if ye from your hearts forgive not every one his brother their trespasses." That great grace of forgiveness of sins, under which you now stand, will be reversed and called in again, by him that hath given it you, if you shall so far tread and trample the glory of it under your feet, as not in consideration and acknowledgment of the greatness of it, to be open and free-hearted in forgiving one another such injuries and trespasses as are done to you. This is the righteous and royal way of that God with the world, "who," as Peter saith, "without respect of persons, judgeth according to every man's work."

I shall not need, I suppose, to caution that which hath been delivered upon this account, with any such item or explication as this: that it was far from our Saviour's intent to threaten, either his disciples, or any other man, that they should incur the sore judgment mentioned, the loss of the forgiveness of sins, or be cast into the prison of hell, by every passionate or sudden heat conceived against a man upon a provocation, or offence given. If this were so, the whole world of saints, in a manner, might cry out, as the disciples, upon occasion of another doctrine taught by Christ, sometimes did, "Who then can be saved ?" But his meaning clearly was, and is, that if they should harbour or nourish thoughts or desires of revenge against any man, that should at any time offend or injure them, and remain implacable, not admitting of a clear and cordial reconciliation with him, and should live and die in this hateful and revengeful posture, that then God would deal no better with them than the lord in the parable did by that servant to whom he had forgiven a great debt, upon his unmerciful dealing by his fellow-servant, when "he delivered him to the tormentors, to be cast into prison, until he should pay the whole debt."

Nor doth anything that hath been asserted concerning the return of the debt of sin upon any man, after forgiveness, upon occasion of cruel, unmerciful, and revengeful dealings by their brethren, bear at all upon that of the apostle: "For the gifts and calling of God are without repentance," Rom. xi. 29. For the meaning hereof is not, that what God once gives he never takes away: we know there are instances in the Scripture without number to the contrary. He took away that integrity and rectitude of nature from Adam, upon his fall, which he had given him in his creation. So in the parable, he commands, "Take therefore the talent from him," *i.e.* the ungrateful servant, Matt. xxv. 28, which before he had given him: yea, and threatens universally, "from him that hath not," viz. by way of improvement or increase, "shall be taken away even that which he hath," ver. 29, viz. by way of stock, or original donation. So that the gifts and calling of God are not in this sense without repentance. Therefore,

1. When the apostle affirms the gifts and calling of God to be without repentance, his meaning may be, (a.) That he never gives anything to any person or people whatsoever, but that he knows and considers beforehand,

all the inconveniences and disaccommodations that will follow upon it, either in reference to his own glory, or to his creature, one or other, in any kind. Insomuch that whatever be the event or consequence of any of his gifts, if they were to be given again, he would give them. Nor doth that expression concerning him, "And it repented the Lord that he had made man upon earth, and it grieved him at his heart," Gen. vi. 6, any way imply, but that if man had been now to make, God would not have made him; or that when he did make him, he did not foresee the inconvenience which now followed upon his making of him. The phrase only imports a purpose of heart in God shortly to destroy him from off the face of the earth, for his wickedness, as he saith, immediately after, that he would do.

The gifts and calling of God are, or may be said to be, without repentance, because, God lets men continue as the same persons, I mean geometrically, or proportionably the same, which they were when the donation, or collation of any gift, was first made unto them. He never changeth or altereth his dispensation towards them, unless it be for the better, or in order to their further good; in which case he cannot be said to repent of what he had given. But in case men shall change and alter from what they were, when God first dealt graciously and bountifully by them, especially if they shall notoriously degenerate, or cast away that principle, or through negligence or otherwise, divest and despoil themselves of that very qualification on which God, as it were, grafted his benefit or gift vouchsafed to them; in this case, though he recalls and takes away his gift, he cannot be said to repent of the giving it, because the terms upon which he gave it please him still.

Only the persons to whom he gave it, and who pleased him when he gave it unto them, have now rendered themselves, by their unworthiness, displeasing unto him, and incapable, by the laws and rules of his righteous dispensations, of any further enjoyment thereof. This is the case between God and such men, who having once obtained remission of sins from him by such a faith, which wrought, or was apt and ready to work by love, afterwards upon the loss or degeneration of this faith, together with the operativeness of contrary and vile principles, are divested by him of that great and glorious privilege, and fall back into their former estate of condemnation.

Therefore, from those quarters of the parable in Matthew which we have lately surveyed, perfect intelligence comes that persons, who have by means of a sound faith received remission of sins upon the account of

Christ's death, may through negligence in not preserving this faith, or the sweetness and soundness of it, so far provoke their glorious benefactor, as to cause him to repeal that his act of grace towards them, and to suffer their former guilt to return, like the unclean spirit with seven worse than himself, upon them. From whence it undeniably follows, that Christ hath purchased remission of sins by his death for those, who notwithstanding, may through their own folly and wickedness perish. Chryostom interprets the place in full consonancy with this inference or supposition. "Although," saith he, "the graces and gifts of God are without repentance, yet malice or wickedness prevailed so far as to dissolve this law. What then is there of more grievous consequence, than to remember injuries which appear to be a subverter, or destroyer, of such and so great a gift of God?"

Amongst our later expositors, Musculus, as orthodox as men can make a man, advanceth the same interpretation, making it his third observation upon the place, "that those sins which are, through the grace of God, pardoned at present, shall not be remitted in the future, unless we will forgive our brother. For it is an unjust thing," saith he, "that he should enjoy the free remitment, or forgiveness of a debt of ten thousand talents, who refuseth to forgive his brother a debt of an hundred pence." Mr. John Ball himself nibbleth also at this exposition, even whilst, for the sake of those that sit at the table with him, he opposeth it. "As in the parable," saith he, "the Lord is said to remit to his servant a thousand talents, when he desired him, viz. inchoately, or upon condition, which was not confirmed, because he did not forgive his fellow servant; so the false prophets are bought by the blood of Christ, viz. in a sort as they believed in Christ, but not sincerely and unfeignedly."[9] A little after, "to these men their sins were remitted in a sort in this world," &c. If he would have brought forth his darkness of inchoately, upon condition, in a sort, into a clear and perfect light, his meaning must have been, that that remission of sins which God gives unto men in this world, he "neither confirms unto them in the hour of death, nor in the day of judgment," the author's own words a little after the former, in case they live and die under an implacableness or unmercifulness of spirit towards those who injure them. Such a sense as this is truly orthodox, whether men vote it such or no. Our English annotators, though they neither buy nor sell this interpretation in expressness of terms, yet interpretatively they buy or confirm it. "This parable," say they upon verse 35, "informs us that they shall find God severe and implacable that do not forgive their brethren, although they have been diversely and grievously

9. Covenant of Grace, p. 240.

injured by them." In these words they clearly suspend the gracious act of God in remission of sins, in respect of the ultimate and complete exercise of it, upon the Christian deportment and behaviour of men in forgiving one another their trespasses.

CHAPTER V:

Several other texts of Scripture (besides those formerly produced in ranks and companies) argued to the clear eviction of truth, in the same doctrine, viz. That the redemption purchased by Christ in his death, was intended for all and every man without exception.

HAVING in our late digression largely vindicated some material proofs from the Scripture, formerly levied for the defence of that great and most important cause, both of God and men, the universality of redemption by Christ, we now proceed to a further levy upon the same account, and shall raise up more Scriptures to plead the same cause.

Let us begin with the parable of the marriage feast, as it is reported by Matthew and Luke. We shall not need, I suppose, to transcribe the whole protasis of the parable, which is very large: but only insist upon some few known passages of it, such as I conceive will jointly, if not severally, give a light of demonstration to the truth of that doctrine, the proof and confirmation whereof is the prize contended for in this discourse. However, if the reader desires an entire review of the parable, he may repair, without much trouble, to the evangelists themselves, Matt. xxii. 2-14 and Luke xiv. 16-24.

First, expositors generally agree, that by those who were the first and second time called or invited to the wedding, the king "sent forth his servants to call them that were bidden to the wedding," Matt. xxii. 3, are typified, or meant, the Jews, whom God had anciently invited and called, by the ministry of his prophets, and several other ways, to partake of that great blessedness, which he intended to confer upon the sons and daughters of men, by means of his only begotten Son Jesus Christ. They were the second, yea, and the third time also (along with gentiles on that occasion), invited hereunto. This was first by John the Baptist and the Lord Christ himself, and afterwards by his apostles.

Secondly, the tenor or form of the invitation, which the servants sent forth to call those that had been formerly invited, were enjoined by the king to use in calling them, is this: "Behold, I have prepared my dinner: my oxen and my fatlings are killed, and all things are ready: come unto the marriage." Matt. xxii. 4. When he saith to those that are invited, "I have prepared my dinner, my oxen," &c.; doubtless his meaning is not that he had prepared his dinner for others, or that his oxen and fatlings were killed for the entertainment of others, and not for those who were invited by him.

Such an intendment as this in his invitation would have been merely delusory, and altogether unmeet to represent the intentions of God, in calling men to communion and fellowship with his Son Jesus Christ, by his ministers of the gospel. He that should invite a man to a feast, and use such an argument or motive as this, to persuade him to accept of this his invitation, and to come accordingly, viz. that he had made very liberal preparations for such and such other men, but had provided nothing for him, should he not render himself ridiculous by such a strain of oratory?

Thirdly, evident it is that very many of those who were invited to this marriage feast by the king, and consequently for whom the feast was prepared, and for whose sake the oxen and. fatlings were killed, never came to partake of the said feast, but were ejected and excluded from it with great indignation, by him that had so graciously invited them. "But when the king heard thereof," (viz. how they had misused and murdered his servants,) "he was wroth: and sent forth his armies, and destroyed those murderers, and burnt up their city," ver. 7. Concerning whom, likewise, the king said to his servants, that had been sent forth to invite them: "For I say unto you, That none of those men which were bidden" (and refused to come) "shall taste of my supper," Luke xiv. 24.

Fourthly, it is no less evident that the true ground or reason why those that were thus excluded from the feast, or suffered this exclusion, was not any precedent purpose or intendment in the king to exclude them, (for had any such intention harboured in him, questionless he would never have invited them) no nor yet that subsequent intendment in him to exclude them, when he saw their great unworthiness; but this unworthiness of theirs itself. "Then saith he to his servants, The wedding is ready, but they which were bidden were *not worthy.* Go ye, therefore, into the highways, &c.; Matt. xxii. 8, 9. This was clearly implying that it was the *unworthiness* of the persons who rejected the invitation, which was the true and proper cause of their exclusion.

Neither the import nor sentence of the law, nor yet the judge, or his just severity in giving sentence according to the law, are so properly the cause of the punishment or death of the malefactor, as the crime committed against the law by himself. It is merely accidental to the law and to the judge, and so to their intentions respectively, that such or such a person becomes a malefactor, and, consequently, that he suffers death. But the suffering punishment, or death, are the natural and proper fruits of the violation of the law, justly inflicting them in whomsoever it be found. And if the matters of fact deserve punishment or death, it would argue a defect in the law and in the judge, if they should not, according to their different capacities, give sentence accordingly.

Neither God, nor any decree or law of his, are any cause, intentionally or directly, of any man's either sin or punishment, but occasionally or accidentally only; and that so, that whosoever sinneth, or comes to be punished for sin, might have avoided both, any purpose, law, or decree of God notwithstanding. And to this purpose pertinent is the observation made by Musculus, upon our Saviour's expression, Matt. xxii. 2. In the Greek, *Ōmoiōthē hē basileia tōn ouranōn*, &c. *i. e.* The kingdom of heaven is made like, or become like (not is like) "unto a certain king," &c. "For," saith he, "the kingdom of heaven is not such a thing, that all the particulars here," in this parable, "reported of it, should belong to the nature of it: but several of them are accidental to it, through the wickedness of men. Otherwise, this kingdom doth not of itself, or in its proper nature, tend to the destruction of any man."

Fifthly and lastly, the pregnant result of the premised particulars is this, that the marriage feast in the parable was provided by the king, and the oxen and fatlings, here spoken of, killed not only for those who upon their invitation were persuaded to come and partake of them, but as well, and with equal, if not with more especial intentions on the king's part, for those also who never came to taste of them. Consequently, the death of Christ, signified by the oxen and fatlings slain, and the blessedness accruing unto the children of men hereby, signified by the feast itself, were equally meant and intended by God for those who perish and for those who are saved, and consequently for all men, without exception of any.

And indeed this purport of the parable lieth so large and full in the carriage of it, that Calvin himself could not but subscribe unto it, as he that shall please to peruse his commentaries upon Matt. xxii. 2, and withal acknowledge what is evident, must needs confess. Amongst several other passages facing this way, having specified some points of difference between Matthew and Luke in recording the parable, he saith, that yet "in the sum and substance of the matter they very well agree, viz. that whereas God vouchsafed this peculiar honour to the Jews, to provide and furnish a table of entertainment for them, they rejected this honour proffered to them." And saith moreover, that "whereas many expositors refer the marriage of the king's son" in the parable "to this point, that Christ is the end of the law, and that God had no other intent in his covenant with this people than to set him" as a king or ruler "over them, and by the sacred band of a spiritual marriage to join a church unto him, I freely accord with them herein."

Afterwards, upon verse 9 of the same chapter, "But," saith he, "if God then spared not the natural branches, the same vengeance hangeth over us at this day, unless we answer when he calleth. Yet shall not the supper provided" or prepared "for us be lost, but God will furnish himself with other guests."[1] In these passages, this great supposed enemy to the universality of redemption by Christ, clearly supposeth, or affirmeth rather, the same to be a truth. He expressly affirmeth that God provided a table of entertainment for those who rejected it and never came unto it, and supposeth that the "supper provided" by God "for us," may, through our neglect of our invitation hereunto, be withheld from us, and that others may be admitted unto it in our stead.

If the death of Christ, and salvation by him, were provided and prepared by God as well for those who reject them as for those who embrace them, doubtless they were intended for all men without exception. This truth, as was lately observed, is so necessary for the due managing of the Scriptures, and many other of the most important affairs in Christian religion, that the professed enemies thereof are ever and anon constrained and forced to make use of it, both in opening the Scriptures, as likewise in their other theological discussions and debates, and so consequently to give testimony unto it. And the very truth is, that it is one of the main pillars that supports and bears up the weighty fabric of that divinity and religion which the Scriptures hold forth unto time world.

Another piece of Scripture rising up in assertion of the same doctrine is that which speaks in these words: *Epephanē gar hē charis tou theou sōtērios pasin anthrōpois,* &c. *i. e.,* word for word, "For there hath appeared the grace of God, which is saving unto all men" or, "being saving unto all men," Tit. ii. 11; that is, which is of a saving nature, property, or tendency, unto all men. The Syriac translation reads, "Servatrix omnium," the saviouress of all men. Our last English translators, rendering the place thus, "For the grace of God, which bringeth salvation, hath appeared

1. Calvin. Harm. p. 188.

unto all men," show themselves more indulgent to their own sense and opinion than will well stand with the ingenuousness and faithfulness required in translators. This is an infirmity too apparent in them at several other turns; though the truth is, that this translation of the words damnifies their opinion one way as much or more than it gratifies it in another.

For in making the apostle to say that the "saving grace of God hath appeared unto all men," they suppose him to be of their judgment, who conceive the gospel and the saving grace thereof to be discovered and preached by God unto men, not only by the ministry of men, or by the letter of the gospel itself, but by the works of creation also, and the gracious government of the world. For certain it is, that the "saving grace" of God, of which the apostle here speaks, had not at this time "appeared unto all men" upon any other terms. But this by the way. Our former translators dealt much more fairly with the Holy Ghost at this place, rendering and pointing the words thus: "For that grace of God, that bringeth salvation unto all men, hath appeared."

The "grace of God," in Christ, is here said to be in the Greek *sōtērios pasin anthrōpois*, salvifical unto all men, not because it is such to all sorts or ranks of men only, or to some men of all sorts and degrees, (as some, not fearing to destroy the clear sense of the Holy Ghost to salve their own, interpret) but because it is such to "all men" simply and without exception of any. This exposition is confirmed,

1. From the context, in the words immediately following, wherein the proper end or ducture of this "saving grace of God," now discovered, is declared thus: "Teaching us that denying ungodliness and worldly lusts, we should live soberly, righteously, and godly in this present world." If, then, this saving grace of God teacheth, *i. e.* be apt to teach, persuade, and lead "all men" without exception, as well one as another, to a denial of "ungodliness" and to "live soberly," then must it needs be alike saving unto all. For if this teaching property in it flows from the savingness of it, which the apostle here clearly supposeth, then must the savingness of it necessarily be of equal extent within that property.

An act of grace, love, or bounty, inviteth, obligeth no more unto thankfulness than those to whom it is meant and intended. Now, certain it is, that the saving grace of God, held forth and proffered unto all men in the gospel, teacheth, inviteth, persuadeth, obligeth all men without exception, as well one as another, to deny ungodliness, &c., to live soberly, &c. Otherwise we must say that there are some men who ought not, who are no ways bound, to learn any of these things from the gospel, nor to practise them upon any account of grace or love tendered herein from God unto them: which, I suppose, is a saying too hard for any considering man to digest.

2. The words themselves in their grammatical, native, and proper signification, give out the sense and exposition specified. The "grace of God" here spoken of is expressly said to be *sōtērios pasin anthrōpois, i. e.* "saving," or salvifical "unto," or apt to save, "all men." And of what dangerous consequence it is to turn the words of the Holy Ghost out of their proper and best known significations into any by, devious, and qualified sense, when there is no necessity of doing it, hath been once and again admonished and declared in the premises.[2]

3. The exposition given fairly accordeth the passage in hand with many other fellow-Scriptures, as where God speaks of "thy salvation which with thou hast prepared," *to sōtērion sou hō hētoimasas,* before the face of *all* people," Luke ii. 30, 31; "who will have *all* men to be saved, and to come unto to the knowledge of the truth," 1 Tim. ii. 4: so again, "not willing that any should perish, but that *all* should come to repentance," 2 Pet. iii. 9; and again, where Christ is said, "by the grace of God should taste death for *every man.*" Heb. ii. 9: to omit several others, which we have demonstratively proved to be of one mind and one heart within the said passage, so understood, as now interpreted.

4. Lastly, the exposition given is attested by orthodox interpreters, so owned and acknowledged by our Calvinistic adversaries. "By name," saith Pelican, "he testifieth (the grace of God) to be common to the universe of men," or to men universally, "because of servants, of whom he had spoken." And presently after: "But we are all one in Christ, we are *all universally* called to the kingdom of God, we were all, after the offence given, to be reconciled unto our Father." Aretius, upon the place, affirmeth that "the gospel offers the grace of God unto *all men;*" and hereupon infers, that "therefore it concerns *all men* to adorn the doctrine hereof with their lives and manners."

If "the gospel offers the saving grace of God unto all men," and "all men" upon this account stand bound "to adorn the doctrine thereof," then must this grace, in the offer of it, and so in the intention of him who offers it in the gospel, be saving *i.e.* of a saving tendency and import unto "all men." Yea, if "all men" stand alike bound, in respect of the alike offer of it respectively unto them, (neither of which alikeness can reasonably be denied, or

2. Chap. I and II.

indeed questioned) it is a plain case that the savingness of it, and salvation by it, is by God alike intended unto all men. But from the universal offer of grace unto men in the gospel, we have formerly argued and evicted real intentions in God of salvation by Christ unto "all men," without exception.[3]

As for those trivial evasions from this and such like Scriptures, as, viz.; that by "all men," may be meant either great numbers of men, or all sorts, or some of all sorts and ranks of men, or Jews and Gentiles; and so again, that the grace of God may be said to be "saving unto all men," because there is a sufficiency of merit in Christ to save all men, though the salvation of all men by him be not intended by God, &c. These, I say, with the like put-offs, we have already, upon like occasions frequently occurring, detected of vanity, and showed their clear inconsistency with the principles, as well of that "wisdom which is revealed from heaven" in the Scriptures, as of that reason and understanding which are naturally ingrafted in men. If any man's judgment be yet tempted with a face of any seeming beauty or strength in any of them, he may, I presume, be delivered from further inconvenience in this kind by a second review of the second chapter of this discourse, at least if he shall diligently consider what is to be seen there.

In the next chapter of the same epistle, the apostle addeth light unto light in the business in hand, expressing himself thus: "But after that the kindness and love of God our Saviour towards men appeared," &c. Tit. iii. 4; in the Greek: *hē chrēstotēs kai hē philanthrōpia:* the goodness and the love (of God) towards man. I here demand, How or whether God can, in any tolerable construction of reason or common sense, be said to be *philanthrōpos*, a lover of men, or to bear an affection of love to men, in case he should hate incomparably the far greatest part of men, and that with the hatred of a reprobation from eternity, leave them without all possibility of escaping eternal misery and torment, and this, when as at the same cost and charge which he hath been at for the saving of a few, he might have provided for the salvation of them all. For this they affirm who grant that Christ died sufficiently for all, but intentionally only for a few.

Can we say that a king or prince is a lover of his kingdom or of his subjects, only because he loves two or three favourites about his court, especially when the generality and great body of his subjects are in imminent danger of perishing, or being undone, unless he provides for their relief, and he in the midst of the greatest abundance of means to relieve them, and this without the least prejudice or hinderance to himself, shall altogether

3. Chap. II

neglect them in their danger and misery? Doubtless there was never a prince or king, since the world began, that ever obtained the name or honour of "a lover of his subjects" upon such terms as these. And yet they make God a "lover of men" in no other sense, upon no whit better terms, who affirm and teach that he loved only that small number of men which they call "his elect," (which the Scripture very frequently affirms to be "few," in comparison to those who perish) when as that great generality, and vast body of men, were, from the greatest to the least of them, in most imminent danger of being undone, and that in the most dreadful manner that can be imagined, to the days of eternity. This teaches withal, that the death of Christ, which was bestowed upon these few only, was sufficient for the saving of the rest also; and that God, upon mere will and pleasure, not to ease his Son Jesus Christ in the least, nor to accommodate himself at all otherwise, implacably resolved from eternity to exclude all these from part and fellowship in that salvation. With a great desire my soul desireth, that men whose consciences serve them to oppose in the present controversy, would seriously and calmly consider, whether that *philanthrōpia* that love to mankind, which the Scripture reporteth to be in God, be at all compossible or consistent within such a dismal design in reference unto men as that now represented.

Again, if God loveth only such a small number of men as the opinion which we oppose supposeth, why is not *philaggelia,* the love of angels, instead of *philanthrōpia,* the love of men, ascribed unto him? For doubtless, if God loves no more men than those who come to be actually saved, he might properly and truly be said to be *philaggelos,* a lover of angels, rather than a lover of men. Because if we shall restrain his love towards men only to those comparative few who will be actually and eventually saved, he will be found to love a far greater proportion of angels than of men; it being no ways probable but that the number of angels who keep their standing and are elect is far greater, being compared within those that fell, than the number of men who, according to the Scriptures, are like to be actually saved, is, being compared within those that perish.

To say that God's love, though but to a few men, expressed in the gift of his Son Jesus Christ to die for them, is more considerable and so a more reasonable ground of giving the denomination of *philanthrōpos* unto him than the love which he bears to angels, though more in number or in proportion, is to say that which no way easeth the matter, or solveth the difficulty.

First, because the angels, the elect angels, as the Scripture calleth them, are partakers with men in the gift of Jesus Christ given unto men, though not in that redemption from sin and misery which accrues unto men by him, unless haply it be by sympathy within their fellow-creatures in their joy and blessedness, yet otherwise, as appears; from Col. ii. 10, and other places; and besides is generally acknowledged by divines.

Secondly, one of the highest expressions I remember, whereby the happiness procured for men by the gift of Christ is set forth in the Scripture, is but *isaggelia*, an equality with the angels, or likeness of condition with them, Luke xx. 36. Therefore God's love to the angels that stand doth not fall short, at least to any such considerable degree, of the love which he beareth unto men that are saved. Therefore the reason why he is styled *philanthrōpos*, a lover of men, not *philaggelos*, a lover of angels, is not because he loves some men more than he doth any angels, but because he loved all men and not all angels.

Besides, if God should love only such a small parcel of men as some imagine, with the hatred of all the rest, he might much more properly be termed *misanthrōpos*, a hater of men, than *philanthrōpos*, a lover of men. The Scripture frequently extols and magnifies the love of God towards all men, yea, towards his enemies, on whom he maketh his sun to arise, and sendeth rain, as well as on his friends, Matt. v. 45, and strictly enjoineth all those that would be accounted his children to resemble and imitate him in this his goodness. But it nowhere suggesteth the least degree of any hatred in him against any person of man, personally considered, nor any other than what doth redundare in personam, as the schoolmen speak, *i. e.* which redoundeth, and, as it were, runs over from the sin which he hateth unto the person in whom that sin is found.

Again, if God should not love the generality of mankind in order to their salvation by Christ, then all the good which he doth unto them in outward things, as in making his sun to arise and his rain to fall upon them, as our Saviour saith he doth upon the unjust as the just, and so his filling of their heart with food and gladness, within the like, must be conceived to be done by him upon such terms and with such intentions as men use to lay scraps for birds or bait hooks for fishes, which they do for none other end but to take and destroy them.

For if God hath no intent in these dispensations of his towards them to do them any good in a saving way, he must needs be conceived to intend their ruin and destruction, at least, the increase of their ruin and destruction by them; it being no ways reasonable to conceive but that he hath higher and more considerable ends propounded to himself in his providential administrations about men, in reference unto men, than about beasts in relation unto them; though it is true he hath the same general and ultimate end, his glory, in all his works and administrations, one or other. But if the generality or far greatest part of men are bound to believe, and bound they are to believe it if it be a revealed truth, that God, in giving them health and peace and prosperity in the world, intends nothing but evil to them, a fuller cup of the wrath and vengeance which is to come, how can the "goodness and forbearance and long-suffering" of God be said to lead men to repentance? (Which yet is the apostle's doctrine, Rom. ii. 4.)

Neither the goodness nor patience of God towards evil men can be said to lead them to repentance but by the mediation or supposal of these three principles: 1. That these dispensations of God, I mean of goodness and patience, towards such men, are proper and sufficient, I mean by the help of that operation of the Spirit of God which always accompanieth them, to bring men to repentance; and 2. That God's intent is that they should bring them actually to repentance, or at least that he hath no intention otherwise or to the contrary; 3. Lastly, that he truly and really intends their salvation upon their repentance.

Wicked men can at no hand of reason, no, nor yet of common sense, be said to be led to repentance by the goodness or long-sufferance of God towards them, unless: 1. It be supposed that there is a genuine, natural, or proper rhetoric or moving tendency in them to persuade and encourage such men to repent; nothing can be said to lead a man to such or such an action or course, but that which is proper to invite or persuade him unto either. Nor unless it be supposed, 2. That God hath an intent that such men should be actually persuaded or made willing to repent by such dispensations, at least that he should have no intentions to the contrary. For how can any man be actually persuaded or made willing by any means, motive, or encouragement whatsoever to attempt or do any such thing which he hath cause to judge or believe that God's intentions stand against his doing or performance?

There is no motive or encouragement against the determinate counsel of God made known. Nor, 3. Lastly, can the said dispensations of goodness or patience in God be said to lead any man to repentance, unless it be yet further supposed that his real intent and purpose is to save him upon his repentance, or in case he shall repent, or at least that they may be such. For what encouragement can any man have to repent, in case he hath sufficient ground to judge that God hath absolutely rejected him and will not save him, no, not upon his repentance? Therefore certainly God hath no intentions of evil, or of condemnation, or of increase of condemnation against the generality of men, no, nor yet against the worst or wickedest of men in those gracious vouchsafements of life, health, liberty, peace, food, raiment, and other the like temporal mercies and accommodations unto them.

Again, how can men look upon themselves as any ways debtors, or obliged unto God in thankfulness, for good things administered unto them with hard intentions, or with a purpose not to bless them, but to make their condemnation so much the greater, and more heavy upon them? If birds and fishes had understanding, and should know for what end, or with what intentions men lay scraps and baits, though made of such things as they love, and stand in need of, in their way, would they thank them for it, or should they have any reason so to do? Or had Amasa any cause to think the better of Joab, who "took Amasa by the beard with the right hand to kiss him"? 2 Sam. xx. 9. Or our Saviour to think the better of Judas, for the kiss wherewith he greeted him? Matt. xxvi. 49.

Besides, it is the duty of the saints to imitate or resemble their heavenly Father, not only in his outward expressions, but much more in his intentions, and frame of spirit towards men, when he doth good unto them, causing "his sun to arise, and his rain to fall upon them." In case his intentions towards them in such applications of himself unto them, were bent, not upon their salvation, but destruction, would it not follow that when they should perform those Christian services unto them, enjoined by our Saviour himself, "But I say unto you, love your enemies, bless them that curse you, pray for them that despitefully use you," &c., Matt. v. 44, they were bound to do all these in order unto, and with an intent to procure, their greater and deeper condemnation, and not within any intent to gain them into the gospel? And if wicked men, enemies to the saints, should know, or have reasonable ground to judge, that when they express themselves outwardly in terms of love, and good-will towards them, they mean them ruin, or increase of punishment and torment hereby, had they not cause to judge them the vilest hypocrites and dissemblers under heaven?

Nor do they represent the glorious God himself any whit better unto the world, who affirm and teach, that in and under his most pathetical and moving invitations, encouragements, and promissory offers of grace, mercy, salvation, unto the generality of men, whereof the Scriptures are full, he intends not the donation, or gift of grace, mercy, or salvation unto them, upon any condition or terms whatsoever, but wrath and judgment, and an opportunity to render them seven-fold more the children of death and condemnation, than otherwise they would or could have been.

Lastly, if God intends the increase of guilt and punishment unto wicked men, or the generality of men, in the comforts and good things of this world providentially disposed and dispensed unto them, he must needs desire the bringing or coming of these accordingly upon them. No man intends anything in order to the accomplishment of such or such an end, but this end is desired by him. Again, certain it is that the increase of guilt and punishment cannot come upon men, by means, or by occasion, of the good things given by God unto them, but only by the intervening of their unthankfulness, and abuse of these good things, in one kind or other.

Further, as there is no man but wisheth and desireth the coming to pass of such things, which are simply and absolutely necessary for the bringing to pass such things as he desireth, so hath no man cause to be offended with any man for the doing of such things, which are simply and absolutely necessary to the effecting of any such end which he desireth. This is especially when his desire in this kind is raised and built upon foundations of righteousness and sound wisdom, which is not questionable in or about any of the desires of God. Now then, if God intends, he must needs also desire, the increase of guilt and punishment upon wicked men, or the generality of men. If he desires this, he hath no cause to be offended with these men, for their unthankfulness, or for any such abuse of his mercies or good things conferred upon them, without which it was impossible for him to attain his desired end, viz., an increase of guilt and condemnation upon them, as was asserted.

The reason is, because, according to our late asserted principle, no man hath cause to be offended with another, for doing that which is directly and absolutely necessary for the bringing to pass of any such end, which is maturely, and according to sound principles of wisdom and righteousness, projected and desired by him. Nor is there the least question to be made, but that if God intends and consequently desires, the increase of guilt and condemnation upon the generality of men, both his intentions and desires in this kind are most regular, in respect of all regularity, that either wisdom or righteousness can give unto them.

Nor will it much, if anything at all, here help to say that though God doth not intend the salvation of the generality of men in giving unto them the good things of this life to enjoy so abundantly, as for the most part he doth, but the increase of their guilt and condemnation, yet inasmuch as no particular man knoweth but that God may intend his spiritual good and salvation, in such dispensations, all are bound to conceive this hope of themselves, and consequently every man stands bound to be thankful unto God for what he receiveth from him in this kind, and to seek more after him. And if any man shall be found neglective of what is his duty herein, or shall turn the grace of God towards him, even in these outward things, into wantonness, and not into thankfulness, he deserves to be punished so much the more severely for it. For to this,

I answer: No man stands bound to believe that, or to conceive hope of that which he hath no sufficient ground of believing, or reason why he should believe it: much less to believe that which he hath much more reason to question or doubt of, than to believe. Solomon informeth us, that "the simple believeth every word." Prov. xiv. 15, viz., as well that which he hath no ground or reason to believe, as that which he hath. And it is commonly said and taught amongst us, that in matters of religion and of salvation, nothing ought to be believed by any man, but what he hath a sufficient ground in or from the word of God to believe. If so, if no man ought to believe, in matters appertaining to salvation, but what he hath a ground or warrant in the word of God to believe; much less ought he to believe any such thing, the truth whereof the word of God administers much more ground to doubt, question, and suspect than to believe.

So that if this be a truth revealed in the word of God, that God doth not intend the spiritual good of the generality, or of far the greatest part of men, in their outward mercies and good things, but the contrary; certain it is that every particular man, at least, that hath no sufficient proof of his regeneration, hath ten, twenty, if not a hundred times more reason to doubt and question, whether his spiritual good be intended by God, or no, in the things we speak of, than to believe that it is intended. As in the business of a lottery, where there are forty, it may be a hundred blanks for one prize, no man hath so much reason or ground to hope, that he shall draw a prize, in case he should adventure his money this way, as that he shall draw a blank.

And upon this account, lotteries have still been accounted little better than cheats, or unworthy devices contrived gin-wise, to catch the money of simple and inconsiderate people, while men of understanding easily discern the fraud, and so keep their foot out of the snare. And whether that doctrine, which teacheth that God intendeth only the salvation of a few, but the condemnation of many, and yet commandeth all to believe that they may be saved, doth not make the glorious gospel of God like unto one of such lotteries, I leave to all understanding and unprejudice men to consider.

In the meantime, evident it is that this opinion, that Christ died not for all men, but for some few only, is, as it were, calculated, and the face of it bent and set, to make the distance between heaven and earth, between God and his creature man, greater and wider than yet it is; to multiply jealousies and hard thoughts in the hearts and minds of men and women concerning God, where they are more than apt enough to engender and multiply, without the irritation of such a doctrine. Yea, whereas God hath put himself into his Christ, ("God was in Christ," saith the apostle, "reconciling the world unto himself," 2 Cor. 5:19) that by the means of him, and by the tender and promise of forgiveness of sins unto men through him, upon the gracious terms of believing he might prevail with the world to love him, to think well and honourably of him. This doctrine seeks to put him out of his Christ again, at least in reference to any such glorious design as that of reconciling the world unto him; yea, and saith, in effect, unto the world itself, Believe him not, though he speaketh ever so graciously unto you: when he promiseth you life and salvation upon the fairest and freest terms, he hath war in his heart against you, and intendeth to destroy you.

If it be yet objected, that, upon the same ground, no particular person should have any particular ground or reason to believe that he is one of those that shall be saved, inasmuch as the number of those that shall he saved is affirmed to be but small; I answer,

True it is, no man is bound to believe, simply and absolutely, that he is one of those that shall be saved, but conditionally only, viz. in case he shall believe, and persevere believing unto the end. All that a man is bound to believe in this kind positively is, that he is one of those that may he saved; and the doctrine asserted by us, viz. that Christ died for all men without exception, administereth a fair ground and full footing for such a faith as this unto every man; whereas the doctrine opposite hereunto, which affirmeth that Christ died for the elect only, leaveth no foundation or ground at all of this faith unto any man whatsoever, at least being yet in his natural condition, and unconverted.

For, 1, if only those men be in a possibility of being saved for whom Christ died; and, 2, if Christ died for the elect only; and, 3, if no unregenerate or unconverted person hath any ground to believe that he is one of God's elect; it roundly follows, and with pregnancy of consequence, that no such person (I mean, who is yet unconverted) hath any sufficient ground to believe that he is one of those that may be, or that is in a possibility of being saved. All the said hypotheses or premises, (as, viz. 1. That no man is in a possibility of being saved, but only those for whom Christ died; 2. That Christ died only for the elect; and, 3. That no unregenerate person hath any sufficient ground to believe that he is one of the elect) are authentic and unquestionable, according to the known principles of our adversaries; therefore the conclusion specified must be admitted and owned by them.

If they will admit the said conclusion, and judge it no way prejudicial, either to themselves or their cause, so to do, I would demand of them what foundation of encouragement they can lay to persuade unregenerate men either to "strive to enter in at the strait gate," to "labour for the meat that endureth to everlasting life," or to apply themselves, seriously and effectually, in one kind or other, to the means of believing. We know that without hope, or an apprehended possibility of obtaining what is endeavoured and sought after, all motives or grounds of persuasion unto action amount to no more than to the beating of the air: the hearts of men are not at all taken or wrought by them. Despair of salvation quencheth all thoughts, all endeavours, all desires of believing. Therefore, if an unregenerate person hath no sufficient ground of hope that he is one of those who are so much as in a possibility of being saved, he is not capable of any impressions from any ground or motive whatsoever to believing.

If it be here said, though an unregenerate person hath no sufficient ground of hope that he is one of God's elect, and consequently, that Christ died for him, yet he hath sufficient ground of hope that he *may* be one of these, and so that there is a possibility that Christ *may* have died for him; and upon the account of such a hope as this, he hath encouragement sufficient to apply himself to the means of believing; I answer,

1. That such a hope, which amounts only, or very little more than, to a bare apprehended possibility of obtaining, hath but a very feeble and faint influence upon the heart of a considering man, by way of encouragement unto action, especially unto such action which is of a laborious and difficult import, and wherein he must deny himself in matters of ease, pleasure, profit, &c., and this to an eminent degree. Now, it is generally known, that that action or course of engagement wherein they must labour and exercise themselves who desire to believe unto salvation, is of such an import as we speak of: it is a course of action wherein men must put forth or give out themselves "with all their heart, and with all their soul, with all their mind, and with all their strength," wherein they must labour, strive, watch, and

pray continually, deny themselves, crucify the old man, &c., or otherwise not expect salvation.

2. Neither is it so clear a truth, especially according to the principles of those against whom we now argue, that an unregenerate man hath a sufficient ground of hope that he may be one of the elect; for if he be not at present one of these, there is no possibility, according to the said principles, that ever he should be such. If it be replied, that the meaning of this assertion, a regenerate man has a sufficient ground of hope that he may be one of the elect, is not that he may be one of these hereafter, whether he be one of them at present or no, but that he may be one of them at the present; I answer, that hope, in propriety of import, respecteth not what is or may be at present, but what may be, or is like to be in the future. Nor do I remember any instance throughout the Scriptures where they make or suppose any other object of hope, but only that which is or may be future; nor that any definition of hope given by learned divines assigneth any other; so that it is very improper, at least, to say, that an unregenerate man hath ground of hope that he may be, at present, one of God's elect. But,

3. A little to indulge impropriety of terms, I demand whether the Scriptures do not constantly represent and make unregeneracy, or an unbelieving condition, especially joined with an habitual practice of known sins, a ground of fear that a man is not at present one of the elect of God; or rather, whether they do not make such a condition a ground of certain knowledge that a man is not at present one of the elect of God? According to the principles of the adverse party in the question in hand, all the elect shall certainly be saved, and inherit the kingdom of God; but in the Scriptures constantly teach and affirm, that unbelievers and unregenerate men, especially living in known sins, "shall not inherit the kingdom of God." Therefore, unless we shall say that the Scriptures are divided in themselves, it is impossible to show or prove that they anywhere exhibit or afford any ground of hope to such unregenerate and unbelieving persons as we now speak of, that they may be, at present, the elect of God.

The Scripture nowhere excludes the elect of God from salvation, but everywhere asserts them as heirs hereof; therefore, those whom it excludes from part and fellowship in this business, are not, at least in Scripture sense, nor, indeed, in any sense consistent with reason, the elect of God.

4. If such unregenerate persons as we speak of have any sufficient ground to hope that they *may* be, at present, the elect of God, then have they the like ground of hope that they are at present of this number, and the elect of

God? The reason of this sequel is plain; because what a man is, and what he may be at present, are one and the same; it being impossible that he should be at present anything besides, or any other than what he is at present, no subject whatsoever being capable of any otherness or alteration in an instant; according to that known maxim in natural philosophy, Motus non fit in instanti, No motion can be in an instant of time; as also that other, Quicquid est, quando est, necesse est esse; *i.e.* whatsoever is, whilst it is, must of necessity be (that which it is). Therefore he that hath ground to hope that he may be one of God's elect at present, hath ground, yea, the same ground, to hope that he is such one at present.

Now if such an unregenerate man as hath been oft mentioned hath a sufficient ground of hope that he is at present one of God's elect, then have the generality of wicked and unregenerate men, respectively, a sufficient ground of hope that they are all, and every person of them, the elect of God. For if any one of this sort of persons hath a sufficient ground of hope in this kind, then have they all and every one the same; for no ground of difference between them in this case is imaginable. But how ill it accords with sundry the grounds and principles of our adversaries to affirm, that all the world, which, as John saith, lieth in wickedness, should have sufficient ground of hope that they are the elect of God, I leave to themselves to consider. Therefore certainly no unregenerate person, such especially as we lately consider. Therefore certainly no unregenerate person, such especially as we lately described, hath any sufficient ground of hope that he is at present one of the elect of God; and consequently, the doctrine we oppose for denying that Christ died for all men without exception, I leaveth no place or ground of any such hope unto unregenerate persons which likely to engage or provoke them unto any gospel inquiry or addressment of themselves to the means of believing; no, nor yet which leaves them in any capacity of being wrought or persuaded hereunto, by any other motives or inducements whatsoever.

5. Lastly, in case unregenerate men should, by the leave and sufferance of the said doctrine, be under any such hope as it asserts unto them, (I mean that they may be the elect of God in that sense of the word elect, which the patrons of this doctrine commonly put upon it) yet would not this hope be apt or likely to animate or encourage them to such applications of themselves as those specified, no nor yet suffer them to be much affected with or wrought upon in this kind by any other motives or means of excitement whatsoever. The reason hereof hath been formerly given, where we

showed and proved that such a hope which hath certainty of success or attainment absolutely and unconditionally insured unto it, is not of that kind of hope which is likely to engage much unto action.

I here add, and have added, that the very genius or import of it is rather to render the subject of it unengageable unto action by other motives. And thus we clearly see, by a thorough examination and debate of the whole business, that the doctrine of our present contest, and which denieth that Christ died for all men, leaveth no ground of hope for any person whatsoever in his natural condition, that he either is or may be one of those, who are in any possibility of being saved by Christ. Consequently it must needs be a doctrine anti-evangelical in the highest. This for the opening and asserting of the philanthropy of God avouched in the Scriptures.

When the author of Hebrews writeth, "For if we sin willfully after that we have received the knowledge of the truth, there remaineth *no more sacrifice* for sins," Heb. x. 26, he clearly supposeth, that they, for whose sins there was an expiatory sacrifice offered by Christ, may by apostasy and a rejection of the grace of this sacrifice, reduce themselves to such a condition, wherein they shall be incapable of any atonement for sin by any sacrifice whatsoever. For this clause, "there remaineth no more sacrifice for sins," evidently implieth, 1. That before the horrid sin of apostasy, here spoken of, the persons that fall into it, have, or had, a sacrifice for their sins, viz., for the expiation and atonement of them, which can be no other but the sacrifice of the death of Christ.

In saying "there remaineth no more" (or, in the Greek *ouketi*, not still, or, not further) a sacrifice for sins, he must of necessity suppose, that till that sad alteration in their spiritual estate here described by their sinning wilfully after, &c. should befall them, they were partakers of a sacrifice for the expiation of their sins, which, as hath been said, must deeds be the death of Christ. Otherwise they should have been in no worse case, as to matter of receiving benefit by the death or sacrifice of Christ, after their apostasy than before. 2. That upon, and after this alteration, they are, either absolutely and altogether excluded from a re-admission into their former grace, whereby they were partakers of the sacrifice of Christ, or at least that they stand upon terms of extreme difficulty ever to obtain such a re-admission. So that this passage of Scripture befriendeth both the main doctrines avouched in the first part of our discourse, with pregnancy of confirmation, respectively.

For, 1. It supposeth that Christ offered the sacrifice of himself for the sins of those, who very possibly may never be saved by him, and consequently, for all men without exception, for concerning those that come to be saved by him, there is no question. And 2. That they who have been partakers of the sacrifice of Christ, and hereby of the grace and favour of God, in the pardon of their sins, may afterwards apostatise into such a condition wherein "there remaineth no more sacrifice for their sins, but a certain looking for of judgment, and fiery indignation," &c. Calvin himself knew not, it seems, how to manage this place, but with full comport of the sense given. "There is a great difference," saith he upon this place, "between particular fallings and such a universal defection, whereby it cometh to pass that we *wholly fall away* from the grace of Christ.

"But because this cannot befall any man, but him who is enlightened, therefore he saith, If we sin willingly after we have received the knowledge of the truth: as if he should say, Who shall willingly *cast away that grace which he had obtained.*" A little after, "He (the author) denies that any sacrifice remains for those, who *depart from the death of Christ*, which is not done by any particular delinquency, but by a *casting away of faith totally.*" Doubtless, they who depart from the death of Christ, were sometimes at it, (*i. e.* partakers of it) and they who cast away faith totally, sometimes had it. And long before Calvin, Chrysostom had declared for the substance of the interpretation given. That which the author saith, saith he upon the place, "is some such thing as this: Thou hast been cleansed, thou hast been discharged from matter of crime, or accusation against thee, thou hast been made a son: if now, thou shalt return to thy former vomit, disinheritance, fire, and all such like (terrible) things abide thee; for there is not a second sacrifice" for thee.

We shall, upon the account of this chapter, produce only one brief passage of Scripture more, wherein the gracious intentions of God towards all men in point of salvation by the death of Christ, are like Solomon's "king upon his throne, against whom there is no rising up." The entire verse, wherein the words we mind are extant, runneth thus: "The Lord is not slack concerning his promise, as some men count slackness; but is long-suffering to us-ward, not willing that any should perish, but that all should come to repentance," 2 Pet. iii. 9. Evident it is, and expositors generally consent, that the apostle in these words propounds a further reason or consideration to satisfy those that, being weak, were apt to stumble and take offence, that the Lord Christ delayed his coming to judge the world and to deliver his saints so long.

No man, saith the apostle in effect upon this account, hath any reason to be offended or take it amiss at the hand of Christ that he makes no more haste in coming to judge the world, seeing that his delay in this kind proceeds not at all from any neglect or backwardness in him to perform his promise in that behalf, (though some men count all delay which is contrary to their minds and desires, to be no better than neglect or slackness unto action) but from his great patience and towards men. His will and desire is that no person whatsoever of mankind, either in present being in the world, or that shall be born hereafter, should perish everlastingly, but that every man of them should come to repentance, whereunto his patience and long-sufferance inviteth, yea, and "leadeth thee," Rom. ii. 4; and by which many are actually led and brought unto it, that so they may be saved.

From the passage thus understood, I argue thus: If Christ be not willing that any man should perish, but that all should come to repentance, then questionless he intendeth the salvation of all, and consequently died intentionally for all. For unless he intended to die for them, yea, and did die for them, it is not possible that he should either will or intend their salvation, inasmuch as no man can will or intend that which he knows to be impossible. But certain it is that Christ is not willing that any man should perish, but that all should come to repentance, the Holy Ghost, in the Scripture in hand, expressly affirming it: Ergo.

Against the sense and interpretation of the words given, and so to the invalidating of the argument built thereon, it is pretended by some that the apostle doth not here assert an unwillingness in Christ that any person whatsoever of mankind should perish, but only that any person of the elect should perish.

To give colour to this exposition, they circumscribe the particle or pronoun *humas*, "us," with the limit or line of their election, so carrying the sense thus: "The Lord is not slack," &c. . . . "but is long-suffering to us-ward," viz. who are his elect, and consequently to all others that are partakers of the same election with us, "not willing that any," viz, of these, the elect of his Father, "should perish, but that all" these "should come to repentance," not any others. This sense of the place is commended by Estius, a Popish expositor. But we shall find Calvin leaning with the truth another way. "So, then, Peter," saith Estius upon the place, "saith that the Lord dealeth patiently, *i. e.* delayeth his promised coming and judgment for the elect's sake, that they might not perish, but, being converted to repentance, be saved."[4] This exposition he labours in the very fire to make to

4. Estius in 2 Pet. iii. 9.

stand; but, as one said in another case, "Oportet aliquid intus esse," an exposition that hath not truth in it, cannot be made to stand.

I would demand of this expositor, and of those who sense with him in the interpretation specified, why, or by what authority, they expound *eis humas*, "towards us" the elect, rather than "towards us" present believers? For if they will needs have the persons here spoken unto to be considered by the apostle not in their natures or general capacities, viz. as they were men, but in some particular or special capacity wherein other men or all men did not partake with them, the capacity of saintship or of faith was as near at hand as that of election. For that the persons we speak of were saints and believers, is far less questionable than that they were elect, in their sense of the word election, who thus interpret. It is true what Estius allegeth to credit his exposition, that this epistle was written to the same persons with the former, who are styled "elect," 1 Pet. i. 2.

But, (a.) Whether his "elect" and the apostle's "elect" be the same, is very questionable; unless, haply, the apostle puts it out of the question that they are not the same, by setting forth his "elect," in the place cited, by such a description which will not agree with Estius's "elect." Estius, with the generality of divines amongst us, by his "elect" understands as well those that shall repent and believe hereafter, though they be at present "sons of Belial," and "to every good work reprobate," as the apostle speaketh, as those who actually do believe. Whereas Peter, in the place now mentioned, estimateth his elect by "the sanctification," *i. e.* the actual sanctification "of the Spirit unto obedience, and sprinkling of the blood of Jesus Christ, according to the foreknowledge," or pre-approbation, "of God;" *i. e.* as God approved and judged it meet, and consequently decreed from eternity to regulate his election of men in time. But this only by the way: for as to this Scripture, with others which treat of election, we shall, God favouring, speak more fully in due time. (b.) Though the epistle was, as this author allegeth, written to the same persons with the former, who in the beginning of the said former epistle are termed "elect," yet are these persons, in this very epistle, and much nearer to the place in hand, described or considered in their capacity of believing: "Simon Peter, a servant and an apostle of Jesus Christ, to them that have obtained like precious faith with us," 2 Pet. i. 1, &c. So that, in this respect, there is much more reason why, in the place in question, he should speak unto them, or consider them, as believers with himself, than as "elect" with himself, in such a notion of election wherein "elect" are distinguished from believers, as was lately declared.

But now to make the apostle to say that God is patient towards us, *believers*, "not willing that any" of us who *believe* "should perish, but that all" *we* "should come to repentance," is to make him speak beneath the line of common sense. For, 1. The patience of God towards believers, who are in a present capacity of salvation, and according to the principles of our adversaries, out of all possibility of perishing, is no means of their non-perishing: neither need he be patient towards them in reference to any such end. 2. Neither have these need to "come to repentance" in order to their non-perishing, unless we shall suppose them in a possibility of a total loss of that faith that is in them, yea, and that they will de facto totally lose it.

2. That the apostle doth not, in the place in hand, speak of the Christians to whom he writes as they were "elect," in the common sense of the word, appears from hence, viz. because, in case there were any "elect" in this sense, the patience of God towards them would be no argument or sign of his non-willing their perishing, or of his willing that they should "come to repentance;" because he shows the same, or greater patience, towards such persons who are not "elect," in that sense, and who never come to believe or repent.

3. The Lord is not here said to be "not willing that any" of the elect "should perish," or, "but that all" these "should come to repentance," but simply and indefinitely, "that any should perish," *mē boulomenos tinas apolesthai* ; and universally, "but that all, (*pantas*) should come to repentance." Now, these indefinite particles, *tis, tinas*, as likewise these universals, *pas, pantas,* do frequently in Scripture (we shall not need to cite places, being so numerous and obvious) signify men, simply and absolutely considered; the former partitively distributively and sometimes interrogatively; the latter universally. But no instance, I presume, can be found, where either the one or the other signifies men in any special capacity, or under any particular consideration, unless haply, it be where such capacity or consideration, is either in the same period, or else in the same contexture of speech, and near at hand, particularly mentioned and expressed.

Now concerning the place in debate, certain it is, that the capacity or consideration of "election" is not only not at all mentioned or specified in time same period, nor yet in the same passage or contexture of Scripture, or any where near at hand, but not so much as in all the epistle from first to last. Therefore, doubtless, *tinas*, "any," and *pantas*, "all," do not here signify any of the "elect," and all the "elect," but any men, and all men.

4. Neither can God, in any tolerable construction or propriety of speech or sense, be said to be patient or "long-suffering" towards those whom he loves with the greatest love that is, and this unchangeable, (for such is the love of election supposed by those against whom we argue to be) especially if it be supposed withal, (which these men suppose likewise,) that though they be wicked, yet they cannot repent, cannot cease to be wicked, until God comes with a strong and irresistible hand to cause them to repent. For when we ardently and affectionately love a person, one or more, we cannot reasonably be said to be patient towards them, though we do not punish them for such miscarriages or actions wherein they are prejudicial unto us, in case we know it to have been impossible for them to forbear such actions, unless we ourselves had effectually restrained them from them. It would not argue any patience in a parent towards his young infant, which he tenderly loves, to forbear correcting it, in case it should let fall and break a Venice glass, or some like brittle commodity, which were put into the hand of it. Patience, we know, is a grace, or virtue, whereby a man is enabled and disposed to moderate the natural passion of anger, and to prevent the exorbitant and undue motions of it.

So that patience hath no place or opportunity to express itself, but only in such cases wherein this passion is apt to be stirred and provoked. Now the passion we speak of, anger, is not apt to be raised or provoked, but only by such actions wherein or whereby we apprehend either ourselves, or some nearly relating to us, to be neglected or despised, according to the philosopher's discourse and description of it, wherein he mentions *oligōria*, the neglect or contempt of a person, or of some related to him, as always the cause of it;[5] The description, if need were, we might show to be very agreeable to what the Scriptures themselves deliver concerning the same passion. So then, in case there be no ground or reason upon which God can judge himself, or any of his, neglected or despised, by the impenitency of his "elect" in their sinful ways, whilst they continue in them, he cannot be said to be patient or "long-suffering" towards them, though he forbears to punish them with death for it. Now when that only is done by a man, which he is, either in one kind or other, necessitated to do, and cannot possibly refrain the doing it, no person whatsoever, what damage soever he may receive by what is done upon such terms, that any sufficient ground to judge himself, or any of his, neglected or despised in such an action, nor consequently to be provoked unto anger by it.

5. Neither can the "elect," in such a sense as many call elect, truly or rea-

5. Arist. Rhet. ii. cap 2.

sonably "account the long-suffering of the Lord salvation" unto them, which yet the persons here spoken of and to are in the sequel of this chapter enjoined to do: "And account that the long-suffering of the Lord is salvation," 2 Pet. 3:15; for they that have salvation infallibly and infrustrably, against and above "death, life, angels, principalities, powers, things present, things to come, height, depth, every creature" whatsoever, ascertained, assigned, or designed, by the irrevocable decree of God unto them, stand in no need of any respite or reprievement from death through the "long-sufferance" of God, in order to the obtainment of salvation. Because, in case they should die, either the first moment that they are born into the world, or after never so much sin committed, yet the decree of God concerning their salvation, being peremptory, absolute, and irresistible, must needs take place, and produce their salvation, against all obstructions and impediments whatsoever. Therefore, as a man hath no reason to set any such high price upon a receipt prescribed unto him by a physician, in order to his health, as to call it "his life," or the emphatical means of his preservation in case his life would certainly have been preserved without it; so neither have the "elect" any competent reason or ground to call or "count the long-suffering of the Lord" towards them "salvation," (*i.e.* a signal means or opportunity of salvation to them,) in case this their salvation might, and certainly should, have been obtained by them, or conferred on them, whether any such "long-suffering" had been vouchsafed unto them or no.

If it be said, that as the salvation of the saints is infallibly decreed, so is it with the like infallibility decreed to be effected by the "long-sufferance" of God towards them, as the means and opportunity thereof, and in this respect they may properly enough be required to "count," or esteem, the "long-suffering" of God towards them "salvation;" I answer, if the decree of God concerning the salvation of the saints be absolute and infallible, in the sense asserted and contended for by our opposers, then cannot the execution of this decree, the actual saving of the saints, be suspended upon any fallible or contingent condition, such as is the saints' accounting the long-sufferance of God to be salvation to them, or their managing this long-suffering of his in due order to their salvation; no more than the standing or continuance of a house, that is well and strongly built upon a rock, depends upon those weak or rotten shores or props which are applied unto it to support it.

Nor can God be said absolutely and infallibly to decree the coming to pass of such things, which are essentially in themselves, and in their own natures, contingent, it being a maxim generally granted by our adversaries themselves, That the decrees of God have no real influence upon their objects, or things decreed, at least no such which altereth their natures, or essential properties of their beings. It is a common saying amongst them, that praedestinatio nihil ponit in praedestinato, *i.e.* predestination putteth nothing in or into either the thing or person predestinated. And if predestination putteth nothing in or into the things or persons predestinated, there is no reason to judge that any other of his decrees doth any whit more.

And if the decrees of God relating unto contingent events should have any such influx upon them, which alters their natures, and changeth the fundamental laws of their beings, transforming them into things absolutely necessary, or necessary with any such necessity which is unavoidable, contingency would be only a name, or matter of mere speculation, God having, with the same infallibility and absoluteness of decree, as say our adversaries, decreed things contingent and things necessary, and consequently made all things, as to matter of event and coming to pass, necessary. So that the salvation of the saints is not absolutely decreed by God to be effected by his long-suffering towards them. Nor could this long-suffering be reasonably by them accounted salvation, in case their salvation were so absolutely decreed unto them, as our contrary-minded brethren suppose. Therefore,

6. Lastly, when the apostle saith, that "The Lord... is long-suffering to us-ward, not willing that any should perish, but that all," &c. his meaning must needs be, that he is long-suffering towards men, simply and indefinitely considered, or towards mankind. It further means this long-suffering of his towards them, proceeds out of a gracious and merciful disposition in him, which inclineth him not to will or desire the destruction of any person or soul of them, but that they may generally, one and other, by the advantage and opportunity of his goodness and long-sufferance towards them, be so overcome, as to repent unfeignedly of their sins, and turn unto him, that they may be saved. This interpretation,

1. Perfectly accords with the words, in their genuine, proper, and best known significations: whereas the other, as we lately proved, requires such a sense and signification of the two particles, *tinas*, and *pantas*, any and all, wherein they are not to be found throughout the Scriptures.

2. The series and story of the context falls in much more genuinely and fairly with this than within that other interpretation; the scope of the words being, as we formerly likewise showed, to vindicate the delay which the Lord Christ maketh, in not performing his promise of coming to judgment

with so much celerity and expedition, as some conceive it meet that he should perform it, from any pretence or plea, that can in a way of reason render it offensive unto any man. Now, look, out of how much the greater, richer, and larger mercy and goodness towards the poor children of men, this delay of his shall be found to proceed, and by how much greater the number of those are, whose benefit and blessedness shall appear to be intended by it and concerned in it. It must needs be conceived to be proportionably so much the further off from being any just matter of offence unto any man, than it would be in case it should be occasioned by any straitness of bowels, or the good intended by it be conceived to relate only to a few.

3. The sense of the words and place, which this interpretation exhibiteth, is more clearly parallel, and consistent with the mind of the Holy Ghost in other Scriptures, than that which is issued by the other. The Scripture no where, or at least no where so much, commendeth the patience or long-sufferance of God determinately towards his elect, or towards believers, in reference to their repentance or salvation, as towards the generality of men, and more especially towards those that are wicked and ungodly. "But we are sure," saith the apostle Paul, "that the judgment of God is according to truth against them which commit such things. And thinkest thou this, O man, that judgest them which do such things, and doest the same, that thou shalt escape the judgment of God? Or despisest thou the riches of his goodness and forbearance and long-suffering; not knowing that the goodness of God leadeth *thee* to repentance?" &c. Rom. ii. 2-4. And God himself, by his prophet Ezekiel, speaketh thus to the wicked and stiff-necked Jews in general: "Repent, and turn yourselves from all your transgressions; so iniquity shall not be your ruin." And further, "For why will ye die, O house of Israel? For I have no pleasure in the death of him that dieth, saith the Lord God: wherefore turn yourselves, and live ye," Ezek. xviii. 30–32. And elsewhere by the same prophet: "Say unto them, As I live, saith the Lord God, I have no pleasure in the death of the wicked; but that the wicked turn from his way and live: turn ye, turn ye, from your evil ways: for why will ye die, O house of Israel?" Ezek. xxxiii.11. Our apostle himself, speaking of the wicked generation of the old world, and of God's patience towards them, saith thus: "Which sometimes were disobedient, when once the long-suffering of God waited in the days of Noah," &c. 1 Pet. iii. 20. Not to multiply places, that of the apostle Paul, formerly opened, is of much affinity with the words in hand: "Who will have all men to be saved, and to come

unto the knowledge of the truth." 1 Tim. ii. 4.

In all these passages, unto which many more of like import might readily have been added, the gracious intent of God in his patience, towards the generality of men, and more especially towards the wicked, are very emphatically asserted, and this by way of encouragement and invitation unto them to repent, that so they might be saved. But concerning any such intentions of God in his patience, determinately towards believers, or his elect, I find the Scriptures silent altogether.

4. Lastly, the sense of the Scripture in hand contended for is attested by Mr. Calvin himself, over and over. "The apostle," saith he, "checketh the too much and preposterous haste" that some made "by another reason, viz. because the Lord doth therefore defer his coming, that" hereby "he may invite all mankind" or the whole of mankind "unto repentance." A little after, thus: "And indeed there is the same consideration to be had, of the duration of the whole world, which there is of every man's life in particular. For God by affording" or enlarging "time to every *particular man*, forbeareth them till they may" or that they may "repent. So, likewise, He makes no haste of putting an end unto the world, that he may give unto *all men* a space to repent."[6] Aretius in his brief commentary upon the place, compares it, for sense and import, within three of those four texts lately cited, viz., Rom. ii., Ezek. xviii., 1 Tim. ii. 4, in all which, as we observed, the patience of God towards the generality of men, or towards sinful men, in order to their repentance and salvation hereupon is clearly avouched. But there is not the least mention or intimation of any confinement or appropriation of this his patience, or intendments either of repentance or salvation therein, unto righteous men, or his elect. Therefore, questionless, this orthodox author also correspondeth with us in the interpretation given. Dr. Ames upon the place acknowledgeth, that "the patience of God in its own nature hath this use and end, viz., to allure" or invite "sinners unto repentance: Rom. ii. 4. And in this sense," he granteth that "their exposition may be admitted, who understand these words, and the like, of all and every particular man."

But whereas he adds that "the apostle in this place particularly respected the elect," and for proof saith that he speaks of the elect, 2 Pet. iii. 9, and numbereth himself with those of whom he speaketh: we answer briefly, 1. That he doth not speak here, of the elect, as such, or in their capacity of election, but only styles those, to whom he there speaks, beloved; which only imports his affection towards them, as they were saints, or believers,

6. Calv. in 2 Pet. iii. 9

or rather as they were so judged by him. 2. Whereas he numbers himself with those to whom and of whom he speaketh, it no ways proveth or supposeth that he numbereth himself in respect of his election, with them, or of his saintship, especially considering that he speaketh not, either to them or of them, as they were elect, as we have proved at large in the traverse of the words. And whereas he grants, that "the patience of God, hath in its own nature this use and end, that it allures" or draws "sinners to repentance;" doth he conceive that this nature of it is altered or changed for the worse, by any intentions of God, in respect of what sinners soever?

Or doth he think that God dissolveth or destroyeth the proper operativeness or tendency of any of his dispensations, in order, either to procure the perpetration of more sin in the world, or to the extenuation of the demerit or punishment of men who live and die impenitent and obdurate in their sins? Or is there any other end imaginable, but only one, or both of these, why the patience of God, which in its own nature, hath this use and end, to draw sinners to repentance, should be divested of them by God?

But against the exposition given, and maintained, some things are objected. First, If the Lord Christ should defer his coming, or be patient towards all men without exception, in order to their repentance, that so they may not perish, he must defer it forever, and so never come; inasmuch as that day will never come, wherein all men will repent.

To this I answer that it is neither the sense of the text, nor yet of the interpretation given, that Christ should be patient unto all men, or defer his coming until all men without exception should actually repent. His intent and desire in his patience towards all men, is that they should repent and be saved, and that he doth by his patience and long-suffering towards all men, afford unto them means and opportunities sufficient to bring them all to repentance.

How such intentions and desires in God and in Christ, which are real and cordial, may yet very possibly never take place, or be fulfilled, remains to be further opened in convenient place.

Another objection levied by some against the interpretation avouched, which yet in part falls in with the former, and is already fallen with it, is this: If Christ certainly knows, knoweth beforehand, that all men without exception will not repent, or will not be saved, how can it be thought that he should will, intend, or desire, that they should repent or that they should be saved? Doth any sober man will, or intend such a thing, which he certainly knows beforehand will never be effected?

We deliver this for a general rule, to direct to a right understanding of Scripture anthropopathies, and attributions of human things unto God; viz. "That it is not necessary that all things accompanying, or relating unto those affections or impressions in men, which are attributed unto God, should be paralleled in him, or have something in his nature corresponding to them. But it is a sufficient ground or reason for the attribution, in case the human affection or impression attributed to him, be, in respect of any one particular, appertaining to it in men, paralleled, or analogised, in the nature of God."

Which rule I explain in the place referred unto by several instances. From hence it follows, though sober men never intend, or will, what they certainly know beforehand will never come to pass, that yet God may, and so Christ, without any reflexion of disparagement unto him in the least, intend and will what he certainly foreknoweth, in such a sense as foreknowledge is appropriable unto him, of which formerly, will never come to pass. The reason is, because intentions, and acts of willing, which are properly and formally in men, and not in God, are not attributed unto God, in all, or every respect, or in respect of all circumstances, which relate unto them in men, but in respect only of such productions or effects, as they ordinarily produce in men.

As for example, when men will or intend such or such a thing, if the act of their will in this case be raised to any considerable strength or height of willing, they engage themselves in the use of such means, for the effecting of what they intend, or will, in this kind, which they judge competent and sufficient hereunto. In like manner God in propriety of Scripture language, is said to intend, and will, the repentance and salvation of men, because he vouchsafeth a sufficiency of means unto them to effect their repentance and salvation hereupon, and chargeth them from heaven to use these means accordingly. And inasmuch as he vouchsafeth this sufficiency of means unto, and imposeth the charge we speak of upon, all men without exception, he may upon good grounds be said to intend or will (*i.e.* desire) the repentance and salvation of all without exception. It is a common saying amongst all expositors of Scripture, as well Protestant as Popish, that "humana transferuntur in Deum, non affective, sed effective:" *i.e.* human passions or affections, are ascribed unto God, not by way of affect, but effect; *i.e.* not because the affections themselves are in him, but because there proceed such effects from him, which are like unto the effects that flow from such affections in men.

If it be here demanded; but if God certainly foreseeth, or foreknoweth that the means and opportunities which he vouchsafeth unto men, to bring them to repentance and so to salvation, will miscarry, and never take effect, but turn to so much the greater condemnation of those, to whom they are vouchsafed, can any vouchsafement of such means and opportunities as these unto men be interpreted, or looked upon, as proceeding from any love or grace in him towards such persons, who he certainly knows beforehand will reject them? Or as any ways obliging such persons unto thankfulness? If I certainly knew that the gift of a hundred pounds unto my son, or friend, would turn to some sad inconvenience unto them, as to the destruction of their lives, to the bereaving of them of their wits, or the like, would it be matter of love, kindness, or respect in me towards them, to give it unto them? Or should I not deal more kindly by them, not to give it in such a case? To this I answer,

1. When God vouchsafeth unto men things which are in themselves and in their natures good, beneficial, and of worthy concernment unto men, and they who receive them very capable of employing them accordingly, he is no ways hindering them from making an answerable use of them, but many ways encouraging, persuading, and pressing them hereunto, is there any reason or colour of a reason why he should be thought less gracious or loving to such men, only because he knows beforehand that they will make no such use of them? Or would the same or the like vouchsafements from him savour of any whit the more grace, love, or goodness, in case it could or should be supposed that he were ignorant what use such men would make of them, or whether they would convert them to their destruction or no? Or is there any reason that the knowledge of God should be turned to the prejudice or disparagement of his goodness?

2. As he certainly foresees that some men *will* turn his grace into wantonness and render themselves liable to the greater condemnation by the abuse of those means which he vouchsafeth unto them for their salvation, so he as certainly knows and foreseeth likewise, that they *may* do otherwise if they please, I mean improve these means to the obtaining of salvation, that his foresight of what they will do notwithstanding. For the foreknowledge which is in God of what men will do neither imposeth nor supposeth any absolute necessity of their doing it;[7] neither have they ever a whit the less liberty or power to refrain from doing it, because of God's foreknowledge that they will do it. Nor would they have ever a whit the more liberty or power to refrain an action or course in case it should be supposed that

7. Rada. Contro. 30. Art. 5.

God doth not certainly foresee what they will do on either hand, refrain, or act and practise. So that God is never the less gracious unto men in his vouchsafement of sufficient means of salvation unto them, because he foresees they will abuse them. But,

3. Lastly, I answer further, that there is not the same consideration of God and of men in respect of such actions or gifts, the issue or consequence whereof, the one and the other are or may be said to foresee that they will prove evil to those that receive them. In case a man should foresee such or such an event in one kind or other that would certainly follow upon any act or gift of his, his foresight would be such literally and properly, *i. e.* he should have knowledge of the event before he had done the action or given the gift, the event whereof he is said to foresee or foreknow. But now God, though he be said to foresee the issue or event of any action or gift of his, yet is not said, properly, or as the word sounds in ordinary acception with men, to foresee it, *i. e.* he doth not first or antecedaneously in respect of time foresee it, or see it before the action be performed by him or the gift given, the event whereof he is said to foresee. For as God himself is not measured by time, so neither are any of his actions; and it is a generally received maxim in theology, admitted by all divines, that God willeth nothing in time,[8] but all things in or from eternity.

Now there is the same reason or consideration of his foreknowledge which there is of his will. As he willeth nothing in time, so neither doth he foreknow or foresee anything *in time:* His foreseeing of things being nothing really but himself, as all his actions are, it must needs be as ancient as himself, and co-eternal with himself. So likewise that act of his whereby he gives or imparts anything unto men, though the gift itself given by it doth not come to the hands of men or to be received by men until such or such a time, yet this act itself of his was from eternity; and consequently is not capable of being *fore*seen by God, because it was as ancient as God himself.

And for the sad event or consequent of this action or gift of his unto men, though he may be thought to foresee it because it happeneth in time, yet inasmuch as that act passed from him from eternity, and so was from eternity irreversible, by which the gift or gifts sorting to so sad an event in the receiver, were conferred upon him in time, there is no reason nor colour of reason why he should be thought to give such gifts, being in themselves good and worthy from his infinite goodness, out of any whit the less love, grace, or mercy towards him who receiveth them, because he foresaw (as

8. Daven. Animadversions, &c. p. 484.

is thought), after his manner of foreseeing, that they would be abused by him to his harm. Especially considering that it was not in his power, I mean in the power of God, to have done more towards the preventing of such an abuse of them by such a man than he did.

It cannot be thought but that God did foresee (i.e. know from eternity) that the Jews of old would mock his messengers and despise his words, and misuse his prophets until his wrath arose against them, and till there was no remedy. Yet the vouchsafement of these means of grace and of repentance, the sending of his messengers, words, and prophets unto them, is expressly attributed unto his compassion, (*i. e.* his love of pity or benevolence of affection) towards them. "And the Lord God of their fathers sent to them by his messengers, rising up betimes and sending; *because he had compassion on his people*, and on his dwelling place," 2 Chron. xxxvi. 15, 16. In like manner our Saviour certainly knew that Jerusalem afterwards would not understand or accept of the things of her peace, the means of her safety and preservation. Yet he ascribes the vouchsafement of them unto her unto a genuine tenderness of love and care in him towards her and her children. "O Jerusalem, Jerusalem, thou that killest the prophets and stonest them which are sent unto thee, how often would I have gathered thy children together, even as a hen gathereth her chickens under her wings, and ye would not!" Matt. xxiii. 37.

But is it not, it is likely you will demand, in the power of God absolutely to prevent the abuse of those good gifts of his we speak of by the receivers, and consequently to do more towards the preventing of this abuse than he doth?

I answer, no. Both reason and religion, which yet is nothing but reason in her exaltation, teach us to judge and say that it is not in the power of God to prevent the abuse of those good gifts of his we speak of in the receivers otherwise than now he doth prevent it, viz. by affording sufficient means unto them for the prevention of it. This, I say, neither was nor is, according to the sound principles both of reason and religion, any whit more in the power of God to do than it is in his power to lie, deceive, oppress, or do any other thing most unworthy of him. For he that is omnipotent must needs be omniprudent also; and he that is omniprudent cannot do anything in the least degree repugnant to the most rigid and strict principles of the most perfect wisdom and prudence that is. God has divine self limitations.

We see it amongst men, that the wiser any man is in reality and truth, the less power he hath to do any thing contrary to the laws and dictates of true wisdom. And the weaker and more defective any man is in this wisdom, the more liberty and power he hath to do foolishly or uncomelily. What was it that made Joseph unable to commit that great wickedness whereunto he was solicited by his mistress? "How than can I do this great wickedness, and sin against God?" saith he, Gen. xxxix. 9; meaning, that he could not do it. Whereas, doubtless, there were men enough in the world that both could and would have done such a thing as that, though he could not. So what was it that made Paul unable to do anything against the truth, and able only to act for the truth? "For we," saith he, "can do nothing against the truth, but for the truth," 2 Cor. xiii. 8: whereas there were, and are at this day, thousands in the world able, *i. e.* at liberty in their wills and consciences, to act ten times more against the truth than for the truth.

The true reason why neither of these men had any power, were not able to do those unworthy things which a thousand other men had power enough to do, was, because they had so much true wisdom in them above other men, which would not suffer them to do such unseemly and unworthy things. And generally we find it, that the more knowingly and prudently conscientious men and women are, the more they are bound up in themselves, and have so much the less liberty or power to do things that are uncomely than other men. So, then, God, being infinitely more wise, and that with the truest and best wisdom that can be imagined, than the wisest of men, must needs in a way of reason be conceived to be more bound up in himself, to have less liberty or power to do anything contrary to any rule, dictate, or principle of the most exquisite wisdom that is his, than any creature whatsoever, whether men or angels.

The apostle, as is well known, breaks forth in a holy kind of astonishment upon his contemplation of the wisdom and knowledge of God: "O the depths of the riches both of the wisdom and knowledge of God! How unsearchable are his judgments;" meaning, that for matter of wisdom and knowledge by which they are ordered, managed, and administered, they are unsearchable, viz. to the bottom, or in respect of all the strains or variety of wisdom that are inn them; "and his ways," in respect of the numberless ingredients of wisdom which he puts into them, "past finding out!" Rom. xi. 33.

So, then, it being contrary to the law and rules of true wisdom, or of that infinite wisdom which rules in God, for him to act in his creatures, at least ordinarily, in opposition to those natural and essential properties and principles which himself hath planted in them. It may easily be conceived how and in what respect he hath no power, *i. e.* no liberty in himself, to prevent the ruin of his creature, man, further or otherwise than by such an interposure of himself or of his grace in order hereunto which will, in respect of any forcibleness or efficacy in working, well consist with the natural and essential freedom and liberty of his will. In respect whereof the utmost line or extent of the liberty or power of God is to proceed no further with men, nor with any man, at any time, in the vouchsafement of grace or means of grace, in order to the preventing of their ruin and destruction, than to leave them a power at least, or possibility, of rejecting the grace offered unto them, and so to ruin and destroy themselves.

Nor, doubtless, did God ever go further or rise higher than this, no, not in the most signal or miraculous conversions which either we read of in the Scriptures, or otherwise have heard of, according to truth. I suppose there is not a greater or more notable instance in this kind than that of the conversion of Paul, which, we know, was effected in a very extraordinary way, and with as high a hand of means as ever was lifted up by God for the conversion of a man, viz. by a vision of the Lord Christ himself from heaven, in splendour and great glory, speaking with an audible voice unto him. Although I know not whether it be necessary suppose that the work of Paul's conversion was perfected, I mean, specifically perfected (for gradually, I presume it was not) by this vision only, or until Ananias, to whom the vision directed him, had made known unto him those things concerning the gospel which he did.

But, whether his conversion was specifically perfected by the vision without Ananias' ministry or no, doubtless there was a liberty or possibility left in Paul himself, to the very last moment or minute of time before his conversion was actually wrought, to have not only resisted, but even frustrated all the means that were used for the effecting of it. Frustrated, I mean, not simply or universally, as if Christ should have been disappointed and lost all he had done in order to his conversion, in case he had not been converted, but frustrated in respect of that particular end, his conversion. For God hath always more ends than one, though but one primary and antecedent, in vouchsafing means of grace and salvation unto men: and whether he obtains the one or the other, it is of much alike concernment unto him, according to that of the apostle: "For we," apostles, or ministers of the gospel, "are unto God," in our ministry, "a sweet," or the sweet, "savour of Christ," *i. e.* we render Christ, or the mystery of Christ, by a diligent and faithful spreading abroad the knowledge of them in the world, as full of satisfaction and contentment unto God as they are capable of being improved unto, "in them that are saved, and in those that perish;" meaning, that the destruction of those who perish through a rejection of his rich grace in Christ offered to them, is matter of good satisfaction unto him, even as the salvation of those is who accept of this grace from him.

So that, let men who have Christ and the means of salvation offered unto them take either the right hand or the left, God will be no loser by them. His counsels and ends, of one kind or other, will be advanced howsoever. How that most serious and solemn profession and oath of God, that he delighteth not "in the death of the wicked," or "of him that dieth," Ezek. xviii. 32, and xxxiii. 11, is of good consistence with the apostles' being the "sweet savour of Christ unto him in them that perish," as also with that profession which himself maketh by Solomon unto wicked men, "I also will laugh at your calamity; I mock when your fear cometh," and "your destruction cometh as a whirlwind;" &c., Prov. i. 26, 27, we shall, I conceive, have opportunity to unfold in the latter part of our present discourse. But this by the way in this place.

Yet give me leave to add one thing further here of necessary consideration for the full clearing of the business in hand. Though it will be consistent with the wisdom of God and the principles thereof to rise sometimes and in some cases in the vouchasafement of the means of grace and of salvation unto men, to the highest pin or degree, in point of efficacy and power, which the native and essential freedom and liberty of the will will bear, yet it is not consistent with this wisdom of his to do it often, much less ordinarily, or of course. The wisdom of a man leads and teacheth him sometimes upon occasion, and in order to some more than ordinary design, to vary from his customary and constant course of acting, yea, though this customary and constant course of his be simply the best and most agreeable to the rules of wisdom, for him ordinarily to follow. Upon this account the wise man informeth us, that there is "A time to kill, and a time to heal; a time to break down, and a time to build up;…A time to cast away stones, and a time to gather stones together;" Eccles. iii. 3, 5 with several other instances of like import. When he saith, there is a time to do this and a time to do that which is contrary unto it, his meaning clearly is, that it is prudential and agreeable to rules of wisdom, for a man, according to time, place, and other circumstances, to vary the manner and kind of his ordinary actions, yea, to act at one time with a kind of contrariety to himself at another.

In like manner, it is perfectly consistent with the infinite wisdom of God, upon some special occasion, and in order to some gracious design, to open the hand of his bounty in the vouchsafement of means of salvation unto men, much wider than will stand with the same wisdom to do ordinarily, or at another time. And as it may be truly said of a wise man, that he cannot cast away stones, when the time is for him to gather stones together; and so, on the contrary, that he cannot gather stones together, when the time and season is to cast them away; such a man cannot mis-time his actions, because his wisdom, which frames and fashions both the consents and dissents of his will, cannot frame or raise a consent of will in him to do anything contrary to itself, or to its own nature and principles, *i. e.* to do anything uncomelily or imprudently. So may it truly be said of God in the matter of granting means of faith and of salvation unto men, that he cannot, in the ordinary and standing course of his providence or dispensation of such means, rise so high, give means of that transcendent nature, efficacy, and power, which he can and doth give now and then, in some special cases, and in order to some great and special end.

As, for example, God was able, no principle of his wisdom opposing, to vouchsafe unto Paul that extraordinary means of believing, or for his conversion, which we spake of, a glorious vision from heaven. But it doth not follow from hence, that therefore he is able (we still speak of his moral ability, or of the ability of his will) to afford the like vision, or any other means like unto that for efficacy and converting power, ordinarily or unto all other men.

When he demands thus concerning his ancient church and people of the Jews, "What could have been done more to my vineyard, that I have not done in it?" Isa. v. 4; he hath not done any such thing in it, or for it, as he did afterwards for Paul. Nor had he multiplied those miracles and great works of wonder, some particulars whereof he did work for them and amongst them, to such a number, or with such frequency, as by his power, simply considered, and without relation unto his wisdom, he was able to have done. And yet he might truly say and profess unto them, as his demand mentioned imports, that he could do no more for them, (to make them fruitful, to bring them to repentance, and so to make them a prosperous and happy people) than he had done: *i. e.* he had done the uttermost which his wisdom, in such a case as their was, permitted him to do.

So, when he vouchsafeth a greater sufficiency of means to one city than he doth to another, as he did to Capernaum above Tyre and Sidon, to one nation than to another, to one age or generation of men than to another; the reason of this difference is to be resolved into the same infinite uniform, though "manifold wisdom of God," as the apostle calleth it, or, which is the same, into "the counsel of his own will," Ephes. i. 11. Not simply into his will, but into the counsel of his own will, (*i. e.* that infinite wisdom or prudence, by which his will is as it were steered and directed in all the motions and actings thereof) according unto which counsel he is said to "worketh all things," Eph. i. 11.

And it may be as truly and as properly said of him, when he vouchsafeth the least and lowest sufficiency of means unto some men, as when he affordeth the greatest and richest of all unto others, that he did or doth what he could, or what he is able to do, as well for the one as for the other. And in such cases of difference as these, that admiration of the apostle, lately mentioned, is most seasonable and proper: "O the depth of the riches both of the wisdom and knowledge of God! how unsearchable are his judgments, and his ways past finding out!" Rom. xi. 33. By his judgments, in this place, we are not, I conceive, to understand only his penal inflictions upon men in one kind or other, but his dispensatory administrations, as he is the judge and great ruler of the world, indefinitely considered, as well such as are munificent as those which are penal. And so the word "ways," in the latter part of the verse, added, it is like, for explication, indifferently implies as well the one as the other.

But how, or in what respect are his judgments, or ways of administration in the world, said to be unsearchable, or past finding out? The former part of the verse clearly informeth us of this; as viz. that they are unsearchable in respect of that abundance of wisdom and knowledge, by which, and according unto which, they are first ordered and contrived, and then executed by him. First, they are unsearchable (viz. unto men, yea, and to angels too) in respect of that most absolute and perfect knowledge which God hath of every particular circumstance, from the least to the greatest, of all the actions and ways of all the men in the world; and so of all cities and of all nations, in all succeeding generations, from the morning of the world until the present hour thereof. It is upon which actions, with all and every their respective circumstances, compared and laid together by God, as by reason of his perfect knowledge of them they readily may be, he builds and forms, by means of his wisdom, of which presently, that entire series, or tenor of his administrations, as well munificent as penal, which from day to day and from age to age take place in the world amongst the sons and daughters of men.

Neither men nor angels are capable of knowing or considering all the infinite and endless multitude and variety of actions, with all their circumstances respectively, which are done in the world, upon which, and according to the exigency of which (not any one of them, from the greatest to the least, omitted or left out) the providential administrations of God in the world, as well of justice as of mercy and goodness, are founded and framed. Hence it is that the apostle concludes, in a posture of admiration, that the judgments of God are unsearchable, and his ways past finding out, in respect of the depths of the riches of that knowledge, which he maketh use of in forming them. Meaning, that no creature who knoweth not as much as God himself knoweth, concerning the grounds and reasons why he ordereth the affairs of the world, of persons, of cities, of countries, of ages, as he doth, and not otherwise, can possibly understand or comprehend the absolute exactness and accurateness of them; however he may apprehend somewhat, yea, much of them, I mean chiefly concerning the equity and righteousness of them.

Again, these "judgments" and "ways" of God are "unsearchable and past finding out," in respect of the "depths of the riches of that wisdom" which is in God, according unto which also they are all calculated and formed by him. For look, as in a judge, who is to administer justice, and to give sentence in the causes of men that are brought before him, there ought to be these two things: (a.) A perfect knowledge of the respective cases wherein he is to give sentence, in all circumstances relating to them, before he doth give sentence; (b.) A principle of wisdom, to weigh and ponder aright every of these cases in all their circumstances respectively, that so he may be enabled to form such a sentence, wherein every circumstance, great and small, relating to every case, may have its due consideration and weight.

So there are, and of necessity must be, in God, to make him an absolute Judge, as he is, of all the world. God has such a perfect knowledge, as we speak of, of all cases that are before him in all the world, with all and every particular circumstance relating to every of them. He has an absoluteness and perfection of wisdom also, (a.) To interpret every particular circumstance relating to every particular action and case in the world, according to true principles of justice and equity, so as to be able to say how much better, or how much worse, such or such an action is, by reason of such or such a circumstance, one or more; (b.) To raise or frame such a sentence, and to administer and execute it accordingly, which shall be made up, as it were, of the equitable results of all and every of those circumstances, which are to be taken into consideration in every award. Now the wisdom which God maketh use of in both these ways, in and about the government of the world, hath so many unfathomable "depths" in it, is so "rich" above measure, so unconceivable, incomprehensible, in the discerning abilities and estimative worth of it, that those judiciary acts and ways which proceed from it, and are moulded and formed by the spirit and strength of it, are greater than all created understanding, above all comprehension, either by men or angels.

By the light of what hath been now argued, it fully appeareth, 1. That all such men who "turn the grace of God," in those worthy means of salvation which he vouchsafeth unto them, "into wantonness," and are not in conclusion saved by them, but perish so much the more grievously, are, notwithstanding, as much obliged in point of thankfulness unto him for them as they could have been in case they should be saved by them. 2. That the vouchsafement and bestowing of such means upon them by God, notwithstanding the certainty of his knowing from eternity that they will not prove saving unto them in the end, are yet arguments and pledges of as much grace, love, and mercy unto them, as they would or could be in case he had as certainly known that they would be of a saving consequence unto them.

3. That God, his infinite wisdom considered, and the obligements thereof upon him, goeth as far, doth as much, to render the means of grace exhibited unto those who perish effectual to their salvation as is possible for him to do. 4. Lastly, that the knowledge which is in God of the future abuse and miscarrying of the means of salvation, in those to whom they are exhibited or vouchsafed by him, doth not precede that act of his by which they are exhibited unto them, this being eternal, or from eternity, as well as that.

CHAPTER VI
Declaring in what sense the former passages of Scripture asserting the universality of redemption by Christ, are, as to this point, to be understood; and, consequently, in what sense the said doctrine of universal redemption is maintained in the present discourse.

THE intelligent and observant reader may, from several passages occasionally inserted here and there in the precedure of this discourse, clearly enough perceive and understand in what sense, and with what explications and provisos, the said doctrine of universal redemption by Christ is asserted and maintained herein. Consequently he would realize in what sense the author understandeth all those texts of Scripture which hold forth the said doctrine unto the world, many of which have been formerly produced upon the account. Yet, that the reader may readily, without either burdening his memory, or spending time in turning over leaves, know where to find his mind and sense concerning both fully explained, I judged it not amiss to devote one entire chapter unto his service herein. Therefore,

To express our meaning in the said doctrine negatively, or rather our non-meaning, when, with the Scriptures, we affirm and teach that "Christ died for all men," *(i. e.* for the redemption and salvation of "all men," without exception of any; for we do not find in Scripture that he died for any for whose salvation he died not) we do not mean or suppose either, 1, that he died sufficiently only for all men, (*i. e.* only that there was price or merit enough in his death for the redemption of "all men;") or, 2, that God, or himself, did every ways, or in every respect, as, viz. both antecedently and consequently intend the redemption or salvation of "all men," in or by his death. Nor, 3, do we mean or suppose, in the said doctrine, that Christ died so, or upon such terms, for all men, that all men shall in time, or at last, be actually redeemed, (from sin and misery) or eternally saved, by his death. Nor, 4, do we suppose that God, or Christ as God, intends the salvation of all men, or of any man or men, by Christ's death, only by the intentions formally or properly so called, or such as are found in men. Nor, 5, do we mean or suppose, in the doctrine avouched, that Christ, by his death, purchased or procured the infusion or gift either of faith or repentance for all men, or, indeed, for any man, or numbers of men, personally considered. Nor, 6, and lastly, for our negative, that by his said death he purchased or procured unconditional pardon or forgiveness of sins for all men, or for any man, or number of men, simply considered, or as such and such individual men by name. But,

1. For our sense and meaning, in the affirmative, we hold and mean, in the doctrine specified, that there was a reality of intention on God's part, (in such a sense as reality of intention is appropriable unto him, which sense we opened at large formerly,[1] and shall briefly again declare in this chapter). There was a valuable consideration, or worth of merit, in the death of Christ, fully competent and sufficient for the ransom or redemption of all men, so it should be equally, and upon the same terms, erogable, or appliable unto all men, in order to their redemption, without any difference, or special contraction or limitation of it unto some more than others.

2. We hold and mean in and about the premises that God did only antecedently intend the actual redemption and salvation of all men in and by the death of Christ; but consequently the redemption and salvation only of some, viz., those who shall believe. What it is to will or intend a thing antecedently, and what consequently, hath been shown formerly in Chap. 2 and shall, God willing, be somewhat further opened in this chapter.

3. When we teach that Christ died for all men, we intend and mean that there is a possibility, yea, a fair and gracious possibility, for all men without exception, considered as men, without and before their voluntary obduration by actual sinning, to obtain actual salvation by his death. So that in case any man perisheth, his destruction is altogether from himself, there being as much, and as much intended, in the death of Christ, for and towards the procuring of his salvation, as there is for procuring the salvation of any of those who come to be actually saved.

4. When, with the Scriptures, we deliver this, for a doctrine of truth, that Christ died for all men, we suppose and mean that God intends the salvation of all men by this death, only so, after such a manner, or with such a kind of intention which is competible to and consistent with his infinite simplicity and perfection of being. Of this kind of intention we shall grant some brief consideration in this chapter.

5. When we teach that Christ died for all men, we mean not only that he put all men without exception into a capability of being saved, as, viz., by

1. See Chap. II.

believing, but also that he wholly dissolved and took off from all men the guilt and condemnation which was brought upon all men by Adam's transgression. So that now no man shall perish or be condemned but upon his own personal account, and for such sins only which shall be actually and voluntarily committed by him, or for such omissions which it was in his power to have prevented.

6. When, with the Scriptures, we affirm that Christ died for all men, our sense and meaning is, that by his death he procured this grace and favour with God for all men without exception, viz., that they should receive from him sufficient strength and means, or be enabled by him, to repent and to believe, yea, and to persevere in both unto the end. In this sense, and none other, he is, or may be said to have by his death purchased the grace of faith and repentance for men; and this upon equal terms in an antecedent consideration for all men.

7. Lastly, our sense and meaning in the said doctrine further is, that Christ by his death purchased this transcendant grace also and favour in the sight of God for all men without exception, that upon their repentance and believing in him they should be justified and receive forgiveness of all their sins. And that upon their perseverance in both unto the end, they should be actually and eternally saved; and that in this sense and in this only, he is and maybe said to have purchased justification or remission of sins, redemption, salvation, &c. for men, for any man, or any number of men: yea, and in this sense, for all men.

The imputation, from the guilt whereof we desire in special manner to wash our hands in innocency by this explication is, that as we speak of universal redemption so we hold likewise universal salvation, or that all men shall be saved by Christ. That such an opinion as this is not consistant with the doctrine maintained in this discourse concerning the death of Christ for all men, sufficiently appeareth from that ground which we have laid and built upon, once and again, in the former part of this discourse, viz.: That such intentions and desires in God and in Christ which are real and cordial may yet very possibly never take place or be fulfilled. This supposed, it may very easily be conceived that God may intend the salvation of all men by the death of Christ, and yet all men not be saved.

Which opinion, I mean that all men shall be saved, as it hath no communion at all with the doctrine avouched in this discourse, so hath it every whit as little with the author's sense or judgment otherwise; who approveth the sentence of the Constantinopolitan Synod assembled under the

Emperor Justinian, wherein this opinion, held, as it seems, by Origen with a surplusage of error joined with it,[2] was condemned. Yea, to me it seemeth not a little strange how any man professing subjection of judgment unto the Scriptures should ever come to a confederacy with such an opinion. For with what frequency and evidence of expression do these rise up against it, ever and anon intimating and asserting on the one hand the paucity of those that will or shall be saved, in comparison of those that will perish, and on the other hand the perpetuity or everlastingness of the perdition and misery of those who do perish? Nor do they give the least intimation or hope of release from misery unto those who die in their sins and perish in their unbelief. "Enter ye in at the strait gate," saith Christ unto the children of men in his doctrine upon the mount, "for wide is the gate, and broad is the way, that leadeth to destruction, and many there be that go in thereat," but we read of none that return or come out thereat: "Because strait is the gate and narrow is the way which leadeth unto life, and few there be that find it." Matt. vii. 13, 14; *i. e.* that find it either first or last, or ever.

For that this is his meaning appears from these and such like sayings: "Wherefore, if thine hand cause thee to offend, cut it off: it is better for thee to enter into life maimed, than, having two hands, to go into hell, into the fire that never shall be quenched," he doth not say into the fire that is hard to be quenched, or which will be long in quenching, but (in the Greek) *eis to pur to asbeston, i. e.* into that fire which differs from all other kinds of fire in this, that whereas they are quenchable, no decree of God interposing to the contrary, this by the unchangeable law of Heaven is made unquenchable. For for the redoubling of the article *to*, hath this import, which is likewise further confirmed by that which followeth, "Where their worm dieth not, and the fire is not quenched," Mark ix. 43, 44. These expressions, "dieth not," and "is not quenched," though according to their precise grammatical import, they only deny the act, the one of dying, the other of quenching; yet according to Scripture dialect, they deny also the very power or possibility of these acts. For there is nothing more frequent here than by the denial of the act to deny the power or possibly of a thing. Thus, Gen. xiii. 6, where our translation readeth "And the land was not able to bear them," the original only saith, "and the land *did* not bear them," as Mr. Ainsworth also translateth the place. So Prov. xxiv. 7, where our last translation, respecting the original, hath it, "he *openeth not* his mouth in the gate," our former translators, rather minding the sense and import of the place, read it thus, "*he cannot open* his mouth in the gate;" to omit many the like.

2. Origen's opinion was not only that all men, but that all devils also should at last be saved by Christ.

So that when our Saviour saith concerning the estate of those that go or are cast into hell, that "their worm dieth not, and the fire is not quenched," his meaning is, that their worm cannot die, nor their fire be quenched; *i. e.* their punishment or torment can never have an end or interruption, viz. because the counsel of the will of the Almighty hath resolved against both, and judged it meet to make them easeless and endless. Upon this account also John the Baptist saith concerning Christ, that "Whose fan in his hand, and he will throughly purge his floor, and gather his wheat into the garner; but he will burn up the chaff with *unquenchable fire*." Matt. iii. 12. So likewise the apostle Paul clearly teacheth, that "the Lord Jesus shall be revealed from heaven with his mighty angels, in flaming fire taking vengeance on them that know not God, and that obey not the gospel of our Lord Jesus Christ, who," saith he, "shall be punished with *everlasting destruction* from the presence of the Lord," &c., 2 Thess. i. 7-9. To this purpose the evangelist John reports it for the saying of an angel unto him in his vision, that "If any man worship the beast and his image, and receive his mark in his forehead or in his hand, The same shall drink of the wine of the wrath of God, which is poured out without mixture into the cup of his indignation; and he shall be tormented with fire and brimstone in the presence of the holy angels, and in the presence of the Lamb: And the smoke of their torment ascendeth up *for ever and ever*." Rev. xiv. 9-11.

These last words are again used in the description of the vengeance that shall be executed upon the "whore:" "And again they," the people that were in heaven, "said, Alleluia. And her smoke rose up *for ever and ever*." Rev. xix. 3. Afterwards, in the same book, we read, that "the devil that deceived them was cast into the lake of fire and brimstone, where the beast and the false prophet are, and shall be *tormented day and night for ever and ever*." Rev. xx. 10. This expression, "for ever and ever," so signally expressed in all the three testimonies last recited, plainly imports that the duration or continuance of the punishment and torment of those who perish in their sins, and are cast into hell, is not commensurable with the continuance of the Mosaical law, long since expired, which in the Old Testament is frequently signified by a word signifying, or at least commonly rendered "for ever," Exod. xxviii. 43; xxix. 28; Lev. xvi. 29, &c., but usually interpreted "for a long time" or for the time of a man's life, &c., but commensurable with the duration of the kingdom of God, of the life of God and of Jesus Christ; for these, in respect of their continuance, are almost constantly said to be "for ever and ever," Psal. x. 16; xxi. 4; Rev. iv.

9; v. 14; x. 6; xv. 7, &c.; i. e. for eternity, or without end.

The notion and term of the "bottomless pit," frequently used in the book of Revelation to signify the state or condition of the damned, plainly enough imports the endlessness or everlastingness of their misery. If we could suppose a ditch or pit without bottom, in the midst of which a man should be thrown, we could not with congruity of notion but suppose also that this person would be always falling, and that his motion or fall would never be at an end. The like apprehension, doubtless, concerning the case and state of those who die in their sins, in respect of their torment and misery, the Holy Ghost seeks to form and plant in in our souls and consciences by the metaphor or borrowed resemblance of a "bottomless pit." It were easy to multiply texts of Scripture to make that voice, which hath now spoken unto us in those last cited, far greater and louder; but those which we have heard speak already in the point have spoken so plainly, that the rest may keep silence at the present without loss or disadvantage to the truth.

Neither do the Scriptures so much as whisper anything of semblance or comport with the opinion now rejected. As for that of the apostle, Eph. i. 10, which some well-willers to the said opinion look upon as sympathising with them in their judgments that way, it will, upon a due inquiry, be found of another spirit. "That in the dispensation of the fullness of times," saith this place, "he might gather together in one all things in Christ, both which are in heaven and which are on earth, even in him," &c. whereunto, for affinity's sake, we may join that from the same pen: "For it pleased the Father that in him should all fulness dwell; And having made peace through the blood of his cross, by him to reconcile all things unto himself; by him, I say, whether they be things in earth or things in heaven." Col. i. 19, 20. From these passages laid together some judge it to be a very legitimate inference that "in the dispensation of the fullness of times," *i. e.* as they understand, in due time, though it be very long before, "all things," *i. e.* all persons of men or mankind, "whether in heaven or in earth," *i. e.* as well those who at present are at the greatest distance from the love and favour of God, whether alive or dead, (the earth containing both) as those that are already in his favour, and therefore in blessedness and glory, shall be "gathered into one by Christ;" *i. e.* shall be "reconciled unto him," and so be invested together in "one" and the same condition of happiness and glory, by virtue of the death of Christ, who died for them all, and that to procure their actual reconcilement unto God, sooner or later, however wickedly and unbelievingly they should either live or die. But that such a gloss as this is quite besides the text and the true import of it, is not hard to demonstrate. For,

Neither of the said passages speak of the event, issue, or success of that glorious design of God by Jesus Christ specified in them, but of the design itself, or what was projected or intended by him. Now, the design or projection of God by Jesus Christ here reported was, as the apostle expresseth it in the former place, *anakephalaiōsasthai ta panta en tō Christō, i. e.* to re-collect, reduce, or gather all things into one head by Christ, or in Christ, "both which are in heaven and which are on earth." In the latter place, this design is said to be the "reconciling of all things to himself by Christ, whether things on earth or things in heaven." By "all things, which are in heaven and which are on earth," by the joint consent of many interpreters, he means angels (holy angels) and men. The neuter gender for the masculine is a frequent construction in the Scriptures, and emphatical. *Pan ho didōsin moi ho patēr, i.e.* "that every thing," meaning, every person of mankind, "which my Father giveth unto me," &c. John vi. 37. So presently after, *ina pan ho dedōken moi, i. e.* "that every thing which he hath given me," &c., verse 39. So, *ta mōra tou kosmou ...kai ta asthenē tou kosmou, i. e.* the "foolish things of the world...and the weak things of the world," 1 Cor. i. 27; for foolish men, and weak men, so esteemed. See also 1 John v. 4; Rev. xxi. 27, &c. The note of universality, *panta,* is better limited to that kind of subject which is properly capable of being headed by Christ, viz. as men and angels; than extended to all things simply and whatsoever; though such a sense as this be passable enough, and is embraced by some.

When the apostle saith, that God's project or design was to recapitulate, or re-collect, or gather all things into or unto a head by Christ, both angels and men, he supposeth, 1. That both stood in need of a head, *i. e.* of one set in place of power and authority over them, who should be both able and willing to govern, order, protect, and direct them so, or upon such terms, that they might not, with any tolerable care over themselves, miscarry in point of greatest happiness, as the one of them, men, had generally done already. And the other, angels, were liable to do, as many of their kind, and of the same creation and nature with them, had done, as Calvin well observes upon the place, affirming, that "as men were lost, so were the angels not out of danger" (of losing). 2. He supposeth further, that God did not intend the effecting of this his design by mere power or prerogative-wise; I mean so as to thrust or force Christ for a head either upon men or angels, nor yet to propound or offer him unto either for a head, in his mere naturals, if I may so speak, unwrought or uncontrived, but as a person orderly and duly fitted and prepared for such a relation, partly by assuming the human nature, or a body of flesh, partly by suffering death, the death of the cross, in this body, and by his rising again from the dead.

For by suffering death, especially the death of the cross, in the human nature, 1. He "made peace," as the apostle expresseth it in the latter of the passages, *i. e.* he did that which was proper and effectual to "reconcile" men unto himself, and consequently unto angels also, who were at enmity with them, because of their enmity against God, yea, and unto and amongst themselves also. The death of Christ in the human nature was upon this account a proper means to "reconcile" men unto God, (*i. e.* to cause men to think holily and reverently of him, to love him, delight in him, &c., who by reason of the guilt of sin cleaving to them were apt before to hate him, as malefactors do their judge). This is because God, the sins of men being perfectly expiated and atoned thereby, freely offereth them, and upon their repentance assureth them, the pardon and forgiveness of their sins. See to this purpose, 2 Cor. v. 19, largely opened by us formerly in Chap. I. So then, the death of Christ being a proper means, as hath been shown, for the "reconciling" of men unto God, it must needs be a means semblably, and by way of consequence, of reconciling them unto angels also, who had no other quarrel against men but for their hatred and enmity against God. Now this reconciliation between men and angels, when actually effected, putteth them into a capacity of being fellow-members in one and the same body, and so of uniting mutually under one and the same head. For as "two cannot walk together except they be agreed," so neither can a plurality of persons kindly, and to the contentment either of themselves mutually, or of their head, incorporate into one and the same community, or walk in subjection under the same head. In which respect the reconcilement of men also to and amongst themselves, as, viz. of Jews unto Gentiles, and Gentiles unto Jews, who through diversity of religious opinions, and outward forms of worshipping God, were at enmity the one against the other, (and there is the same reason of other men distanced in affection whether upon the hike occasions or otherwise) was as necessary as that of men unto angels, in order to the accomplishment of the said great design of God. Now Christ by his death, and by the general promulgation of the gospel throughout the world, which dependeth thereon, and was a fruit thereof, both took away the ceremonial observations of the Jews, with their notions and opinions hanging thereon, as also the idolatrous and superstitious rites and observations of the Gentiles, with such conceits as they built hereon, which together made, as it were, a double "partition wall" between them.

Thus he was endeavouring, with a high hand of grace, to reduce both the one and the other of them into one and the same way of worshipping God, viz. that prescribed in the gospel, as also both to think and speak the same things concerning God, and so to cause the enmity and alienation of mind between them to cease, that by this means they might be prepared and fit to make as fellow-members one body. See the apostle's discourse on this point, Eph. ii. 11-16. The same, or the like course, he hath taken also by his death, and the publication of his gospel thereupon, to reconcile all other persons of mankind among themselves, viz, by calling them into communion in one Spirit, in one faith, in one hope, in one baptism, in one God, in one Saviour, &c., that so there might be no occasion of any such differences or distances between them, but that they might be every ways meet to associate in one and the same spiritual body, and live sweetly together under one and the same Head, Jesus Christ. This then is one consideration wherein the death of Christ was necessary for the bringing about the glorious projection of God, I mean the "gathering of all things, whether in heaven or on earth," under, or "into a head," the same head, Christ.

Secondly, this death of Christ did accommodate the design of God in another respect also, viz, as his voluntary subjection hereunto was an equitable foundation or consideration whereon God might, as he did, exalt him to the transcendent honour of that glorious headship and principality. "Who," saith the apostle, meaning because, "being in the form of God," an estate wherein "thought it not robbery," as he had no reason to do, "to be equal with God: But made himself of no reputation, and …humbled himself, and became obedient unto death, even the death of the cross." In consideration of this wonderful humiliation and condescension, saith he, "God also hath even highly exalted him, and given him a name above every name," &c., Phil. ii. 6-9, &c. Hence it is that the Scriptures still mention that glorious investiture of his which we speak of, headship over men and angels, as conferred upon him, not till after his rising again from the dead, "according to the working of his mighty power, Which he wrought in Christ, when he raised him from the dead, and set him at his own right hand in the heavenly places, Far above all principality, and power, and might, and dominion, and every name that is named, not only in this world, but also in that which is to come: And hath *put all things under his feet*, and *gave* him to be the *head* over all things to the church," &c. Eph. i. 19-22.

From these last words, "and hath put," &c., it is observable, that though God hath by a strong hand "subjected" all things whatsoever under and unto Christ, yet he hath "given him to his church," and to his church only, consisting of men and angels, Col. ii. 10, to be a head. From whence it follows, 1. That neither men nor angels are necessitated or compelled by God to accept of Christ for their head, or in the relation of a head, though they be necessitated and compelled, with all other creatures, to subject to his will and pleasure in the exercise of his power. For that which is properly given to a man he is not forced to accept or take, but receives it freely. If men or angels be unwilling, or; shall refuse to be or to continue as members of his church, as they are at liberty to do, (for their wills in this kind are not compelled or necessitated by God) they shall discharge themselves, though to their infinite loss and misery, from their relation or subjection unto Christ as their head. 2. That Christ stands in the relation of a head, and so performs the offices of a head only unto such, whether angels or men, who are members of that body which is called his church. So that though the nature and compass of God's great projection by Christ, and his death, was, as we heard the apostle expressing it, *anakephalaiōsasthai ta panta*, &c., to "head," or "rehead, all things" whatsoever, viz, that are headable, as we interpreted, "whether in heaven or on earth," (*i. e.* all men without exception, and all standing angels) yet it doth not follow from hence that all men without exception, ever will or shall be actually headed by Christ, and so be saved by him, because many will not accept of, or submit unto, those terms, upon which only the declared will and purpose of God is to interest his creature actually in so great and blessed a privilege.

For though God's purpose and design was to head all men without exception, with or in Christ, as well as all his good angels, (*i. e.* so to give and contrive his Christ, that all of both sorts of these creatures, without exception, might be put into a capacity and have opportunity of being brought into the relation of members under so glorious a head) yet it was no part of either, that any one particular, whether of the one kind of creature or of the other, should actually come into this relation otherwise than by a free and voluntary acceptation of Christ for their head. The Pharisees and lawyers rejected the counsel or projection of God (intended by him for good unto them) in baptism against themselves *(i. e.* to their own great damage and loss) in refusing to be baptised by John, Luke vii. 30. In like manner the greatest part of men voluntarily reject the great counsel of God for the reducing of them under so infinitely desirable a head, as the Lord

Christ is, to their own unconceivable misery, by refusing to subject themselves unto him in the relation of members.

Nor doth it follow from such a rejection of that counsel of God we speak of by men, that therefore this counsel of his, or his intention in it, should be frustrated or made void. As hath been said, the tenor, frame, or import of this counsel was, not that all men without exception should absolutely and without condition be actually invested with the benefit or blessing therein intended unto men; but that all such men without exception, and such only, who should *believe* in Christ, and freely submit unto him as a head, were they all without exception, or were they never so few or never so many, should actually partake of the said benefit. Therefore from neither of the two passages of Scripture cited towards the beginning of this chapter, can any such conclusion be evinced, that all men without exception shall first or last be saved by Christ; because it cannot be evinced from either of them, that all men without exception will believe in him first or last, without which there is no salvation supposed in either of them.

Neither of the places speak of any such reconcilement of all things unto God, which was actually to take place in any person of man, without the intervening of faith. Nor yet do either of them supposeth an absolute necessity, that all men or that any man should believe, so as to be actually and completely reconciled unto God, by means of the projected reconciliation here spoken of, is evident from this applicatory discourse of the apostle, subjoined to the latter of them: "And you that were sometime alienated, and enemies in your mind by wicked works, yet now hath he reconciled, In the body of his flesh through death, to present you holy and unblamable, and unreprovable in his sight: If ye continue in the faith grounded and settled, and be not moved away from the hope of the gospel." Col. i. 21-23. In this clause, "If ye continue in the faith grounded," &c., he clearly supposeth, 1. That their present reconciliation unto God was obtained by the intervention of their faith; and, 2. That the perfecting and completing of it in glory did depend upon their perseverance in this faith unto the end. Which latter clearly implieth, that notwithstanding that reconciliation which God made of all things to himself by Christ, yet they might very possibly not have been reconciled unto him or saved in the end. We observe from Doctor Prideaux, "That such conditional sayings, upon which admonitions, promises, or threatenings are built, do at least suppose something in possibility, however by virtue of their tenor and form they suppose nothing in being."

For those words, in the former of the said places, "That in the dispensation of the fulness of times he might gather together all," &c., they no ways import any such time yet to come, wherein all men should be actually gathered together in one, or be saved by Christ; but only that God made choice of the most convenient time, as, viz, when many ages and generations of the world had first passed, to bring his Son Jesus Christ into the world to suffer death, and so to raise him again from the dead, and upon this to anoint him within that precious oil of joy and gladness. By this he was consecrated into the great honour and dignity of that glorious headship we speak of, and whereof he stands possessed at this day. And that for this end, this intent on God's part is that all men without exception that should for the time to come be born, and live in the world, should by believing in him, and submitting to him, have the opportunity to enjoy him in the blessed relation of a glorious head, by whom they might be preserved and kept in peace and blessedness for ever.

If it be yet demanded, how God, in the latter of the said passages, may be said to reconcile all things (*i. e.* as well angels as men, as we formerly expounded) unto himself by Christ, when as between him and his elect angels there was no enmity or distance; I answer,

1. It is not necessary, upon the account of any expression here used by the apostle, to suppose that the angels were in particular reconciled unto God by Christ, but those words, "Whether they be things in earth or things in heaven," may be taken emphatically, and import only such a sense as this, that as God's project in Christ was for reconcilement, so was it so gloriously vast and comprehensive in this kind, that it compassed and took in not only the inferior world, the earth, and all things therein, but even the superior also, the heavens themselves, and all things herein, viz. as far as they were reconcilable, or stood in need of reconcilement unto him. So that in case there had been any distance, more or less, between God and his angels, the course which God had taken by his Christ was abundantly sufficient and proper to have healed it. When the same apostle exhorts Timothy in "Preaching the gospel, to be instant in season and out of season," he doth not suppose or imply that there is any time out of season, or unseasonable, for the work. But the expression is emphatical, and imports that he need not be curious or solicitous to distinguish between times and times for the preaching of the gospel, as if there were any danger that he might preach it unseasonably, or at any time or times that were not fitting for such a work: meaning, that all times were seasonable for it. The two

expressions, I conceive, do somewhat parallel one the other. Yet,

There is a sense, and this not altogether improper, wherein the angels themselves may be looked upon as reconcilable unto God, yea, and as actually reconciled unto him by Christ. For, 1. As Calvin upon the place well observes, "The obedience which the angels perform unto God, is not in every respect so complete or absolute as to satisfy God, without a pacifier coming between." And to this point he citeth that of Eliphaz in Job: "And his angels he charged with folly," Job iv. 18. He reads the words, "In his angels he will find iniquity," (agreeable whereunto is that other saying of the same author, "Yea, the heavens are not clean in his sight." Job xv. 15), which he is confident cannot be meant of the evil angels or devils. 2. He observeth further, and that with more unquestionableness of truth, that the angels being creatures are not out of all danger of falling, and so have need of confirmation by the grace of Christ. From whence he concludes that there is not so much righteousness in the angels themselves which sufficeth for their perfect and full conjunction with God, but that they also stand in need of a peace-maker by whose grace they may thoroughly and entirely cleave unto God. When he ascribeth their obnoxiousness to fall unto their being creatures, he plainly supposeth that they have no such confirmation by Christ, but that they are in a possibility, at least, of falling, this notwithstanding, inasmuch as they are creatures still, as well as they were before, or should have been without this confirmation by him, though it is true their condition is eminently bettered by that benefit of confirmation which they have by Christ, being hereby become out of danger, though not out of possibility of falling. But this by the way.

Whether the present righteousness or obedience of angels be every ways so absolute as to satisfy God without any further satisfaction from another or no, in case without that confirmation which now they have received by Christ, they had been liable to offend God and make him their enemy, but are by means thereof delivered from this danger, they may properly enough be said to be reconciled unto God by him. For as such a recipe, which is taken to prevent a disease may be as properly called physic as that which is used to recover a man out of sickness, in like manner I see no reason but that that gracious and friendly act by which a breach likely to happen between two is prevented, may be called an act of reconcilement as well as that whereby actual enmity between them is healed. Or,

3. Lastly, the best interpretation of the place may very probably be this, which leaveth no place for the difficulty or demand propounded, viz., to

expound these words, *eis auton*, not terminatively, or, to himself, but causally, for himself; which construction the preposition *eis*, with an accusative case, frequently admits. *Eis touto gar exēlthon*, "for therefore came I forth," Mark i. 38. So again, *egō eis touto gegennēmai kai eis touto elēlutha eis ton kosmon ina marturēsō tē alētheia*, *i.e.* "for this cause came I into the world, that I should bear witness unto the truth." John xviii. 37[3] Besides many the like. The words *eis auton*, thus understood, render the sense of the place clearly this: That God by the cross, or death of Christ, reconciled men on earth and angels in heaven (viz. between themselves, angels being enemies unto men because of their sinning against God, which cause of enmity being taken away by the death of Christ, the angels become friends to them, as we lately showed) not to himself, but for himself, *i. e.* for the effecting of his own gracious design in advancing Christ to be head unto both, being incorporated and united in the same body, which without the healing of the enmity or disaffection between them, could not have been, as we lately proved. This exposition differs not much from that of Augustin, in Cap. lxi. lxii. "Enchirid. ad Laurentium." By what hath been argued upon the two passages, it appears, I presume, sufficiently that there is nothing to be found in either of them from which the salvation of all men can with any colour of reason be concluded.

Much less can any such conclusion be regularly drawn from that of our Saviour, "Verily I say unto thee, Thou shalt by no means come out thence," meaning out of the prison of hell, "till thou hast paid the uttermost farthing," Matt. v. 26. For threatening men that they shall not come out of hell till they have paid, &c., he no ways supposeth that in process of time they will suffer to the uttermost of what they have deserved in punishment by sinning against God, and that then God will deliver them. The emphasis of the expression rather carrieth a sense of a contrary import, viz. that they must never expect to come out from this prison, inasmuch as they will never be able to pay in punishment what they owe to the just severity of God for sinning against him, especially after such a rate as they have done.

For they are only obdurate and finally impenitent sinners that are cast into this prison. A promise of receiving anything being made or implied upon the performance of an impossible condition is equivalent to a threatening that a man shall never receive it. When God expresseth himself thus to Jerusalem, "When thy sisters, Sodom and her daughters, shall return to their former estate, and Samaria and her daughters shall return to their former estate, then thou and thy daughters shall return to your former estate."

---

3. John xviii. 37. *Eiz, pro heneka,* propter, ob. Rob. Constant. Lexic. In verbo *Eis.* Vid. et lexicon Joh. Scapulae in eodem verbo.

Ezek. xvi. 55, he rather threateneth this city with a non-returning to her former estate than promiseth any such thing to her. So in case our Saviour should promise unto those that are cast into the prison of hell for the debt of their sins that when they have paid the full debt they shall be released and come forth, it would rather have the import and force of a threatening that they should never be released, than of a promise of releasement after any time whatsoever.

Yea, such promises as these are more emphatically interminative or threatening than plain and formal threatenings themselves. The reason is, because a plain and bare threatening only imports the purpose of him that threateneth to bring the evil mentioned in the threatening upon the person threatened. Whereas such promises as we speak of, wherein deliverance from evil is promised upon the performance of an impossible condition, the reason or cause why the evil threatened should be executed or inflicted upon the person threatened, commonly is implied. As when our Saviour promiseth, for the words in hand have a kind of promissory import, that they who are cast into hell shall come forth when they have paid the uttermost farthing, (*i. e.* discharged the full debt) he plainly intimates the reason or cause why they shall never come forth out of this prison to be because they will never make such payment. Now a threatening upon an equitable and just ground for the execution of it is much more piercing and convincing than when it is simply and without any mention or intimation of such a ground, denounced.

If it be demanded, but why should not men who are cast into hell for sin be able, in continuance of time, to pay the uttermost farthing, and so be delivered from thence, at last? Or, how can it stand with the justice or equity of God's proceedings against men for sin, to inflict everlasting punishments upon them for sinning only for a short time? I answer,

1. Sin, especially such sin for which men are sent to hell, being an injury or base affront, offered to an infinite majesty and goodness, the demerit of it must needs be great and indeed inconceivable. The reviling of a magistrate or the smiting of a prince in the face are misdemeanors of a higher nature, and justly more punishable by men than the like injuries done to meaner men. Yea, it is the sense of all men, that the greater the person is in dignity, especially when his worth and merit is every ways answerable, to whom an injury or indignity is offered, the greater proportionably is the offence committed, and obligatory to the greater punishment. When the standers-by said to Paul, "Revilest thou God's high priest?" Acts xxiii. 4,

they clearly intimated that the sin of reviling a person invested with so great a dignity as the high priesthood was signally demeritorious, and deserving exemplary punishment.

Now, then, allowing proportionably for the incomprehensible and endless dignity, sovereignty, majesty of God, all in conjunction with eminency of worth and goodness every ways commensurable to them, the injury which men offer unto him by voluntarily sinning against him and his laws, plainly appears to be of infinite demerit, and so binding over the sinner to an infinite punishment. Infinite, I mean, either intensively, in respect of the nature or quality; or extensively, in respect of the duration of it. Now, the creature not being capable of suffering punishment infinite in the former consideration, the just severity of God imposeth upon him that which is infinite in the latter. To speak or think slightly or lightly of the guilt or demerit of sin, or to look upon the punishment of hell fire as exceeding the proportion thereof, proceedeth either from a profound ignorance of the nature, majesty, infinite goodness and sweetness of God, or else from a profane neglect of an intense and due consideration of them.

2. The infinite purity of the Divine nature, and most perfect hatred of sin ruling and reigning therein, may well be conceived little less than to necessitate him, (a.) To the denunciation and threatening of that most severe punishment we speak of, for the restraint and prevention of it; and, (b.) Consequently, to the execution hereof, when the sinner shall despise his atonement, and neglect to wash himself in that fountain which he hath most graciously opened for sin and uncleanness, (*i. e.* for men to purify and wash themselves in, from the defilement of sin, and whatsoever polluteth) unto the world. In what degree the nature of a man abhorreth anything, and apprehendeth a contrariety in it, either to its being or well-being, he riseth proportionably in his care and use of means for the prevention of it. The devil, it seems, had made observation of this principle in men, when he said, "Skin for skin, (or rather, skin after skin,) yea, all that a man hath will he give for his life," Job ii. 4. Death being, as Bildad styleth, him, "the king of terrors," Job xviii. 14; *i. e.* a thing which men generally are more afraid of than anything, than all things in the world besides, engageth the generality of men proportionably to withstand his approaches, and to do the uttermost they are able to deliver themselves out of his hand. Now, that which death is to men, in point of abhorrency, sin is unto God. Therefore, it ought not to seem strange unto, or offend any man, that he should make the strongest and sharpest bridle he could for the restraint of it in the world.

Or consequently, that he should impose by law a penalty as deep and dreadful as the vengeance of eternal fire itself, upon the perpetrators of it. Any thing beneath this doth not answer the degree, or rather the degreeless infinity, of his hatred and abhorrency of sin.

3. The severity of that punishment of sin, which is now under consideration, will be found the more equitable and just, if we consider, on the one hand, how graciously and bountifully above measure God dealeth with men, in order to their escape and deliverance from it; and, on the other hand, how wilfully, how desperately, and with what senseless irrationality, men must go to work and act to bring themselves into the suffering of it.

(a.) God hath discovered unto men, as by a vision of the noonday, the great deformity, foulness, filthiness and most detestable abominableness of sin. The devil was never presented to any man's sight, mind, or imagination, in any such monstrous, uncouth, horrid, affrighting form or shape, as sin is exhibited to the judgments and consciences of men in the Scriptures.

(b.) He hath discovered likewise, upon the same terms, that most viperous, violent, that most pernicious and keen antipathy which sin carrieth in it against the peace, comfort, well-being, and sovereign blessedness of men. Poverty, shame, sickness, pains, tortures, and torments in the flesh, death, the grave, putrefaction, rottenness, &c., are but as the hummings of a gnat or bitings of a flea, of light and inconsiderable enmity to the comfort and happiness of men, in respect of that most enormous execrable, devouring, and confounding contrariety thereunto, which the word of God informeth the world to be in sin.

(c.) As concerning those accommodations to the nature of man, as in pleasures, profits, or contentments otherwise, by the promise whereof sin is wont to commend herself and her service to the children of men, and to draw them aside into folly, God hath undertaken and engaged himself, partly by promise, partly by oath, to confer the same, either formally or eminently, upon them, in ways of righteousness and of honour, if they will be persuaded to walk in them.

(d.) In case men, either through ignorance, in any degree hard to be overcome and expelled by coming to the knowledge of the truth, or through human frailty or incogitancy, shall be prevented with sin, or entangled in any sinful course, God hath, as it were, at the cost and charge of his Son Jesus Christ, in most bitter sorrows and sufferings, reared up a golden altar, I mean that of repentance, for them to flee unto, and to take hold of. This is from whence he hath most magnificently promised never to take, or pluck, any man to destroy him, how unrighteous, wicked, or unworthy soever his ways have been.

(e.) That law, by the observation and keeping whereof, men may, and shall, be free from sinning, and so from guilt contracted hereby, is, in all the respective branches and parts of it, "holy, and just, and good ;" holy, *i. e.* honourable to those that keep it. It requires nothing, no act of obedience from men which is any ways ignoble, servile, base, or reflecting disparagement upon them. Just, *i. e.* tempered, framed, and fitted to such principles which God hath planted in the natures of men, so that there is nothing commanded in it (the law) which unjustly crosseth or thwarteth any impression, disposition, or inclination, which is natural to them, or which God hath planted in them; or which requireth any other, any further strength, to perform it than what God either had actually conferred upon them, or is ready to confer, upon such an application of themselves unto him for the obtaining hereof, of which they are very capable. Lastly, the said law is, in all parts of it, good also, *i. e.* commodious and beneficial to the observers, according to that of David, "in keeping of them there is great reward," Psal. xix. 11. So sin, especially such sin or sins which, in the end, bring the vengeance of hell fire upon them, if men be not extremely careless, negligent, and slothful, may very well be prevented.

(f.) God hath plainly forewarned men of that eternal wrath and vengeance which he is determined to bring and execute upon all persons who shall be found finally impenitent. Whereby he hath taken a very gracious and effectual course, not only to bring sin, especially continuance in sin, out of credit and request with the hearts of men, but to make it as the shadow of death unto them, the dread, and first-born of abhorrings to their consciences and souls.

(g.) Unto all those, who shall be found obedient unto his laws, refraining ways of sin and of unrighteousness, he hath promised, and that upon such terms that men may very well come to be fully satisfied upon clear and evident grounds, of the reality and truth of these promises, the most magnificent, bountiful, and glorious reward of life and immortality, and all the desirable and great things of the world to come. By this he hath taken a like gracious and effectual course to exalt righteousness and sinlessness of life and conversation, in the hearts and souls and consciences of men.

(h.) To put himself into a capacity of making such promises as these, as also of performing and making them good, not men, and so generally of treating with them so graciously as now he doth, about the great things of their peace, he hath delivered up unto death, the most bitter and ignominious death of the cross, his only begotten Son, in whom his soul greatly delighted. Hereby he hath given all possible evidence and assurance unto men, within what height and ardency of affection and desire he seeketh their salvation and eternal happiness, how transcendently great his love, how tender above measure his compassions are towards them.

(i.) Lastly, over and besides all these gracious administrations and expressions of himself towards them, he vouchsafeth unto them the monitory, assisting, and strengthening presence of his infinite Spirit with them, and that upon such terms, that if they regard and comport with him in his first and lower motions, they shall have an advance and increase of such his presence, and be stirred up and strengthened mightily to oppose temptations unto sin, to walk in paths of righteousness, and generally to act in due and regular order, as to the escaping of the wrath and vengeance which is to come, so to the obtaining of that life and glory, which God hath promised to those that love him. Now the consideration of these particulars, within some others of like import, that may be added, maketh it fully evident that men have all the real engagements upon them as well as the most efficacious means vouchsafed unto them, that they are capable of, to refrain from sin, and to love and practise righteousness: in which regard the most severe punishment that can be inflicted upon them for a wilful obdurateness in ways of sin, is but equitable and just.

Lastly, concerning the pretended disproportion between the practice of sin, as being but for a short time, and the punishment of hell fire, continuing for ever, it hath been sufficiently atoned, and the seeming hardness thereof taken off by the premised considerations. The demerit of a sin, which may be suddenly, and in the twinkling of an eye, committed, may be such, and so enormous, as to deserve punishment of a long continuance. The act of murder is, or may be committed almost in an instant. Yet all men judge it but equitable that the murderer should have his life taken from him, which, in truth and strictness of consideration, is a perpetual punishment, being a perpetual deprivation of that, which is, or was most dear to the offender. And generally the law of retaliation, which requireth "an eye for an eye, a tooth for a tooth," &c., is, I suppose, judged by all men most reasonable and equal. And yet this law, in the ordinary process and execution of it, inflicteth punishments very disproportionable, in respect of continuance, to the time wherein or whilst, the transgression was in acting.

A man may in an instant of time, well nigh strike out the eye of another, and yet the loss of one of his own eyes, which according to the exigency of the law we speak of, he must suffer for such a misdemeanor, would be a punishment to him whilst he lives. When a labourer receives his hire, or wages, for his day's work, there is no proportion between the time of his labour and the time wherein or whilst he receiveth his wages. The proportion which in this case is, in equity, to be considered, is not between the time or continuance of the one and the other, but between the value or worth of the one and the other. A man may receive in the fortieth part of an hour, the full value of his twelve hours' labour. In like manner, the proportion which reason and equity requireth to be observed between sins and punishments, consisteth not in an equality of time between the committing of the one, and the inflicting or suffering of the other, but in an equality between the degrees of demerit in the one, and of suffering in the other. Now it hath been clearly proved, that such an equality as this is to be found between sin, which is practised or committed, but within a short space of time comparatively, and between the punishment of hell fire, though continuing forever. And let me here add this; that the shortness of the time, wherein men are and know themselves to be, in a capacity or possibility of sinning, knowing withal that their punishment for sinning will be sore and endless, is, in justness of account, rather an aggravation than extenuation of the demerit of their sinning.

For of the two, it is much more irrational and unworthy of men, knowingly and voluntarily to bring an eternity of most grievous punishment upon their own heads, by sinning for a short space only, than it would be to incur the same misery, upon the account of a larger time of sinning; as it is a point of greater folly and indiscretion, for a man to waste a fair estate, and to bring poverty or beggary like an armed man upon him, by the vain luxury, and excess of one day, or one hour only, than it would be to continue in a spending posture for ten or twenty years together, and to come to beggary at the last. The Holy Ghost in Scripture, frequently insinuates the irrationality of sinning, by the consideration of the short and inconsiderable continuance of the accommodations accruing unto men thereby. "Wilt thou," saith Solomon, "set thine eyes upon that which is not?" *i. e.* the being whereof is inconsiderable, and next to that which is not, or which hath no being at all for time short continuance of it, "For riches certainly make themselves wings; they fly away as an eagle towards heaven." Prov. xxiii. 5. Now every whit as certain it is, that the fruits or contentments which accrue unto men by other ways and means of sinning, are every whit as perishable, of as short and uncertain a continuance, as riches, which are the birth that covetousness travelleth with, and is pained to bring forth.

So that all particulars relating to the business in hand, being put to account, and truly summed up together, amount to this, that there is no unrighteousness, or hardiness in it at all, that God for the sins which men impenitently and with wilful obdurateness of heart commit within the short compass or space of mortality, should inflict a punishment of an everlasting continuance. Nor is this his severity against sin any whit the more obnoxious or disparageable, because he himself suffers no inconvenience thereby in the least, his estate in blessedness and glory being liable to no breach, or disaccommodation. This rather commends the equity of such his proceedings against sin and sinners, and clearly evinceth that what he doth in punishing the one and the other with that severity of punishment, which hath been oft mentioned, he doth not out of any spirit of revenge, properly so called, or as it is frequently found in men, nor out of any desire of self-reparations, but out of the most absolute and perfect righteousness, holiness, and purity of his nature, in conjunction with that most exquisite, sedate, and dispassionate knowledge which he hath of the just demerit of sin.

Whereas, in the explication of our doctrine, concerning Christ's dying for all men we signified that intentions, and so reality of intention, are not competible unto God, in all and every respect, wherein they are ascribed unto men: though we have sufficiently accounted for our sense and meaning herein formerly, yet we shall here, for the reader's satisfaction, briefly review that account, that so it may clearly appear, how and in what sense we affirm and hold, that God intended or intendeth the salvation of all men, in or by the death of Christ. The actions of men, and so of angels, and of any creature whatsoever, as well immanent as transient, inward as outward, not being really the same things with their respective natures, essences, or beings have their peculiar and appropriate forms really distinct from their said natures and beings, so that they may be actually separated from these, and yet these continue and remain.

As for example, David once had a purpose or intention to build God a house or temple. But upon a discovery made unto him by God, that his will was otherwise, and that not he, but his son Solomon should do it, his purpose and intentions that way expired, and had no longer a being. Yet David, after this purpose and intention of his were fallen, continued the same person, for nature and essence, which he was before. Now because that which we call an intent, or intention in created subjects, as men, has a peculiar nature or form, really distinct, as hath been said, from the subject and nature thereof, and names and words were at first imposed upon things, according to what men generally knew or apprehended to be in them, hence it is, that these words, "intent, intention," &c. properly, and in ordinary discourse between men, signify such an act of the mind or will of the reasonable creature, which is in his power as well to let fall and lay aside, as to conceive, or raise up within him; yea, and which falleth and ceaseth constantly and of course, when the thing intended is effected.

Therefore, in his strict and formal signification of the word, intentions are altogether inattributable unto God, inasmuch as all his acts and actings, in one kind or other, are divisim et conjunctim, jointly and severally, one and the same thing within his nature, essence, and being, as we have heretofore demonstratively proved, and that from the express principles and constant assertions of our adversaries themselves, as likewise from the doctrine concerning the nature of God, generally received amongst us, and, consequently, are not perishable, or liable to any expiration, fall, or change, upon any events, accomplishments, or effectings of things whatsoever, more than himself, or his simple essence and being. So that when with the Scriptures we ascribe intentions unto God, our meaning, with theirs also, is, that God, in and by that one great indesinent, unintermittable, inconceivable act of his, which is himself, and wherein he put forth himself from eternity, and by which he gave and gives being to all creatures, motions, and actings of creatures whatsoever successively, acteth and expresseth himself in order to the effecting or obtaining of such ends, or things as he is said to intend, after some such manner as men do, when they intend the effecting or procuring of what they project or desire. Therefore as men, when they intend such and such ends, are wont to levy and use means proper and likely, at least in their judgments, to effect and bring them to pass: in like manner God is said to intend such and such things, when he providentially acteth in due order towards, and with a sufficient proportion of strength in acting for the effecting and procurement of them. And thus, and in this sense, we desire to be understood, when we affirm and hold, that God intendeth the salvation of all men without exception, in and by the death of Christ; viz. that upon the account of Chist's death, he vouchsafeth a sufficiency of means unto all men (considered as men, and before their wilful sinning that most heinous and unpardonable sin) whereby to be saved. So if any particular person, man or woman, perish, or be not saved, the cause or reason hereof is not any want of sufficient means from God for their salvation, but their own voluntary neglect, or non-improvement of the means vouchsafed unto them in order thereunto. Yea, such a neglect they were no ways necessitated unto, neither by any decree of God, nor by any strength or subtilty of temptation from the devil, or from the world, nor yet by any weakness or strength of corruption in themselves, but might, all these notwithstanding, very well have prevented, and not have incurred the guilt or danger of it.

When, in the premised explication of our doctrine, we say that God did only antecedently intend the actual redemption and salvation of all men, in and by the death of Christ, and not consequently. Our meaning is, that he so far, and upon such terms, intended the salvation of all men, without exception as to vouchsafe unto them all sufficient grace and means for their salvation, not purposing or intending to interpose, by any providence of his, either positive or private, but that every man, without exception, may, or might so improve or use the grace and means vouchsafed unto them, as to obtain salvation thereby; this, with the ancient fathers Chrysostom and Damascene, I call, his willing or intending the salvation of all men, antecedently. Of this intention, or will of God, the apostle speaks plainly, 1 Tim. ii. 4, "Who will have all men to be saved, and to come unto the knowledge of the truth." But this antecedent intention of his notwithstanding, he may and doth intend and will likewise, that whosoever shall *not* use the said grace and means so graciously vouchsafed unto them to truly repent and believe, yea, and persevere, thus repenting and believing unto the end, should perish everlastingly.

So that, according to this latter, this consequent intention of his, he intendeth the salvation only of those who shall believe and persevere, believing unto the end (which is not a work), and the condemnation of all others: (we speak now of persons actually capable of faith and unbelief, not of infants, who admit of a peculiar consideration by themselves.) This, with the forementioned authors, I call his consequent will or intention. The former of these is not called his antecedent will or intention, either because it precedes the other in time or in eternity, or in worth or dignity, or the like. No precedency in any of these kinds, hath place amongst the decrees, wills, or intentions of God, which are all equally eternal, equally honourable and worthy of him. But the reason of this denomination is, because it is so ordered, and cometh to pass by Divine dispensation, that grace and means for the obtaining of salvation, are always in the first place vouchsafed unto men, before either salvation be actually conferred upon any man that believeth, or anything penal, I mean, spiritually penal, or any ways tending either to obduration or condemnation, be inflicted upon unbelievers, and much more before actual destruction is brought upon them.

So that the latter of the said two wills or intentions in God is therefore termed consequent, because he never acteth in order to or with any tendency towards the condemnation or destruction of men, but consequently to and after such gracious actings of his which were of a saving tendency and import unto them, these being resisted or rejected by them. This distinction of the intention or will of God, into antecedent and consequent, as it hath been now opened, is founded upon clearness and expressness of Scripture in sundry places. "O Jerusalem, Jerusalem, thou that killest the prophets, and stonest them which are sent unto thee, how often would I have gathered thy children together, even as a hen gathereth her chickens under her wings, and ye would not! Behold, your house is left unto you desolate. For I say unto you, Ye shall not see me henceforth, till ye shall say, Blessed is he that cometh in the name of the Lord." Matt. xxiii. 37-39.

The Lord Christ, by his prophets, word, Spirit, providences, and administrations of sundry kinds, first endeavoured, and sought with much tenderness and greatness of compassion, to put the Jews into an estate and condition of peace and safety, as well temporal as spiritual (viz. by attempting to bring them to repentance and to a holy and humble walking with their God). So that his intention, will, or desire of their peace and safety were antecedent, *i. e.* antecedently expressed or put in execution, to his intention or will concerning their destruction, which were not expressed or executed but upon and after those gracious applications of God unto them in order to their peace, and their rejection and contempt of them in those words, "and ye would not;" in which respect these may properly be termed consequent. The Scriptures abound with passages of this kind; I mean, which mention the gracious addressings of God unto men for their wealth and safety, as exhibited unto them in the first place, and his penal inflictions upon them afterwards, and not till their abuse or neglect of the said addressments of grace. See upon this account, Revel. ii. 21, 22; 2 Chron. xxxvi. 15-17; Isa. v. 2, 4, 5; Ezek. xvi. 6-8, &c. compared with verses 35-38, &c. (not to mention other places of like consideration, without number) all which are clear and pregnant for the justification of the said distinction of the will of God into antecedent and consequent, according to the premised explication. The antecedent will or intention of God is frequently in authors, and with good propriety, termed his primary or principal intention or will; the other, his secondary or less principal. That antecedent intention of his we speak of, is, in respect of the subject matter of it, or things intended, the exhibition of sufficient means for salvation, absolute and unsuspended upon the actings and movings of the creature. My meaning is, that a sufficiency of grace and means for the obtaining salvation is always, and without any respect or consideration had either of the merit or demerit, worthiness or unworthiness of men, vouchsafed unto them all by God.

That which I call his consequent will or intention in this kind, is in respect of the subject matter thereof or the things intended, viz. the collation of actual salvation, and so the infliction of actual condemnation or of spiritual judgments in order hereunto, suspended upon the behaviour of men: so that, for example, this intention or will of his notwithstanding, salvation is never conferred upon any man but upon his believing and continuance in believing unto the end. Nor should it be conferred upon any man, in case no man should be found so to believe. Nor is condemnation or destruction, or anything tending hereunto, inflicted upon any man but upon his neglect or abuse of the means of salvation exhibited unto him; nor should they ever be inflicted upon any man, in case no man were found neglective or abusive of the grace of God, in the means of salvation vouchsafed unto them. So that the consequent intention or will of God is of like nature and consideration with the politic laws of men, which either assign rewards to those that shall deserve well of the state where they live, in such or such a way, or decree the infliction of punishment upon malefactors in several kinds.

Neither of these laws suppose any absolute or positive necessity that there will be any either so deserving as to have right of claim to the rewards promised, or so wicked as to incur the punishments ordained by the said laws. So neither do the consequent intentions of God suppose a determinate necessity either that there will be any who shall have right to the great reward of salvation intended by him hereby unto those that shall believe perseveringly; or any that will incur damnation by final impenitency and unbelief, although, it is true, the Scriptures otherwise suppose and declare, 1. That there will be some saved, by believing unto the end. 2. That there will be many condemned for their final impenitency and unbelief. 3. Lastly, that all persons of mankind, without exception, will either believe unto salvation, or remain impenitent to condemnation. But as the said politic laws of men are not therefore useless or impolitic, because they suppose no absolute necessity, either that there will be men found to deserve the rewards proposed in the one, or to incur the penalties imposed by the other, inasmuch as the former serve to excite and strengthen men to do worthily. And it is very probable that some will accordingly be provoked to do worthily, by the rewards promised therein; and the latter are useful and proper to prevent the being of such persons in the state who are wont to practise such misdemeanors as are therein threatened: in like manner, though that consequent will or intention of God we speak of supposeth no necessity either that some will believe to salvation, or that any will remain unbelieving and impenitent to condemnation. Yet is it through the manifestation of it unto men, of singular benefit and blessing unto the world, because in the former part of it, by means of the great recompence of reward, salvation promised therein, it is of marvellous efficacy and force to quicken men to believe, yea, and to continue believing unto the end. In the latter part of it by means of the dreadful punishment threatened therein, it is of like efficacy to awaken men out of the deep sleep of impenitency and unbelief.

Nor do we all this while, in discoursing the antecedent and consequent intention or will of God, suppose that there are two wills or intentions in God, properly so called, (no, nor yet so much as one) much less that there are two contrary wills in him, the one unto the other. But intention and will are, as hath been already said, ascribed unto God in respect of his administrations or efficiencies, which have some kind of likeness with those actings which proceed from men, when they intend or will any thing by virtue of such their intendments. So to say that God willeth or intendeth one thing with one kind of will or intention, and another either contrary to it or differing from it, with another kind of will or intention, amounts to no more, truly interpreted, than to this, that some of his dispensations have a tendency towards the producing of such and such ends; and others, towards the producing of such and such other ends, either differing from them or contrary to them. Nor doth it follow from God's acting in order to differing, yea, or contrary ends, that he is therefore divided in himself, or inconsistent with himself; no more than it follows that he that mourns at one time and upon one occasion, and rejoiceth at another time and upon another occasion suitable to such a passion or expression, is inconsistent or any ways in contradiction to himself.

For a close of this chapter, I shall endeavour the assoiling of a special difficulty, at least as it seems to some, concerning the intentions of God. It hath been said, that God in Scripture is said to purpose, or intend a thing, when he affordeth means that are proper and sufficient to bring it to pass, especially if he commands them to be used accordingly, this being a dispensation of like consideration with the deportment of men, who are wont to provide a sufficiency of means, at least so apprehended by them, for the effecting of what they purpose or intend. Upon this explication of intentions in God, this question is moved, whether, according to the purport hereof, it may not be said that he intended the offering up of Isaac by death; because, 1. By his providence he furnished Abraham with all things sufficient and necessary hereunto. And, 2, gave an express command unto him, that he should offer him accordingly. Now if he did not intend the oblation we speak of, which by his prohibition of it by an angel before it was performed, and by means whereof it never came to be performed, he seemed not to have done, then cannot the said explication stand; nor are the intentions of God to be judged of by his vouchsafement of means proper for the production of an effect, no, not though he commands them to be used in order thereunto. To this I answer,

1. That the intention of God in commanding Abraham to offer up his son Isaac, having otherwise furnished him with means sufficient hereunto, was a thorough trial of Abraham's love and faith, not the actual offering up of Isaac by death. This is evident from Gen. xxii. 1, and Heb. xi. 17, &c., compared.

2. In order to the accomplishment of this his intention, he commands Abraham: "Take now thy son, thine only son Isaac, whom thou lovest, and get thee into the land of Moriah; and offer him there for a burnt offering," &c., Gen. xxii. 2. Therefore,

3. This command of God unto Abraham concerning the offering of his son, is none otherwise, nor in any *other* sense, to be understood as directed by God unto him, as Abraham's obedience or disobedience to it was, or might be a sufficient trial either of the soundness or unsoundness of his faith and love towards God. So then,

4. The soundness and sincerity of Abraham's faith and love, being sufficiently tried and discovered by a discovery of his readiness and willingness to obey the said command of God, and to offer up his son, and this discovery being sufficiently made by that which Abraham did towards the offering up of his son by death, though he was not actually thus offered up by him, it roundly follows, that the meaning of the command given unto Abraham in the case in hand, was not that he should actually offer up his son by death, but that he should proceed so far towards the offering him up

in that manner, until his willingness thereunto were sufficiently manifested, and God would take him off, and stay his hand from acting further herein. Such constructions or forms of speech wherein the consequent is put for the antecedent, and so, again, where the end or effect is named to signify the means proper for the procurement of either, are familiar and frequent with the Holy Ghost in the Scriptures. An instance of the former we have, Psa. xxii. 26, in this clause, "They shall praise the Lord that seek him," *i. e.* they shall be graciously entreated by him, and receive good from him, and hereby be occasioned or provoked to praise him. So Deut. x. 17 the phrase, "taketh reward" describes payment for doing unjustly, which commonly follows such payment. So again, to "make the son of the beloved first-born," signifies the conferring of the inheritance, or a double portion, upon a person, this being a usual consequence of primogeniture to carry the inheritance, or a double portion, Deut. xxi. 16. So to "offenders" or "criminals" signifies to be guilty, or liable to punishment, 1 Kings i. 21; guilt, or obnoxiousness unto punishment, being a consequence of wickedness. To pass by many other places of like construction, instances of the latter are frequent also. Thus, "salvation" is put for the Scriptures, or knowledge of God, as being the means of salvation, John iv. 22, "For salvation is of the Jews." Upon a like account, Peter exhorteth men to "account that the long-suffering of our Lord is salvation," *i. e.* a means of salvation, 2 Pet. iii. 15.

See more places of like character, Rom. xiv. 20; 1 Tim. iv. 16; Deut. xiii. 5, according to the original, &c. According to either of these constructions, the command of God unto Abraham to offer up his son Isaac for a burnt-offering, may import only a doing of such things which were precedaneously necessary to an "offering him up" after such a manner, as, viz, to provide wood and fire for the burning of him, a knife for the slaying of him, a cord, or the like, wherewith to bind him, an altar on which to lay him, and so again, actually to lay the wood provided upon the altar, for the burning of him, actually to bind him, to take the knife into his hand, to stretch forth his hand with the knife in it with an intent to slay him. All these things, with the like, being requisite to the actual offering up of Isaac by death, might well be signified, and doubtless were signified, yea, and were all that was signified or meant by that command of God, so oft mentioned, unto Abraham, concerning the offering up his son. Therefore,

5. Look what God commanded Abraham to do about the offering up of his son, that he really intended he should do, yea, and Abraham did it accordingly. He commanded Abraham to offer up his son; and in such a

sense as he commanded, Abraham obeyed, the Scripture testifying thus of him, in these words, "By faith Abraham, when he was tried, offered up Isaac: and he that had received the promises offered up his only begotten son." Heb. xi.17.Therefore certainly God commanded Abraham no other kind of offering up of Isaac than that which Abraham performed, and what himself really intended that he should perform. Whether Abraham at first understood the command of God in such a sense as that wherein we have now interpreted it, is not material. By that inhibition which was served upon him by the angel, to surcease all further proceedings in and about the offering up of his son by death, before he was thus offered, he clearly enough understood that to have been the sense and mind of God in the said command, which we have asserted. So that,

6. Lastly, it is a clear case, that the explication and account, given formerly in this treatise, concerning the intentions of God, or rather concerning the ground and reason why intentions are attributed unto him, is no ways encumbered or disabled by the instance of God's command given unto Abraham concerning the offering up of Isaac, notwithstanding Isaac's non-oblation by death. There is nothing in this example to prove that God doth at any time vouchsafe means competent and proper for the bringing of any thing to pass, especially when he commands that these means be used accordingly, but that he truly and really intends, as he is capable of intending any thing, the coming to pass thereof.

Nor can it here, with any face of reason, be replied, that, by such a construction as we have put upon the words of God in his command unto Abraham concerning the offering up of his son, when he vouchsafeth means of salvation unto men, and commandeth them to use them accordingly, it cannot be concluded from thence, that, therefore, he really intendeth the salvation of men, but only that they should use the said means to obtain salvation. This is because, though God, in Abraham's case, did, in his intentions, separate the means of offering up Isaac from the actual oblation of him, this not being the end of his command given unto him, as was said,—yet he did not separate between the said means and that which was his true end in the command, which was the trial of Abraham's faith. It was also for the effecting whereof, the said command, and all that which was meant thereby, and was as natural and proper a means as it was for the actual oblation of Isaac by death.

In like manner, when he vouchsafeth means of salvation unto men, and commandeth the use of them accordingly, he cannot be supposed to divide or separate, in his intentions, between the use of these means and their proper end, salvation.There being no other end proper to be effected by the use of the means of salvation but salvation itself, or, at least, none but in conjunction with salvation. And certain it is, that there is no man of wisdom who intends the use of such means, which are determinately appropriate to the production of one end, and no more; or, however, of no more, but only by and through the production of that one, but that he intends the production of this end peculiarly. How God may intend the salvation of men, and yet men never come to be saved, may be yet further opened upon occasion.

CHAPTER VII
Exhibiteth several grounds and reasons whereby the universality of redemption by Christ, or Christ's dying for all men, without exception, is demonstratively evicted.

SCRIPTURE *authority* is greater than all demonstration otherwise, for the eviction and confirmation of any doctrine or tenet in matter of religion as simply and in itself. So also it is with those whose faith mainly or solely beareth upon the foundations of the Scriptures, yet have arguments and grounds of reason, if they be pregnant and clear, a very acceptable influence upon the judgments and consciences of men, when they are levied and drawn up in the nature of seconds or assistants to the Scriptures, and plead the same cause with them.

For when a doctrine or opinion is held forth as the mind of God in the Scriptures, and Scripture authority produced and insisted upon, either singly or in consort, for the proof thereof; in case this doctrine shall be found to have a fair and clear consistence with the unquestionable principles of sound reason, there remains no place in the consciences of men for fear or jealousy, concerning the truth thereof. God himself being the author of those noble endowments in men, reason and understanding, must needs be conceived the author also of whatsoever truly consorteth with them. But in case the authority of the Scripture shall be urged and pressed upon the consciences of men in defence of such a doctrine, which grates or bears hard upon the common and clear dictates of that light which God hath planted in the souls of men, it is impossible but that a considering man should much question such a sense or interpretation which is put upon the Scriptures in such a case.

The premises considered, I judge it a matter of signal consequence in order for securing the judgments and consciences of men about the truth of the main doctrine maintained in this discourse, to demonstrate the perfect and clear consistency of it with grounds of reason, though substantially proved already from the Scriptures. Yea, and satisfactorily also, I trust, unto those who so understand the Scriptures as not to make either the wisdom or justice of God sufferer by them. My reasons, then, for the universality of redemption by Jesus Christ, in reference unto men, are these following:

If Christ died not for all men without exception, in the sense formerly declared, then is that great covenant of grace, which God hath made with the world, and ratified in his blood, made with unknown persons, and such who are no ways expressed in this covenant, neither by name nor by any other character or qualification by which they may, at least for a long time, be known or distinguished. But this great covenant we speak of is not struck, or made with unknown persons. I mean with such who, for a long time, if ever, neither can tell themselves whether they be the covenanted or no, nor are capable of any reasonable information hereof by others: Therefore, Christ died for all men, without exception.

The reason of the former proposition, and the consequence therein, is this: because the elect, so called in the common notion of election, with whom only this covenant of grace is pretended to be made, and for whom only Christ is supposed to have died, are persons no ways distinguishable from others, neither *before* at all, and often after their regeneration and conversion unto God. That they are not at all discernible from others, before conversion, is evident from several places. "For we ourselves," saith the apostle to Titus, meaning, who are now so much altered and changed by a work of grace and regeneration in us, "were sometimes," viz., before our conversion, "foolish, disobedient, deceived, serving divers lusts and pleasures, living in malice and envy, hateful, and hating one another," Tit. iii. 3. Certainly, these are no appropriate or distinguishing characters of the elect, but such, which do evidently prove the elect, in the common signification of the word, before conversion, and the non-elect, to be indiscernible the one from the other, as well by themselves as by others. We shall not need to cite any more places for the proof of this. You may peruse the second chapter of the epistle to the Ephesians at your leisure, which speaks, almost throughout, to this point. Again,

That after regeneration itself, the elect, so called, are often indiscernible, either to themselves or others, from hypocrites and those that shall perish, is no less evident neither. First, that they are not at all discernible from hypocrites, in respect of others, at least for a time, and many times for a long time, will, I suppose, readily be acknowledged. The apostles did not know Judas to be a hypocrite or a traitor, no not after long acquaintance and converse with him; for then they would not have suspected every man himself, when Christ told them that there was one of them that would betray him.

Nor did Philip know Simon Magus to be "in the gall of bitterness and in the bond of iniquity," Acts viii. 23, when he baptized him; nor Paul, Demas, whilst he made him his companion. And how should others infallibly know who are elect and shall be saved, when, as the Lord Christ saith, that "many that are first shall be last;" *i. e.* many that for a time march in the head of profession, and make a show of more zeal and forwardness in the ways of religion than other men, yet wheel off again to the world, and become like salt which "have lost his savor," and "is thenceforth good for nothing, but to be cast out, and to be trodden under foot by men." Matt. v. 13.

Again, that such persons as we speak of, the elect, I mean such who shall actually be saved, at least a great part of them, are not able always, no, nor ordinarily, after the work of regeneration in them, to distinguish or discern themselves from those who shall perish, is abundantly confirmed, partly by the continual fears, jealousies, and doubtings of their spiritual condition, wherewith many of them are exercised even to their dying day. This is partly also by those great and good opinions which they have of others, as being worthy and sound Christians, who yet afterward are like "the dog" who "is turned to his own vomit again; and the sow that was washed to her wallowing in the mire." 2 Pet. ii. 22. So that the truth of the major proposition is unquestionable; viz. that if Christ died not for all men without exception, but for the elect only, then is the covenant of grace in his blood made with unknown persons, such who neither can certainly say of themselves (in this life), nor any for them, that they are the covenanted ones.

As to the minor proposition, the truth hereof is evident also. The tenor of it was this: That the covenant of grace is not struck or made with unknown persons, or such concerning whom it is either impossible or next to impossibility to know plainly and certainly who they are. It is contrary to the nature and intent of a covenant, especially of a covenant of grace, that the parties interested in it, and whom the covenant concerns and relates unto, should not be discernible or known from all other persons whatsoever, or that it should minister any occasion of controversy or debate who these persons should be. Look into all covenants that are drawn up and made between man and man, and you shall find, for the most part, the names of the covenanted as well as of the covenanters expressed in them. Or, howsoever, if all their names be not expressed, yet are they sufficiently declared otherwise, as viz. by such and such characters, relations, or the like, whereby they may be as plainly known as if their names themselves were mentioned. As for example: When one man covenanteth with another who is named in the covenant, and with his heirs, executors, administrators, or assigns, these words of relation do as plainly and clearly point out the persons intended and meant as if they had been expressed by their names.

Yea, doubtless, the reason why these persons are usually expressed by such terms of relation, and not by their names, in covenants between men, is, because neither of the covenanting parties, at the time of the making of the covenant, knew or were able to call them by their names. This cannot be said of God in his covenant of grace, inasmuch as all men's names were known unto him when he made this covenant with the world. Look into the Scriptures; in all the covenants specified and recorded here, you will find the persons covenanted with either named or else so described that there is no place left for any doubt who they be. When Caleb made this covenant, proffered these terms: "He that smiteth Kir- jath-se-pher, and taketh it, to him will I give Achsah my daughter to wife," Josh. xv. 16, it is and was easy enough to conceive who they were with whom this covenant was made, viz. all the people or men that were with him, expressed in that pronoun "he," which in the dialect of the Scripture hath the signification and force of the universal particle "whosoever," as, "He that believeth," *i. e.* whosoever believeth, "shall be saved," Mark xvi. 16. So in that of our Saviour, John vi. 37, "Him that cometh unto me," *i. e.* whosoever cometh unto me, "I will in no wise cast out;" with many the like.

A like covenant or offer of grace it seems that Saul also made upon occasion of the affront which the giant-like Philistine, Goliah, put upon him and his whole army: "And it shall be that the man who killeth him, the king will enrich him with great riches, and will give him his daughter, and make his father's house free in Israel," 1 Sam. xvii. 25. It is evident, likewise, in this covenant, who the persons were that were covenanted with upon the terms mentioned, viz. all the persons, without exception, in Saul's army. I choose rather to give instance in such covenants as these, because they are of the same form and tenor, mutatis mutandis, as lawyers use to say, with the covenant of grace itself, which is founded in the blood of Jesus Christ. But the like is every whit as apparent in other covenants also, as you may please to consider at your leisure.

If we weigh the end or intent of a covenant, we shall clearly find that this requires a determinate and clear knowledge or a distinct designation of the parties covenanting or covenanted with. The principal and main end or intent of a covenant, is, to insure unto the party or parties covenanted with such and such terms or things as are specified in the covenant according to the tenor and conditions thereof. The end of a covenant is not the simple collation or donation of any thing to a person, one or more, but the securing or insuring persons that such and such things shall be given unto them, or conferred upon them, upon the performance of such and such conditions as the covenant specifies. And this, clearly and without controversy, is the end (I mean, the proper and immediate end, for there are several ends besides this) of the covenant of grace established in the blood of Christ, viz. to give assurance unto the sons and daughters of men, that upon their faith and repentance, and their perseverance in both unto the end, they shall have salvation and eternal life conferred upon them.

If so be a man hath an absolute, unlimited, and right-out purpose or intent to confer such or such things upon men, a covenant is but an unsavoury and superfluous thing; because a man may confer or give what he pleaseth to another without it. So if God had a simple and absolute intention to confer the great things of heaven upon men, I mean, without the performance of such and such articles or conditions as we speak of, the making of a covenant with them had been in vain. Therefore, the proper end of a covenant is to assure or to secure those that are covenanted with, that upon the performance of the articles of the covenant, the good things mentioned therein, if it be a covenant of good things, shall be exhibited and given unto them. Now, then, this being the end of a covenant, if the persons interested and concerned in it, or covenanted with, should not be known who they are, they cannot partake of this end, nor be any whit the better or more secure in their minds touching the enjoyment of the good things mentioned in the covenant upon any performance whatsoever. This is because the good things mentioned in a covenant cannot be claimed or expected by any but only by the persons covenanted with, though they should perform the terms or conditions specified in the covenant tens times over. "For if the trumpet," saith the apostle, "give an uncertain sound, who shall prepare himself to the battle?" 1 Cor. xiv. 8.

In like manner, if the covenant of grace speaks unto persons unknown both to themselves and others, and holds forth life and salvation only unto such, both men and women, as no man can say or tell who they be, how shall any man or woman be excited, provoked, or engaged, either by the tender of the covenant unto them, or by the great and excellent things therein promised conditionally, to "take hold of the covenant," as the Scripture speaketh, *i. e.* to perform conditions therein required?

If it be said, yes, the covenant is to be preached, and tendered unto all, without exception of any; and assurance is therein given unto all, that upon performance of what is there required, the good things there promised shall be given unto them. So that there is ground and encouragement enough howsoever, for every man and woman without exception to believe. To this I answer,

It is true, the covenant is to be preached and tendered unto all, without exception; and there is ground and encouragement enough for every man without exception to believe. But both these clearly suppose, that the covenant is made with all men, without exception of any; and consequently that the death or blood of Christ, which is the ground-work and foundation of this covenant, extendeth unto all. No covenant offereth anything, insureth anything, upon what terms soever, but only unto those that are covenanted with and comprehended in the covenant. When a man covenanteth with such or such a workman, to give him so much or so much, as suppose five or ten shillings by the day, this covenant doth not bind him to give the like wages to another. What is the reason why the covenant of grace, or the gospel, doth not offer or insure grace and salvation to the devils, as well as to all manner of men whatsoever upon their believing? Doubtless, because the devils are not within the number of the covenanted ones, nor of those unto whom grace and mercy were intended upon the terms of the gospel. And this because the death of Christ, which is the ground of the covenant, doth not in the atoning virtue of it reach unto them; the sphere of whose activity (in this kind) is limited and bounded by the will and pleasure of God.

And certainly, if reprobates (so called amongst men) I mean such who in time perish everlastingly, had no more interest than the devils have in the death of Christ, there was no more ground or reason why the covenant, or the grace thereof, should be more preached unto them, than to the devils. Nay, there were less reasons of the two, why it should be preached unto them, than why it should be preached to the devils, (at least according to the principles of that opinion which we oppose) because, if preached to the devils, though it did them no good, it would do them no harm, it would not increase their condemnation; whereas the preaching it to such men as we speak of, can only increase their misery and torment. This for our first argument. If Christ died not for all, then is the covenant in his blood made but with some men, and these altogether unknown even to themselves; which (as hath been shown) is contrary to the nature, end, and scope of a covenant.

I shall not trouble the reader with that impertinent objection, and uncouth notion, of Christ's being the only person with whom the covenant is made. What other covenant soever may be found to have been made by God with Christ, certainly that covenant we speak of, viz. wherein remission of sins, and deliverance from the wrath to come, are promised upon repentance and believing in Christ, was not made with Christ himself. God never said unto Christ, Repent and believe, and thou shalt have thy sins forgiven, and be saved. Therefore the covenant made with Christ, if any such thing be or were, is altogether irrelative to our present argument. Nor doth that of the apostle, Gal. iii. 16, prove that Christ, in a personal consideration, is the only person, or, indeed, any person at all, with whom the evangelical covenant is made. The tenor of the place is this: "Now to Abraham and his seed were the promises made. He saith not, and to seeds, as of many: but as of one, And to thy seed, which is Christ." First, it is evident from this place, that Christ is not the only person to whom the promises here spoken of are made; because they are expressly said to be made to Abraham, as well as to Christ. "Now to Abraham and his seed were the promises made," &c. Therefore, the word *Christ* (in the latter clause) is to be taken metonymically, for those who spiritually descend from him, and are born of him by faith; in such a sense as the words Jacob and Israel frequently signify Jacob's seed or posterity, *i. e.* the whole nations of the Jews, in the Old Testament. In such a sense the same word also, Christ, is to be understood, 1 Cor. xii. 12. "For as the body is one, and hath many members, and all the members of that one body being many, are one body: so also is Christ:" *i. e.* so also is it with believers, who in respect of their spiritual being, are from Christ; meaning, that though they be many personally distinct, yet they make one spiritual or mystical body with Christ their head. Now when the promises are said to be made to Abraham, and his spiritual seed, believers; the meaning is not, as if they were so, or upon such terms made to them, that none but they had any right to receive them, or believe them: for then it must follow, that men must or ought to be believers before they receive or believe the promises, which is impossible. But the promises are made to Abraham and his seed, *i. e.* the great inheritance of life and salvation promised by God, is promised as touching the actual exhibition or collation of it unto believers only, such as Abraham himself was, and such as those who desire to be accounted his seed must be.

But this supposeth not but that the said promises are, in this sense, made to Adam and his seed, *i. e.* to all mankind, viz. that all and every person of mankind, as well as Adam, yea, or Abraham himself, have a right to believe them, so that in case they should believe them, they should do no unjust or unrighteous thing. Nay, they have not only a right, but a grand necessity likewise lying upon them to believe them, as well in respect of the commandment of God, who commands no unjust or unrighteous thing, as of their own eternal peace and safety, whereof they will certainly make shipwreck, unless they do believe them.

A second demonstration, whereby Christ's dying for all men is evinced, is this: "If Christ died not for all men without exception, then he died for the elect only: But he died not for the elect only: therefore for all men without exception." I presume the former proposition will be granted without further proof; because they who deny that Christ died for all, generally suppose and grant that he died for some, and by name for the elect, and, indeed, for these only. So that if it be proved, either that he died not for the elect at all, or not for the elect only, then, according to their own principles and grounds, it follows that he died for all. Now then, that he died not for the elect, and much more not for the elect only, which was the minor proposition, appears thus. If the state and condition of the elect were such, that Christ needed no more to die for them, than he needed to die for the holy and elect angels, then Christ died not for these, much less for these only. But the state and condition of the elect was such, that there was no more need that Christ should die for them, than for the elect angels: Ergo.

In this argument, I reason, I confess, upon my adversaries' grounds, not mine own, concerning elections: but howsoever, such a process of arguing as this is very serviceable for the confirmation of a truth in opposition to an error; and the apostle Paul himself sometimes useth it in a like case, as 1 Cor. xv. 29. The major proposition in this last argument, standeth upon this ground, that there was no need that Christ should die for the holy or elect angels. I suppose this will not be denied or doubted of by any; but however it is clearly enough asserted by the apostle, in that saying of his, Gal. ii. 21, "I do not frustrate the grace of God; for if righteousness" *i. e.* justification, "come by the law, then Christ is dead in vain," *i. e.* without any necessity or reasonable cause moving thereunto. But now, if there had been a necessity that Christ should have died for the elect angels, it would not have followed that his death had been in vain, though men might have been justified by the law. Therefore if there were no more reason, no more need why Christ should die for the elect of men, than for the elect angels, certainly he did not die for them, much less for them only.

But now that there was no more reason, no more need why Christ should die for the elect of men, than for the elect angels, which was the substance of the minor proposition, appears by this double consideration: 1. Because God loved the elect, I mean the elect of men, and that as such, as elect, without any consideration had of Christ's dying for them, with as great a love as he did the elect angels yea, with as great as it was possible for him to bear to them. 2. Because salvation and eternal glory were decreed and adjudged to them, and consequently were made truly and properly theirs, in and by God's purpose in electing them. God, in electing them without any consideration or respect, had unto Jesus Christ's dying or to die, for them, or unto their believing in him, did irreversibly appropriate and consign over unto them eternal life. From these two grounds it follows undeniably, that there was no more need for Christ to die for the elect of mankind, than for the elect angels. For,

(a.) If God loved the elect of men with as great a love as he loves the elect angels, or as he is capable of bearing towards them, what occasion, what necessity was there that Christ should die for the one more than for the other? The same love affords the same favours, the same privileges, without any mediation to equalize it in this kind. If God loved the elect of men as much, as intensely as the holy angels, considered only as elect, or before their election, —for this is the notion and sense of our adversaries in the point in hand,— then the offence and distance occasioned by sin between him and them was wholly ceased and taken out of the way, before the blood of the covenant was sprinkled on them, before the atonement came at them; as the "Hebrew women," in the story, "are delivered ere the midwives come in unto them," Exod. i. 19. And if so, if the offence and distance caused between God and his elect, by means of sin, was swallowed up in the love of election, so that he loved them now, considered only as elect, or to be elected, as much as he did or could do upon their actual ingrafting into Christ and participation of his death, to what purpose should Christ die for them? Or what profit is there in the blood of Christ as to them? God thought every whit as well of them, loved them as much, intended to do as much for them, yea, irreversibly decreed, adjudged as great things unto them before and without all consideration had of the death of Christ, as he did or could do upon the consideration of it.

(b.) God, out of his love of election, as the doctrine of election is commonly taught and received amongst us, did in the very act or decree of his election, freely, and of his mere good will and pleasure, irrevocably assign, adjudge, make over, and give, to his elect, justification, salvation, glorification, and what not in this kind? And if so, Christ could not die to purchase or procure these things for them; because they were truly, properly, and by right of free donation, theirs before. It were ridiculous for any friend of mine to go and lay down a great sum of money to purchase or procure that on my behalf, which I have already assured unto me by the free and stable and irrevocable gift and donation of him that hath a full right and power to give it unto me. Therefore, whereas many amongst us cry out of Socinianism as a most dangerous heresy, and the great abomination of their souls, the truth is, that they themselves teach and hold as rank and right down Socinianism in their opinion about election, as the greatest Socianians themselves can do. For what is the master-vein in the body of this heresy, but to deny that Christ truly satisfied or made any atonement for sin, and that upon this ground, because God freely and of his mere grace gives forgiveness of sins unto men, without any satisfaction? And how little doth this differ from that doctrine of election, which passeth for current amongst us; teaching, that forgiveness of sins, and all the great things depending hereon, are assigned and decreed unto men in their election, without any consideration had of Christ's dying for them, or their believing in him?

If it be there said, that they who hold election in the most absolute and peremptory way, do not say or hold that God intends actually to confer remission of sins, or eternal life, upon the elect, otherwise than for and through the satisfaction made by Christ for them in his death, though they hold that he intends, without any respect had to the consideration of Christ's death, actually to confer them upon them. They exclude the satisfaction of Christ from having anything to do in God's purpose of election, not from having anything to do in the execution of this his purpose; here they acknowledge it to have much to do, to be upon the matter all in all. To this we answer,

That this distinction, or explication of the opinion, doth no ways relieve it, but rather burdens it more and more. For,

1. Certain it is, that God doth not purpose or project one way, and act or execute in another: but his executions do exactly answer the tenor, purport, and form of his purposes or intentions. Men who are subject to oversights, and consequently to repentance, may, and many times do, vary from their model or platform, when they come to action, because some better thing, it may be, hath come in their way, than they thought upon in the first pro-

jection of their work. But nothing can come in God's way either more satisfactory, or better pleasing unto him, than what was present with him in the first contrivance or projection of his affairs. Therefore, if, in point of execution, he actually confers remission of sins and salvation upon men, because of and with respect unto the death and satisfaction of Christ, it is a certain sign that he purposed this collation of them in his purpose of election, upon no other terms. And consequently that in God's very purpose of electing men unto salvation, he had respect unto the death of Christ, yea, and to their ingrafting into him by believing; and that he never purposed salvation unto any, without interesting the death of Christ in his intentions in this kind, as well as in his executions of what he thus intends.

If God might intend and purpose salvation unto men, without the consideration of the death of Christ, certainly he may as well actually confer and give this salvation without any respect had thereunto. For this is a general and plain rule, that what a man may lawfully will or intend to do, without such or such a consideration, he may as lawfully act or do it without this consideration. For there is every whit as much required to justify a man in his will or purpose of doing a thing, as to justify him in his act or deed according to this will. Certainly, that which a man may lawfully will or purpose, he may lawfully do. In like manner, if God might lawfully—I mean, with the consistence of his wisdom and justice—purpose, will, or decree forgiveness of sins and salvation unto men, without considering them as believers in Christ, he may as well actually confer these things upon them without any such consideration. If so, the death of Christ is no ways necessary either to justify or commend either the justice or the wisdom of God in the actual justification or salvation of men. So that evident it is, that the doctrine of election, as it is ordinarily, entertained amongst us, doth abrogate the grace of God in Christ, and makes his death to be in vain. But the Scripture teacheth this doctrine upon other terms, and maketh Christ, *i. e.* the consideration of Christ, and of faith in him, the foundation of election, and that upon which God raised, as it were, and built it. "Blessed be the God and Father of our Lord Jesus Christ," saith the apostle, "who hath blessed us with all spiritual blessings in heavenly places in Christ. According as he hath chosen us in him before the foundation of the world, that we should be holy," &c. Eph. i. 3, 4. Observe these words, "According as he hath chosen us in him." Here are two things very considerable as to our purpose, in these words. The first lies in that word, *kathōs*, "according as," or, even as. "Who hath blessed us," *i. e.* actually and de facto blessed us "with all spiritual blessings in heavenly places in Christ, according as," or, even as "he hath chosen us."

This clearly shows that God's actings, his actual and present dispensations, are adequately and exactly conformable unto his purposes or projections. God, saith the apostle to them, in effect, in all that he hath done for us by the gospel, and by Christ, as in the enlightening of us, in sanctifying of us, in justifying of us, in comforting of us, &c., hath but acted that which he had modelled and formed out for us in his purpose, or counsel of election, before the world began. The second thing to be observed in the words, is, that God is here said to have "chosen us in him," *i. e.* in Christ, "before the foundation of the world." How, or in what sense, is God here said to have elected or "chosen us in Christ?" First, I suppose the apostle here speaks, not of the act, but of the purpose or decree of election or choosing. So the sense of the words, "according as he hath chosen us in him, before the foundation of the world," is this: according to that model, platform, or purpose of election (in which whoever believes will be saved), which upon the happy advantage or opportunity he had of his Christ, and that most gracious and wise contrivance of him in order to such a purpose which was before him, he framed and made within himself from the days of eternity, or before the "foundation of the world."

The purposes or intentions of God concerning such and such acts or dispensations, are very usually in Scripture expressed by the names of the acts or dispensations themselves, as likewise the purposes or intentions of men are after the same manner. Thus, Rom. viii. 30, God is said to have glorified those whom he intends or hath decreed to glorify. Thus, also, 2 Tim. i. 9, and again, Tit. iii. 5, he is said to have saved those apart from their works, but only under his purpose of saving them, to omit many the like. So in the Scripture in hand, he is said to have "chosen us before the foundation of the world:" because he purposed or decreed, before the foundation of the world, to choose us. Well, but what was the nature or tenor of this purpose or decree of his concerning our election? Or how, and in what sense is it said to have been in Christ, as the apostle here asserts it to have been? According to the most usual and proper signification of the preposition *en*, in, (in such a construction) that is said to be done *in* Christ, which is done by means of him, or for his sake, or by the meritorious influence or contribution of his death and sufferings, by way of motive, towards the doing of it. In this sense the preposition is used a verse or two after; a place that will give light to the phrase in hand. *Eis epainon soxēs tēs charitos autou en hēs exapitōsen hēmas en tō ēgapēmenō, i.e.* "To the praise of the glory of his grace, wherein he hath made us accepted in the beloved;" Eph. i. 6; *i. e.* hath made us dear, and near, and precious to himself, by means of the death, satisfaction, and atonement made by his beloved Son for us.

By the way, if the grace of God itself—and that in the glory of it, in which consideration the apostle here speaks of it—doth no other ways, upon no other terms, render us accepted with him, but only in "and through the beloved," viz. as having made our peace by the atonement of his death for us, then were we not so highly accepted with him through any purpose of election, (especially if we shall conceive this purpose of election to have been conceived in God before, and without all consideration of the death of Christ) as the common notion of election suggesteth. So, then, God is said to have purposed our election or choosing in Christ, because his purpose was to separate, elect, and choose those who should believe in Christ, for his sake in whom they believe, to salvation. This interpretation might be much cleared and confirmed by the opening of these words, which we had not long since in hand, Rom. ix. 11: "That the purpose of God according to election might stand, not of works, but of him that calleth." The purpose of God according to election, *i. e.* that purpose, counsel, or decree of God, according unto which, or in conformity whereunto he ordereth and manageth his election of persons in time, is here described, (a.) Negatively, "not of works." (b.) Affirmatively, in these words, "but of him that calleth."

When the apostle denies "the purpose of God according to election" to be of works, his meaning clearly is, that God did not purpose to elect, separate, or choose those men to eternal life, who should seek their justification by the works of the law. Again, when he affirmeth this purpose of God according to election to be of him that calleth, (meaning, of God himself, who calleth men to justifications and salvation) his meaning as clearly is, that the tenor of God's purpose, according unto which he means to elect and choose men and women to eternal life, is this; viz. to make choice of those for this blessed end and purpose, who shall believe in his Son Jesus Christ, or seek their justification by faith. This purpose is said to be "of him that calleth," in opposition to a being "of works;" because a purpose according to election, which should be of works, is the purpose of them that are called, viz. men; they conceive and think that God should purpose and intend to choose those only unto life, who should be diligent observers of the law, and seek their justification that way. But now "the purpose of God according to election," is not formed or shaped according to the sense or notion of those that are called, who generally pitch upon works, but according to the sense and mind of God himself, who calleth; who, as we know, hath declined works for such a purpose, and hath chosen faith.

So that the apostle's meaning in this antithesis, "not of works, but of him that calleth," is plainly this, "not of works," but of faith; faith and works being famous antagonists or competitors in the writings of this apostle for justification, the one as set up by God, the other by men. The same interpretation of the phrase, "who hath chosen us in Christ," may be yet further strengthened by that in Peter. "Elect according to the foreknowledge of God the Father, through sanctification of the Spirit, unto obedience and the sprinkling of the blood of Jesus Christ," 1 Pet. i. 2. First, he saluteth them as persons elect, or chosen, "according to the foreknowledge" (or pre-approbation) "of God the Father;" *i. e.* as persons so qualified, or as having obtained such an estate and condition, wherein "God the Father" from eternity judged it meet to "elect" or choose the persons of men unto salvation, or to estimate and account men for eternal life. In this sense he terms them "elect according to the foreknowledge," or fore-approbation, "of God;" meaning that their present condition in believing did, according to the tenor of the eternal counsel and purpose of God in that behalf, separate between them and the generality of the world, who in respect of their unbelief were looked upon by him and adjudged as the refuse of men in comparison of them, and in their present posture unmeet to have salvation conferred upon them.

2. He particularly describeth what that qualification or condition is, which God foreknew or fore-approved, as meet for him to regulate his election of the persons of men by, and wherein now they were invested, and consequently, "elected," in those words, "through sanctification of the Spirit unto obedience, and the sprinkling," &c. His meaning is, that they, through the assistance and gracious co-operation of the Spirit of God, were now brought to yield obedience unto the gospel, to believe in Jesus Christ, as he who by his death had purchased remission of sins for them, &c. implying that such an estate and condition as this, sanctification by the Spirit, &c. is that very estate wherein what person or persons of men soever should at any time be found, God in his eternal counsel judged it meet to confer the honourable title of "elect," or chosen, together with the grace and privilege of justification, upon them. So that to choose us in Christ, doth not signify to choose us personally considered with Christ, or in the same act of elections wherein or wherewith Christ was chosen, or the like,

but to intend, purpose, or decree to choose us, as being, or when we should be in Christ by believing. Having once obtained this being, a being in Christ by faith, we may truly and in good propriety of speaking be said to be chosen, by means or by virtue of that purpose or decree of election which was in God "before the foundations of the world," whereby he decreed to choose all those unto salvation, how many or how few soever they should prove, who should at any time be found in Christ by faith. In such a sense, Othniel, having smitten and taken Kir-jath-se-pher, may be said to have been made Caleb's son-in-law, by virtue of that declaration, law, or promise, which Caleb had made before, viz. that "He that smiteth Kir-jath-se-pher, and taketh it, to him he would give Ach-sa my daughter to wife," Judg. i. 12.

In such a sense likewise all those of Aaron's posterity, who came to be priests, though many generations after, may be said to have attained this office and dignity by virtue of the law concerning persons admittable into this office, which was enacted and made by God long before the Scripture itself ascribeth a virtue or power unto the law to make priests. "For the law maketh men high priests, which have infirmity," Heb. vii. 28. In like manner, that law, purpose, or decree of election, wherein and whereby God before the foundations of the world determined to choose all those that should believe in Christ, may be said to make all those elect or chosen who do thus believe. Yea, and God himself, by means of this his purpose or decree, may be said to have elected or chosen all those who do at any time believe, "from before the foundations of the world." Thus we have done with our second argument, wherein we have fairly and clearly proved, (a.) That Christ needed not to die at all for the elect, in the common Calvinistic notion of the word elect. (b.) That he did not die for the elect only, in any sense or notion of the said word whatsoever; and consequently, that he died for all men.

A third demonstration of the point is this: "If Christ died not for all men, then all men are not bound to believe in him or on him for salvation, or as a Saviour: But all men are bound to believe on him for salvation: Ergo." The reason of the major proposition is clearly this: no man is bound to lay out his silver for that which is not bread; nor to stay himself, with any confidence or assurance, upon any person whatsoever, for help or succour in any kind, concerning whom he knoweth not whether he hath wherewith to help him or no. Therefore, except all men had a sufficient ground to believe that there is redemption and salvation for them in Jesus Christ, they were not bound to believe on him as a Saviour, or to depend upon him for sal-vation. And if men have a sufficient ground to believe that there is redemp-tion and salvation for them in Christ, and that if they come unto him for it, they shall partake of it, then must it needs be a truth, that he hath these things for them indeed, and consequently that he died for them: because no man can have a sufficient ground to believe that which is not, or that which is false. This proposition is so plain, so obvious to every man's capacity and understanding, yea, to common sense itself, that I cannot well suspect the least question or doubt in any about the truth of it: If Christ died not for all men, then all men are not bound to believe on him for salvation.

Notwithstanding, if any shall object and say, It is true, if Christ died not sufficiently for all men, all men were not bound to believe in him for sal-vation; but we grant that in this sense, viz. sufficiently, he did die for all men. And this is a sufficient ground to oblige all men to believe on him for salvation, though he died not intentionally for them. To this I answer,

1. By demanding what men mean in saying that Christ died sufficiently for all men, in opposition to his dying intentionally for them. If they say, they mean that the death of Christ, simply and in itself considered, was or is sufficient to redeem and save all men, as well as those who are redeemed and saved by it, but was not intended by God or by Christ, for any such end or purpose as the redemption of all; I answer; if so, then was that redun-dancy or overplus of merit or atonement in the death of Christ, which remains over and above what is necessary for the redemption of those, for whom it was intended, and who are actually redeemed by it, suffered by God to run to waste, and to be "like water spilt upon the ground." And if so, then was there but a very small quantity or proportion of the worth and value of the death of Christ intended by God for use, or to do either him-self or his creature any service, in comparison of what vanisheth into the air, and is thrown behind his back, as good for nothing. For if there be a sufficiency in it for all those who are not redeemed by it, these being a far greater number than those who are, or are supposed to be actually redeemed by it; it must needs follow, that if that proportion of it, which was sufficient for them, was not designed or intended by God for them, then far the greater part of it was designed by him unto vanity, and to no more hon-our than that which is not. Thus we see how they that deny the death of Christ for all men intentionally, and yet grant it sufficiently, count "the blood of the covenant at least the far greatest part of it, as "an unholy thing," as that which us consecrated to no holy use, end, or purpose; yea,

and that which is yet worse, make God himself and Jesus Christ, the drawers or makers up of this account to their hand.

If they reply and say, that that remainder of the value and price of the death of Christ, though it was not intended by God for the salvation of those who are not actually redeemed by him, yet was intended for their condemnation, and so not lost; I answer, that this is yet worse and more unreasonable than the other. For, (a.) Might not men as reasonably say, that God made the sun, and put it into the midst of the firmament of heaven, to bring night and darkness upon the world, as that he gave his Son Jesus Christ unto death for the condemnation of the world? "For God sent not his Son," saith Christ himself, "into the world to condemn the world, but that the world through him might be saved," John iii. 17. And elsewhere, "I came not to judge the world, but to save the world," John xii. 47. And John the Baptist clearly expresseth the end and intent of Christ's death, "Behold the Lamb of God, which taketh away the sin of the world," John i. 29. Men may as well say that the end and intent of the sacrifices offered up by the priests under the law, was not to make atonement for men, or to purge them, but to bring more guilt upon them, as say that the intent of Christ in sacrificing himself was not to save, but condemn men. (b.) It is not the manner of God, nor is it agreeable either with his wisdom or his goodness to make things proper and fitting for the bringing to pass of good and gracious ends, and then to consign them over to the effecting of ends of a quite contrary nature and import, as, *v. g.* to create wholesome and savoury meats, which are apt and proper to nourish and make the lives of men comfortable to them, and to design these, being thus created, to the destruction or discomfort of the lives of men. Indeed, when men abuse their tables, and are unthankful to him that spread them for them, it is agreeable with his wisdom, and no ways disagreeing with his goodness, to make them to become snares unto them.

And in this sense only are all those places and expressions in the Scriptures to be understood where anything penal, or that is contrary to the peace and comfort of men, is presented as the end of Christ's coming into or going out of the world by death: as where he saith that he "came not to bring peace, but a sword," and to "put fire on earth;" that he "came for judgment into the world;" that he "was set as well for the falling as for the rising of many in Israel;" with the like. All such sayings as these import only the event or secondary intentions of God in sending Christ into the world, not those which were primary and predominant in him. Or, to speak properly, they do not import any intention at all, on God's part, in or about the sending of Christ into the world, but only show partly how unworthily some men will or possibly may behave themselves towards Christ, being come into the world. And partly, what the intentions of God are concerning those who shall behave themselves thus unworthily towards him. See what hath been formerly delivered in upon this account, and subscribed by Calvin himself, Chap. I.

If it be yet further said, Yea, but if God had had an intent to save though but a smaller number than now he intends to save, yet he could not have saved them by a sacrifice of less value and merit than that by which he now intendeth to save, those who shall be saved by Christ, and consequently not by a sacrifice of less value than that which hath in it a great surplusage or redundancy of merit above what was barely necessary or sufficient to save those whose salvation was intended. Therefore, this overplus of merit cannot be said to be lost or to be cast aside by God as unserviceable, inasmuch as it is essential unto, and absolutely inseparable from, that sacrifice which was simply necessary for the salvation of those whom he intended to save. As, suppose two or three men were in such a strait for meat to eat, being ready to perish through extremity of hunger, and could make no provision for their lives but only by slaying of an ox or a sheep that came in their way, and, when they had slain them, could not tell what to do with nine parts of ten of them. In this case, so much of the flesh of this ox or sheep as these men knew not how to dispose of to any serviceable end, cannot properly therefore be said to be lost, or to be cast aside by them as good for nothing, because it was a natural part of that beast which they were necessitated to slay for the preservation of their lives. To this objection also we answer,

By way of concessions: It is true, if God had intended to save but the one half, or had it been a far less proportion than so, of those persons, men and women, who now shall be saved, he could not have done it in that way of wisdom and justice wherein he now intends to save men by any sacrifice or atonement of less value than hath now been offered for those who shall be saved. Consequently, it should not have had a overplus and redundancy of merit in it sufficient to save many millions of persons besides those who in such a case, and under such a supposition, should be saved by it. But,

I answer further, by way of exception, that notwithstanding this, if God should have given such a sacrifice or atonement for the saving of a few only, which was sufficient to save more, yea all, without exception, and not intended the saving of all those who were capable of salvation by it, he should voluntarily and without any necessity at all, may, contrary to the importunate cries of the extreme misery of so many thousands in his ears, have made frustrated and void the far greatest and richest part of that sacrifice or atonement. As, suppose in the instance given of the men that in an exigent were necessitated to slay the ox or sheep spoken of for the preservation of their lives. It is true, they could not be charged with spoiling or making waste of that which remained of the flesh of either besides what was sufficient for themselves, simply because they slew the ox for their own necessity, being in a condition of imminent danger of their lives otherwise. But suppose there had been many poor souls hard at hand in as much danger of starving as themselves, in case they had refused or neglected to have given unto them of the remaining flesh we speak of, and would rather have buried it under ground, where they might not find it, or make it any ways unfit for meat and nourishment unto them. In this case they might justly be charged with making spoil and waste of that flesh which remained unto them when they had eaten, and that upon terms of the greatest unmercifulness and unworthiness. In like manner do they, who acknowledge the death of Christ sufficient for all, and yet affirm it to be given or intended by God only to some few, charge him, and that upon terms of much unworthiness and very dishonourable to him, to evacuate or make of no use or effect the far greatest part of this death, there being so many millions of souls before him in the utmost extremity of misery, to whom it might, and that with double and treble honour both to his wisdom and goodness, be disposed. Therefore, certainly, if the death of Christ was sufficient for all, it was intended by God for all. But,

Suppose it were granted that Christ died sufficiently for all, yet unless it be granted withal, that he died intentionally for all, the sufficiency of his death is no sufficient ground for all men, nor indeed for any man, to believe on him, or to cast themselves upon him, for salvation. Nabal was a rich man, and had sufficient means to have relieved David and his men in their necessity, and his sheep-shearers too. But yet David and his men had no sufficient ground to depend upon him for relief in their extremity; nor is it like they would have repaired to him for relief, if they had known his churlish and inhuman disposition before. In like manner that opinion which represents God as minding only, and intending the salvation of a few peculiarly relating to him by a purpose of elections, in the death of Christ, but altogether averse from so much as hearing of the saving of all others thereby, what doth it else but dissolve and loose all bounds of engagement or oblig-ement upon men, to believe on Christ, or on God through Christ for salva-tion? For who is bound to seek water from a flint, or to repair to thorns in hope to gather grapes from them? For they who deny that God intendeth the salvation of all men by Christ, represent him to the generality of men upon no better terms of comparison, than of a flint to him that wanteth water, and of thorns to him whose soul lusteth after grapes.

If it be said, yes, there are reasons and grounds sufficient for all men without exception to believe on Christ for salvation, though it be not sup-posed that he died for all men. Because the promise of God howsoever is general and free unto all: Whosoever believes on him shall be saved. To this I answer;

It is true, the promise is general and free unto all. And this generality and freeness of the promise plainly showeth the generality and freeness of the salvation promised to all men, to be commeasurable with the promise, and extensible to as many as it. Otherwise the ministers of the gospel shall be found liars and false witnesses. For if they shall promise salvation unto all men, in case they shall believe, when as there is no salvation for far the greatest part of men, whether they believe or not believe, or in case they should believe, for their believing or not believing doth not alter the inten-tions of God in the death of Christ, nor multiply salvation, do they not undertake more in the behalf of God than God himself, according to notion, is able or willing to perform? But this point we have debated more liberally in the third chapter of this book.

If it be yet said, Yea, but God who orders and frames their commission, may without danger will them to preach and promise salvation, to all that will believe, though salvation be not purchased for all men, because he knows beforehand that those only will believe for whom there is salvation purchased in the death of Christ. To this I answer;

If God had kept his intentions in this kind to himself, and had not declared that he intended salvation only to a few, there might be some more colour or pretence for such a plea. If he had not let the world know any-thing, but that he really intended the salvation of them all, though he should in the meantime have intended but the salvation of a very few, he might with far less dishonour, at least for the present, cause the heralds of his grace, his ministers I mean, to make such a general proclamation, as now he hath given them in charge to make throughout the world, of grace and salvation prepared for all flesh, for all comers whatsoever. But to imagine and suppose that first he gives the world to know and understand that he intends to save but a very few of them; and yet this notwithstanding, and, as it were, in the very face of such a declaration, to cause the great year of Jubilee to be proclaimed throughout the world, eternal liberty and redemption to be offered unto all flesh, unto all persons without exception, must needs be most unlike him, and unworthy of him, yea, and have a direct tendency to make him that which a reverential sense of his majesty makes hard to be uttered, the hatred and abhorring of all his creatures.

David, to present his hollow-hearted and treacherous friends hateful both to God and men, describes them thus; "The words of his mouth were smoother than butter, but war was in his mouth: his words were softer than oil, yet were they drawn swords." Psa. lv. 21. And doth not that opinion turn the glory of the ever gracious God, that great lover of mankind, into the image of such a vile and abominable creature as David here describes, which saith of him, that he comes indeed unto men, and opens the bosom of love unto them, speaks sweet and loving and gracious words unto them, offers them, yea, and that with much importunity of urging and pressing them to an acceptance, terms of mercy and great compassions, forgiveness of sins, adoption, life, salvation, glory, the great things of the world to come, and yet all this while, under all these sweet droppings of his lips, hath in his heart that most bloody and irreconcilable war of reprobation, a purpose and resolution taken up and conceived within him from the days of eternity, never to be altered upon any terms whatsoever, of casting them into hell, and tormenting them with the vengeance of eternal fire?

Certainly that opinion, which representeth God unto men upon such terms, in such a shape as this, flatters or rather befriends the devil, and makes him to have much of God in him. And if God should conceal for the present that intention of his we speak of, viz. of saving only a few, and of destroying the generality of men, and yet proceed in that method which now he doth, in inviting the whole world to grace and favour with him, except he should conceal it to the days of eternity, whensoever it should break forth and be discovered, it would occasion the same reflection of dishonour upon him; yea, and doubtless would comfort and ease the damned in hell, if ever the knowledge of it should come amongst them. But this for the proof of the major proposition in the argument propounded; If Christ died not for all men, then all men are not bound to believe on him for salvation.

The minor, I conceive, needs little proof, being this: But all men *are* bound to believe on him for salvation. However the truth of this proposition is as clear as the light at noonday, partly from the commandment of God directed unto all men to believe on him. This is partly from the threatenings of God denounced against all men that shall refuse to believe on him; partly from the promises made unto all men, who shall believe on him; partly also from the encouragements which are administered by God unto all men to believe on him.

First, it is evident that God commands all men without exception to believe on Christ. "And the times of this ignorance," saith Paul preaching to the idolatrous Gentiles at Athens, "God winked at; but now commandeth all men every where to repent," Acts xvii. 30. If to repent, then certainly to believe in Christ; without which there is no true repentance. The reader for his further satisfaction on this point (if he be in any degree yet unsatisfied) may at leisure peruse and ponder the following Scriptures: 1 John iii. 23; Matt. xvi. 24; Rom. x. 3, 16; Luke xiii. 23.

Secondly, as God commandeth all men to believe on Christ, (which is indeed sufficient to prove that they are bound to believe on him) so doth he severely threaten all those that shall not believe on him. "But he that believeth not, shall be damned," Mark xvi.16. The Scriptures likewise abound with passages of this import: a first-fruits whereof are here presented, John iii. 36, viii. 24; Acts iii. 23.

Thirdly, as God commandeth all men to believe on Christ, and threateneth all with death, which shall not believe; so he promiseth life and salvation unto all without exception, who shall believe on him. This assertion, I conceive, is no man's question, the Scriptures being so particular and express in the frequent delivery of it, John iii. 16; xi. 25, 26; 1 Pet. ii. 6.

Fourthly, and lastly, as God commandeth all men to believe on Christ; threateneth all with death, who shall not believe; promiseth life and salvation, unto all who shall believe; so doth he encourage all to believe on him. My meaning is, he tendereth and suggesteth reasons and motives of an encouraging and sweetly-persuading nature and import unto men to believe. For otherwise the commands and promises of God made unto those who shall believe, are grand encouragements (in a large acception of the word) unto men to believe; and his threatenings are more engaging to the servile tempers and dispositions of men to believe, than any encouragements whatsoever. But my meaning in the particular in hand is this; that besides commands and promises, God lays before the hearts of men such considerations, which are apt and proper in a sweet and encouraging way to induce men to believe on Christ, or on himself through Christ for salvation.

As for example: sometimes he presents them with his great love to them, as John iii. 16; Tit. iii. 4, &c.; sometimes with his mercy and his compassions, the greatness and tenderness of these, as Exod. xxxiv. 6; Luke i. 72, &c.; sometimes with his delight or pleasure taken in showing mercy, as Mic. vii. 18; Ezek. xxxiii. 11, &c.; sometimes with his faithfulness, as Heb. x. 23; 1 Cor. x. 13, &c.; sometimes with his oath, for their greater security in his promises, as Heb. vi. 17, 18; Luke i. 72, 73; otherwhile, with his desire of their salvation, as 1 Tim. ii. 4; Ezek. xxxiii, 11; otherwhile again, with the grief and trouble of his soul at their stubborn courses, and that because they are and will be destructive unto them, as Ezek. xviii. 31; Jer. xliv. 4; sometimes with the abundant provision he hath made for their salvation and peace, as Matt. xxii. 4; Heb. ix. 14; sometimes likewise (to omit many other particulars in this kind) with the consideration of that special glory which will accrue unto himself and to his grace, by their believing and salvation thereupon, Ephes. i. 6, 12, and elsewhere. Now to think or say, that under all these commands, threatenings, promises, and all this great variety of encouragements directed unto all men to believe, yet all men are not bound to believe, is to me the thought and saying only of such a man, who is resolved to stand by his own thoughts and sayings, against any light or evidence of truth whatsoever.

A further argument, evincing the death of Christ for all men, is this: If God really and unfeignedly intends or desires the salvation of those who perish, then he really intended the death of Christ for all men. This proposition we shall not need to prove, but only by this brief account. All men (without exception) are either such who are saved, or such who perish; and that God really intended the death of Christ, for those that are saved, is no man's doubt or contest. Therefore if he really intended the salvation of those also who perish in or by the death of Christ, he intended this death of Christ for all. This proposition then being undeniable, I proceed and assume thus: But God really and unfeignedly intends or desires the salvation of those who perish: Therefore he intended the death of Christ for all men. This latter proposition, that God really and unfeignedly desires the salvation of those that perish, is clearly proved by this consideration; viz. that God so frequently, so fervently in the Scriptures professeth his desires of the peace and salvation of such men, yea, and a holy regret of soul in himself, when they will stubbornly run courses destructive to their salvation, contrary to his desires and endeavours with them in this kind.

Let us give instance in some passages of such an import as we speak of.

"O that there were such a heart in them, that they would fear me, and keep all my commandments always, that it might be well with them, and with their children for ever!" Deut. v. 29, (saith the Lord himself concerning the great body of the children of Israel, whose carcasses soon after "fell in the wilderness" through unbelief, as the inspired writer observeth. Heb. iii. 17.) So again by David, "Oh that my people had hearkened unto me, and Israel had walked in my ways! I should soon have subdued their enemies, and turned my hand against their adversaries," &c. Psal. lxxxi. 13, 14. Thus the Lord speaks concerning those, "whom" as he had immediately before said, "he had given up to their own hearts' lusts, and who walked in their own counsels." That expression also of the Lord in Isaiah is of the same character. "Thus saith the Lord, thy Redeemer, the Holy One of Israel; I am the Lord thy God, which teacheth thee to profit, which leadeth thee by the way that thou shouldest go; O that thou hadst hearkened unto my commandments, then had thy peace been as a river, and thy righteousness as the waves of the sea." Isa. xlviii. 17, 18. Whereunto this also in the same prophet may be joined; "I have spread out my hands all the day unto a rebellious people, which walketh in a way that was not good, after their own thoughts; a people that provoketh me to anger continually to my face, that sacrificeth in gardens," &c. Isa. lxv. 2, 3.

By "spreading forth the hands," saith Calvin, upon the place, "he signifies a daily summoning of them, and that to draw and unite them unto himself." A little after: "The Lord never speaks unto us, but he therewithal stretcheth forth his hand to unite us unto himself, and causeth us to feel that he is near unto us. Yea, he so manifests his fatherly love, and so willingly accepts of us, that if we yield not obedience unto his voice, we ought justly to impute the same to our own forwardness." So that Calvin's judgment clearly is, that in this and such like places, God professeth a reality of intention and desire in him "*to draw and unite unto himself*" (*i. e.* to sanctify and save) such who, through their own forwardness, never come to be actually united unto him, or saved.

Add hereunto only two places more for the present, though there be many others to be found. The former of these shall be that in Jer. xliv. 4, 5: "Howbeit I sent unto you all my servants the prophets, rising early and sending them, saying, Oh, do not this abominable thing that I hate. But they hearkened not, nor inclined their ear to turn from their wickedness, to burn no incense unto other gods." The latter place is in the New Testament. "O Jerusalem, Jerusalem, thou that killest the prophets, and stonest them which are sent unto thee, how often would I have gathered thy children together, even as a hen gathereth her chickens under her wings, and ye would not! Behold, your house is left unto you desolate." Matt. xxiii. 37, 38. Upon the former of these places, Calvin makes the prophet to say, "that God was watchful, because *he was solicitous for the people's safety*. Even as a man that is intent upon his business, will not stay till the sun shines upon him, but will prevent the morning itself." Upon the latter place he saith, that "God attempted, in a way of gentleness and fair speaking, *to allure* the Jews unto him; that his *benignity*, or kindness, was great towards them; that his invitations of them were more than mother-like;" with much more of like import.

Now to say that God should profess and express himself unto men and women with so much vehemency and patheticalness of affection, as these gestures, phrases, and expressions (our chiefest adversaries themselves being judges) imply, spreading forth his hands all the day long, endeavouring to gather people with as much care and tenderness as a hen gathereth her chickens under her wings, crying out, Oh, do not this abominable thing, &c., and yet have no desire at all, no intention at all of their salvation, nay, on the contrary, have settled and grounded intentions to destroy them forever, is to render him like to that generation of men in the world, whom his soul most abhorreth, and who are indeed, and that most justly, the hatred and abhorring both of God and men, hypocrites, I mean, and dissemblers.

Christ commands us to be merciful, as our heavenly Father is merciful, Luke vi. 36; but if we should be merciful, as those represent the mercifulness of our heavenly Father, who deny that Christ died for all men, we should be the first-born children of hypocrisy, and the most notorious dissemblers under heaven. This is many degrees worse than those whom James speaks of with reproof: "If a brother or sister be naked, and destitute of daily food, And one of you say unto them, Depart in peace, be ye warmed and filled; notwithstanding ye give them not those things which are needful to the body;" James ii. 15, 16. For though such merciful ones as these do their poor brethren and sisters little good with their merciful words, yet it no ways appears, nor is it likely that, under such words as these, they hide or harbour intentions of evil, or of a further increase of misery unto them. Whereas they that shall be merciful like unto their heavenly Father, as the opinion which we oppose lays the pattern before us, shall under the most affectionate protestations of love and kindness unto men, under the most earnest asseverations of intentions and desires of their good, conceal settled projects, purposes, desires, and intentions of doing them the greatest mischief they can imagine.

That which is wont to be excepted against this argument is so empty, except it be of contumely and dishonour unto God, that it neither deserves consideration nor confutation. And I believe all that can be excepted against it is of very little more weight. Some, as to the Scriptures cited for the confirmation of the argument with their fellows, wherein God (as we heard) professeth with so much earnestness the sincerity of his desires to the welfare and salvation of those who perish, answer somewhat to this purpose,—for it is hard indeed to make any regular or good sense of what they answer at this point,—that God in such expressions useth *sancta quadam simulatione*, a kind of holy simulation: others, that he doth *duplicem personam induere, i. e.* that he takes upon him a double person. Others, that God is presented in such Scriptures as speaking *secundum voluntatem approbativam, non efficacem, i. e.* according to his will of approbation, not according to his will of efficacy or execution. Others, that such wishes or desires as are expressed in the said Scriptures are attributed unto God anthropopathically, and according to the rate of human capacity, &c. But what uncouth and hard-faced allegations are these? Or what salt of interpretation is there that will make them savoury? Or what do they that use them but as it were to beg bread out of desolate places to support the life of an opinion that is guilty, and deserves to die?

First, I would know of those who take sanctuary from the pursuit of the Scriptures mentioned, under the wing of *sancta quaedam simulatio in Deo*, a kind of holy simulation in God. What do they mean by this *sancta simulatio*? As far as my short understanding is able to reach, to talk of a holy simulation, and of a sunshine night, or of a beast endued with the reasonable soul of a man, would make discourses of a parallel consistence. If simulation, counterfeiting, or professing one thing, whilst the contrary is intended, be holy in God, why or how should they not be holy in men also? But in men we know they are abominable. Yet the tenor of God's injunction unto men is, "But *as he which hath* called you is holy, *so be ye holy* in all manner of conversation." 1 Pet. i.15. Or if some things in God may be holy, which are abominable in men, how or by what rule shall men distinguish between such holy things in God, which are holy also when found in men, and such other holy things in God, which, when found in men, are abominable? Besides, the Holy Ghost attributes the honourable title of *apseudēs*, one incapable of lying, unto God, Titus i. 2.

If God cannot lie, much less can he counterfeit or dissemble; simulation and dissimulation always including lying, and adding somewhat besides that is evil to boot. And doubtless he that so much loveth or "desireth truth," *i. e.* conformity in reality of purpose and affection, unto words and outward professions "in the inward parts" of men, Psal. li. 6, and commands them to "not love in word, neither in tongue; but in deed and in truth," 1 John iii. 18, is himself fully commensurable in heart and soul, in the most real purposes and intentions that can be conceived, with all that goeth out of his lips. His mouth is not so wide opened unto the world, but that his heart is enlarged accordingly; nor is he at any hand to be judged like unto him whom David brandeth with this character of wickedness, "The words of his mouth were smoother than butter, but war was in his heart: his words were softer than oil, yet were they drawn swords," Psal. lv. 21. Such a simulation or dissembling as we now speak of, and which some most unworthily attribute unto God, is by the very light of nature execrable and accursed. Homer puts these words into the mouth of his Achilles[1]:

To me he is abhorred like death,
Whose heart accords not with his breath.

But this subterfuge of *simulatio sancta* is, it seems, so broadly obnoxious, that the greatest part of those who wish themselves safe from the pre-mentioned Scriptures, are afraid or ashamed to trust to it. Therefore,

2. Some others of them attempt an escape by the new, but dead way of this distinction. God, say they, wisheth the peace and salvation of those that perish, *voluntate approbativa*, with or according to his approving will, *i. e.* He approveth of the salvation of such persons as good; but he doth not wish it *voluntate efficaci*, *i. e.* with his efficacious will. Are not men, think we, sorely afraid of the truth, who can accept deliverance from it by the unworthy hand of such distinctions as these? For, is it a thing of any reasonable resentment in the least, that God should positively and peremptorily determine and decree from eternity that which is directly contrary to his will of approbation? Or, is not the destruction of those who perish contrary to their salvation? Therefore, if God approveth of their salvation, and yet peremptorily decreeth their condemnation (whether positively or permissively only, as these men count permission, is not material), doth he not decree that from eternity which his soul hateth or abhorreth, or, which is the same, which is contrary to his will of approbation?

And whoever decreed such a thing which is contrary to what he

1. Iliad. I.

approveth, taketh pleasure, or delighteth in? No man ever yet, being in possession of his senses, though but common and ordinary, decreed his own sorrow, or anything contrary to what he approveth. In what sense Christ is said to have been "delivered up, taken, and crucified," with wicked hands, "by the determined counsel of God," is by the tenor of which explication it plainly appeareth, that in or about the crucifying of Christ there was nothing decreed or determined by God, but with perfect accord to his will of approbation. When the said distinction teacheth us that God doth not will the salvation of those that perish voluntate efficaci, with his efficacious or effectual will, I would gladly know what it meaneth by this efficacious will of God.

Certainly he willeth the salvation of these men with a will efficacious to a degree, yea, to a very considerable and great degree; with a will, I mean, exerting itself upon such terms in order to the promoting, furthering, and procuring their salvation, that, unless they resisted the Holy Ghost, they should be actually saved. Yea, upon such terms, that God himself professeth that he knoweth not what to do more to effect or procure their salvation than what he doth: " What could have been done more," saith he, "to my vineyard, that I have not done in it?" Isa. v. 4; to interpret, "what could have been done more," by, "what would have been more," is to dissense the place, and to make hay and stubble of good silver and gold. In what sense God is, and properly enough may be, said not to be able to "do more" than what he actually doth to promote the salvation even of those who perish, hath been formerly opened in Chap. V. Yea, the most learned abettors of that doctrine which we now oppose, generally grant that God vouchsafeth means of salvation, yea, sometimes means very rich and powerful in this kind, unto those who in the event are not saved. Doubtless, such dispensations as these argue a will in God some ways, and in some measure, operative and efficacious in order to the salvation of such men, which is more than a will of mere approbation.

If by the efficacious will of God, the said distinction meaneth such a will which acteth irresistibly, or necessitatingly, in order to the saving of men, and that God with such a will as this doth not will the salvation of any of those who perish; my answer is, (a.) That if this be meant particularly of the initial or first applications made by God unto such men, that will of his from which these proceed may, in a sense, be said to act irresistibly and necessitatingly towards their salvation; not indeed as if by these exertions or actings of this will of his the salvation of these men must necessarily follow, but because such applications of God unto them in order to their salvation cannot be prevented, nor God hindered, by any means whatsoever, from or in the making of them unto them. God will either will or nill men themselves, or who ever besides, at first, before they have corrupted themselves with the ways and manners of the world, graciously apply himself unto them in the things of their eternal peace, by writing the effect of his law in their hearts, by enlightening them with the knowledge of himself, to a good degree, as of his being, "his eternal power, and godhead," &c., which we may call the elements or first rudiments of salvation. But, (b.) If by the efficacious will of God, the distinction meaneth such a will in him which acteth upon such terms, in order to the salvation of a man, that there is no possibility for him to miscarry or perish under these actings, I grant that God doth not will the salvation of those that perish with such a will as this, but deny, withal, that there is any such will as this in him, or that he willeth the salvation of any man or men whatsoever upon any such terms, but that all the time of their sojourning in the flesh, and till salvation be actually vested in them, they are, such actings notwithstanding, in a possibility of perishing. This possibility is no ground, nor reasonable occasion, unto those who believe, of any fear that hath torment, but only of care that hath conscience, as hath been shown formerly. But,

Concerning those who inform us that the Scriptures specified, wherein God presenteth himself, as affectionately wishing and desiring the salvation even of those who perish, are figurative, and to be understood anthropopathically, conceiving that by saying thus, they shake off the argument built upon these Scriptures against them. The truth is that their information in this kind is steady and good, but their conceit upon it weak and worthless. For what though a Scripture passage be figurative, and contains in it an anthropopathy, one or more, is it therefore non-significative? Or doth it hold forth nothing of a spiritual import to the judgments and understandings of men for their edification? When God saith of himself, "If any man draw back, my soul shall have no pleasure in him." Heb. x. 38; so again when he saith, "For all those things hath mine hand made..." Isa. lxvi. 2; so when he is said to have given unto "Moses...two tables of testimony, tables of stone, written with the finger of God," Exod. xxxi. 18, with others more of like character, without number, are such sayings as these barbarian unto us, or like so many trumpets giving an uncertain sound? Or are they not as significant and expressive, as full of edification and instruction in the knowledge of God, as other sayings in the same volume with them?

Or could the same subject or matter of truth, which they hold forth, have been delivered within more grace, or with better advantage to the understandings of men, in other terms or forms of expression than those specified? Yea, the truth is that very little, if anything at all, concerning God, can be conveyed by words unto the minds and understandings of men, but by expressions which are figurative, the reason whereof hath, I remember, been formerly observed by us. And for the Scriptures, questionless there is in them more of the knowledge of God, and of his attributes, taught by anthropopathies, and that kind of dialect, which borroweth things proper unto men to make known unto us things proper unto God, than by all other kinds of phrases or expressions whatsoever. Now then this I would demand of those who of the anthropopathies found in the Scriptures under present consideration, think to make shields and bucklers against the dint and force of the argument drawn from them, I would, I say, willingly demand of these men, what other sense, or what other matter of information, instruction, edification, they can make of the said places. It can only be this, or that which is equivalent to it, viz. that there is that eminently or transcendently in God, or in the Divine Being, which relateth unto the salvation of those, who notwithstanding in time perish, after the same manner, wherein the earnest wishes, and most serious and cordial desires in men, relate unto their respective objects, or things so wished and desired by them.

3. They, who to salve their opinion of Christ's non-dying for those whose salvation God professeth with so much seriousness and solemnity in the passages in hand that he desireth, without charging him with hypocrisy, apply this plaster, viz. that in this place God expresseth himself, pro captu humano, *i. e.* with a condescension to human capacity, these men, I say, spin the same thread of vanity with the former. For be it granted, that God in the said passages condescends to the infirm and weak apprehensions of men, and teacheth them mysteries, as they are able to hear and understand, doth it follow from hence, that therefore he teacheth them nothing at all, speaks nothing at all to their understandings in these places? If it be granted that in them he speaks anything at all to the understandings of men, I demand, as lately, what can it else be, but that he truly, really, cordially, affectionately, wisheth, willeth, desireth, (in such a sense as he truly, really, cordially, affectionately, wisheth, willeth, desireth any other thing) the salvation of such men, who yet through their own voluntary negligence and unworthiness, in conclusion perish and are not saved? And if so, then doth that doctrine either arraign the most holy and blessed God of the foulest

hypocrisy and dissimulation that lightly can be imagined, which affirmeth that notwithstanding the solemnity and frequency of such protestations, yet he never intended that his Son Christ should die, and make atonement for them; or else that he intends and desires their salvation otherwise than by Christ's death.

A fourth demonstration of the doctrine asserted. "That doctrine which directly tends to separate and divide between the creature and his Creator blessed forever, or to create and raise jealousies and hard thoughts in the former against the latter, cannot be evangelical or truth: But such is the doctrine which denieth that Christ died for all men without exception: Ergo." The major proposition in this argument carrieth a sufficiency of light in it for the manifestation of its own truth. The clear and known project and intent of the gospel is "to reconcile all things both in heaven and on earth into one," as we lately heard from the apostle; to slay and destroy that enmity which is so apt to arise and work in the minds and thoughts of men against God, through a consciousness of their sinful lives and ways, in conjunction with those strong impressions upon their conscience of his infinite holiness and majesty; and so to create and plant in their stead worthy and honourable thoughts of God, full of love, sweetness and peace, in the inward parts of men, as we argued and proved at large from 2 Cor. v. 19, as we noted in Chap. I. Therefore that doctrine, the face whereof is set a quite contrary way, as viz. to multiply, foment and increase those evil and hard thoughts of God, which the sense of sin, and guilt, as hath been said, are marvelously apt to engender in the hearts and spirits of men, must needs be anti-evangelical, and of another inspiration much differing from that whereby the gospel was given unto the world. So that to clothe this proposition with light, we shall not need to labour or spin.

Nor need we be put to much trouble for proof of the latter proposition, had not the adverse doctrine gotten the advantage of possession against the clear truth, in the judgments of men. For what can be more apparent, than that such a doctrine, which manifestly importeth the causeless, peremptory, irremediable, and unremoveable hatred of God against far the greatest part of men, and this burning to the bottom of hell: the persons against whom this hatred is supposed to be lodged in him, being unknown. What, I say, can be more apparent than that such a doctrine as this, directly, and with open face tends to a most sad, horrid, and desperate alienation of the heart and soul of the poor creature, man, from his dear and ever blessed Creator, God? Or is it possible that such a creature should truly, cordially, or entirely love, or delight in him that made him, in case he either knows, or otherwise hath strong grounds of jealousy and fear, that before he made him, and without any offence taken at, or respect had unto, any of his future sins, or unworthy carriages in the least, he so far hated and abominated him, as to resolve, against all mediation whatsoever, to cast him out of his sight, to devote and doom him to suffer the vengeance of eternal fire?

Or doth not that doctrine, which denieth that God intended the death of Christ for the salvation of all men, manifestly import and suppose that God to such a degree hated and abhorred, or however purposed and decreed to hate and abhor, the far greatest part of men from eternity, as to resolve against all means possible to be used by them, or purposed to be used by himself, for prevention, to pour out the fierceness of his wrath upon their heads in flames of unquenchable fire? The Holy Ghost teacheth us, that loving of God, *i. e.* love towards God, must or ought to be kindled in the hearts of men, by a sense or apprehension of a precedency of this affection in him towards them. "We love him,"saith John, "because he first loved us;" or, as the original *agapōmen*, will indifferently bear, as Calvin himself observes and grants, "Let us love him, because he loved us first." 1 John iv. 19. According to either of these constructions of the words, the intimation is pregnant, that the love of God towards men apprehended and believed, is and ought to be the proper seed of a reciprocal affection in men towards him.

And the Scripture most frequently conjures men to love God, upon the account of his great love towards them manifested by the gift of his Son, Jesus Christ, unto them. Now if love declared and represented be the natural and proper seed of the same affection in another, then hatred discovered and apprehended, must needs be a seed of a contrary import, and of like aptness to beget in its own likeness also. For though God chargeth men to love their enemies, and those that hate them, yet he doth it upon the account of that great and signal love which he hath first shown unto them in the gift of his only begotten and dear Son. And we see, notwithstanding this great commandment imposed by God upon men, and that upon the advantage of such a rational and equitable ground or motive for the performance of it, yet with what difficulty and renitency of the flesh, even in men truly sanctified, yea, and with what rareness of example, it is effectually, if at all, performed. How impossible then must it needs be, that men should truly love God, whilst they apprehend him as an enemy, bent in an implacable and unappeasable manner, to destroy them, and that with the most formidable destruction they are capable of enduring, and this to the days of eternity. Especially considering, that they have no advantage or motive, of any love shown unto them by another, any ways considerable, whereby to be strengthened or enabled to love him, against so sore a stumbling-block and obstruction in the way of this affection, as a reprobating of them from eternity. This demonstration is so pregnant of proof and conviction, that certain I am nothing can with any strength, scarce with any face of reason, be alleged against it. But meet it is that the poor should be heard in his cause, as well as the rich. Therefore,

1. To the argument now urged, it may be objected, that the doctrine which affirmeth that Christ died only for the elect, and not for all men in general, hath no such tendency or aptness in it as the said argument chargeth upon it, to separate between God and any of his creatures; because it leaveth a hope to every person of mankind, distributively considered, that they may be of the number of the elect, and consequently of those for whom Christ died. There is no man or woman but may, the said doctrine notwithstanding, be of a good and comfortable hope that Christ died for them, and so have no ground to conceive hardly of God, or to be alienated in their minds or hearts from him. To this I answer,

Be it granted that the doctrine we blame leaveth a degree of hope to every person that he is one of those for whom Christ died. Yet it is a hope very faint and feeble, and which must needs be sick at the heart, as being overbalanced many degrees by contrary jealousies and fears; and so can at no hand be termed a good or comfortable hope, or give any advantage by way of motive unto the creature to think well and honourably of God. The truth is, it is rather a possibility of conceit than any well-grounded hope that such a doctrine leaveth or affordeth unto any man, being yet in his unregenerate estate, that he is one of those for whom Christ died. Suppose forty or a hundred men should be arraigned and found guilty of high treason against their prince, and he should declare, without naming any of their persons, that he would graciously pardon the offence of one or two of them, but was resolved, against all possible interveniences whatsoever, to inflict in the most severe manner the penalty of death upon all the rest. Would such a hope of escape or of finding favour in the eyes of their prince as should be afforded or left unto these men in this case, be any considerable encouragement or ground of motive unto them respectively to conceive honourably of their prince for clemency, goodness, and mercy? Or would not the severity and peremptoriness of his resolutions to take away the lives of the generality or far greatest part of them, rather represent him to their minds as a man of rigour and extremity against those that provoke him? Much more should these men and all others have just ground to judge this prince to be a person of a hard spirit, addicted unto cruelties and blood, in case they should know, especially from himself and by his own profession, that long before any of the said persons were touched with the least guilt, yea, or thought of treason, he was peremptorily resolved to have the blood and lives of them all, one or two only excepted?

And as for his granting pardon unto this one or two, there being no ground in reason or equity why he should respect these more than the other, may it not seem rather the working of a mere humour, or a conceited and groundless action, than any fruit of an habitual goodness or clemency of disposition, or of any mature or considerate deliberation? And doth not the doctrine which we condemn for that capital crime of denying that Christ died for all men, draw a portraiture of God resembling in all the lineaments of his face the hard-favouredness of such a prince? First, it represents him as engaged, and this against all possibility of relenting, yea, and this to the days of eternity, in counsels and purposes of blood, yea, of the blood of the precious souls of men. Secondly, it representeth him as thus engaged against millions of millions of these souls, yea, against the whole mass or element of mankind, a small remnant comparatively only excepted, and these for a long time, if not during the whole term of their mortality, undiscernible from the rest; within the compass of which term, notwithstanding, they must be prevailed with to love God, or else they are lost for eternity.

Thirdly, the said doctrine portrays him engaged as aforesaid, before, and without any consideration or respect had to, any future sins, impenitency, unbelief, or any other, of those against whom it supposeth him so implacably and unmercifully engaged. Fourthly and lastly, it holdeth him forth unto the world as purposing and intending, without any reasonable or equitable cause, only upon his peremptory and mere will, to make that vast difference between that small remnant of men mentioned and the numberless multitudes of them besides, which consists in the unmeasurable blessedness of the former, and the inconceivable misery and torment of the latter. Now, whether this forms the most blessed God in the minds, judgments, souls, and consciences of men as amiable and lovely, as attractive of their hearts and affections, as worthy to be delighted in, to be depended on, by all persons of mankind, without exception of any, for all and all manner of good, temporal, spiritual, eternal, I am not much afraid to make it the arbitrary decision of those that dare so much as pretend to ingenuousness, fairness, and freedom of spirit amongst our adversaries themselves.

If it be here objected and said, that our doctrine also representeth God as irreversibly engaged, and this from eternity, upon the same destruction or punishment, and this of the same numbers of men with the other, inasmuch as it granteth or supposeth that God from eternity unchangeably purposed the eternal destruction of all those, without exception, that shall remain finally impenitent and unbelieving, which are the same men, both for numbers and personality, which the other doctrine, so much opposed by us, presenteth as the objects of those unalterable reprobating purposes or intendments of his from eternity and that consequently, the one doctrine representeth God as little lovely or desirable unto his creature as the other; To this I answer,

(a.) Though the doctrine asserted by us supposeth such a decree in God from eternity whereby all persons that should remain finally impenitent and unbelieving are decreed or adjudged unto the vengeance of eternal fire, yet doth it not adjudge to this account any such who are either through defect of years, as children dying as infants, or defectiveness in discretion otherwise are not capable of faith or repentance, of which we have already in part given an account, Chap. II. We shall, God willing, account more fully in the latter part of this discourse: whereas the doctrine impugned by us includeth as well infants of days as defectives of years, especially the former, in that decree of reprobation which it notioneth in God. So that this doctrine doth at no hand engage God so deep in the blood of mankind as the other; and consequently, in this respect, rendereth him unto his creature far more gracious, lovely, and desirable than the other.

(b.) The doctrine we plead, though it sets the face of God's reprobating decree against all finally impenitent and unbelieving, and so materially, and in a consequential way, against the same persons, capable of impenitency, which the other doctrine subjecteth unto it; yet, 1. It subjecteth no person of mankind, as such, or by name, unto it, but supposeth all men, as men, in a capacity, and under a fair possibility, of being elected, this decree of reprobation notwithstanding; though it concludeth from many prophetical Scriptures otherwise, that a very great number of men will in time be reprobated for their wickedness and unbelief. Whereas, the doctrine opposed bends this decree against the persons of men personally considered, and so leaveth such and such men, from first to last, irrecoverably doomed to destruction. 2. The doctrine asserted by us presenteth God in his decree of reprobation as truly and really intending the salvation of men as in his decree of election itself; yea, and questioneth not but that his decree of reprobation, according to his gracious purpose and intendment therein, hath occasioned, and doth occasion daily, the salvation of many. The principal intent of the law, threatening such and such malefactors, as traitors, murderers, &c. with death, is not to take away the lives of such persons, who shall commit these foul crimes and misdemeanours, by death, this is but the subordinate intention or end of it, but to prevent the perpetration of these crimes in all that live under this law, and consequently, their suffering of death for them. Much less is it any part of the intent of such a law to make any person or persons, by name, traitors, murderers, or the like, that so they may be cut off by death. In like manner, we judge and teach, that the sovereign and primary intent of this decree of God, "he," *i. e.* whosoever "believeth not, shall be damned," Mark xvi. 16. Besides which, in respect of the substance and import of it, which may be expressed in other terms, we find no decree of reprobation in God mentioned, no, nor yet so much as intimated in the Scriptures, in which the goal is to bring damnation upon those who shall not believe, much less to expose any man, or numbers of men, to an unavoidable necessity of a non-believing, that so they may be damned, but to prevent the sin of unbelief in all men, in order to their non-damnation, and that they may be saved.

(c.) The doctrine which avoucheth that Christ died for all men clearly resolveth the reprobation of all that are, or ever come to be reprobated, into themselves, or their own voluntary and deliberate course of sinning, or persisting in unbelief, as the cause thereof. And so, this fairly dischargeth God and his decree as no ways accessary unto it. Whereas, the adverse opinion resolveth it into the mere pleasure or peremptory will of God in his decree of reprobation, affirming this to be the principal, if not the sole and adequate cause of it. So that there is a very vast difference between the one opinion and the other in their respective representations of God unto his creature, in point of grace, goodness, and loveliness on the one hand, as of rigour, hardness, and unloveliness on the other hand. It is true, God is very severe, terrible, and unrelenting, in the execution of his penal decrees upon those who voluntarily expose themselves to the doom and dint of them; in which respect the Scripture speaketh oft of his severity. But, in the framing of them, his primary intentions were, as hath been said, gracious, no ways inconsistent with or repugnant to the peace and comfort of any of his creatures, but calculated with dueness of proportion and respects for the advancement of them. Yet,

Against the main argument last insisted upon, it may be further object-ed: They who deny that Christ died for any but for the elect only, represent God altogether as gracious and lovely unto his creature as they who affirm that he died for all. Because the former hold and teach withal, that God really intends that all those for whom Christ died shall be actually saved hereby; whereas (the argument says) the latter hold, that though Christ died for all, yet he died only so, or upon such terms for them that, notwithstand-ing his dying for them, they may all perish. Now, doth it not argue as much, or more, grace and goodness in God, to provide certainly, and above all possibility of miscarrying, for the salvation of a few, than to provide a bare possibility only of salvation for all or for the salvation of all after such a manner, and upon such terms only, that all, notwithstanding this provision made for them, may very possibly perish? To this, also, I answer,

(a.) That they who teach that Christ died for all men, do not teach that he died to make provision only for a bare possibility that all may be saved, but such a provision which is fully and richly sufficient for the salvation of all men; yea, so sufficient, that all men, if they be not intolerably and unex-cusably negligent and careless in a matter of so transcendent a concern-ment unto them, may, and most certainly shall, be saved. The provision which God hath made, by the death of Christ, for the salvation of all, is so redundantly plentiful that there is no place or possibility left for the mis-carrying of any man, but by a neglect of it only. "How shall we escape," asketh the inspired writer, "if we neglect so great salvation," &c. Heb. ii. 3, clearly implying, that if they did not neglect it, but seriously and dili-gently mind and look after it, they *would* escape, (viz., the wrath of God and the vengeance of hell fire,) and, consequently, be saved. Otherwise, in case their regarding or esteeming of this salvation should be accompanied with the same danger or destruction which their neglect should bring upon them, the writer might as well, or, indeed, rather, have said, "How shall we escape," whether we "neglect this great salvation," or no?

(b.) There is no comparison, for matter of grace, goodness, or bounty, between such a provision for the salvation of all men, without exception, whereby all and every person may, if they be not wilfully bent upon their own destruction, be saved; and such, whereby there is no possibility, save only for a few, a number inconsiderable compared with the whole, to be saved. Nor is that certainty or necessity of the salvation of a few, which is pretended to be consulted or intended in this latter provision, being accompanied with the exposure of so many millions of millions of precious souls to inevitable damnation, any ways considerable, in point of grace, with that great and blessed opportunity which, by the former provision, is put into the hand of the world, and of every person of mankind, without exception, to escape the vengeance which is to come, if they please, and withal to be crowned with an incorruptible crown of glory; especially, if it be considered withal, that he that makes such a provision for a few, had wherewithal in abundance, and this disposable, contrivable to no other use or purpose, to have provided upon the same terms for all; and that all the reason he had for his non-disposing of it this way—I mean, for the benefit and blessing of all—was only his mere will and pleasure.

Suppose a man had a thousand quarters of wheat, or the like, which he knows not what to do with, or to what use to convert it, but only to the relief of a company of poor indigent creatures ready to be affamished and perish through hunger. In case this man should actually relieve only two or three persons in this distress with part of this abundance, there being a thousand before him in the same extremity, and in no possibility of being relieved from any other hand, but should rather choose to cast the residue of his grain into the sea, or bury it under ground, or some ways or other destroy the serviceableness of it unto man, than dispose of it towards the relief of any of the rest. Would not such an act as this, by reason of the unnaturalness and affectate unmercifulness of it, quite drown the grace and loveliness of his charity in relieving those few? In like manner, they who pretend the exaltation of the grace and love of God towards men, in giving Christ to die for them, whose death they grant to be sufficient, in point of merit, to save all men without exception, and yet teach that God intended only the salvation of a few, the whole lump or body of mankind standing in the same need of salvation with these few, and that he chose to suffer the merit of this death of Christ rather to vanish into the air, or to be like water spilt upon the ground (excepting only the salvation of those few by it), than to accommodate and relieve thereby the residue of mankind in their saddest and utmost extremity. What do they less than bury all that which is lovely in that act of grace or mercy towards a few, under the imputation of so great an unmercifulness or hardness of bowels towards many?

At this turn it is commonly pleaded that God is no debtor to any of his creatures, and consequently that he is and was at perfect liberty, whether he would show mercy unto any, or make provision for the salvation of the smallest number of all. Upon which account, it could not have been termed an act of unmercifulness in him, in case no provision had been made by him for the salvation of any, much less that he should not make provision for all. As this argues no unmercifulness at all in him, that he hath made no provision at all for the salvation of the devils, because he was no ways bound to it. Whereas upon men, in case they have means and opportunity to relieve the necessities of those that are in misery, and neglect to do it, the imputation and charge of unmercifulness justly lieth, because they are under a law in this behalf. So that the grace of God, in his merciful provision for the salvation of a few, is no ways obscured or disparaged by his non-providing for all. To all this I answer,

1. That neither the argument yet in hand, nor the answer given to the former objection, intermeddles little or much with the liberty or rightfulness of power vested in God to deny mercy where he pleaseth, as to show it likewise where and to whom he pleaseth. But the one and the other insist upon the demonstration of this, viz. that they who ascribe unto God reality of intentions to make provision for the salvation of all men without exception, in and by the death of Christ, upon these gracious terms for the enjoyment of it, which have been specified, render him far more gracious, lovely, and attractive to the hearts of men, than they who present him with intentions of providing only for a few thereby, upon what terms soever, with the hardening of himself against and neglect of all the rest, being incomparably far the greater number, in their greatest extremity. And this, I suppose, we have made good against all rational contradiction. But,

2. Whereas we reflected upon such an act, which our adversaries imagine to be in God, whereby they say, notwithstanding a sufficiency of merit before him, in the death of Christ, for the salvation of all as well as of a few, yet he rather suffered this precious sufficiency, in respect of the redundancy of it over and above the provision made by it for a few, to vanish or be split, than to intend any help or healing by it unto the generality of men. Whereas, I say, we censured such an act as this, as ill consisting with or obscuring the beauty and loveliness of that gracious act of God in providing for the salvation of a few, we did not herein reflect prejudice in the least upon any liberty or rightfulness of power truly competent unto or vested in God. We only showed and asserted the deformity or moral contradictiousness between two acts, which notwithstanding our adversaries ascribe, as well the one as the other, unto God.

3. Concerning that liberty of showing and denying mercy where and to whom he pleaseth, which the objection in hand asserteth unto God, we

answer, that how absolute soever this liberty in him may be conceived to be, simply or in respect of any engagement from men or any creature, yet, (a.) It is confined and subjected unto such declarations and promises which himself hath freely made; so that, for example he is no more at liberty, nor hath he any more right of power to withhold or deny mercy from and unto any of those to whom he hath promised mercy, or to whom he hath declared that he will show mercy, however otherwise they may seem unworthy or unmeet objects of mercy. He hath no more liberty, I say, to do either of these, than he hath to lie, deal unfaithfully, unjustly, and the like. Upon this account the prophet David acknowledgeth it unto God, as a signal engagement upon him, to praise and worship him, that he "hast" still "magnified thy word above all thy name." Psal. cxxxviii. 2; meaning, that whatever attribute of his (which is, either in whole or in part, his name), at any time seemed to oppose or stand up against the performance of any promise or declaration of mercy made by him, yet he always magnified his promise, by giving real, full, and seasonable performance thereunto.

He passeth not for the vailing or obscuring any other part of his name, so that his truth and faithfulness in his word may be advanced. (b.) As he hath no liberty, as some men count liberty, of showing or denying mercy, contrary to his word, so neither hath he any liberty of acting in one kind or other, and consequently neither of showing or denying mercy, in opposition to his wisdom, which is, as it were, the steerage of all his dispensations in one kind or other, according to that of the apostle formerly considered, "who worketh all things *after the counsel* of his own will," Eph. i. 11; *i. e.* according to the exigency or requirement of that most absolute, infinite wisdom of his, by which his will, and consequently his power, which is always exerted and moved unto action by and according to his will, is directed and led forth in all the movings and actings of it. Insomuch that, as we lately argued and proved in Chap. V, God is at far less liberty to decline, in any his ways and actions, the most district rules and principles of the most accurate wisdom that is, than any creature whatsoever, man, or angel. Therefore to conceit or plead for such a liberty in God of showing and denying mercy to whom he pleaseth, which is inconsistent with that determination of himself in either kind, which he hath declared in his word, is to conceive and speak unworthily of him, yea, and to shake the foundations of that hope upon which the saints and sound believers are built by the gospel. For if God be at liberty to deny mercy, contrary to his word, or will revealed therein, what assurance can the best believers have that they either are or shall be justified or saved by him? So that until our adversaries have first proved that God hath made no such declaration in the gospel as that he hath made, and is still willing to make, provision for the salvation of all men without exception, by the death of Christ, which hitherto they have not done, it is in vain for them to pretend a liberty in him of denying mercy to whom he pleaseth, by way of proof or confirmation of their opinion.

It would have been no act of unmercifulness in God, but of districtness of justice only, in case no provision had been made by him, either by the death of Christ or otherwise, for the salvation of any. Yet such an act as this would not have rendered him so gracious and lovely in the eyes of his creature, or so attractive of their hearts and souls, and consequently not so evangelical, as that act of grace hath now done and doth, whereby he hath made that blessed provision for them. And if a providing for the salvation of some, doth (in the judgment of our adversaries) render him more gracious and evangelical, than such an act or course would have done, whereby he had refused to make this provision for any at all; certainly the greater the number shall be supposed, for whom this gracious provision is made by him, so much the greater and more evangelical must that act of grace necessarily be, by which such provision is made.

And in case God had provided (whether by the death of Christ, or in any other way) but for the salvation of one man only, and had left the whole posterity of Adam, this one man excepted, to have perished everlastingly, it could be looked upon but only as such an act of grace, which is next to none at all. And wherein little of that evangelical spirit, which abounds and reigns in God, could have been discovered, yea, and would doubtless commend itself unto the intelligent creature, less for wisdom than for grace.

Proportionably, the fewer or smaller number they are supposed to be, for whom provision of salvation is now made by God, the lesser and more contracted, and so the less evangelical, must that grace needs be concluded to be, by which this provision is supposed to be made. For what proportion one, or a single person, beareth unto those few, whose salvation is (in the sense of our adversaries) now provided for by God; the same do these few bear unto all, or unto the whole body of mankind. Therefore if they judge that God showeth more grace in providing for the salvation of that number of men, which they call the elect, than he should have done in providing for one person of this number only; they have reason to judge also, in case God maketh this provision, not only for their small number of elect, but for them and all others with them, that he showeth far more grace in such a provision as this, than in that which their doctrine confineth him unto.

Nor doth it from these debates any ways follow, that in case God had made provision for the salvation of the devils, he should have manifested more grace or evangelicalness of spirit, than now according to our principles, he hath done, in providing salvation for men only, though for all men, although, it is true, the number of those for whom provision of salvation should have been made in this case had been greater, than now we suppose it to be. The reason is, because grace, especially divine grace, is not to be measured or judged of simply or merely by any beneficialness accruing unto the creature of one kind or other, but by a beneficialness accruing in an honourable and prudential way, in respect of him from whom, or by whom, this beneficialness is supposed to accrue. Acts of prodigality are, or may be beneficial to the receivers of what is thereby given, yet are they no acts of grace. Nor would it be any act of grace in a judge to spare the life of a murderer, or traitor, though this act of his, in the nature of it, is beneficial to him whose life is spared, and may possibly turn to a further benefit unto him.

The reason why these, and such like acts as these, though they may be very beneficial to their objects respectively, are notwithstanding not to be reputed acts of grace, is because grace evinces such a principle which is every ways regular and savoury; and as comely and honourable in the fruits and actings of it unto him in whom it resides, as beneficial, helpful, or refreshing unto others. Whereas prodigality, and so injustice, or inconsideration in a judge, though beneficial unto many, are yet unworthy principles, and justly dishonourable unto their subjects. So then, in case it were not, or be not well consisting with the principles of true and divine wisdom, and so would not have been truly honourable unto God to make provision for the salvation of the devils, the making of this provision for them would not have been any matter of grace in him. And consequently, upon such a supposition, he should have been never the more gracious, though in making provision for salvation, he should have taken the devils into part and fellowship with men. And that it is no ways consistent with his wisdom or honour, to spread a table of salvation before the devils, as he hath done for men, may by this clear argument a posteriori be evinced, viz. that he hath not done it. It being reasonable in the highest to conceive, that God never was, never will be wanting to himself in point of honour or glory.

Besides, that of the inspired writer, *Ou gar dēpou aggelōn epilambanetai,* Heb. ii. 16, *i. e.* for in no wise, or at no hand, doth he help, or relieve the angels (meaning, the lapsed angels), carrieth this import pregnantly and distinctly in it, that to reach forth a helping hand unto them, was not simply a thing which God was not pleased or willing to do, but such a thing which lay at a great distance from his thoughts or intentions to do. Which distance imports a signal inconsistency with or repugnancy unto his wisdom, honour, and glory. How or in what consideration or respect, the providing for the salvation of the fallen angels or devils, is or would have been repugnant to the wisdom, and so no ways consistent with the honour of God, is (haply) not unworthy a sober inquiry. But because it is somewhat eccentric to the main business in hand, and the body of our discourse begins to swell to an unacceptable bulk already, we shall decline the penetration of it at present. Only offering to consideration, whether their prodigious unnaturalness, or height of misdemeanor in sinning, above what is to be found in the sin of men, either as sinning in Adam, or by actual and personal perpetrations (ordinarily), may not upon a very reasonable account be deemed the cause or reason why it was not honourable for God, or of any good consistence with his holiness or wisdom, to stretch forth a hand of grace, or of salvation unto them.

We see in the case of men themselves, that if they sin with a high hand, especially after any considerable means of grace vouchsafed, and turn their head against the light which hath shone clearly to them, or upon the ways of holiness, wherein they have sometimes walked, that God "taketh no pleasure in them," *i. e.* that they are an abhorring to his soul; and that against all such men who shall commit that most hideous and enormous sin against the Holy Ghost, God sayeth "I swear in my wrath, that they shall not enter into my" eternal "rest." Heb. iii. 11. Now if God judgeth it a matter unbecoming his grace, holiness, or wisdom, and no ways consistent with his honour, to impart of that salvation which he hath provided in Christ for men, unto those for whom it was provided, in case their misdemeanor in sinning shall rise to such a height as hath been mentioned, and as a total and persevering apostasy importeth; can it seem any ways improbable, the devils having desperately apostatised from a far greater light, from a richer and more sensible experience of the grace, love, and bounty of God, than apostates amongst men lightly can do, that his soul should so far abominate them, together with such their stupendous apostasy, as to judge it altogether unmeet for God, unworthy that "inaccessible light" of wisdom, grace, holiness, and glory "wherein he dwelleth," to conceive so much as a thought within him in order to their salvation?

The schoolmen resolve the irremediablesness, as they term it, of the sin and misery of the devils into several causes or grounds, most of which, and these the most material, respect the greatness of their sin, the rest the quality or condition of their natures. Yet if that be true which they assign, among other reasons, why no course should be taken or thought upon by God for or about their salvation, viz. that their wills or appetites are naturally, and by the principles of their creation, unflexible, or unremovable from that object, whether it be good or evil, which they have once chosen, it is a consideration of strength enough alone to carry the business under inquiry clear before it. For if this be an essential property of their natures not to be in any capacity of changing when once they have chosen, it follows at once that, having now chosen apostasy and defection from God, they are by their own act irrecoverably, and against all possibility of redemption, concluded under sin and misery for ever. And if this were the frame and condition of their natures, and themselves conscious and privy to it (and conscious doubtless they were to the law and terms of their own creation), it renders their sin unmeasurably sinful and inexcusable above the sinfulness of the sin or sins of men.

For though Adam, and so all men in him, knew not, in case he did or should sin, whether he should obtain from God the grace of a Redeemer or no, yet neither did he know the contrary, but probably knew that he was capable of redemption. So that, though his sin was exceedingly great in many considerations otherwise, yet in this behalf it was the more rational, and so the more pardonable and excusable, viz. that he knew himself in a capacity of being restored. Whereas the angels, in case they understood the inflexibility of their wills after an election, and consequently that they were simply and absolutely unredeemable after sinning, and yet presumed to sin, must needs be the more irrational, and so the more insufferable and inexcusable in their sin.[2] But whether this doctrine of the school, concerning the unchangeableness of the wills of angels, after their first determination, be square and stable, or no, I am at present, in a fitter posture to query than determine. Only herein my thoughts are all made, that the wills of both sorts of angels, as well of those who at first chose righteousness, as of those who made a choice contrary hereunto, remain to this day unchanged; the one in their adherency to the good, the other to the evil, which they chose respectively in the beginning.

But this unchangingness doth not necessarily flow from any unchangeableness in either of them, but may, in the former, arise from the native lib-

2. Th. Aquin. Sum. Part. I. qu. 64, art. 2.

erty of their wills, which, as they had power at first to choose that which was good, so have they power, and this with enlargement by means of the sensible experience they gain continually of the sweetness of the good chosen by them, to persevere in this their choice. In the latter, this is partly from the just judgment of God denounced against them, and made fully known to them, viz. that he will upon no terms whatsoever be reconciled unto them to the days of eternity; partly also from his absolute and total withdrawing of his Spirit of grace from them. Nor do I apprehend anything considerable to oppose my belief but that they will, both the one and the other of them, remain upon the same terms unchanged to the days of eternity. Yet were I to build, I would rather choose the former of these for my foundation, because I conceive Scripture evidence more pregnant and clear for it. To say that the will of a creature should and will remain unchanged in that which is good, is no elevation of it above that sphere of excellency which is made for it to move in. But to affirm that at any time it is, or ever will be, thus *unchangeable*, is to make it a companion of his who, in the height of his pride, said, "Ero similis Altissimo," I will be like unto the Most High.

But concerning the unredeemableness of the devils, I much rather approve another reason which the forementioned authors, the schoolmen, give of it. "Diabolus," say they, "peccavit in termino; homo, in via:" *i. e.* The devil sinned being at his journey's end; man sinned (only) by the way. The meaning is, that the devil sinned in an estate of perfect blessedness, under a full fruition of God, in which respect his sin was provoking in the highest. Whereas man, when he sinned, was but in his progress towards such a condition, and was not as yet possessed of it; and in this respect sinned, though at a very high rate of provocation, his sin simply considered, yet at a far lower rate than the devil, because against a far lower light, and less grace received. But of this enough, if not more than enough, our main business being no more interested in it than we formerly intimated it to be. Nor did the difficulty laid in our way exact of us anything more than only to prove that it had been no act of grace in God to provide for the salvation of the devil, which, I suppose, hath been done with measure heaped up. Therefore,

4. Lastly, to the plea made for a liberty in God to show and to deny mercy, as and to whom he pleaseth, I answer yet further, that in case it be found a thing utterly and clearly inconsistent with the wisdom of God, or with the goodness and graciousness of his nature, having provided means

of salvation as sufficient and proper for the salvation of all as of a few (which our adversaries neither do, nor with any face of reason can deny), to limit himself in the consignment or designment of them to the salvation of a few, with a disserviceabling of them as to all the rest, then hath he no liberty to confine or limit himself after any such manner, nor to evacuate the usefulness or beneficialness of these means in respect of the generality of men. This consequence hath been sufficiently argued and proved already, and however, is of itself lightsome enough to make every denier, yea, or questioner of it ashamed. Therefore I assume, for God to limit himself in the consignment of those means of salvation unto a few, which he hath provided with a sufficiency and aptness for the salvation of all, or to disintend the salvation of the greatest part of men by them, is a thing clearly and utterly inconsistent with the wisdom of God and graciousness of his nature. Therefore he hath no liberty in the case specified to straighten himself within the narrow bounds of such a consignment as that mentioned. In this argument we suppose, and take for granted, that the death of Christ is a means as sufficient for the salvation of all men, and as proper and meet for the salvation of all, as of a few. And in this, I presume, we have no adversary; or, however, the generality of those who are adversaries in the main of the controversy depending, accord with us therein. The reason of the assumption, in the argument now propounded, is, as to the former part of it, because it is notoriously repugnant to the principles of sound wisdom to make waste of anything which is serviceable or useful for any honourable or worthy end and purpose. And the more precious and difficult of procurement a means is, the more honourable and excellent the end or purpose is for which it is appropriately and peculiarly serviceable. The more repugnant it is to all principles of wisdom to sacrifice it upon the service of vanity, and to do nothing with it at all.

Now, questionless, the death of Jesus Christ is a means most choice and precious; not another of like preciousness, efficacy, or worth, to be procured or levied by God himself: the end for which this death of Christ is most appropriately serviceable, is the salvation of the whole world, which is an end most honourable and worthy. Therefore it must needs be notoriously inconsistent with the wisdom of God to dispose of this means only in order to the procurement and effecting of an end far less honourable, as, namely, the salvation of a few, the obtaining whereof the excellent worth and weight of the said means doth incomparably over-ponderate and transcend. So that a non-disposal of it towards the obtaining of the just and adequate end for which it is appropriately useful and serviceable, is to evacuate and make useless, though not in whole, yet in part, the super-transcendent excellency, worth, and virtue thereof. But of this lately.

The reason of the latter part of the said assumption, is, because it is every whit as repugnant to the nature of grace, goodness and bountifulness of disposition, not to relieve the miserable, who are every ways capable of relief. And this with honour to him that shall relieve them, when a man hath abundantly in his hand wherewith to relieve them, especially when withal he hath no other end or use whereunto to dispose what he hath in this kind but only towards the relief of such persons. And as the apostle John argueth and demandeth concerning men, "But whoso hath this world's good, and seeth his brother have need, and shutteth up his bowels of compassion from him, how dwelleth the love of God in him?" 1 John iii. 17. In like manner we may well reason, and demand concerning God: If God, having the good of the world to come, means of salvation for his poor lost creature, man, and yet shutteth up his compassion from him, how dwelleth the love of man in him? And yet the Scripture, as we formerly heard, speaketh very excellent and glorious things of his love unto men, no where confining it within the narrow circle or sphere of the elect or some few particulars. Nor, indeed, can he, with any congruity of expression, be called *philanthrōpos*, a lover of men, or of mankind, in case he loveth some few particular men only; as he is no where in Scripture called *philaggelos*, a lover of angels, although he loves a very considerable number of this kind of creature, as viz. all his elect or holy angels, because he loveth not all particulars. But of this more largely in the premises, Chap. V. To the point in hand: Certain it is, 1. That God hath no other use or occasion of contrivement of the death of Christ save only for and in order towards the glorifying of himself in and by the salvation of men, or, at least, none other but what would be as effectually promoted and attained by it though it should be intended by him for the salvation of the generality of men.

2. That this death of Christ is every whit as proper and as sufficient a means to bless the whole generation of mankind with salvation as those few whom our adversaries suppose to be only blessed by it in this kind. 3. That it would be no ways dishonourable unto God, nor of any harder consistence with his justice, wisdom, hatred of sin, or with any other of his attributes whatsoever, to intend the salvation of any others, or of all men, by the death of Christ, than it is to intend the salvation of those few whom our adversaries grant to be the objects of his intentions in this kind. 4. That

the generality of men, or those whose salvation our adversaries suppose not to be intended by God in or by the death of Christ, are every whit as miserable, and stand altogether in as much need of salvation, as those whose salvation they suppose to have been intended thereby. By the light of these grounds laid together, it plainly appears that it is a thing signally inconsistent with the grace, goodness, mercy, bounty of the Divine Nature or Being to consign the death of Christ to the salvation only of a few, and to suffer the far greatest part of men (being in every respect as salvable, and this by the same means and with the same proportion to any end whatsoever as they), to remain miserable and perish everlastingly for want of a like consignment unto them for the same end.

To reply and say that God gains the manifestation of his sovereignty, or prerogative of showing mercy and denying mercy to whom he pleaseth, by intending the salvation only of a few, which he could not have gained by intending the salvation of all, is to flee to a polluted sanctuary, and which hath been in this very chapter razed to the ground, and not so much as one stone thereof left upon another that hath not been thrown down.

Fifthly, that Christ died for all men, without exception of any, I demonstrate further by the light of this argument: "That doctrine whose tenor, frame, and import are of a direct and clear tendency to promote and advance godliness amongst men, is, questionless, evangelical and the truth. But such is the tenor, frame, and import of that doctrine which teacheth that Christ died for all men without exception. Therefore, questionless, this doctrine is evangelical, and none other but the truth." The major proposition in this argument needeth no more proof than the sun needs a candle whereby to be seen when he shineth in his might. Yet, if a proof be required, we open that signal character or description of the gospel delivered by the apostle, Tit. i.1, where he calls it *alētheias tēs kat eusebeian*, "the truth which is after godliness;" meaning a body or system of truth, calculated and framed with the most exquisite proportion, efficacy, and aptness that can be imagined, for the promotion, propagation, and advancement of godliness in the world, as we formerly interpreted. So that what particular doctrine soever is found to be of the same tendency, must of necessity be a member of the same body, a branch of the same truth, or, however, clearly and fairly comporting with it, and so a truth. For there is nothing accordable with truth but truth.

The truth of the minor proposition, also, hath been set before the reader in a clear and perfect light, in the precedure of this discourse in Chap. V, where we evinced, above contradiction, that the doctrine of our adversaries, asserting only a limited redemption by Christ, leaveth no hope at all, or at most but a very cold, feeble, and faint hope, to any ungodly or urregenerate man of being saved by Christ. And, consequently, it hath nothing in it much quickening or provoking unto godliness, at least, in respect of such persons who are at present ungodly, who are the far greatest part of the world, but is full of a spirit of antipathy and opposition hereunto; inasmuch as whatsoever is of a destructive or discouraging import to any man's hope of obtaining upon endeavours, is obstructive and quenching to these endeavours themselves. Whereas the spirit and genius of the doctrine maintained by us is, to fill all men whatsoever with the richest and greatest assurance of hope they can desire, that, upon their diligent and faithful endeavours to repent and to believe, repentance and faith shall be given unto them by God; and that, upon the like endeavours to persevere in a course of repenting and believing (these are not works), they shall have perseverance also given, and so in the end be unquestionably saved.

What is commonly alleged in defence of the doctrine of limited redemption, against the argument now propounded, hath been fully answered in the place last referred unto, together with whatsoever, I conceive, can lightly be alleged further upon the same account. If I were conscious unto, or could suspect anything, that with any competent show of probability might be yet objected to the disabling of the force of the said argument, I call God for a record upon my soul that I would not conceal or dissemble it out of any indulgence to mine own opinion. This, in brief, for my fifth argument.

Sixthly, "If Christ died for the elect only, and not for all and every man, then will there no man be found culpable of judgment, or liable unto condemnation or perishing, for or through unbelief, or for not believing on Christ for salvation. But there are many that will be found liable to condemnation, yea, and will be actually condemned for their unbelief: Ergo." The reason of the consequence in the former proposition is pregnant and clear. First, the elect will not be found liable to condemnation for unbelief, because they, according to the principles of our adversaries, shall be all infallibly drawn or brought to believe. Also, no reprobate can be liable to condemnation for not believing on Christ for salvation, because he transgresseth no law or precept of God by such his unbelief; for, doubtless, God commandeth no man to believe on Christ for salvation but only those for whom there is salvation in him; as he commandeth no man to gather grapes of thorns or figs of thistles.

Nay, his constant manner and method of teaching, charging, admonishing, and treating with men in other like cases imports that, in case there were no salvation for men in Christ, he would be so far from admonishing or charging them to believe on him, that he would take them off, and dissuade them from believing or depending on him in that kind. For, if we search the Scriptures, we shall still find that God, upon all occasions, counseleth and chargeth men to take heed of uncertain, empty, and vain dependencies, and to seek for help, peace, and safety where they are to be found. Places of this import are obvious and frequent. "And Samuel said unto the people, Fear not: ye have done all this wickedness: yet turn not aside from following the Lord, but serve the Lord with all your heart; And turn ye not aside: *for then should ye go after vain things which cannot profit nor deliver: for they are vain*; for the Lord will not forsake his people," &c. 1 Sam. xii. 20-22.

So again: "Trust not in oppression, and become not vain in robbery: if riches increase, set not your heart upon them," Psal. lxii. 10. Immediately before, speaking of God, he had said: "Trust in him at all times; ye people, pour out your heart before him: God is a refuge for us. Selah. Surely men of low degree are vanity, and men of high degree are a lie: to be laid in the balance, they are altogether lighter than vanity." Elsewhere: "Wilt thou set thine eyes upon that which is not? For riches certainly make themselves wings;" Prov. xxiii. 5. So also: "Thus saith the Lord; Cursed be the man that trusteth in man, and maketh flesh his arm, and whose heart departeth from the Lord; for he shall be like the heath in the desert," Jer. xvii. 5, 6, to omit other passages of like consideration without end. It being, then, the constant manner of God in his addressments unto men to dissuade them from begging their bread in desolate places, from laying out their silver for that which is not bread, from leaning upon broken reeds, from expecting rain from clouds without water, from putting their trust in things that cannot help or profit, &c. It is at no hand to be believed that he will counsel or command any man to acquire "gold," or "white raiment" of Jesus Christ, unless he knew that he had both the one and the other for them; to depend upon him for salvation, unless this great and blessed commodity were in his hand ready for them. Yea, it is the manner of God, and so of the Lord Christ also, to take men off, and turn their expectations and dependencies aside even from himself, in respect of a receiving such things from him which he finds them inclined to expect from him, and himself in no posture of mind or will to give them. Upon this account he speaketh unto

Jeremiah thus: "Therefore pray not thou for this people, neither lift up cry nor prayer for them, neither make intercession to me: for I will not hear thee." Jer. vii. 16.

The emphasis of all this variety of expression, "pray not, lift not up cry nor prayer, make no intercession," &c. standeth, I conceive, in this: viz. to declare that when he is fully purposed and resolved not to do a thing, he would not have anything at all, little or much, in one kind or other, done by the creature for the obtaining of it at his hand. He expresseth himself once and again to the same prophet in words of like effect and almost of the same tenor, Jer. xi. 14; xiv. 11. So when he perceived that Amaziah and the men of Judah expected and depended upon his presence with those hundred thousand men of valour, which they had hired with a great sum of money out of Israel to assist them against the Edomites, and he was fully purposed not to be present with them or to prosper them in battle, he gave knowledge unto Amaziah and those with him accordingly, and by an express from himself, by the hand of a prophet, advised him to discharge this army, which accordingly he did, and prospered, 2 Chron. xxv. 6, 7. In like manner our Saviour, in the gospel, knowing that the scribe who came unto him with this profession, "Master, I will follow thee whithersoever thou goest," Matt. viii. 19, expected some great accommodations by him in the world, quenched his expectations in this kind with this water cast upon them, "The foxes have holes, and the birds of the air have nests; but the Son of man hath not where to lay his head." Matt. viii. 20.

That passage also of his to his disciples savours much of the same spirit: "In my Father's house are many mansions: *if it were not so, I would have told you.*" John xiv. 2. This was clearly implying that his disposition and spirit stood to deal clearly and plainly with them about such things which they might and might not expect from him; and that he would not suffer them to look for more from him than what he was fully able and provided of, and withal ready and willing to confer upon them. And it being, as we all know, the determinate counsel and most fixed will and purpose of God not to give salvation unto final impenitents and unbelievers, he hath openly and aloud proclaimed the thing accordingly in the hearing of all the world, that men might not be deceived, frustrated, or undone, by any their expectations from him in this kind. So that we may, without the least regret of mind or thought, conclude, that God enjoineth no man, requireth no man to believe on Jesus Christ for salvation, or to expect salvation by him, but only those for whom he hath purchased or provided salvation, and is accordingly ready and willing to give it unto them. Therefore if the doctrine of our adversaries be orthodox, which teacheth that Christ died not for all men, but for the elect only, certain it is that none but the elect are enjoined by God to believe on him for salvation. And consequently no other person who believeth not on him transgresseth any commandment of God in this his non-believing, and so cannot be liable unto any condemnation at all thereby, much less to the condemnation of hell. This for proof of the major proposition in the argument last proposed.

The tenor of the minor was this: But there are many that will be found liable to condemnation, yea, that will be actually condemned, for unbelief. This proposition hath, I conceive, such pregnant affinity with the express and unavoidable letter of the Scripture, that the mention of a place or two, speaking to the point, will be proof in abundance. "He that believeth on him, is not condemned: but he that believeth not," (viz. in case this Son of God hath been declared or preached unto him; for it is a non-believing in this case only of which he here speaketh,) "is condemned already, because he hath not believed in the name of the only begotten Son of God." John iii. 18. "Is condemned already;" *i. e.* his sin in not believing is so notorious, and so provoking in the sight of God, that it carries condemnation, as it were, in the very face of it, and renders the person guilty, as good as condemned, before the sentence of condemnation passeth from the mouth of the Judge upon him: according to the ancient saying,

"Illo nocens se damnat, quo peccat, die." i. e.
"The self-same day wherein he sinneth,
The person guilty, himself condemneth."

Yea, the Scripture itself, the better to set forth the greatness and great danger of the sin of unbelief, speaketh of it much after the same manner. "It was necessary," say Paul and Barnabas with great boldness unto the Jews, "that the word of God should first have been spoken to you: but seeing ye put it from you," *kai ouk axious krinete eautous tēs aiōniou zōēs, i.e.* and judge, (or, adjudge, decernitis,) "yourselves unworthy of eternal life," *i. e.* saith Beza, by this your own fact pass sentence, as it were, and give judgment against yourselves, "lo, we turn to the Gentiles," Acts xiii. 46. Their rejecting or non-believing in Christ, revealed by the ministry of the gospel unto them, is interpreted by the Holy Ghost as a sentence of condemnation pronounced against themselves by themselves. So again: "He that believeth not shall be damned," Mark xvi. 16; meaning not only, if so much, for his other sins, as for his non-believing; as is fully evident from other places, where the high-provokingness of the sin of unbelief, in the sight of God, is very plainly and significantly asserted. "For if the word spoken by angels was steadfast, and every transgression and disobedience received a just recompence of reward; How shall we escape if we neglect so great salvation; which at the first began to be spoken by the Lord..." &c., Heb. ii. 2, 3. When he saith, "If we neglect so great salvation," he expresseth or points at unbelief in the ordinary and most proper cause of it, viz. negligence or contempt of the gospel, and of the grace therein offered by God unto the world; which neglect or contempt are sins highly offensive and displeasing unto him. This appears yet more plainly in the parable of the marriage-feast or great supper, where, upon the report of the servant sent forth to invite the guests, of their slight pretences for their not coming, the master of the feast is said to have been angry, and, in the heat of his anger, to have said, that "none of those men which were bidden should taste of my supper." Luke xiv. 24.

Besides, the sin of unbelief is interpreted by the Holy Ghost himself, as a giving of the lie to God, or, which is the same, the making of him a liar. And in this respect it must be a sin highly exasperating and provoking him, and consequently must needs be a sin exposing the sinner unto condemnation. "He that believeth not God hath made him a liar; because he believeth not the record that God gave of his Son." 1 John v. 10. This proposition, then, being unquestionable, viz. that unbelief, and that by way of demerit, as well (if not rather) as any other sin, and not by the mere pleasure or appointment of God only, rendereth men justly obnoxious unto condemnation. The argument of the last proposal stands impregnable against all assaults; and therefore Christ died for all men without exception, and not for the elect only.

The truth of this conclusion I evince by this demonstration also: "If Christ died not for all men, but for the elect only, then did God put the world (I mean, the generality of mankind) into a far better and more desirable state and condition, in the first Adam and under the law of works, than he hath done in the second Adam, or under the law of grace. But this is not so. The world was not at first put by God into a better condition in the first Adam, or under the law of works, than it is in the second Adam, and under the law of grace: Ergo."

In this argument, I do not apprehend what, according to the principles of our adversaries themselves, can reasonably be denied. The consequence in the proposition opposeth none of these principles; for doubtless none of them gainsayeth any of these propositions, either: 1. It is a better and more desirable condition to be in a capacity or under a possibility of being saved, than to be in an utter incapacity, or under an absolute impossibility of obtaining this blessedness; or, 2. In the first Adam all men were alike salvable, being all furnished with gracious abilities for the doing of the will of God, and for the observing of that law upon the observation whereof their life and peace depended, even as Adam himself was furnished in this kind, with whom all men stood in one and the same condition; or, 3. Lastly, that the generality, or far greatest part of mankind are not brought into a capacity of salvation by the second Adam, no satisfaction or atonement being made for their sins by him. They who grant these three conclusions, if they be willing to be led by their own light, cannot stumble at the consequence in the major proposition.

Nor can I conceive wherein the minor should offend them. For it is the uncontroverted sense of all divines, as far as yet I understand, that the second Adam is a far greater benefactor to mankind than the first Adam was, even whilst his innocency remained with him. And that the condition of men in general is much better under the second covenant, the covenant of grace, than it was under the first, the law, or covenant of works. Nor is it at any hand worthy belief, that God should put the world into a better estate, or posture of well-being in the first man, who "was from the earth, earthy," than in the second man, who "is the Lord from heaven;" especially considering that it is the constant method of the Almighty in his works and dispensations to begin with that which is less perfect, to proceed unto that which is more, and to conclude with that which is most perfect of all.

"First the blade," saith our Saviour, "then the ear, after that," in the last place, "the full corn in the ear," Mark iv. 28. And the apostle tells us, in another case, that "when that which is perfect is come, that which is in part," or imperfect, "shall be done away," 1 Cor. xiii.10. So that, it seems, that which is perfect is still hindmost in the retinue of God's proceedings, as Rachel and her children were in Jacob's march when he went to meet his brother Esau, Gen. xxxiii. 2. Thus "God, who at sundry times, and in divers manners spake in time past unto the fathers by the prophets, Hath in these last days hath spoken unto us by his Son," Heb. i. 1, 2. But the path we now speak of hath been so much occupied and beaten with the feet of the providence of the most wise God, that it is visible enough to all the world. As to the particular in hand, viz. that the grace of God abounds to the world much more in the latter, the new covenant, which he hath struck with it in Jesus Christ, than it did in the former covenant made with it in Adam, appears, as in general by those glorious things that are everywhere spoken of the latter covenant, above anything so much as intimated concerning the former, so more particularly from that consideration which the apostle suggests unto us in this passage: "And not as it was by one that sinned, so is the gift: for the judgment was by one unto condemnation, but the free gift is of many offenses unto justification." Rom. v. 16.

Whereas he saith that "the judgment was by one (*i.e.* by reason of or upon the commission of one sin only, as appears from the antithesis in the latter clause, "but the free gift is of many offenses") unto condemnation," he plainly informeth us, that the first covenant made with the world in the first Adam was so narrow, peremptory, and strict, that in case any person of mankind should at any time, and though but once, have tripped or stepped aside from anything commanded therein, he became presently a dead man hereby, wholly bereft of all hope or possibility of being ever recovered or restored to the favour of God by means of this covenant. This is according to that cited by the same apostle: "Cursed is every one that continueth not in all things which are written in the book of the law to do them." Gal. iii. 10. Whereas the covenant of grace made with the world in Jesus Christ is (as we are taught in the words, "but the free gift is of many offenses unto justification") so above measure gracious, that though a man sinneth oft, yea, and this very grievously, yet he is not hereby cut off from a hope of re-enjoying the love of God. Nay, by the express tenor of this covenant, he hath assurance from God that, upon his repentance, his sins, how many soever, of what nature soever, shall be forgiven him; yea, and this sealed unto him by baptism, according to that of the evangelists, "John did...preach the baptism of repentance for the remission of sins," Mark i. 4; Luke iii. 3; *i. e.* preached this doctrine, that by that "baptism" which he was commanded to administer, God did confirm or seal unto men "the remission of their sins" upon their repentance, in such a sense and manner as Abraham is said to have "received the sign of circumcision, a seal of the righteousness of the faith which he had yet being uncircumsized..." &c. Rom. iv. 11, *i. e.* of that justification, or forgiveness of sins, which God, upon and by means of his believing had conferred upon him. This by the way.

At what door of evasion an escape can be made from the hand of this argument I cannot readily imagine. If the cause we oppose be any ways defensible against it, it is by some such plea as this: The world, or mankind, may be said to be put into a better condition by Christ, or by the covenant of grace, than it was by Adam, and by the covenant of works, inasmuch as a considerable part hereof is by Christ put into such a capacity of salvation which shall certainly be actuated, and so a great number of men certainly saved. Whereas in Adam, though all men were in a capacity, or under a possibility of salvation, yet this capacity was so narrow, weak, or remote, that there was little hope, or probability, that any man would be saved by the means or advantage thereof, which accordingly, as we know, came to pass. Now is it not better for a family, or other community of men, to have good assurance that some of their members shall have great matters of honour and estate bestowed upon them, though all the rest were made incapable of such privileges, than to be at an uncertainty whether any one of them shall be preferred in this kind or no? To this I answer,

It is at no hand to be granted, that the whole species, or generality of mankind, were in Adam invested only with a narrow, faint, remote capacity of salvation or of happiness. For, (a.) They were created in an actual possession of happiness, and with the light of God's countenance shining brightly upon them. They were all made "upright," or righteous, Eccles. vii. 29, and "in the image of God," Gen. i. 27, and so could not be miserable, and consequently in no danger or likelihood of becoming miserable. For such a condition as this had itself been misery. As for the possibility of becoming miserable with and under which they were created, it imported neither danger nor likelihood of their becoming miserable, being nothing else but an essential distinguishing badge of their creatureship, without which they could no more be made than water without moisture, or the earth without a shadow projectible from it. (b.) Concerning the matter of event, nothing can be inferred from hence touching any slipperiness of the place or ground on which they stood in Adam.

The greatest unlikelihoods sometimes take place when probabilities vanish, and turn to nothing, as in the fulfilling of that pair of predictions by our Saviour, "Many that are first shall be last; and the last shall be first." Matt. xix. 30; "The kings of the earth," saith Jeremiah in his Lamentations, "and all the inhabitants of the world, would not have believed that the adversary and the enemy should have entered into the gates of Jerusalem." Lam. iv. 12; and yet we know they did enter. Who would have said that David, a man attested by God, for "a man after his own heart," and "one that would fulfill all his pleasure," a man who said of God, "thou has hast taught me from my youth," Psa. lxxi. 17; to whom the "statutes and judgments" of God "were sweeter also than the honey and the honey-comb," Psa. xix. 10;

"more to be desired than gold, than much fine gold," ibid.; a man that had "rejoiced in the way of thy (God's) testimonies, as much as in all riches," Psa. cxix. 14; who said he was "afflicted and ready to die from my youth up," Psa. lxxxviii. 15, *i. e.* sorely, deeply, and constantly exercised with afflictions from first to last; who, I say, would have said that such a man as this would, together with adultery, have committed murder, and this upon the vilest and most execrable terms, that such a sin, I suppose, was ever known to be committed by any man?

And yet we know that such a thing was done even by this man. So again, who would have said, but only he, to whom "the darkness and the light are both alike," Psa. cxxxix. 12, that Peter, a disciple so zealously devoted unto his Lord and Master, whose heart a little before was set to stand by him, though "all men" besides "should forsake him," yea, rather to "die" with him, than "deny" him, Matt. xxvi. 35, should, all this notwithstanding, soon after, not only "deny" him. And that upon no great account of danger, but forswear him also once and again, and this with a "curse?" Matt. xxvi. 70, 72, 74. But David and Peter both repented. By these and many like experiments that may be added, it appears that the miscarrying of all men in Adam is no sufficient argument of any irreconcilable deficiency in the foundation of their standing and remaining happy in him. Yea, (c.) and lastly for this, they stood upon as good terms in Adam for the continuance of that happiness, in the fruition whereof they were created, and consequently for escaping death and misery, as men ordinarily wish or desire for the security of their lives, their estates, and what otherwise is dear unto them.

For who desireth any better terms of assurance for his life or estate, than to be able to defend and make good the one and the other against all assailants that can possibly invade or endanger them; and withal to be in a sufficient capacity of knowing or discovering when any attempt or assault shall be made upon them? Such a security as this had all mankind in Adam for the perpetuation of that good and happy condition, which was their portion from the gracious and bountiful hand of their Creator, in the day wherein he created them. They were endued with strength every way sufficient to withstand all tempters, and temptations unto sin, yea, and were in a regular capacity to have discovered the approach of any temptation, and of whatsoever might endanger them; and so to have preserved the unspottedness of their native integrity, and consequently to have maintained themselves in an uninterrupted possession of that rich and happy inheritance, which was vested in them by the law of their creation. Therefore,

The comparison of the family or community specified in the objection is altogether irrelevant to the case in hand; and besides, it demands that, as reasonable to be granted which is nothing less. For it is not better for the generality of a family or greater community of men, that some few of the members, either of the one or the other, should have the greatest assurance that can be given of the greatest things that can be enjoyed, all the rest of their members being left to unavoidable beggary, torment, and misery, than that all particulars of either should be put into such a capacity and way of being all honourable and happy, that by a regular, prudent, and careful behaviour of themselves and managing the opportunities which are before them, there should none of them miscarry, nor fail of such enjoyments. For thus the comparison ought to be stated, to make it truly representative of the great business whereof we are in travail.

Now it is not better for the generality of a state, or great commonwealth, that some two or three, or some small and inconsiderable number of the members or inhabitants thereof, should be great favourites of the prince, or of those in chief places, and have riches, honours, offices, and places of power heaped upon them without end, all the rest being made slaves, and divested of all capacity, so much as of any tolerable subsisting in the state, than it would be, that all and every of the said members, or inhabitants, should be put into a hopeful and ready way, by their regular industry and honest demeanour of themselves, to thrive and lift up their heads, and live like men. Although in the meantime they might, either through voluntary and supine carelessness and sloth, or through some vile practices otherwise, deprive themselves of such happiness. That cannot be better for the generality of any community of men, which induceth an absolute necessity of extreme misery upon the far greater part of them, though attended with all imaginable advantages to some few, than that which is as an effectual door opened unto them all, unto all happiness, although it be not so opened, but that they may, through a supine negligence, and unfaithfulness to their own interest, shut it against themselves. That which is worse for the greater part, cannot be better for the whole. So then our argument last propounded remains still in full force: Christ certainly died for all men; because otherwise the world or generality of mankind, should have been better and more graciously dealt with, and provided for by God in the first Adam, than in the second. But Christ's blessings are far greater.

The same doctrine I confirm yet further by the seal and warrant of this argument: If Christ died not for all men without exception, then no man whatsoever, in his unregenerate estate, stands bound to believe in him, or to depend on him, at least with any certainty of faith or hope for salvation. But there are many men who, in their unregenerate estate, stand bound thus to believe in him and depend upon him. Yea, all men without exception, at least all that have not yet sinned the sin unpardonable, stand bound thus to believe and thus to depend; Ergo.

The reason of the sequel in the former proposition, is, because no man stands bound to do that which he hath not a sufficient ground or reason to do; or, to speak somewhat more warily, for the doing of which there is no sufficient ground or reason. Yea, the doing of anything upon such terms, I mean without a sufficient ground in reason for the doing it, is an act irregular, sinful, and displeasing unto God. "Also, that the soul be without knowledge," saith Solomon, "it is not good: and he that hasteth with his feet, sinneth." Prov. xix. 2. The former clause was rendered somewhat more plainly in our former translation, thus; "Without knowledge the mind is not good;" *i. e.* though a man in what he doth, means or intends never so well, yet unless he knows or apprehends a sufficient reason or ground for what he doth, his good meaning will not justify him, or make him sinless in his action; according to what followeth in the latter clause, "But he that hasteth within his feet," *i. e.* that is forwarder in his affections than in his judgment, that falls upon action, before he knows a good cause why and wherefore he so acteth, "sinneth."

Upon this account our Saviour reproveth the man that saluted him by that honourable and divine title of, good: "Why callest thou me, good? there is none good but one, that is God." Matt. xix. 17. Doubtless the meaning of the man, in styling him, "good," was good, and proceeded from a reverent opinion of him; yea, in styling him, "good" he spake nothing but truth, and that according to our Saviour's own principles, inasmuch as he was indeed God. Yet because the man had not this knowledge of him, and so no sufficient reason for what he did, or said, in calling him, "good," therefore he reproveth him for so doing or speaking. To this point also lieth that of the apostle, "Whatsoever is not of faith, is sin;" Rom. xiv. 23, *i. e.* whatsoever a man doth, not having a sufficient ground in reason, one or more, on which to ground a belief or persuasion of the lawfulness of it, is sinful; viz. quoad hominem, in respect of the doer, not always, or necessarily, quoad rem, or in the nature of the thing itself. Yea, to believe anything, without a sufficient ground in reason to satisfy or convince a man of the truth of it, the Holy Ghost termeth the belief of the simple or foolish, according to that of Solomon, "The simple believeth every word," Prov. xiv. 15; or, as our former translation read it, "The foolish will believe every thing," *i. e.* as well that, for which there is good reason why it should be true, as that for which there is none, which is a lash, loose, and unsavoury kind of faith, and such as God relisheth not, regardeth not, no not when the object of it, or the thing believed, is a truth. For God, as the wise man informeth us, "hath no pleasure in fools." Eccles. v. 4. So that if there be no sufficient ground in reason, why any unregenerate person should believe or depend on Christ for salvation with certainty of faith, most certain it is that he stands not bound in duty hereunto. Now if Christ died only for the elect, and no unregenerate person certainly knoweth, or can know, that he is one of the elect, it is a clear case that he can have no sufficient ground in reason to believe or depend upon him upon such terms. That no unregenerate man certainly knoweth, or can know, that he is one of the elect, hath been proved formerly, and that ex abundanti; viz. where it was fully evinced, that no unregenerate person hath so much as any probable ground whereon to judge that he is elected.

If it be objected, yes, an unregenerate person hath the command of God to believe or depend on Christ for salvation, and this is a sufficient ground in reason for him to do accordingly. To this I answer, by granting the whole argument; but retrench, that if unregenerate persons have the command of God to depend on him for salvation it is upon the ground lately evinced in this chapter above all contradiction, viz., that there is salvation in God for them, and, consequently, purchased by him for them by Christ's death. For he hath salvation for no man upon any other account, John xii. 24. So that this objection rather strengtheneth than weakeneth the doctrine we maintain.

The minor proposition in the argument last advanced by us, which only affirmeth, as to the exigency of our cause, that many unregenerate persons stand bound in duty to believe on Christ for salvation, is too rich in evidence to stand in need of proof. For, 1. The Scripture saith expressly, that "God… now commandeth all men every where," and, therefore, unregenerate men as well as others, "to repent," Acts xvii. 30. If to repent, then to believe also; inasmuch as there can be no sound repentance, such as God commandeth, without faith. And if so be men yet unregenerate stand not bound in duty or conscience to believe on Christ, then is it no matter of sin in them to make God a liar. "He that believeth not God maketh him a liar, because he believeth not the record God gave of his Son." 1 John v. 10; meaning, that whosoever justifieth or believeth God in the record he hath given of his Son, must needs believe on him: viz. because the tenor of this record is, that "whosoever believeth on him should not perish, but have everlasting life." Now, he that believeth this, can no more refuse or forbear to believe on Christ than he can be content eternally to perish, or refuse everlasting life, as not worthy his believing for the obtaining of it. But, doubtless, it is sinful in any man to make God a liar, (*i. e.* either to do, or to neglect to do, any act, by the doing or neglect whereof God is any ways represented as untrue of his word, as he is by any man's non-believing on Christ) and consequently, every man, except the before excepted, stands bound in duty and conscience to believe on Christ. Again, secondly, if no unregenerate men had any band of duty or precept from God lying upon them to believe on Christ, whosoever of this sort of men should at any time believe on him should supererogate, and do more than what he is by God commanded to do. Consequently, all believers, without exception, should be supererogators in their first act of believing, because, until now they were unregenerate persons. But the proof of this proposition is, I suppose, supererogatory, and more than any darkness or doubtfulness in it, yea, and haply, more than our adversaries themselves require. Therefore, we pass on to another argument.

"If God intended not the death of Christ for all men, and that in order to their salvation, then have not all men a sufficiency of means vouchsafed unto them whereby to be saved. But all men have a sufficiency of means in this kind vouchsafed unto them; Ergo:" The consequence in the former proposition is pregnant without proof. For it is greater than contradiction, that they who have no propitiatory sacrifice offered up for them, nor atonement made for their sins, have no sufficiency of means for salvation. So that if God intended no such oblation, no such atonement for any man or number of men, most certain it is that such men are in no capacity of salvation; and, consequently, can have no sufficiency of means whereby to be saved.

The truth of the minor proposition, which avoucheth a sufficiency of means vouchsafed by God unto all men whereby to be saved, might be evidenced by sundry demonstrations.

First, if all men have not a sufficiency of means vouchsafed unto them whereby to be saved, then God dealeth with men far more strictly, and with greater severity in the new covenant, the covenant of grace, than he did in the first covenant, which was a covenant of works. The reason hereof is, because in, or under the covenant of works, men were invested by God with sufficient means for the performance of that covenant, and so for the obtaining of the great reward promised or covenanted therein, which was no less than eternal life, though possibly, not a life so rich in blessedness as that covenanted with men in the covenant of grace. That all men, without exception, had a sufficiency of means in Adam to have persisted in innocency, and to perform all the articles and terms required of them in that covenant, which was made with them in him, is the sense of all men learned in the Scriptures, as well modern as ancient, that yet I have heard of; nor will it, I suppose, be denied by our adversaries themselves. If it should, there is proof upon proof at hand to make it good; but what needs a levy of men to gain that by force which is voluntarily offered? Now, then, it being far greater rigour and severity to impose such terms or conditions upon a man, in order to the saving of his life, or for the obtaining of any desirable good, which are of an impossible performance unto him, than to impose only such which he hath competent abilities to perform. Evident it is, that God must needs be more rigorous and hard unto men in the covenant of grace, made with them in and by Christ, than he was in the covenant of works made with them in Adam, in case it be supposed that he required impossible conditions of them in the former, and only such which were possible in the latter.

But that God dealeth more graciously and bountifully with men in the second covenant, made with them in Christ, than he did in the first, which was made with them in Adam, is the pregnant result of all things (in a manner) that God hath spoken unto the world by his Son in the gospel. Nor can our adversaries themselves deny it without the loud reclamation of evidence and truth. To pretend that God dealeth more graciously and bountifully with his elect in the covenant of grace, than he did in the covenant of works, but not with the generality of men, is but a slim evasion. This supposeth, either that the covenant of grace is not made with the generality of men (which is a notorious untruth, and hath been detected accordingly once and again already), or that this covenant is not made upon the same terms and conditions, with all those interested or included in it; which is a conceit of no whit better an accord, either with reason or truth.

Secondly, if all men have not a sufficiency of means granted unto them by God, then God dealeth with the generality, or far greatest part of men, more rigorously and with less mercy, and this under the covenant of grace, than he doth with the devils themselves. The reason is plain; because, in case men have not a sufficiency of means whereby to be saved, they have only means given them whereby to increase their condemnation. Yea, such means, and so and upon such terms given them, that they cannot but use them to their greater and more heavy condemnation, than that whereunto they should or could have been liable, had no such covenant of grace been made with them or tendered unto them. For if they be not enabled by God to repent and to believe the gospel, they must needs be subjected to an absolute necessity of despising or neglecting it; there being no medium between accepting the great salvation brought unto them therein, which is done by faith, and the neglecting of it, which is always accompanied with unbelief. Now a neglect of the gospel, and of the great salvation tendered therein by God unto men, is the first-born of provocations in the sight of God, and maketh men seven-fold more the children of wrath and of death, than otherwise they would have been. "How shall we escape," saith the inspired writer, "if we neglect so great salvation?" &c. Heb. ii. 3; implying that this sin is unquestionably more exasperating, incensing, enraging the Almighty against his creature man, than any other sin or sins whatsoever.

Yea, if a man by means of the gospel and the grace offered unto him therein be not brought to repentance, and to a forsaking of ways and practices of sin, the sins themselves, which he shall commit under the gospel, will turn to a far deeper and more dreadful account in condemnation unto him, than the like sins without the gospel would have done. So that it is clear on every side, that in case men be not enabled by God to repent and believe the gospel, the exhibition and tender of the gospel unto them must needs be a heaping of coals of fire upon their heads by God, a project and design to render them two-fold or rather a hundred-fold more the children of hell, misery, and torment, than otherwise they had been. Whereas most certain it is, that God hath designed nothing, acted nothing, in one kind or other to increase the punishment or condemnation of the devils, especially in any way of an unavoidable necessity, above the demerit of their first sin.

Thirdly, if God doth not vouchsafe sufficient means unto all men, whereby to repent, believe, and so to be saved, then will he condemn and destroy (or at least increase the condemnation and destruction of) far the greatest part of men, for that which is no sin (I mean impenitency and unbelief). For, 1. I suppose that it is no sin at all in the creature, not to perform or do any such act, which is proper only for God himself to do, or which requires the lighting down of his omnipotent arm to effect it. 2. I suppose (that which hath been both lately and formerly proved) that God doth and will condemn and destroy men for impenitency and unbelief. So then if to repent and to believe, be such acts or works in the soul which cannot be produced, raised or performed by men by means of that strength or those abilities which are vouchsafed unto them, but absolutely require the omnipotent power of God to effect them, it is no ways more sinful in the creature not to exert or perform them, than it is not to be God. Consequently, if God should punish men for the non-performance of them, he should punish them for that which in such a case, and upon such a supposition would be no sin. Yea, if God should punish men for not endeavouring or not doing that which is in their power to do, in order to repenting and believing, he should punish them for not attempting to make themselves equal in power unto God.

Fourthly, if God, hath not vouchsafed a sufficiency of power to believe unto those, who notwithstanding do not believe, then did our Saviour without any ground or cause in the least, wonder at the unbelief of many in the gospel: yea, and at the faith of others: "And he could there do no mighty work, save that he laid his hands upon a few sick folk, and healed them. And he marveled because of their unbelief." Mark vi. 5, 6. On the other hand, "When Jesus heard it," *i. e.* the answer of the centurion, "he marveled, and said to them that followed, Verily I say unto you, I have not found so great faith, no, not in Israel." Matt. viii. 10. First, there is not the least cause or occasion why any man should marvel that creatures or second causes should not act above their sphere, yea, though there be the greatest conjunction of such means which are proper and helpful unto them in order to such actings which lie within their sphere.

As for example: though the year be never so seasonable and fruitful, yet there is not the least occasion to marvel or think it strange that the thorn should not bring forth grapes, or the thistle figs. So in case there be twenty great lights shining in a room, it is no matter of wonder at all that a blind man seeth nothing at all that is before him. In like manner, in case it be supposed that men are utterly destitute of a power of believing, there is not the least air or colour of an occasion why any man should think it strange that they should not believe, what helps or advantages soever for or towards believing they have otherwise. So again, when causes, or means which are known to act necessarily, uniformly, and constantly in their way, do move and act accordingly, there is not the least occasion given why any man should marvel or wonder at it. When the sun shineth or fire burneth, when birds fly, or fishes swim, no man is tempted or provoked to the least degree of admiration. Nor is there any whit more reason or cause of marvel that any person at any time should believe, though under the greatest disadvantages for believing, in case it be supposed and known that that cause which worketh or produceth faith in men, as viz. the power of God, by which faith is always produced in men, when they do believe, should always work or act necessitating or irresistibly in the production of it.

Possibly the grace of God, by which men under signal disadvantages are, according to our adversaries' principles, necessitated to believe, may be just matter of admiration unto men; but the vouchsafement of such grace supposed, the act of believing in men is no ground of admiration at all; no more than it was under the law to see a man making haste to his city of refuge, being hotly and closely pursued by the avenger of blood; or than now it would be to see a young infant a mile from home being carried along in the parent's arms. However, to add this by the way, I incline to think that the reason of our Saviour's marveling upon the centurion's answer was not simply and absolutely the excellency or greatness of his faith discovering itself thereby, but in part, the strangeness of the stupidity and unmanlikeness of spirit in those of Israel, which he was occasioned to remind and consider, by the notableness of that faith, which shined in a man who was, and had been, in all likelihood, a pagan, and a soldier, and an officer of rank amongst soldiers. All these in their respective natures, and according to common experience, which still follow the nature of things and discover them, are disadvantages to believing. The words mentioned have a breathing of such an import: "When Jesus heard it, he marveled, and said, I have not found so great faith, no, not in Israel." If believing depends upon the omnipotent exertions of God, after any such manner, as our adversaries imagine, our Saviour could have no competent reason to marvel, either that it should be found where it was, or not found where it was not; unless this should be a ground of marvelling unto him, that God by his omnipotency, should be able to work faith in whom he pleaseth. Or that man should not act and do more than he hath power to do, yea, or than all the creatures in heaven or in earth can enable him to do, I mean, believe.

Fifthly, if they who believe not have no sufficiency of power vouchsafed by God to believe, then is the faith of those who do believe no reasonable or just matter of reproof or shame unto those who do not believe. But the Scripture often puts those who do not believe to rebuke and shame, by mentioning unto them the examples of those who do believe: Ergo. This latter proposition needs no other proof but only the sight and consideration of these and such like passages. "For John came unto you in the way of righteousness, and ye believed him not: but the publicans and harlots believed him: and ye, when ye had seen it, repented not afterward, that ye might believe him." Matt. xxi. 32. "The men of Nineveh shall rise in judgment with this generation, and shall condemn it: because they repented at the preaching of Jonah: and, behold, a greater than Jonah is here." Matt. xii. 41. "By faith Noah, being warned of God of things not seen as yet, moved with fear, prepared an ark to the saving of his house; by the which he condemned the world..." &c. Heb. xi. 7. From such places as these, it is evident that the faith, repentance, and obedience of the saints, or of such persons who do believe, repent, and obey, are a just matter of condemnation unto those who believe not, repent not, obey not, and represent them as inexcusable.

But now, to make good the sequel in the major proposition, these worthy actings and deportments of those in whom they are found would be no ways considerable for any such end or purpose as the shaming or condemning of unbelieving, impenitent, and disobedient persons, unless it be supposed that these have, or had, or at least might have had, and this upon the same terms with those other, the like power and abilities whereby to believe, repent, and obey, as they did or do. The casting great matters into the treasury by rich men was no disparagement or matter of shame to the poor widow that cast in two mites only, because these two mites were her whole substance. She was not able to cast in more; in which respect our Saviour himself gives her this testimony, that she "hath cast more in than all they which have cast into the treasury." Mark xii. 43.

Their casting in great matters would have been matter of just disparagement unto her in case she had been as wealthy as they, and should have cast in her two mites only. Nor is the flying of a fowl in the air any disparagement to a man in that he doth not the like. Nor is the speaking of Greek and Hebrew by him who hath been seven years at school to learn these tongues, and hath had the help of men expert and skilful in them to direct him, any matter of disparagement to an infant of days who is not as yet capable of such education, though he speaketh them not. And generally where there is not an equality of strength, means, and abilities for the performance of an action that is commendable, the performance of it by him or them who have the advantage of strength and means in this kind doth no ways reflect disparagement upon the others, though they perform it not. If those who do believe have the omnipotency of Heaven to assist them in believing, nay, to necessitate them to believe, certainly their believing is no matter of disrepute or disgrace unto those who believe not, especially if it be supposed that they have no power at all to believe.

Sixthly, if God's purpose and intent be to stop the mouths of all such persons, and to leave them without excuse who shall prove wicked, ungodly, unbelieving, &c., then doth he vouchsafe sufficiency of power and of means to repent and believe, and so to be saved. But the consequent is true and most unquestionably evident from the Scriptures: therefore the antecedent is true also, viz. that God doth vouchsafe a sufficiency of power or means unto all men whereby to believe, &c. That God's purpose is, and that he maketh provision accordingly, to stop the mouths of all wicked and ungodly men, so that they shall have nothing with any colour of reason or equity to plead for themselves why the sentence of eternal death should not pass upon them when they come to appear before his tribunal, is, for truth, as clear as the light at noon-day from these and such like places: "For the invisible things of him from the creation of the world are clearly seen, being understood by the things that are made, even his eternal power and godhead, *eis to einai autous anapologētous*, *i. e.* "to the intent they should be without excuse." Rom. i. 20, as our former translators rendered, meaning, in case they should neglect the "glorifying of God" by depending upon him, serving, and obeying him. Our last translation maketh no difference as to our purpose, rendering the words thus: "so that they are without excuse:" for if they, the heathen, be "without excuse," by the means vouchsafed unto them by God, whereby to glorify him, certainly it was his intent to render or make them so by the said means.

So again: "Now we know that what things soever the law saith, it saith to them that are under the law: that every mouth may be stopped, and all the world," viz. of ungodly persons, "may become guilty before God," Rom. iii. 19; or subject to the judgment of God, as our former translation rendered the original Greek *upodikos*, *i. e.* found guilty upon such terms that the judgment of God in their condemnation may appear every ways equitable and justifiable. I omit other places. Light enough shineth from these cited to discover this for a certain truth, that God intends the inexcusableness of all impenitent and unbelieving persons.

Upon this foundation of truth I build this inference, in the major proposition, that therefore it must needs be that he vouchsafeth a sufficiency of power or means unto all men to repent and believe. The reason of this consequence is plain, viz. because the plea of insufficiency or want of strength for the doing of what is commanded, is the first-born of apologies or excuses in the case of non-performance. Yea, it is an excuse passable not only with all ingenuous and well-composed men, but even with those that are of rough, stern, and severe principles, if they be not absolutely bewitched or besotted with the senselessness of express tyranny. The person whom the king found amongst his guests without a wedding garment, being demanded by him how he came in thither not having this garment, "was," saith the parable, "speechless," Matt. xxii. 12. Doubtless, if he could with truth, or with the consent of his conscience, have made such an answer as this, that he had not wherewithal, or that he wanted means, to procure a wedding garment, he would have pleaded it, yea, would have been excused by the king upon such a plea: whereas now the king's servants must "bind him hand and foot, and take him away, and cast into outer darkness." verse 13. So in the parable of the talents, if the "unprofitable servant" could have given this account unto his master with truth or with the verdict of his own conscience, that he had not a sufficiency of power granted unto him to improve his talent, as the rest of his fellow-servants had, or, that it was not possible for him to have given his master content in the improvement of it, or the like, it had been another manner of excuse or plea than that which he insisted upon, to his further entanglement, as the purport of the parable in that behalf declareth. Matt. xxv. 14-30.

To pretend that men are sufficiently inexcusable before God for neglecting or not doing many other things which they have power to do, though it be not supposed that they have sufficient power to believe, is to serve the glory of God with an inexcusableness of their own devising, and which falls short many degrees in reaching the counsel and purpose of God for the advancement of his glory in that behalf. For his purpose is not to bring an inexcusableness upon the heads of wicked and impenitent men only in respect of some lesser or lighter, whether omissions or commissions, but in respect of that great and capital sin also, unbelief, yea, mainly and chiefly in respect of this. Now, men cannot appear before God inexcusable upon the account of their infidelity or unbelief, unless it be supposed that they had been sufficiently furnished by him with means, abilities, and opportunities for believing.

If men since Adam have power from God to believe that God is and that he is a rewarder of those that seek him, then have they power to believe justifyingly, or to acceptation with God. But men have this power: Ergo. The consequence in the major proposition the inspired writer makes where he saith, "For he that cometh to God must believe that he is, and that he is a rewarder of them that seek him." Heb. xi. 6. By "coming unto God," it is clear, by the whole carriage of the context round about, that he meaneth a coming unto him with acceptation, and so as *euarestēsai*, to please him. And Calvin himself, all along his commentaries upon the place, taketh it for granted that the writer speaketh of such a faith, or believing, quae gratiam apud Deum conciliet, which procureth grace and favour with God.

The minor proposition is the sense of learned men generally, especially of such who have acquainted themselves with the writings of philosophers, and other studious and learned men amongst the heathen. In these writings they find many sayings, wherein the authors do not only avouch the certainty and unquestionableness of the being of God, but that very property also, the belief whereof the author here principally requireth to give a man access with acceptation unto God, viz. his being "a rewarder of those who seek him." And besides the apostle himself expressly affirms, that *to gnōston tou theou, i. e.* that which is knowable of God, (or, as Calvin interprets it, "Quod de Deo cognosci operae-pretium est," *i. e.* that which is worth a while to be known of God,[3]) was *phaneron estin en autois*, is manifest in them; yea, and further, that God himself "hath shown it unto them." Rom. i.19. A little after, he chargeth them thus, that "when they knew God, they glorified him not as God, neither were thankful; but became vain in their imaginations," &c. Rom. i. 21, assigning this for the ground and cause of that most severe and dreadful proceeding of God in judgment against them, in delivering them up to "a reprobate mind," "vile affections," "uncleanness," &c.

Now, questionless, 1. This "glorifying of God as God," imports, amongst other things, a believing, trusting depending on him, as "a rewarder of those who seek him." For they who do not thus believe or depend upon him, cannot be said, whatsoever they shall measure unto him besides, to "glorify him as God." 2. Had they not had a sufficiency of power thus to have "glorified him," (I mean, as God, and as "a rewarder of those who seek him,") the neglect or non-performance of it would have been no provocation in the sight of God so signally exasperating or provoking, as to have kindled a fire of such high indignation in his breast against them, which should burn so near to the bottom of hell as that specified. The servant, saith our Saviour, "that knew not" his Lord's will, "and did commit things worthy of stripes, shall be beaten with few stripes." Luke xii. 48. Yea, doubtless, had not this servant been in a capacity of knowing "his lord's will," in case he had been duly inquisitive after it, he had not been "beaten with" any "stripes" at all, though he had committed such things

3. Calv. Instit. lib. i. cap. v. sec. 1.

which had been "worthy of stripes" in other men. This is evident from that great principle of equity attested by our Saviour in the words immediately following, "For unto whomsoever much is given, of him shall be much required," ("of him," *i. e.* of him only,) and consequently not of others, to whom little hath been given. And if we shall go along with the said principle whither it will directly lead us, we shall be brought by it to this conclusion, that unto whomsoever nothing is given, of him nothing will be required.

As in the parable of the talents, we hear of no servant called to account but only such who had received talents, one or more. Therefore, without controversy, the heathen generally had, and have power, means, and opportunities sufficient to come to the knowledge of this gracious property in God, that "he is a rewarder of those who seek him," and consequently of "coming to him" with acceptation. And let me add this by the way, that he that hath a sufficiency of power and means to come to the knowledge or belief, 1, that "God is," 2, that "he is a rewarder of those who seek him," is not by this sufficiency simply necessitated either to believe the one or the other. It is with the generality of men in this respect as it is with God himself; as well the one as the other have power to do many things which yet they do not, and therefore are not by a power of acting necessitated unto action.

Yea, it is a principle owned by our adversaries themselves, that men generally have power to do more than they do; and it is an unquestionable rule in the art of reason, that a negatione actus, ad negationem potentiae, non valet argumentum. So that in case it should or could be proved, (which I believe never yet was, nor ever will be proved) that no heathen wanting the letter of the gospel, and the oral ministry of it, ever yet believed on God to justification, or was accepted with him, yet would it be no sufficient proof that therefore they had no power thus to believe on him, or to do that upon the doing whereof they should have been accepted with him. But that the heathen had, and have, power vouchsafed unto them by God whereby to repent and to believe, if their will were answerable to their power in this kind, might be yet further evidence by a far greater vote from the Scriptures, but that in levying this here we should anticipate a considerable part of our intentions relating to the second part of this work.

And besides, three of the most considerable passages, Rom. x. 18; Acts xiv. 16, 17: Rom. ii. 4, pregnant with the truth we now contend for, have, I remember, been largely opened and argued by us upon the same account elsewhere.[4] I shall, at the present, conclude the point in hand with a parcel of discourse from the writings of Mr. Calvin, who, in "An Epistle, showing how Christ is the end of the Law," prefixed before the French New Testament, discourseth to this effect: "After that Adam was left in such confusion, he was fruitful in his cursed seed, to bring forth a generation like unto him; that is to say, vicious, perverse, corrupted, void and destitute of all good, rich and abounding in evil. Nevertheless, the Lord of his mercy, who doth not only love, but is himself love and charity, being yet willing by his infinite goodness to love that which is not worthy of love, hath not altogether dissipated, lost, and overwhelmed men, as their sin did require; but hath sustained and supported them in sweetness and patience, giving them time and leisure to return unto him, and set themselves to that obedience from which they had strayed. And though he did dissemble and was silent (as if he would hide himself from them), suffering them to go after the desires and wishes of their lust, without laws, without government, without any correction by his word; yet he hath given them warnings enough, which might have incited them to seek, taste, and find him, for to know and honour him as it behoved them.

"For he hath lifted up every where, and in all places and things, his ensigns and arms, yea, so clearly and intelligibly emblazoned, that there was no one could pretend ignorance of the knowledge of so sovereign a Lord, who had in so ample a manner exalted his magnificence, viz. That in all parts of the world, in heaven and in earth, he hath written, and even engraven, the glory of his might, goodness, wisdom, and eternity. Saint Paul therefore saith very true, that the Lord never left himself without witness, even towards them unto whom he hath not sent any knowledge of his word. Forasmuch as all the creatures, from the firmament to the centre of the earth, might be witnesses and messengers of his glory unto all men, to draw them to seek him, and after having found him, to welcome him, and do him homage, according to the dignity of a Lord so good, so powerful, so wise, and eternal; and also did help each one in its place to this quest.

"For the birds singing, sung God; beasts cried aloud unto him, the elements stood in fear of him, mountains reasoned with him, rivers and fountains cast their eyes upon him, herbs and flowers smiled on him. Although that indeed there was no necessity to seek him very far, by reason that each one might find him in his own self, being that we are all kept up and preserved by his virtue dwelling in us. In the meanwhile, for to manifest more amply his goodness and infinite clemency among men, he hath not content-

4. Divine Authority of the Scriptures Asserted, p. 183-185, &c.

ed himself to instruct them all by such documents as we have expressed, but hath specially given to understand his voice to a certain people," &c.

To this so large and lightsome an acknowledgment of sufficient means vouchsafed by God unto the heathen, whereby to come to the knowledge of him, of his goodness, power, &c., and consequently to repent, and believe in him, I shall not need to subjoin such sayings as these, "That the knowledge of God is naturally inbred" or implanted "in the minds of men;"[5] "that this knowledge is stifled or corrupted, partly by their foolishness, partly by their malice;"[6] with other passages of like import extant without number in this author.

Lastly, if wicked men and such who perish in their sins through impenitency and unbelief, have not sufficient power and means to repent and believe, then, when God most graciously, most affectionately, most earnestly invites them to repent and believe, and this in order to their peace and salvation, he rather insults over them in their extremity of weakness and misery, than really intends any thing gracious or of a saving import to them. But to conceive thus of God is most unworthy of him, and dishonourable to him, and not far from blasphemy: Ergo. The reason of the connexion in the major proposition is, because to profess love to a man that is in imminent danger of his life, and upon this account to persuade, press, and be earnest with him to do that for the safety of his life which the persuader in this case absolutely knoweth to be impossible for the persuaded to do (as suppose it were to make him wings, and fly in the air beyond the seas, or to turn himself into a fish, and live in the seas, or the like) such an addressment as this to such a poor wretch would be basely illusory and insulting, nor could it admit of any better interpretation.

In like manner, if God, knowing that a natural and ungodly man is in the utmost danger of perishing forever, and withal, that he hath no power to repent or believe, shall yet vehemently and affectionately urge, press, and persuade such a man to repent and believe, that he may not perish, can such an application as this bear any other construction than as derisory, and proceeding from one who doth not simply delight in the death of a sinner, but to make the death of such a miserable creature as full of gall, and bitterness, and misery as he well knows how to do? Therefore, certainly, when God "stretcheth out his hand all the day long" to wicked men; when he saith, "Turn ye, turn ye from your evil ways: why will ye die," &c.; when he saith, "Repent, and turn yourselves from all your transgressions, so iniquity shall not be your ruin,"; and again, "Turn at my reproof," with the like,

5. Calv. Instit. 1. i. c. 3, in titulo.
6. Idem, Institut. 1. i. c. 4, in titulo.

he knoweth that what he thus earnestly and affectionately requireth of them, and presseth them unto, they have power to perform. Otherwise, in such expressions as these, he should be like unto a judge or king, that, having sentenced a lame man to death for treason or some other crime, should promise him his life in case he would run twenty miles within an hour's space, and accordingly press him with much seriousness unto it. I have met with nothing, to my best remembrance, from the pen of any defender of the contrary faith to obstruct or check this argument in the course of it; nor am I able to imagine what can with any face of reason or of truth contest with it.

To say, that when God, with the greatest earnestness of expression, calls upon wicked men to repent, he only signifies unto them what would prevent their destruction, were it found in them, but supposeth not any principle or power in them to exhibit or perform it. Such an allegation, I say, as this hath neither salt nor savour in it. For, to what account can it be brought, that God should inform wicked men how or which way they may escape destruction, if it be supposed withal that they are in no capacity, no, not so much as under a possibility, of receiving any benefit by such an information? Besides, God cannot truly and cordially profess that he "desireth not the death of a sinner," or "of him that dieth," upon the account only of an information directed to such a man concerning the way or means of his escape, unless it be supposed withal that he is made capable by him of benefit by such an information, and in a condition to make use of it in order to an escape. And, to conclude, mere informations are not wont to be given in exhortatory or preceptive language, as, "Turn ye, turn ye," &c., nor in such pathetic strains as "Why will ye die, O house of Israel?" nor with such promises annexed as "So shall not iniquity be your ruin;" nor, lastly, where they are of no use neither to those to whom they are given nor to him that giveth them, nor to any others; which, upon consideration of particulars, would plainly appear to be the case before us.

To say that in such affectionate exhortations and expressions as those under present consideration, God only expresseth his will of approbation, signifying that righteousness, and repentance after sin, and so the peace and salvation of his creature, upon and by means of these, are things simply agreeable to his nature, mind, and goodness, but doth not intend to signify any will or purpose in himself to work repentance in the persons to whom he thus speaketh, nor yet that they have power to repent without him, is an allegation as inconsiderable, and inconsistent with reason, as the former. For,

1. If righteousness, and repentance after sin, and the salvation of the creature hereupon, be simply agreeable to his nature, mind, and goodness, then why should not the repentance, and, upon this, the salvation, of those persons to whom he particularly addresseth himself in those gracious and earnest compellations and exhortations of which we now speak, be every whit as agreeable to his nature, mind, and goodness as the repentance or salvation of any other persons in their case? He no where signifieth any difference in this kind. Or, if the repentance and salvation of some sinners be agreeable to his nature, mind, and goodness, and not of others, it is a plain case that the repentance and salvation of the creature, simply considered, are not the things that are so agreeable to him, but the repentance and salvation of such and such particular subjects. For repentance and salvation are the same things, and of the same nature, in what persons or subjects soever: no personal consideration whatsoever altereth their natures or essential properties. Again,

2. If the intent of God were to express or signify his approbative will of the repentance and salvation of his creature, or the agreeableness of these to his nature, mind, and goodness, he would rather have expressed it in applications of himself unto such persons or subjects whose repentance and salvation he really intendeth and desireth, than in addressments made to those whose repentance and salvation he desireth not, nay, whom he was resolved from eternity (for this is the voice of the oracle consulted by our adversaries) to destroy forever. It were very improper and hard for a judge or prince to make a feeling and affectionate discourse of their clemency, goodness, and sweetness of nature, their great averseness to acts of severity, &c., unto such persons whom they had been of a long time resolved, and before any cause administered by these persons of such a resolution against them, to put to a terrible, torturing, and ignominious death, especially at or near the time when this most severe execution is intended to be done upon them.

Lastly, the argument propounded by us, and with whose vindication we are yet in labour, doth neither suppose that God will work repentance, as our adversaries call "working repentance," in the persons there spoken of, *i. e.* that he will work it upon any such terms that it shall necessarily or infallibly be effected, nor yet that the persons themselves can repent without God. That which it supposeth is this, that God is so far moving and assisting the hearts, wills, and consciences of these men in order to their repentance, that, if they were but willing to do what he enableth them to do in reference and order to the same, their repentance would be effected, and they saved upon it. In which case, I mean, if they should repent, this repentance were most justly ascribable unto God, not to themselves, inasmuch as it is he that, (a.) giveth them power and abilities to repent: (b.) secretly forms and fashions their wills so as to make them willing actually to repent: (c.) supports their wills, thus framed, to and in the production of the act itself of repentance. Whereas that which men themselves do, in, towards, or about their repentance, is so inconsiderable in comparison of what God doth, that the greatness of his grace and interposure herein, deserves, in a manner, all the praise and honour that belongs unto the action. It be true, however, that the person himself who repenteth, or in whom repentance is wrought, must of necessity be so far, or to such a degree, interested and active in the work, that the work itself may be as truly and properly ascribed unto him, or called his, as it is ascribed unto God, and termed his. For it is man that repenteth, not God, though what he doth in repenting he doth by the operating and assisting grace of God; in which respect it is said to be his gift. But all men without exception have a sufficiency of power vouchsafed unto them by God whereby to repent and to believe unto salvation; and that it is through want of will, or rather willingness, not of power, that any man perisheth.

At present, to the further confirmation of the main doctrine commended in this discourse, we argue thus,

"If God intended not the death of Christ as a ransom or satisfaction for all men, then are there some men whom he never intended to save, but to leave irrecoverably to everlasting destruction and perdition." This proposition, I suppose, stands firm and strong upon its own basis, and needs no prop of proof or argument to support it. For, God intending to save no man but by the death of Christ, evident it is, that if there be any man or number of men for whose salvation he did not intend this death, that he never intended their salvation. Therefore I assume: "But there are no such men or number of men whose salvation God never intended, or whom he intended to leave irrecoverably to everlasting perdition. Ergo." The reason of this proposition is, partly because whatsoever God at any time intends he intended always, yea, from eternity. This is partly also because there was a time when all men were righteous and holy, viz. during the whole time of Adam's integrity, in whose loins all men then were, and so must needs be partakers of the same holiness and integrity with him. So that unless we shall say and hold that God never intended the salvation of just and holy men, but to leave them irrecoverably to everlasting perdition, we cannot say that there are or were any men, or any number of men, whose salvation he never intended, or whom he intended to leave irrecoverably to everlasting destruction. Yea, all men had a being in God himself before they received or had a being in Adam, in which respect Adam himself is called "the son of God," Luke iv. 38; viz. because he received his being from him, as (though not after the manner that) children receive their beings from their parents or fathers. Now, wheresoever, or in what estate or condition soever, Adam was, there were all men in the same estate and condition with him.

So, then, all men considered as being in God, were nothing but God, *i.e.* a part of God, himself, according to the common and most true maxim of divines:

"Quicquid in Deo est, est Dens;" whatsoever is in God, is God. The truth of this maxim refers to the absolute simplicity of the Divine Essence, or God. Therefore, if God purposed from eternity to leave any man or number of men irrecoverably to eternal destruction, this purpose was conceived or taken up by him against these men whilst they were yet only in his will and power, and consequently, whilst they were nothing but himself. But that God should peremptorily resolve and decree never to save, nor to intend to save, but to design and consign over irrevocably, irreversibly, irrecoverably, to eternal misery and destruction millions of men whilst they were yet perfectly righteous and holy, yea, whilst they were yet nothing but himself, is, doubtless, a notion hardly incident to the judgment or thoughts of any man who trembles to think irreverently or unworthily of God.

It is like it will be here pleaded, that God, in his purpose or decree to leave the men we speak of to everlasting perdition, doth not look upon them, or consider them, as being in himself, nor yet as being righteous and holy in Adam, but as men that would in time prove corrupt, sinful, and abominable. For God to decree to leave men thus considered to irrecoverable destruction is no ways unworthy of him. I answer,

1. If God, in his decree of reprobation, considered men as sinful and wicked, then he passed over, and took no knowledge or notice of them, whilst they were yet righteous and innocent, or if he did take knowledge of their righteousness, yet, this notwithstanding, and, as it were, with the neglect and contempt of it, he passed that most dreadful doom or decree of an eternal reprobation against them. Whereas the Scriptures everywhere commend and highly magnify the constant love, care, and respects of God

towards the righteous: "For the righteous Lord," saith David, "loveth righteousness; his countenance doth behold the upright." Psa. xi. 7. And again: "For thou, Lord, wilt bless the righteous; with favour wilt thou compass him as with a shield." Psa. v. 12. So again: "The eyes of the Lord are upon the righteous," Psa. xxxiv.15; (to omit many other places of like assertion.) From whence it evidently appears that (a.) God beholds and sees, and cannot but behold and see, those that are righteous; (b.) Seeing and beholding them such, he always loves them, and delights in them. Therefore it is impossible that God at any time should not see and behold the persons we speak of, being righteous, and whilst righteous; and (c.) That, seeing and beholding them such, he should not love them, and intend graciously to them; and consequently, that all this while he should intend or decree the extremity of all evil and misery against them.

It is altogether inconsistent with the righteousness and equity of God's proceedings, to neglect or pass by the present condition or ways of men, either of righteousness or unrighteousness, and to respect them, or measure out unto them, either grace or displeasure, either reward or punishment, according to their future condition, or according to what he foresees their ways will be afterward. All God's purposes and decrees relate unto men according to the nature and exigency of their present conditions, not of their future. If a man be at present in a condition of righteousness, he is under the gracious influence and benediction of that decree of God, whereby he hath decreed life, and peace, and blessedness to righteous men. And suppose it be known unto God that this man, righteous at present, will afterwards forsake his righteousness, and turn aside into ways of unrighteousness. Yet whilst he remaineth righteous he is not under the dint or danger of that decree of God which respects unrighteous men, whereby wrath and judgment are decreed against them.

That disposition or principle which we now ascribe unto God is most clearly asserted in the Scriptures by himself, and that by way of vindication of his righteousness from the unworthy conceits of those who judged otherwise of him: "If a man be just, and do that which is lawful and right; And hath not eaten upon the mountains, neither hath lifted up his eyes to the idols of the house of Israel,... he is just; he shall surely live, saith the Lord God." Ezek. xviii. 5, 6, 9. During this posture, or course of righteous walking, he is under the blessing of that gracious and unchangeable decree of mine, wherein life and peace are decreed unto righteous men. "But when the righteous turneth away from his righteousness, and committeth iniquity, and doeth according to all the abominations that the wicked man doeth, shall he live? All his righteousness that he hath done shall not be mentioned: in his trespass that he hath trespassed, and in his sin that he hath sinned, in them shall he die." Ezek. xviii. 24, *i. e.* perish forever, viz. unless he repents, and turns back again to his former course of righteousness. So again: "Therefore, thou son of man, say unto the children of thy people, The righteousness of the righteous shall not deliver him in the day of his transgression: as for the wickedness of the wicked, he shall not fall thereby in the day that he turneth from his wickedness: neither shall the righteous be able to live for his righteousness in the day that he sinneth. When I shall say to the righteous that he shall surely live; if he trust to his own righteousness, and commit iniquity," as many being in an estate of grace, upon a presumption that they cannot possibly fall away, too frequently do, "all his righteousness shall not be remembered, but for his iniquity that he hath committed, he shall die for it. Again, when I say unto the wicked, Thou shalt surely die; if he turn from his sin, and do that which is lawful and right; If the wicked restore the pledge, give again that he had robbed, walk in the statutes of life, without committing iniquity; he shall surely live; he shall not die." Ezek. xxxiii. 12-15.

By these, and very many more places of like consideration, in reference to the business in hand , which might be added, it is fully evident, that particular men, or the persons of men, from time to time, come under the eternal decrees of God, either of life or death, of salvation or condemnation, not according to the nature, exigency, or import of their potential or future, but of their actual and present conditions respectively. Consequently, if the generality of men were either from eternity righteous (and righteous they must needs be whilst they were in God, and in him only, and were nothing but God), or at any time after their creation, as they were in Adam during the time of his innocency, they must needs, whilst they were in these capacities or conditions, be under that eternal decree of God, by which or wherein life, and peace, and happiness are decreed unto righteous men, and so could not be from eternity under a decree of reprobation.

2. Lastly, if God from eternity looked upon the far greater part of men (all those I mean who are reprobates, so called) as persons that would in time prove sinful, or as persons in time proved sinful, and, under this prospect of them, passed a decree of reprobation upon or against them, then was this sinfulness wherein he beheld them the ground or cause of this decree of reprobation, or not. If not, to what purpose is it pleaded or stood

upon in reference to the said decree? And why is it not plainly and right-down affirmed that God reprobated them out of his mere will and pleasure, without the interveniency of any consideration of sin, to incline or move him thereunto? And if this be so, he need not in his decree of reprobation look upon them as sinful, but simply as men. If he looked upon them simply as men, then he looked upon them as the pure and perfect workmanship of his own hands. If so, then the perfect workmanship of his own hands must be the object of his reprobation, and consequently that which is good: "And God saw every thing that he had made, and behold it was very good." Gen. i. 31. But impossible it is that that which is good, especially "very good," should be the object of God's reprobation. Again, if that sinfulness, wherein it is pretended that God looked upon men when he reprobated them, was any ground or cause of such his reprobation, then was it a ground or cause morally moving him hereunto, for other influence or efficiency upon him it could have none. If so, then, (a.) The will of God may have a cause superior to it, and productive of it; which is generally taken for an impossibility.

(b.) If the sinfulness of men foreseen moved God morally to conceive or make a decree of reprobation against them, then was this decree made by him in a way of justice and equity; yea, upon such terms that, had he not made or passed such a decree upon the grounds and reasons that were before him, he had been unjust. If so, there being the same reason why he should pass a like decree against those men also who are now called his elect, inasmuch as a like sinfulness in them was foreseen likewise by him from eternity, he must be unjust, because he hath not passed a like decree against these. The truth is, that such a decree of reprobation as men commonly notion in God, involves so many inextricable difficulties, palpable absurdities (that I say not intolerable blasphemies also), that my hope is it will shortly, *mole mali sui ruere*, fall and sink with the insupportable weight of its own evil in the minds and judgments of men.

As it is with those, who have arrived at years of discretion, and actually believe: they carry original defilement still about them. They were, in respect of what was derived unto them from Adam in their natural conception and birth, wholly lost, and are still, notwithstanding their faith, in the rigour and strictness of justice, worthy of eternal death. And yet, by means of their faith and the gracious compact and covenant which God hath made with those that believe, they are not in an estate of condemnation, or liable to eternal death. In like manner children may possibly be conceived, and so born into the world, with original sin, and yet not with or under the guilt of it. This may be dissolved and taken away by the superabounding grace of God vouchsafed unto the world by Jesus Christ, though the sin itself remaineth. So again, children, as soon as conceived or born, may be, and are, in strictness of account, worthy of eternal death by reason of that communion they had in Adam's sin, being in his loins when he sinned. Yet this worthiness may not be imputed unto them, or charged upon them, being, as we suppose it clear from the Scriptures, expiated or atoned by the great sacrifice of Christ in his death. We recalleth that Christ said, with children gathered around him, "For of such is the kingdom of heaven." Matt. xix. 34. But we have gone beyond the line of our late intentions in following this chase. We retire, with a purpose to conclude this chapter, with the addition only of one argument more for the confirmation of our main doctrine.

Therefore, the universality of redemption purchased by Christ I further argue and demonstrate from the consideration of some of the principal types under the law, by which the compass and unlimited extent of it were prefigured. I shall insist only upon two: the brazen serpent, and the feast of jubilee.

First, concerning the brazen serpent: Our Saviour himself owneth and asserteth a typical correspondency in the creation and usfulness hereof with himself in respect of that great and gracious design and purpose of God in sending him into the world: "And as Moses," saith he, "lifted up the serpent in the wilderness, even so must the Son of man be lifted up: That whosoever believeth in him should not perish, but have everlasting life." John iii. 14, 15. A type being a kind of similitude, and the property or condition of this not being, in the proverbial expression, "to run on all-fours," *i. e.* to answer or hold proportion in all particulars, indeed, many times not in more than one only, therefore our Saviour, to prevent all misunderstanding in the interpretation or application of the type mentioned, particulariseth that very respect or consideration in himself, and his sending into the world, which was prefigured and expressed in the type alleged by him, in these words, "That whosoever believeth in him should not perish, &c."

To understand clearly what there was in the type answering, in a way of prefiguration, that consideration in Christ's coming or sending into the world, which himself here insists upon as presignified hereby, we must have recourse to the history concerning the erection of the brazen serpent, unto which also himself sendeth us in that particle of comparison or resemblance, "as;" "As Moses lifted up," &c. The original of this brazen serpent, together with the counsel and intention of God in his erection, Moses recordeth thus: "Make thee," saith the Lord to Moses, "a fiery serpent," viz. in similitude or form, "and set it upon a pole: and it shall come to pass, that *every one that is bitten*, when he looketh upon it, shall live." Num. xxi. 8; from which words it is most evident, that this "fiery serpent" (in form as Christ came "in the similitude of" that "sinful flesh," whose sting is so mortal to the world) was not intended by God as a means of healing or preservation to a certain, definite, or determinate number of persons, or that such and such by name, and no other, should look upon it in order to their healing, or that whosoever in the event did look upon it, and no other but these, should be healed by it. But it means whosoever would, might look upon it (for which end also Moses was commanded to set it up on high upon "a pole," where it might be readily visible unto all), and that whosoever should or did hook upon it, being bitten or stung with any "fiery serpent," might be healed thereby. Now, all men without exception being, as we all know and confess, stung, and that mortally, with the "fiery serpent" sin, unless Christ should be lifted up, upon the cross, *i. e.* suffer death, with an intent on God's part, 1. That every man, if he pleased, might believe in him; and, 2. That every man that should believe in him should be saved by him; he should altogether disanswer that famous type we speak of, and that in that very consideration and respect wherein he pleads a special conformity to it.

If it be replied, the correspondency between Christ and the brazen serpent is sufficiently salved in this, that as the will and ordinance of God in and about the brazen serpent was, that whosoever, being stung, should look up to it, should be healed; so is it his good pleasure in and about Christ, that whosoever believeth in him should be saved from that death which sin exposeth him unto; but this doth not imply or suppose Christ to be an universal Saviour, or Redeemer. I answer,

1. That the brazen serpent was not ordained by God to be a condition or means of healing, by a looking up to it, only unto those, or for their sakes, who actually did look up to it and were healed by it (unless we shall suppose that all those, without exception, who were stung of serpents, did look up to it, and were accordingly healed, which would be a supposition without sufficient ground) but unto all those, without exception, and for their sakes, who were, or any time after should be, thus stung, whether they would or should look up to it for healing or no. Nor do we find in the words of the institution of it, lately specified, the least whisper or intimation of any exception of persons in this kind. Therefore, unless it be admitted that Christ died as well for those, or for their sakes, who, being sinners, as all

are, do not or shall not believe in him, as for those who do or shall, he will not fulfil the type we speak of, no, not in that consideration wherein the richness and fulness of his grace was in special manner typified, as himself, in the words lately transcribed from his own mouth, plainly enough declareth.

2. If it be granted, that this is the will or intent of God, that whosoever believeth or shall believe in him, shall be saved, it amounts to as much in expressness of consequence and import as we contended for; viz. that there is salvation purchased and procured by him for all men without exception. For that which is to be had upon the performance of such a condition, which, being performed, gives no being to it, must of necessity have a being there, where or from whence it is to be had upon the performance of this condition, whether this condition be performed or no. If it be true, that in case I shall go up into the chamber, I shall meet my friend or brother there, it must needs be true that my friend or brother is there, whether I go up to meet him there or no. In like manner, if this be a truth, that in case I shall believe on Christ, I shall find salvation for myself in him, it must of necessity be every whit as true that there is salvation in him for me, whether I believe in him or no: because my believing in him would not create any salvation in him more than what was in him before. So that if it were not in him before my believing, I could not have it, I should not find it in him, though I should believe. But the legitimacy of the consequence we speak of, from the premises unto which we relate it, and which are our adversaries' own resolute doctrine, we have argued and evicted at large, and this more than once, in our former discussions in Chap. III and IV.

Again, the other great type we mentioned, of the redemption purchased by Christ for the world, the feast of jubilee, plainly proveth this redemption to have been, in the purchase and procurement of it, general or universal. However, in the actual possession or enjoyment of it, it proves the benefit or blessing only of a few (at this time in history), by means of the non-acceptation of it by the greatest part of those for whom it was purchased. That the feast of jubilee under the law was a type, and that of a most clear and significant import, of the spiritual liberty and freedom from sin and misery, purchased by Christ, and proclaimed by God in the gospel unto the world, is the standing notion and sense of all parties in the present controversies. The tenor of the institution of this feast, as far as concerns the business in hand, runneth thus. "And ye shall hallow the fiftieth year, and proclaim liberty throughout all the land unto all the inhabitants thereof: it shall be a jubilee unto you; and ye shall return *every man* unto his possession, and ye shall return *every man* unto his family." Lev. xxv. 10. And a little after: "In the year of this jubilee ye shall return *every man* unto his possession." ver. 13. "This returning of every man to his possession is," saith Mr. Ainsworth, "a figure of our restoring by Christ into paradise, the possession whereof Adam lost by sin." And, by proportion, the returning of every man to his family (*i. e.* to his civil liberty and freedom), is a figure of our restoring by Christ unto that spiritual liberty, or freedom from under the dominion and power of sin, with all the hard consequences of such a bondage, whereof we were all deprived by Adam's sin.

Now the tenor of the counsel and intentions of God, in the erection or institution of this feast, we see expressly to be, the ease, benefit, restitution to possessions and liberties of *every man*, without the exception of any. Yea, all servants that had refused their liberty at the end of the seventh year of their service, which their masters were expressly enjoined by the law, Exod. xxi. 6, to grant unto them, if they desired it, had the benefit and indulgence of the jubilee, and were then to be manumitted or set at liberty, if they desired it, as well as others. This plainly signified the riches of the grace of God in the gospel to be so great, that even willful sinners, and such that waxen old in ways of provocation, are hereby made capable of the love and favour of God in the pardon of all their sins. For, to note this by the way, the intent of this feast was not, I suppose, to compel, or necessitate every man, no, nor yet any man, to return either to his possession, or to his family, whether they would or no, but to afford them an opportunity, and to invest them with a liberty, or right of returning unto either, if they please. Because otherwise, it had been less matter of gratification, ease, or indulgence unto men, yea, possibly unto some, as viz. unto those, who had been found unwilling to return unto either, it had been matter of trouble and discontent. *Pan gar anagkaion pragm aniaron ephu*, (as the Greek epigram hath it) *i. e.*

Whate'er necessity imposeth,
The mind necessitated troubleth.

But to the point in hand. It being the clear and unquestionable intent of God, in and by the great and solemn feast of jubilee, to loose the two sore yokes of bondage and poverty from off all necks whatsoever, without any difference or distinction of persons. In one kind or other, he should be far more gracious and munificent in type or shadow, than in substance, in case he should not be every whit as large, free, and comprehensive in his intentions of affording means and opportunity unto men for deliverance from sin and death by Jesus Christ.

If it be objected it is true, the intent of the jubilee was to invest every man (viz. who was a Jew, and of the natural seed of Abraham) with a right of power to return to his possession or family; but not to gratify every man simply, or to indulge the like privilege unto all the world. Therefore this rather proves the confinement of the intentions of the grace of God in Jesus Christ, unto his church or elect only, than the enlargement of them unto all the world; especially considering that the whole body of the people and nation of the Jews, were typical, and presignified the church or churches which were afterwards to be raised up amongst the Gentiles. To this I answer,

1. Be it granted, that the body or nation of the Jews did typify the church or churches of the Gentiles, yet did not every single person of this nation typify a true member of these churches. As, for example, Ahitophel did not typify a true saint, or a believer under the gospel, nor did Korah, Dathan, and Abiram typify so many godly or holy men among the Gentiles. Nor had any unrighteous or wicked person of this nation the honour of typing out any true Nathaniel, or elect person, under the New Testament. If ungodly persons among the Jews were types of anything, it was of such hypocrites or profane persons that should be found in the churches under the gospel. And if so, the intent of the jubilee being, as we have proved from the express letter of the institution of it, for the benefit, comfort, and ease of every man amongst them, as well of the wicked and unholy, as of the holy and righteous, it follows roundly, that this typified and taught, that the intentions of God, in and about the salvation afforded and exhibited by Jesus Christ unto the world, stood equal and indifferent towards all men without exception, without any distinction of holy and unholy, righteous and unrighteous, elect and reprobate, or the like.

Although the law of jubilee, as the whole ceremonial law, in all the parts and branches of it, was given particularly unto the Jews, yet was it not given particularly for the Jews, *i. e.* for the sake or benefit of the Jews only, but for the accommodation and benefit of all the world besides. And upon this account, I suppose, the apostle Paul calleth the ceremonial injunctions by Moses, the elements, or rudiments, not of the Jews, but of the world, Col. ii. 8-20; viz. because they were given with an intent, on God's part, to nurture and breed up the world. This meant all nations as well as the Jews, in such a measure or degree of the knowledge of the Messiah, then to come, which he judged meet to impart unto the world until his coming. So that howsoever the Jewish nation was honoured by God above all other nations, in being made by him feoffees in trust, as it were, for the world, and had the keeping of the oracles of life committed unto them, yet had they no right or lawfulness of power, to deny any person under heaven part or fellowship with them, in any of their spiritual privileges, who should desire it of them in a due and regular way, and turn proselyte.

Now there was no person of any nation, that was made by God incapable of the benefit or blessing of proselytism. Consequently, the joy and privileges accruing unto menu, by virtue of the law and feast of jubilee, did, though not in so immediate and direct a way, concern all other nations and persons as well as the Jews, or natural seed of Abraham. Even as the gospel and sacramental administrations annexed thereunto, in these days, are only possessed and enjoyed in and by the churches of Christ; yet they are so, upon such terms possessed and enjoyed by them, that whosoever from amongst the most idolatrous and heathenish nation under heaven shall believe, may and ought to have communion within them in such their possessions and enjoyments. Either of these answers is sufficient to loosen the joints of the loins of the objection.

The arguments and grounds laid down and managed in this chapter, together with those passages and texts of Scripture which we have heard speaking so distinctly and aloud the same things with them, have turned my thoughts and judgment about the intentions of God in the death of Christ upside down, and have filled me, mind, heart, soul, and conscience with this belief, that these intentions of his stand, and always stood, equally, impartially and uniformly bent for or towards the salvation of the world without any difference or variation in respect of any man, or numbers of men, considered simply as men, or as having done neither good nor evil. Yet are there three things more that have made my belief in this kind, measure heaped up, pressed down, and running over. The first is, that conjunctio magna, that great conjunction of all, or far the greatest part of the chief luminaries in the firmament of the Christian church, whilst the constitution of it was yet more athletic, healthful, and sound, I mean during the primitive times, the multiplied rays or beams of whose light concentrated in the same point of doctrine with us. Of this we shall, God assisting, give some competent account in the forepart of the chapter following.

The second is, the frequent testimony given to this doctrine by those who are so esteemed, the chief adversaries and opposers of it, who, as appears from their writings, are oft necessitated to assert or own it as a principle, without which they know not in many cases, how to make a consistent discourse, or manage the theme they have before them. Somewhat of this also we shall show in the latter part of the said chapter. The third, and last, is the apparent inconcludency and weakness of those arguings and reasonings, whether from the Scriptures or other principles, by which the cause of the contrary opinion is wont by the ablest patrons it hath, as far as men of this engagement are yet known unto me, to be pleaded and maintained.

CHAPTER VIII
Wherein the sense of antiquity, touching the controversy under discussion, is truly and impartially represented

FOR the sakes of those afraid to believe anything, what pregnancy of ground soever there be to evince the truth of it otherwise, but only what they know (or at least think), that many men honourable in their sight have believed before them, I have subjoined this chapter to those large debates which finished their course in the preceding chapters of this book. Our discourse has established the scriptural position on Christ's atonement, I trust, to the satisfaction of all such who count it more safe to stand upon a rock alone, than upon a quagmire or quicksand with a greater company.

But because all men have not this faith, I shall show those that want it a group of as honourable persons, as any that have inhabited mortality since the apostles' days, standing upon the rock of that doctrine which hath been asserted and recommended in our former discussions. For who within that compass of time we speak of have had a spirit of greater glory resting on them than those that sat in the apostles' chairs next after them, and were pillars of light and fire in the Christian church in her primitive and purest days?

And that these in their respective stations and successive generations were not only partakers, but defenders and assertors of the same faith with us in the doctrine of redemption hitherto maintained, is legible enough in the next ensuing testimonies. After them we shall show how fluctuating and inconsistent with themselves the judgments of later writers have been about the said doctrine, and how impossible it is for any man to be of an established conscience therein, that shall build himself upon their authority.

We shall begin with Augustine, the first-born amongst the fathers, though not in time, yet in worth and name; and from him proceed first unto those that lived before him, by a gradual ascent; and then to those that succeeded him, by a descent answerable. That Augustine's doctrine concerning the intentions of God about the extent of Christ's death, was the same as the orthodox and sound assertions stated by us in our present discourse, needeth, I suppose, no greater proof than an impartial and due consideration of these and such like sayings, scattered up and down in his writings from place to place upon occasion. In that discourse wherein he makes answer, *ad articulos sibi falso impositos*, to certain articles falsely fathered upon him, he insisteth upon this, in the first place, as laid to his charge, that he should hold, "That our Lord Jesus Christ did not suffer for the redemption of all men."

The second he mentioneth is this: "That God should not be willing to save all men, though all men were willing to be saved." In purging himself upon the former of these, he writeth thus: "Against the wound of original sin, wherewith in Adam the nature of all men was corrupted and become dead, and from whence the disease of all manner of concupiscence groweth, the death of the Son of God our Lord Jesus Christ is a true, potent and the singular remedy, who being not liable to the debt of death, and the only person without sin, died for those that were sinners and debtors" in this kind. "Therefore as to the greatness and potency of the price, and as far as concerns one" and the same "cause of mankind, the blood of Christ is the *redemption of the whole world*. But they who pass through this world without the faith of Christ, and the sacrament" or sacred work "of regeneration, are strangers to" or estranged from "this redemption. Therefore, whereas by reason of one" and the same "nature of all men and, by" one and the same "cause of all men truly undertaken by our Lord, all men may truly be said to be redeemed, yet all men are not" actually "brought" or delivered "out of captivity. The propriety," *i. e.* the actual possession and enjoyment "of redemption, is, doubtless, with them, out of whom the prince of this world is cast forth, and who are now not vessels of the devil, but members of Christ: whose death is not so bestowed upon mankind, that they who never come to be regenerate, should belong to the redemption thereof," *i. e.* should actually partake of this redemption, "but so that what by one only example" or exemplary act "was done for all men together," or at once, "might be celebrated in all particular persons, by a particular sacrament:" *i. e.* might by a particular administration of the sacrament of this redemption, meaning, I suppose, baptism, to each particular man, be plainly declared to relate unto, or to concern all particulars.

"For that cup" or potion "of immortality, which was tempered and made of our infirmity, and the divine power" or virtue "hath in it wherewith to profit all men; but it profiteth no man unless he drinketh it." What testimony from a man concerning his judgment in any point, can be imagined more pregnant, satisfactory and clear, than such wherein he expressly complains of being falsely charged with the contrary, and vindicates and explains himself accordingly? Beza, because of this testimony, so full and particular against his opinion of limited redemption, and being loath to have this his opinion encumbered with the opposite authority of this father, dischargeth it of the burden, by pretending that the book, or tract, wherein it standeth is supposititious, and not Augustine's. But besides the genius, phrase, and style, every ways *omoiazonta* resembling the author, whose name it beareth, Calvin, who of the two was a man of greater discerning abilities, acknowledgeth it accordingly.[1] Nor is there any piece in all those writings, which pass under the name of Augustine's works at this day, but may, upon a pretence every whit as plausible, be traduced as illegitimate.

Before I pass from this testimony, I desire the reader to take knowledge that the worthy author thereof, towards the beginning of the said tract, and a few lines before the recited testimony, professeth, that what he should deliver therein, was his sense and judgment in the respective articles, in opposition to the Pelagians and their doctrine. From whence it manifestly appeareth, that in Augustine's days, it was no orthodox doctrine, but a Pelagian error, to hold that Christ died not for all men; inasmuch as the father complaineth (as we heard before) that he was falsely charged by some abettors of the Pelagian faction that he held, that Christ the Lord suffered not for the redemption of all men. Therefore they who traduce the doctrine maintained in this discourse, under the odious name of Pelagianism, either declare themselves notably ignorant of what Pelagianism meaneth, or else asperse that father, who, questionless, knew better than all his fellows what belonged to Pelagianism, with the blot of this ignorance. By his vote and verdict, the doctrine which contradicteth that asserted by us, is Pelagianism.

Another testimony from the same father, upon the same account, may be that formerly cited. Having rehearsed these words, "For God sent not his Son to judge the world, but that the world through him should be saved:" he infers thus: "Therefore as much as lieth in the physician, he came to heal the sick. That man slayeth himself, who will not observe the precepts of the physician. He came a Saviour unto the world. Why is he called the Saviour of the world, but *that he should save the world*."[2] Elsewhere, addressing himself in his private devotions unto the Lord Christ, he speaketh to him thus: "I know thee to be true God, and our Lord Jesus Christ, the only begotten Son of God, the Creator, Saviour, and Redeemer of me, and of *whole mankind*."[3] Again: "O thou unclean world, he cometh that should

1. De occultâ Dei Provid. in Respons. Ad Præfat. Opusc. p. 851.
2. Aug. in Joh. Tract. 12.
3. Aug. Soliloqu. c. 32.

redeem thee, and thou art troubled: and him thou wilt destroy, when he was *minded to deliver thee*."[4] Concerning Judas he demandeth, "What did the sin of Judas, who sold him, by whom he *should have been*" or, was to have been "*redeemed?*"[5]

Afterwards he presenteth Christ, after his resurrection, speaking to the unbelieving Jews, who had crucified him, thus: "Behold the man whom ye have crucified; behold that God and man, in whom you refuse to believe. You see the wounds which you have inflicted, the side which ye have pierced: because by you, *and for you*, it hath been opened, and yet you will not enter."[6] In another place, thus: "Mankind falleth sick, not of bodily diseases, but of sins. This great patient" or sick man "lieth all along the world, from the cast unto the west. *For the healing of this great sick man, the omnipotent physician comes down.*"[7] The same father (in another part of his works, comparing the first and the second Adam together) discourseth to this effect. "What therefore was justly due from Adam, Christ unjustly by suffering death, paid. He stretched forth his hand to the sweetness of the apple: Christ to the bitterness of the cross. He showed the tree of death; Christ the tree of life. He lift up himself against God and fell; Christ *humbled himself that he might lift up all*. Adam brought death upon all men universally; and Christ hath repaired" or, restored "life unto all men. Every one therefore looked towards the brazen serpent and was healed" of the wounds received "from the poisonous serpents. The brazen serpent set upon a wooden pole, overcame all the venom of the living serpents: and Christ being hung upon the cross, and dying, quenched the old poisons" or venoms "of the devil, and *delivered*" or freed "*all that were struck*" or stung "by him."[8]

This father, in his dialect and manner of expressions could not more significantly declare for general redemption than he hath done in the now-recited testimonies. And the truth is, that passages and sayings of like import are very familiar and frequent in his writings. In one place he saith, "Judas cast away the price of silver for which he sold the Lord, and acknowledged not the price *with which himself was redeemed by the Lord*."[9] In another, " Unless he (Christ) had been crucified, *the world* had not been *redeemed*."[10] In a third, " For the blood of Christ is so" or, upon such terms "shed for remission of *all sins*" or for remission of the sins of all men "that it is able to blot out that very sin by which it was shed."[11]

In a fourth, " We read in the Scriptures that the safety" or salvation "*of all mankind is purchased*" or bought "with the blood of our Saviour, as the

4. Aug. de Symb. 1. ii.   5. Ibid.   6. Ibid.   7. Aug. de verbis Domin. Serm. 59.   8. Aug. de Temp. Serm. 101. 9. Aug. in Enar. Psal. lxviii.   10. Aug. de Symb.   11.. Aug. Tract. 92. in Joh.

apostle Peter saith," &c. In a fifth, "If therefore the price of our life be the blood of the Lord, see then how it is not the earthly uncertainty of a field that was redeemed therewith, *but the eternal safety* of the *whole world*." [12] In a sixth, "God in no" other "way provided more beneficially" or bountifully "for mankind, than when the very wisdom of God, that is, his only Son, consubstantial and co-eternal with the Father, attempted to assume whole man."[13] In a seventh, "What then is the meaning of, God is in the midst of her? This signifies that God is equal" or equally affected "unto all, and accepteth no man's person. For as that which is in the midst, is alike distant from all the extreme parts, so God is said to be in the midst" inasmuch "as he consults and provides equally *for all*."[14] In an eighth, speaking in a rhetorical apostrophe unto Thomas, he expresseth himself thus: "Thomas, look well on our price, deligently consider the prints of the nails, and in his very wounds acknowledge" or take notice of "the medicine or treasure of mankind."[15] And not long after, "Death was given unto one, *that it might be taken away from all*."

It were easy to make this pile of testimonies far greater, but that we judge these specified abundantly sufficient to convince any man, that hath not abjured ingenuity, that Augustine's habitual and standing judgment was, that Christ by his death atoned the sins of all men without exception. Nor can there, I verily believe, so much as one saying be produced out of all his writing, wherein the contrary is asserted by him. Many places, I grant, may readily be found, wherein he denies the possession, and actual enjoyment of the redemption or salvation purchased by Christ, unto many, as viz. to all final impenitents and unbelievers: of such an import as this is that saying of his: "The Lord did not by his resurrection repair" or restore "unto forgiveness, all" or any "unbelievers, and such who for their heinous sins were adjudged to eternal punishments."[16]

Such sayings as this, are of perfect accord with the doctrine asserted by us, Chap. VI of this discourse, where we acknowledged and proved at large, that notwithstanding the redemption purchased by Christ for all men, yet no man dying in impenitency and unbelief shall be saved. Now if Augustine were of this judgment, that Christ died for all men, there is little question to be made, but that this opinion or doctrine reigned generally in the Christian church in his days (and so had done before him) as orthodox and catholic. Recall that he was, as the ablest, so the strictest and closest defender of that faith, which was more generally esteemed orthodox, and professed, taught, and held throughout the Christian world.

12. Aug. de Temp. Ser. 128.   13. Aug. de ver. Relig.   14. Aug. in Psal. xlv.
15. Aug. de Temp. Ser. 138.   16. Aug. de Temp. Serm. 137.

Nevertheless let us hear other learned, pious, and orthodox writers delivering their sense about the said point, in their own words.

Ambrose, with whose ministry and eloquence Augustine was much affected, asserted the same doctrine without fear. "The sun," saith he, "is commanded to arise upon all men. And this sun doth indeed arise daily upon all men. But that mystical Sun of righteousness is risen unto" or, for "*all men*, is come to *all men*, hath suffered *for all men*, and is risen again *for all men*, and hath therefore suffered, that he might take away the sin of the world. But if any man believeth not in Christ, he depriveth himself of the *general benefit*, as if a man by shutting the windows, should shut out the beams of the sun, it doth not prove that therefore the sun is not risen upon, or unto all, because such a man depriveth himself of his heat. But as for what concerneth the sun, he keeps his prerogative: but this man acteth the part of an unwise man shutting out" from himself "the favour of the common light." And a little before he had said: "The earth is full of the mercy of the Lord, because forgiveness of sins is granted" or given "unto *all men*,"[17] *i. e.* offered as a gift unto all. In another place thus: "The brazen serpent was (in a figure) as it were fastened to a cross, because it was" hereby "declared that the true serpent was to be crucified for mankind, who should frustrate" or, make void, "the poison of the serpent, the devil, being" indeed "cursed in the figure, but yet in truth was he, that should take away the sins *of the whole world.*"[18]

Once more: "So then he" the apostle Paul "saith, that there is a Saviour left to us for a suffrage of life," meaning, by whom life is voted in heaven for us "which the law could not provide: which" Saviour "God from the beginning decreed should be born: who because he was the only person that could be found without sin, having overcome the enemy of mankind, *abolished*" or, blotted out "*the sins of all men.*"[19]

Jerome, who also was contemporary with Augustine, though somewhat his senior, gave the right hand of fellowship unto him in the doctrine now under inquest. We shall only taste his judgment in this behalf, in a few testimonies from amongst many. "The Lord," saith he, "being about to suffer *for all the world*, and *to redeem all the nations* on the earth with his blood, makes his abode in Bethany, the house of obedience."[20] Elsewhere, having recited that of our Saviour, "So God loved the world, that he gave his only-begotten Son," &c., John iii. 16, he goeth on thus: "But if now a considerate reader shall in his secret thought answer, or reply, Why are there many who are not saved, if he saved them, and loved them, and spared their chil-

17. Ambr. in Psal. cxviii. tom. ii. p. 948. edit. Paris.   18. Ambr. Apolog. David. 1. c. 2.
19. Ambr. Epist. ad Rom. c. 9.   20. Hieron. in Matt. xxvi.

dren, and redeemed them with his blood, and assumed them" or, their nature, "and exalted them, being assumed? There is a plain reason to be given; for they believed not, and grieved," or, exasperated, "the Holy Spirit."[21] A little after, speaking of John Baptist, of whom it is said that "he came to be a witness to bear witness of the light, that all men through him might believe; he subjoineth, "He is not presently in fault, if many refused to believe; for the will of him that came, was that *all men* should *believe* and be *saved*."

Once more, writing to Oceanus, he challengeth some erroneous person for suggesting unto him "that there are some sins which Christ cannot purge with his blood, and that the scars of men's old sins stick so deep in their bodies and souls, that they cannot be healed," or, made less, "by his medicine." Concerning whom he demandeth, "What else doth such a person but make Christ to have died in vain? For he died in vain, if there be any whom he cannot quicken," or, give life unto. "And John, pointing at Christ with his finger and voice, 'Behold the Lamb of God! Behold him that taketh away the sins of the world,' should speak an untruth, if there were any such persons in the world whose sins Christ had not abolished," or, blotted out. "For they who are not taken into consideration by the indulgence of Christ, must be proved not to belong to the world; or if they be of the world, one of the two must take place: if they be delivered from their sins, they give testimony to the power of Christ: if they be not delivered, they do in effect demonstrate the weakness of the thing; which God forbid that we should believe concerning him who is omnipotent."[22] He that remains yet unsatisfied whether this father held general redemption or no, may, if he please to seek, find more ballast for his thoughts in this kind, in what he hath written upon chap. xliii. and chap. xlv. of the prophecy of Ezekiel. I confess, that when he speaks of the application or actual enjoyment of the redemption purchased by Christ, he then limiteth it (as all the fathers generally do, and as we expressly did Chap. III of this discourse) to the particular society of believers. We shall not need to cite places upon this account.

Chrysostom, who lived some years before Augustine, was not at all behind him in avouching the same doctrine concerning the extent of the redemption of Christ. Writing upon those words, Heb. ix. 28, "So Christ was once offered to bear the sins of many," he demandeth thus: "Why doth he say, 'of many,' and not of all? viz. because all have not believed. For he indeed *died for all men*, and *to save all men*, as much as was in him. For

21. Hieron. in Isai. liii.
22. Hieron. Epist. 83, ad Oceanum.

that death" of his "did counterbalance the destruction of all men. But he did not bear" or, offer up "the sins of all men, because they themselves *would not*."[23] So that he clearly resolves the perishing of men, not into any want of atonement made by Christ for them, but into themselves, and their own wilfulness in not believing. For he expressly saith, "that Christ died for all men, and that to save them."

Again, commenting upon chap. ii. 9, of the same epistle, and having rehearsed these words of the author, "That he through the grace of God should taste death for every man." "Not," saith he, "for believers only, *but for the whole world*: for he died for all men. For what though all do not believe? He hath fully done that which was proper for him to do."[24] Much to the same purpose in another place: "Although Christ did not gain all men, yet he died for all men," so "fulfilling that which belonged unto him."[25]

Elsewhere, comparing the lamb offered in the Levitical sacrifices, with Christ the Lamb of God; concerning the former, he saith, that "it never took away any one man's sin so much as once; whereas the latter" taketh away "the sin of all the world;" and that "when it was in danger of perishing, it presently delivered it from the wrath of God."[26] To reserve many other testimonies offered by this author in the case in hand, to another occasion, in case it be offered, upon Rom. iv., he hath these words: "That thou mayst not say, How can we, being under the guilt of so many and such great sins, be justified? he showeth thee him that hath abolished" or, cancelled "all sins."[27]

Athanasius lived somewhat above a hundred years before Augustine, and yet was full of the spirit of that doctrine concerning the redemption by Christ, which we contend for. "Since," saith he, "the debt due from all men was meet to be paid, (for all men ought to have died) for this cause chiefly he came," as it were, "on pilgrimage to us, and after the demonstration of his godhead by" his "works, it remained that he should offer up a sacrifice *for all*, delivering up his temple unto death for all men, that so he might discharge and free *all men* from that old transgression."[28] Elsewhere: "with the blood of his passion," or, mactation, "he simply redeemed *all men*."[29] In another place: "There was need of death, and it was requisite that death should be endured for all, that what was due from all might be satisfied. Wherefore the Word, for that it could not die, or it was immortal, assumed to itself a body capable of dying, that he might offer that as his own for all men, and that suffering for all by means of his coming thereunto, he might destroy him that had the power of death, that is, the Devil."[30] In another

23. Chrys. in Heb. x. Hom. 17.   24. Idem in Heb. ii. 9.   25. Chrys. ad Rom. xiv. 15.
26. Idem. in Joh. 1. 29.   27. Idem. in Rom. iv. 25. Hom. 9.   28. Athan. de Incarn. Verbi.
29. Athan. in Passionem Salvatoris.   30. Athan. de Incarnat. Verbi Dei.

tractate the same author thus: "It became the Lord, being desirous to make a renovation, to make new the first Adam, that, his sin being dissolved, he might take away sin on all hands *from the universe of mankind*."[31] In another, thus: "For the coming," or, presence, "of the Saviour in the flesh, was the solution of death, and the safety" or, salvation "of every creature."[32] If the reader desires to know more of the mind of this author, touching the point in question, he may please to peruse his learned tract, entitled, "Do Incarnatione Verbi Dei," wherein he hath frequent occasion to declare his judgment therein.

Hilarius, another orthodox father, who lived not long after the former, writeth upon Matthew to this effect: "He," Christ, "admonished them to learn what this meaneth, 'I will have mercy, and not sacrifice,' viz. that the law bound up," or consisting only, "in the observation of sacrifices, could afford no help" unto men, "but that safety," or salvation, "was reserved *for all men whatsoever* in the indulgence of mercy." And presently after, speaking of Christ: "He came unto," or for, "ALL MEN: how then doth he say that he came not to," or for, "the righteous?"[33] His answer is, that there were none such, but all were sinners. Elsewhere he discourseth thus: "The Son of God was born of a virgin for the sake of mankind, and the Holy Ghost himself assisting him in this operation, and overshadowing with his power (being the power of God), he planted the beginnings of a body for himself, that, being made man of a virgin, he might receive that nature of flesh in" or upon "himself, and that by the fellowship of this conjunction the whole body of mankind might be sanctified; that as *all men were hid*" or built "*in him*, by means of his willingness to assume a body, so again he might be related unto *all men*," or carried back into all men, "by that which was invisible in him,"[34] meaning his divine nature. Once more: "For he did this once, offering himself a sacrifice unto God, being to redeem" or recover "*the whole salvation of mankind* by the oblation of this holy and perfect sacrifice."[35]

Lastly, (because this testimony, being somewhat more emphatical than its fellows, would not be omitted): "For he took the flesh of sin, that in the assumption of our flesh he might forgive sins, being made a partaker hereof, by assumption, not by sinning, by" his "death blotting out the sentence of death, that *by a new creation of mankind*, he might *abolish the constitution of the former decree*, suffering himself to be crucified, that by the curse of the cross he might strike through," dissolve, or make void, "all the curses of that terrene" or earthly "damnation."[36] Whether he calleth that

31. Athan. in Passionem Domini Segment. t. ii. p. 626. Edit. Paris.
32. Idem in Epist. ad Adelphium contra Arianos.   33. Hilar. In Mat. can. 9.
34. Hilar. De Trinit. l. ii.   35. Idem in Psa. liii.   36. Idem de Trinit. cap. 1.

"damnation," whereunto men became subject by Adam's transgression, "earthly," because he judged the extent of the penalty of it to consist only in the dissolution of the body by death, as if the punishment of hell fire came in upon the account of the gospel, in case it should be rejected, (which is the judgment of some amongst us) I shall not dispute, nor undertake to determine. I will will pass on to hear the sense of other learned, orthodox, and pious fathers, much about the same time with the former.

Cyril of Jerusalem, much about the same times, delivereth his sense about the redemption of Christ thus: "The crown of the cross is this: it led by a light those that were blind through ignorance, it set at liberty those that were detained under sin, and *redeemed the whole world of men.* And wonder not that the *whole world* should be redeemed, since he was not a bare man, but the only begotten Son of God that died for it."[37] And again: "Knowest thou why" or for what end "the kind Lord did not decline death? It was that the *whole world* might not be destroyed through sin."[38] *i. e.* as appears from the former sentence and the scope of the place, that the whole world might be saved by him. In another place the same author saith, "Heaven and earth are full of his glory, the ends of the world are full of his goodness, full of his praise, the *whole nature of man* is full of his condescension," &c. A little after, speaking of Christ: "He," saith he, "that is the offerer is the same that is offered up *for the world.*" And not long after: "Let Adam rejoice, saying unto Christ, by Simeon, 'Lord, now lettest thou thy servant depart in peace, according to thy word.' Now dost thou dismiss" or loose "me from eternal bands, now dost thou deliver me from corruption, now dischargest thou my sorrow."[39] Evident it is, that in this last testimony he bringeth in Adam speaking, not only, nor so much, in his own name, personally considered, but in the name of his whole posterity also.

Eusebius, another author of note about these times, attesteth the same doctrine, by affirming that "the saints of old, by the teachings of the Divine Spirit, came to learn long before that there was a certain venerable and great sacrifice, that should be highly accepted with God, which should in time come unto men, and which would be the *expiation of the whole world.*" And a little after: "This was the Christ of God, concerning whom it was said of old that he should come unto men, and should be slain, after the manner of a beast," or sheep, "*for all mankind.*" And again, not long after: "According to the testimonies of the prophets, there was found that great, and greatly to be esteemed price, for the redeeming both Jews and Grecians, I mean that expiation" or atonement "*for the whole world,* that

37. Cyril. Hierosolym. Catech. 13.
38. Ibid.
39. Cyril. Hierosolym. De Prophetû Simeone, &c.

sacrifice for the souls *of all men*, that offering for *every spot and for every sin*, that Lamb of God."[40] Elsewhere he saith, speaking of Christ, that "he took care for the salvation *of all men that had been born from the beginning of the world*, and to destroy him by his death who had the power of death, the devil."[41] This author abounds with sayings of like import.

Arnobius, another Christian writer about the same times, of good account, bringeth in the heathen arguing and demanding of Christians thus: "If the Saviour of mankind be come, as you Christians affirm, why doth he not, by the same bounty, deliver all men? He doth not deliver all alike, who calleth all alike. He doth not keep back or reject any person from his sovereign grace," or, indulgence, "who affords the same power unto high, low, servants, women, children, of coming unto him." To this, this author answereth: "The fountain of life is open *for all men*, nor is any man denied the right" or, power "of drinking nor driven away" from it. "If your pride" or, disdain "be such, that you reject the benefit of the gift offered, nay, if your wisdom be so great as to call those things which are offered by Christ, pastime and toys, how doth he offend who inviteth you" notwithstanding "who hath only this to do, viz. to expose the fruit" or, blessing "of his bounty to the arbitrement" or, free choice "of that right" or, power of choosing "which is given you?"[42]

Didymus, another author of note in this century, and who was Jerome's tutor, in his third book concerning the Holy Ghost, writeth to this purpose: "Wherefore the Father, even for their salvation not sparing his own Son, delivered him up unto death, that by the death of his Son, he being destroyed who had the power of death, that is, the devil, he might *redeem all those* that were held in the bands of captivity by him." Not long after, speaking of the Jews, "They," saith he, "rising to the highest pitch of impiety, betrayed and crucified the Lord the Saviour, who vouchsafed to come down to the earth *for the salvation of all men*." Afterwards, he calls "Judas the betrayer of his Master and *Saviour*."[43]

Basil, surnamed the Great, about the same time, or not long after, judged it a point of faithfulness unto him whose ambassador he was, to concur with his fellows in the same doctrine. "What," saith he, "could man give of so much value for the redemption of his soul? Yet was there found for *all men together* one worthy price of the blood of our Lord Jesus Christ, which he shed" or, poured out "*for us all*." Soon after: "If we consider his kindness and love to us, he calleth us brethren, and descendeth to the nature of man, who gave himself a propitiation *for the whole world*, and not for him-

40. Euseb. De Demonstrat. Evangel. lib. i. c. 10.   41. Euseb. De Demonstrat. Evangel. lib. iv. c. 12.
42. Arnob. lib. ii. contra Gentes.   43. Didym. 1. iii. de Spiritu S.

self.["]44 In another place he saith, "David, prophetically foreseeing the future grace of the loving-kindness of the Lord towards men, saith, that it is meet to serve and love him, who hath bestowed such and so great a benefit upon mankind, that he hath not spared his own Son, but hath delivered him up *for all men*."45 More testimonies from this author are at hand, if need be.

Gregory Nyssen, brother to the last-named father, stands by his brother in the pre-asserted doctrine, saying, that "as the beginning of death being first" only "in one, passed through the whole nature of man: in like manner the beginning of the resurrection, by means of one, extendeth itself unto the *whole nature* of man."46 More plainly in another place: "He" (speaking of Christ) "sanctifieth unto God and the Father not only the first born of men, but even the *whole tribe*" or generation "*of mankind*, by means of the first-fruits of our lump being in him, that is, by means of that flesh which he took of us, enlivened with a rational" or, intellectual soul, "whereby he did, as it were, leaven the *whole mass*" or, concretion "of the essence" or, substance "of mankind with holiness."47

Gregory Nazianzen, another great light burning and shining in the house of the living God (the church) about these times, gave forth the light of the same doctrine in his ministry. Speaking of Christ, he saith, "To the Jews, he becomes as a Jew, that he may gain the Jews: to those that are under the law, as one under the law, that he might redeem those that were under the law: to the weak" he became "as weak, that he might save those that were weak. He is made all things unto *all men*, that he may win" or, gain to himself "*all men*."48 In another place he saith, "There is no matter of wonder like unto that of my salvation: a few drops of blood refashioning the *whole world*, and, like that which causeth the coagulation of milk, knitting and gathering us together one *with all men*."49

Elsewhere, in his Christian Poems, he speaketh to this effect:

From one we all proceed, we all one breath
Breathe out; to one we all incline;
God unto all alike, his birth, his death,
*His resurrection, and heaven, doth consign.*50

Epiphanius, a little before the two last-named Gregories, writing against heresies, asserteth the doctrine we contend for, as orthodox. "First," saith he, speaking of Christ, "He offered himself that he might discharge the sacrificing of the Old Testament, presenting" unto God "a more perfect living" sacrifice "for all the world." Afterwards: "How vain" and bootless "is all

---

44. Basilius M. in Psal. xlviii.   45. Basilius M. in Psal. lxi.   46. Greg. Nyss. Orat. Catechet. c. 16; Etiam c. 22, 23.
47. Greg. Nyssen. de occursu Domini, &c. circa medium.   48. Greg. Nazianz. Orat. 81. In initio.
49. Greg. Nazianz. Orat. 42. paulò ante finem.   50. Idem. Carm. 3. Præcept. Ad. Virgin.

the understanding that accompanieth heresy? for they" (heretics) "even deny their own Lord, that bought them with his own blood."[51]

Tertullian, who lived in the age next before the last-mentioned authors, though in some other points he declined the judgment of his orthodox predecessors, yet, in the doctrine under inquiry, he was one spirit with them. "What," saith he, speaking of the wood, by the casting of which into the water, the prophet Elisha caused the iron to swim which was sunk, "is more manifest than the sacrament," or, mystical signification "of this wood?" As, namely, "that the hardness of this world," meaning the obdurate world itself, "being sunk in the depth of error, is by the wood of Christ, that is, of his passion, delivered" or recovered "in baptism; that so that which long since perished by wood," or, by a tree, "in Adam, might be restored by the wood," or, tree, "of Christ." A little after, applying unto Christ the story of Isaac carrying the wood, wherewith he was to have been offered, had not God recalled the command given to Abraham on this behalf, and of the ram caught by the horns in a thicket, which was offered, he doth it in words to this effect: "Christ, in his own time, carried" his "wood upon his shoulders, sticking," or, hanging "upon the horns of the cross, having his head compassed about with a crown of thorns: For it became him to be made a *sacrifice for all nations:*" and afterwards he saith, that he "was made a sacrifice," or, offering, "in," or through, "all things for us all."[52]

Origen, about the same time, held forth the same doctrine in the world, affirming that "our Lord and Saviour, being led as a lamb unto the slaughter, and offered up as a sacrifice of" or, upon "the altar, procured remission of sins *for the universal world.*" A little after: "So then the world is trained up, first to seek remission of sins by divers sacrifices, until it should come to a perfect sacrifice, a complete and absolute sacrifice, a lamb of a year old, perfect, which should take away the sins of the *whole world.*"[53]. Elsewhere he maketh the apostle Paul to have said, that "Christ had given himself for the redemption of *whole mankind,* that he might redeem those that were kept in bondage by sins, by tasting death without deceit, *for all men.*"[54] I present the reader only with a little from these authors respectively, in comparison of what upon the same account might be transcribed from them.

Cyprian, a worthy author and martyr of this age, counted it no injury to the truth to abet the same doctrine. Having mentioned some examples, as he termeth them, of a propagation of creatures otherwise than according to the common course of nature, he advanceth this demand to salve the possibility, or rather to evince the probability of the virgin's conception.

51. Epiph. adversus Hæreses, 1. ii. t. 1; Hæresi 55.   52. Tertul. Adversus Judæos. c. 13.
53. Origen. in Num. Hom. 24.   54. Origen. in Rom. iii. 25.

"Shall, then," saith he, "that seem incredible to be done by the power of God for the redintegration," or new-making, "of the *whole world*, examples whereof are to be seen in the propagation of animal creatures?" Afterwards: "Christ then suffered not in the flesh with any detriment or injury to his Godhead, but that through the infirmity of the flesh, he might work salvation *in the midst of the earth*,"[55] meaning, for all the world round about him. In another place he saith, "The corruption of nature, even in our first beginnings, deserved to be cast away and abandoned" by God. "But because the will was not in fault, God provided a remedy *against that general condemnation*, and tempered," or qualified "the sentence of his justice, removing that hereditary burden from the posterity," or children, "and mercifully purging out the leaven of original corruption by the washing" of baptism "and anointing.

"But indignation and wrath deservedly returns back upon them, who, after the grace of this indulgence" from God, in the forgiveness of their sins, "voluntarily go astray and wander by sinning, abusing their own freedom, being led, not by necessity, but by will; nor doth there remain for them any benefit," or anything gotten, "in the death of Christ, but the benefits" hereof "being despised by them, do most justly condemn them."[56] This passage is pregnant with the assertion of both the main doctrines vindicated in the present discourse, as viz., 1. That Christ hath died as well for those that shall be condemned and perish as for those that shall be saved, and, consequently, for all men. 2. That those also may be condemned and perish, who had sometimes obtained remission of sins by Christ.

That further may be taken into consideration, by occasion of the former part of this quotation, that it was the judgment and sense of the ancient fathers and Christians generally (I know none to be excepted,) that in baptism there was always a particular application made to the person baptized of the general redemption purchased by Christ. So (they believed) he that was baptized, if an infant, received thereby exemption and deliverance from the guilt of original sin derived from Adam: if a person of mature years, not only this, but forgiveness also of all his actual sins committed formerly. For which opinion, though I do not as yet see any demonstrative ground, either in the Scriptures or in reason, and, God sparing me life, I shall in one particular declare my sense in opposition to it. Yet the opinion, I confess, so far taketh with me, partly for the proofs' sake which are produced, with some probability, for it; partly for the signal learning, gifts, sharpness of judgment, quickness of apprehension, and, above all, for the

55. Cypr. In Exposit. Symboli.
56. Cypr. De Ablut. Pedum.

singular piety and zeal for the truth, found in so many assertors of it; partly also for those degrees of inevidence and inconcludency which are found in the arguments usually insisted upon to prove the contrary, that my soul cannot enter into the secret of those, who, upon a confident presumption that the said opinion is erroneous, refuse to offer their children unto baptism. They are hereby, according to the sense of all the fathers, as hath been in effect said, exposing their precious souls to a certain loss of salvation by Christ, in case they die before they come to years of discretion.

Certainly it is no point of Christianity to lay such wagers as these upon the truth of any opinion which hath such a cloud of enemies and opposers of it, as all the ancient fathers, without exception, as far as yet I understand, and together with these (for we cannot reasonably imagine the contrary) all the Christian churches in the primitive times, with all the knowledge, parts, zeal, and faithfulness of both. Yea, and some of our late Protestant writers themselves, and these of eminent worth and note especially when men have no better or more satisfactory grounds for their opinion than have yet been produced against the lawfulness of infant baptism. But this by the way.

Clement of Alexandria, another famous champion of Christianity about these times, was of the same faith in the point in hand with his fellows. In one place he demands, "How is he," speaking of Christ, "a Saviour and Lord, if he be not the *Saviour and Lord of all?*" In another he termeth Christ the "disposer" or administrator "of all things according to his Father's will, governing" or taking order for "the *salvation of all men.*" Elsewhere he argueth thus: "Either the Lord doth not take care for all men, and this either because he is not able, which is not right" to suppose, "or because, though able enough, yet he will not: but this is not incident to him that is good: nor is he backward," or indisposed hereunto, "through voluptuousness, inasmuch as for our sakes he assumed flesh exposed to sufferings; or else he *doth take care of all;* which indeed becometh him that is made *Lord of all:* for he is a *Saviour, not of some, and not of others,*" &c.[57] In an oration to the Gentiles he calls unto them thus: "Hear ye that are afar off, and hearken ye that are near: the word is not hid" or concealed "from any: the light" thereof "is common, it *shineth unto all men.*"[58]

Justin Martyr, whose writings, amongst those that treat of Christian religion, and are judged authentic, and not spurious, are the most ancient that I know since the days of the apostles, giveth frequent testimony to the truth of the same doctrine. In one place he presenteth the saints "as knowing" or acknowledging "that he that hath wrought that great salvation *for mankind,*

57. Clem. Alexand. Strom. 1. vii.
58. Clem. Alexand. in Orat. and Gentes.

is praiseworthy, greatly to be feared, and the Maker" or Creator "of heaven and earth."[59] In another, speaking of Christ, he saith, that "now through the will of God, being made man *for the sake of mankind,* he submitted himself to suffer whatsoever the inconsiderate Jews were inspired by the devil to inflict upon him."[60] In a third he saith, that "Christ neither submitted himself to be born, nor yet to be crucified, as if he needed these things" for himself, "but for that kind" or generation "of men which in" or by "Adam was fallen under death and the deceit of the serpent."[61] By "mankind," or the "kind of men," he cannot mean a few, a circumscribed number, a small parcel of men, as the elect, so called, are known to be: these in no propriety of speech can be called *to anthrōpeion genos,* "the generation" or "kind of men:" or, if in one place he should have meant "the elect" by such an expression, it is no ways like but that in some other he would have expressed himself more plainly. But what he means (in the Greek) by *to genos to tōn anthropōn,* "that genius" or "general kind of men," appears evidently enough by this descriptive character which he gives of it, *ho apo tou Adam upo thanaton epeptōkei, i.e.* "which from Adam," or through Adam, "was fallen under death." This, we know, is the adequate and appropriate character, not of some men, but of all mankind without exception. But the sun is visible enough without a candle.

Ireneus, not long after the former, avouched the doctrine of our contest over and over. "As Eve," saith he, "becoming disobedient, became" hereby "the cause of death both to herself and to the universe of mankind; so Mary, having the man predestinated" by God, meaning Christ, "notwithstanding" her being involved in the death brought upon all mankind by Eve, yet, "becoming an obedient virgin, she proved the cause" or means "of salvation *unto the universe of men.*"[62] His meaning is, that by submitting unto the pleasure of God, signified unto her by the angel, concerning the bearing and bringing forth of his Son Jesus Christ in the flesh, she had the grace accordingly vouchsafed unto her to bear and bring him forth who was the "author or cause of salvation to universal mankind;" by which submission and service she, in a sense, became the cause or means also of this salvation.

Elsewhere the same father saith, that "Christ recapitulated" or gathered into one "in himself *all nations* dispersed" up and down the world "even from Adam, *all tongues and every generation of men* together with the person of Adam himself."[63] In another place he gives this reason why Paul saith that "we are reconciled through the body of his flesh," viz. "because

59. Just. Martyr. in Dialogo cum Tryph. P. 300. Edit. Morel.   60. Idem, Apol. 2. Pro Christianis.
61. Idem, in Dial. p. 316.   62. Iren. lib. iii. adversus Hæres. cap. iii.   63. Iren. adversus Hæres. 1. iii. c. 33.

his righteous" or just "flesh reconciled *that flesh which was detained in sin*, and brought it into favour" or friendship "with God."[64] Now, that flesh which was detained in sin, was not the flesh only of the predestinate or elect, but of all mankind without exception.

These are the principal fathers and writers of the primitive times, and before Augustine, that are now extant or known. All these with one mouth (as we have heard) and with a "nemine contradicente" give testimony to the truth of that great doctrine, which hath been avouched in this discourse, viz., that the redemption purchased by the death of Christ, was for all men, considered as men respectively, and not for the elect only or those that shall actually partake of it, and be saved.

The writers of best note and repute, since Augustine (until these later times of reformation) and from whose writings the best and steadiest informations are to be had, what doctrines or opinions ruled in the churches of Christ, and amongst those Christians that were judged orthodox and sound in the faith, in their days, are these: Prosper, Cyril of Alexandria, Theodoret, Leo, Fulgentius, Primasius, Gregorius, Beda, Theophylact, Anselm, Œcumenius, and Bernard. Let us briefly hear what is resolved by these respectively, upon the question concerning the intentions of God about the extent of Christ's deaths.

Prosper, well known for a thorough disciple of Augustine, and who served his generation not long after him, declareth his sense in the business in hand plainly enough, in words to this effect: "All men are truly said to be redeemed, yet all men are not gotten out of captivity. For that cup of immortality, which is tempered" or compounded "of the infirmity of men and power of God, hath in it wherewith to profit all men; but it helpeth not unless it be taken" or drank. "And the Lord Jesus expressly saith, that his flesh is bread from heaven" or, an heavenly bread *"which giveth life unto the world*. But except it be eaten, it giveth no life: as in the parable in the gospel, the marriage" feast "was prepared for all that were called; but they only enjoyed it, who came with a wedding garment unto it."[65]

Elsewhere he saith: "Our Saviour is most truly said to have been crucified for the redemption of the whole world, both in respect of the human nature truly assumed by him, as also because off the common destruction" of men "in the first man: and yet" in a sense "he may also be said to have been crucified only for those, who receive benefit by his death," *i. e.* that his crucifying was, in the consequent intentions of God, intended only for such. "For the evangelist saith, that Jesus was to die for that nation; and not

64. Idem, lib. v. c. 16.
65. Prosp. ad Capp. Vincent. c. 1.

for that nation only, but that he might gather the sons of God dispersed into one, &c. He gave his blood *for the world*, and the world would not be redeemed, because the darkness received not the light."[66] These last words plainly interpret his meaning in those, wherein he had said, that "Christ may be said to have been crucified for those only who reap benefit by his death:" and imply, that his meaning herein was only this, that God by his consequent will or intention, intended the death of Christ, or the benefit of his death only for such who come in time to partake hereof, viz. by believing. Concerning the antecedent and consequent will or intentions of God, see before, Chap. VI.

He that yet questions the judgment of this author in the point, may please to peruse the brief sentence which he gives upon the ninth chapter or head, *Capp. Gallorum*; and especially those two books *De Vocatione Gentium*, (which though some ascribe unto Ambrose, yet are they discernible enough by some characters to be the writings of Prosper, and are cited under his name by the Synod of Dort). In these he shall find general redemption by Christ, asserted ten times over, the main scope of these books being to prove, that there is no person of mankind simply excluded from participating in the saving grace of redemption purchased by Christ.

Cyril of Alexandria (about the same time with Prosper) filleth his writings with the same truth. "They," saith he, speaking of the Jews, "unjustly desire his death, wickedly lie in wait for him; unmercifully slay him, thrust him out of their land and city, who is the life, the light, the *salvation of all men*."[67] Elsewhere: "Since it became" him "to suffer that corruption, sin and death, which man brought in" to the world "being by this means to be turned back," or, destroyed, "he gave himself a counter-ransom for the life *of all men*."[68] Once more: "It is without controversy that the whole world is saved, Immanuel having died for it."[69] See more in this author upon the same account, *De Recta Fide ad Reginas*, &c. c. 22. circa initium. In Joh. lib. ii. c. 1, and in iii. cap. Joh. ver. 17, &c.

Theodoret, somewhat before the two last-named authors, conceived that he found the universality of redemption by Christ in the Scriptures. For commenting on the fifth chapter to the Romans, he maketh the words of the apostle equipollent to these: "The munificence of grace overcometh the decree of justice. For when man sinned, the whole kind" or race "is punished. But now when all men behave themselves impiously and unjustly, he doth not inflict punishment" upon them "but granteth life" unto them.[70] Afterwards in the progress of his exposition upon the same chapter, he

---

66. Idem, ad Object. Vincent. cap. 10.   67. Cyril. Alexand. 1. ii. in Joh. c. 5.
68. Idem, in Joh. 1. v. c. 3.   69. Idem.   70. Theodoret. ad Rom. 5.

presents the apostle speaking thus to his Romans: "doubt not of the things I speak with relation unto Adam. For if these things be true, as they are, and that when he sinned, his whole race received a decree" or sentence "of death, evident it is, that the righteousness of" our "Saviour procureth *life for all men*."

Leo, commonly styled the Great, very frequently bewrayeth his judgment to stand to the same point. Comparing the death of the Lord Christ with the deaths of other holy men, he saith, that "there were but single" or particular "deaths in every of these respectively, nor did any of these persons discharge the debt of any other by dying, whereas amongst the sons of men, our Lord Jesus alone was found, in whom all men were crucified, all men died, all men were buried, yea, and all men rose again."[71] Elsewhere thus: "That general and deadly hand-writing of our being sold" under sin and death "was" cancelled, and "made void, and the bargain of" our "captivity passed into a right of redemption."[72] Once more: "That he" Christ "might repair the life of *all men*, he took on him the cause of all men; and that which he of all men was not bound to do, he made void the force of the old handwriting, by "making payment" of the debt due thereby "*for all men*."[73]

Fulgentius, about the year 500, succeeded his predecessors in the inheritance of their judgment concerning the universality of redemption by Christ. "As the devil," saith he, "smote" or wounded "whole man by deceiving him, so God, by assuming whole man, saved him, that so one and the same might be acknowledged both the Maker and *Redeemer of the whole creature*," or creation, "who was able both to make that which was not, and to *repair*" or restore "*that which was fallen*."[74]

Primasius, who lived somewhat more than a hundred years after Augustine, helped to keep the doctrine we plead alive in the world. "As Christ," saith he, "suffered reproach from his own," he means the Jews, "whom he *came to redeem*, when they said unto him, 'Thou hast a devil,' and offered him all other indignities, even to his passion itself;[75] so did Moses likewise." If Christ came to redeem those who charged him with having a devil, with casting out devils through Beelzebub, and who maliciously prosecuted him with all manner of injuries and evil-entreaties, and this unto death, doubtless he came not to redeem the elect only, or such who in conclusion repent, believe, and are saved. For some of these, and particularly those that said he had an unclean spirit, were charged by him with that sin which he saith shall not be forgiven, neither in this world nor

71. Leo. Serm. xii. de Passione Domini.   72. Idem, Serm. x. de Passione Domini.
73. Idem, Epist. 72.   74. Fulgent. Ad Thrasimund. l. i. c. 14.   75. Primas. ad Heb. c. 11.

in the world to come. Matt. xii. 32, compared with Mark iii. 28-30. The same author elsewhere saith, that "Christ, as much as lay in him, *died for all men*, however his death profiteth none but only those who are willing to believe in him."[76] And yet again: "The Father, Son, and Holy Ghost is" or are "the God of all men, and therefore desireth that *all that he hath made should be saved.*" A little after, "The blood of Christ hath verily been shed *for all men*, benefiteth them that believe."[77]

Gregory, surnamed the Great, about the year 570, counted it neither heresy nor error to teach the same doctrine. "The Father then," saith he, "being just, and punishing him who was just," meaning Christ, "disposeth all things justly: because upon this account *he justifieth all*," or all things, "because he condemneth him for sinners who was without sin."[78] Elsewhere he termeth Christ "*The Redeemer of mankind*;"[79] and in another place expressly saith that "Christ *redeemed all men* by his cross; but yet that it remaineth, that he that endeavours to be redeemed," *i. e.* to enjoy the redemption purchased for him by Christ, "and to reign with God, be crucified."[80]

Bede, somewhat above a hundred years after Gregory, propagated the same doctrine in the world for truth. "Joseph," saith he, "in the Egyptian language, signifieth Saviour of the world. This is manifest in Christ, since under the figure of Joseph, he is declared to be the Saviour, not of the one only land of Egypt, but also of the *whole world.*" And soon after, "But in our Joseph," meaning Christ, "the *whole world* deserved to receive increase."[81]

Theophylact, who lived more than two hundred years after him, viz. about the year 930, (as some of our best chronologers calculate the time of his mortality) is a sufficient witness that the same doctrine was alive in the church in his time. "He verily," saith he, speaking of Christ, "died for *all men*: and canst not thou endure to pray for them?"[82]

Elsewhere we have words to this effect from his pen: "As by the offence" or fall "of one, the curse came upon all men, (that which before he called judgment," or condemnation, "he now calleth an offence, that is, the sin of Adam) even so by the righteousness of one, Christ, grace is come unto *all men*, giving *unto them* both *justification* instead of sin, *and life* instead of death."[83] In another place he saith, that "the apostle showed how that all men were indeed condemned from" or by "Adam, but were saved" *i.e.* had salvation provided for them "from" or by "Christ."[84]

Œcumenius, somewhat above a hundred years after him, favoured the

76. Idem, ad Heb. c. 2.   77. Idem, in 1 ad Tim. c. 2.   78. Greg. Mag. Moral. 1. iii. c. 11.
79. Idem, Moral. 1. ix. c. 21. Vid. et 1. xxxiii. c. 10.   80. Idem, in 1 Reg. cap. ix. 24.   81. Bed. in Gen. c. xli.
82. Theophylact. in 1. Tim. ii. 6.   83. Idem, ad Rom. v. 18.   84. Idem, ibid, in vers. 20.

same doctrine, as truth. "Judgment," saith he, "*i. e.* condemnation, came from" or by "one Adam, upon all men: but the free gift and donation of God prevailed so far, that it even abolished" or blotted out "the sin of Adam: and not this sin alone, but all others likewise which men sinned after that sin: yea, and did not this only, but also brought them into a state of justification, that is, unto righteousness."[85]

Anselm, not long after the last-mentioned author, appeared in defence of the same doctrine. "He alone," saith he, speaking of Christ, "as by dying paid," or discharged, "so did he blot out" cancel and make void "that hand-writing, which in a kind of hereditary way passed along from our proto-plast," Adam, "through *all generations*."[86] Elsewhere, he exhibiteth God inviting "all men to come unto him, and declaring that *no person* whatso-ever *needs fear a repulse*, since he desireth not the death of a sinner, but that he should live."[87] In another place he saith, that "Christ is become a means of safety, and this not of any inferior kind, but of that which is eter-nal; and this not to a few, but *to all*."[88] And again, that "God the mediator, which God hath placed between himself and men, underwent death for all men, that he might redeem all men from death."[89]

Bernard, somewhat after the year 1100, followed the tract of the same doctrine. In one place he saith, that "Christ wept for the sins of the *sons of Adam*, and afterwards shed his blood for them." In another, having repeat-ed the words of the apostle, "If one died for all, then were all dead," he glosseth thus: "That namely the satisfaction of one might be *imputed unto all*, as this one bare the sins *of all*."[90] Once more, "And that is the profes-sion of a Christian's faith, that he which liveth, should not now live unto himself, but unto him who died *for all*. Nor let any man say unto me, I will live unto him, but not unto thee; since he did not only live unto all men, but even died *for all men* also."[91]

Nor hath the doctrine asserted by us been thus fully and clearly attested only by that successive generation of orthodox and learned antiquity, which we have heard speaking, as it were, with one mouth the same things with us therein, in their particular and respective writings. It hath received credit and countenance, also, from all councils and synods of any ancient date, as far as my reading and memory are able to inform me, which have had occasion to take cognizance thereof, or of that which is contrary to it.

The first general council after the apostle's days, was that assembled at Nice, about the year 325, by the authority of Constantine the Great, in the twentieth year of his reign; a council that hath always been of sovereign

85. Œcum. ad Rom. c. 7.   86. Anselm. in 1 ad Cor. c. 15.   87. Idem, in Medit. de Passione Christi.
88. Idem, ad Heb. v.   89. Idem, 1 ad Tim. c. 2.   90. Idem, Epist. xc. post medium.
91. Idem, Serm. in verba Psal. xxiii. Quis ascendit, &c.

esteem in all Christian churches. This council, in that symbol of faith, or creed, composed by the members of it, make this profession, or confession of their faith, in the point we speak of, "We believe that the Lord Jesus Christ, the Son of God, for *us men*," not for us elect, or for us believers, saints, or the like, but for *us men*, "and for our salvation descended, and was incarnate and made man, suffered, and rose again."[92]

Evident it is, that the council drew up this form, or confession of faith, for the use of the generality of those who professed, or should afterwards profess Christianity, with an intent and desire that every Christian respectively should make the same profession with them. Now, then, if their meaning in the said symbol were, that Christ was incarnate, made man, suffered, &c. only for such persons who were elect, as some call election, such, I mean, who should be actually saved, and not for the generality of men; one of the two must necessarily be supposed: either, 1. That they judged all professors of Christianity to be elect, in this sense, and, consequently, such as should be saved: or else, 2. That they intended that men should make profession of their faith at peradventure, and profess that they believed that, which they knew not whether it was true or no, and so could have no sufficient ground to believe it. Yea, and that many should make such a profession, wherein the event would certainly prove them to have lied both unto God and men when they made it. For certain it is, and demonstrable from the Scriptures, that all that profess Christianity in the world will not at last be saved.

When, therefore, any of these shall profess and say, "I believe that Christ, the Son of God, was made man, and suffered for me," in case he did not suffer for him, which, say our adversaries, the event of his non-salvation will evince, in that profession of his, he must needs be found to have been a liar. Therefore, without controversy, the sense of the Nicene fathers, in the mentioned passage of their creed, was, that Christ became man, and suffered death for all men without exception. Now this Nicene creed, (as is well known to those that are a little versed in ecclesiastical history) was attested and subscribed by the three Œcumenical councils next following; the first at Constantinople, the second at Ephesus, the third at Chalcedon. Nor do I remember that it was ever censured or rejected by any council or synod, esteemed orthodox. I shall not insist upon that epistle of Cyril of Alexandria (an author lately mentioned,) written to Nestorius, the heretic, approved by three general councils: in which epistle Christ is expressly termed the Saviour of us all. Gerardus Johannes Vossius, a late Protestant

92. Symb. Nicen. vid. Athanas. in Epist. ad Jovianum de Fide.

writer of good note, a diligent searcher into, and impartial relater of matters of antiquity, reporteth, that by a synod assembled at Mentz, in the year 848, of which Rabanus Maurus was president, and at which Haymo was present, Goteschalcus the monk was condemned, who, amongst other erroneous opinions held, "That they who perish, although they sometimes believed, and were baptized, yet were not redeemed by Christ, but only sacramentally," or as far as the sign of redemption reacheth, "nor ever separated from the mass of perdition."[93]

The same author addeth further, that soon after this Moguntine Synod, there followed a council of the church of Rhemes, and of many other bishops in France, whereof Hincmarus, a learned man in these times, was president. This council, he saith, approved the judgment of the former, touching their censure of Goteschalcus. Yea, he proceedeth, and saith yet further, that the church of Lyons, although in many things it rather inclined to Goteschalcus than to the two late-mentioned synods, yet in the particular in hand it approved the sentence of the said synods. In a large transcription which he exhibiteth from the acts of this last synod, he citeth words to this effect: "How then when they are baptized in the death of Christ, and are washed from their sins in *his blood*, is that true renovation and true purgation wrought, if they yet remain in the mass of damnation and perdition concrete, and not severed?"[94] He speaketh, as appears all along the discourse, of such persons who finally apostatise and perish. Therefore the clear sense of this council also was, that those who are washed from their sins in the blood of Christ, and consequently who were redeemed by him, may notwithstanding perish.

The same doctrine, as the same author reporteth, was approved and further established by another synod held at Valentia, in France, consisting of the bishops or ministers of the fore-mentioned church of Lyons, and of two other churches; who professed that "They did believe it, as a thing meet to be held with the firmest belief, that as some of those who are truly regenerate and truly redeemed, are eternally saved by means of their continuance, through the grace of God, in their redemption; so that others *of them*, because they would not abide in the safety of that faith which they once received, and chose rather, whether by embracing corrupt doctrine, or by wickedness of life, to reject and *make void the grace of redemption* than to preserve it, are never able to arrive at the fulness of salvation, or to attain eternal happiness."

If my library would hold out, it is like I might be able to produce other

93. Gerar. Joh. Voss. Hist. Pelag. lib. vi. Thesi. 12.
94. Ibid.

councils and synods, besides these insisted upon, interested in the same doctrine which these, as we have heard, avouched for orthodox. But the joint testimony of those which have been produced is, I suppose, matter enough and proper enough to stop the mouth of that, whether ignorant or worse-conditioned calumny, which traduceth the opinion or doctrine of general redemption, as if it were an old rotten popish opinion that had been from time to time rejected and thrown out of the church by all orthodox and sound men. The truth is, I have not in all my reading, which I confess is of no considerable compass for my years, to my best remembrance met with the censure or rejection of the said doctrine in the acts or records of any one council or synod whatsoever, unless, haply, it be in the acts of the nuperous Synod of Dort. For to a man of an erect judgment, and whose spirit hath more of God and of a man in it than to suffer itself to be yoked with prejudice or base partiality, reading and weighing some passages in the records of this synod, it cannot lightly but be a matter of some difficulty, and which will cost him some of his thoughts to resolve himself clearly what the resolutions of this synod were touching the extent of the gracious intentions of God in, or about the redemption purchased by Christ, at least in case these resolutions of theirs be only estimated by their expressions. Do not such sayings as these distinctly sound universal atonement by Christ? "God, commiserating *mankind* being fallen, sent his Son, who gave himself a price of redemption *for the sins of the whole world.*" And a little after:

"Since that price which was *paid for all men*, and which will certainly benefit all that believe unto eternal life, yet doth not profit all men," &c. Again: "So then Christ *died for all men, that all and every man* might, by the mediation of faith, through the virtue of this ransom, obtain forgiveness of sins and eternal life." I know no Remonstrant that holds more or otherwise in the point now under contest. Yet again they say, that "Christ by his death did not only found the evangelical covenant" between God and man, "but also obtained of his Father, that wheresoever this covenant should be preached, there should ordinarily such a measure of grace be administered" or given "with it which is sufficient to convince all impenitents and unbelievers of contempt or neglect, at least, in their non-performance of the condition."[95]

Questionless if men be duly and sufficiently convinced, or be in capacity of this conviction, that negligence is, or was, the only reason or cause why such or such a thing is not, or was not performed by them, it must be

95. Act. Syn. Nation. Dordrect. part. ii., p. 78.

supposed that such men have, or had, sufficient strength or means to have performed it. For if men certainly know that they have not, or had not, a sufficiency of means or strength for the performance of a thing, it is impossible that they should even be convinced that only negligence was the cause of their non-performance of it. The reason is, because a knowledge or persuasion that the performance of a thing is impossible, in respect of a man's weakness, or want of strength to perform it, is a certain cause of his non-attempting it, and consequently of his non-performing it. So that negligence in this case cannot be the only cause of his non-performance; nay, the truth is, that negligence is no cause hereof at all. Suppose a man doth neglect to try or to use means that he may fly like a bird in the air, yet this neglect of his cannot reasonably be looked upon as any cause of his not flying; but his inability to fly, in conjunction with a certain knowledge of such an inability in him, and of the invincibleness hereof, is the adequate and sole cause of his not flying.

The same synod elsewhere by other of its members expresseth itself thus, using the distinction of antecedent and consequent: without the knowledge whereof, the true state of the controversy in hand can hardly be understood. "But when we say," saith the synod, "that Christ died for believers and for his friends, this is to be understood *consequently*, so that the term" *i. e.* the event of his death; for what else they should mean by terminus, I understand not, "is hereby signified; as, on the contrary, he is said to have died *antecedently* for his enemies and unbelievers, (the word "unbelievers" being taken negatively)."[96] What the mystery of their meaning should be in these last words, wherein they restrain their sense in what they had said to a negative unbelief, is above the reach of my understanding. But when they say that Christ died consequently for believers, and antecedently for unbelievers, they speak the whole heart of their adversaries, the Remonstrants, touching the intentions of God in and about the death of Christ, as far as so few words can express it.

For neither do they in any of their writings, that ever came in my way, anywhere affirm or say that Christ died consequently for unbelievers, *i. e.* with any such intention that unbelievers continuing such unto the end should be saved. And for such who, though unbelievers at present, yet shall afterwards repent and believe, these Synodians themselves will not deny but that Christ died consequently. Concerning the distinction of antecedent and consequent, as it relates to the present controversy, we spake formerly, Chap. II, VI. But how that assertion of the men we speak of, wherein

96. Act. Syn. Nation. Dordr. Part. ii. p. 99.

they grant that "Christ died antecedently for his enemies and unbelievers," will find quarter at the hand of their own thesis, soon after subjoined," wherein they say that "Christ died *adequately for* all and *only the elect*," I leave to themselves and their friends to consider.

I speak it with all simplicity of heart, and without the least touch or tincture either of prejudice or partiality (impressions to which I am far from being a debtor for any part of my contentment), that to the best of my memory and understanding, I never met with a piece of discourse from the hand of any judicious or learned man more full of broad and pregnant inconsistencies, than the decisions of this synod in the points cognizanced by them. Only the writings and preachings of men interested in the same principles with them I find deeply baptized into the same spirit of self-digladiation, whereof we shall, God willing, give instances by way of proof, to a sufficient proportion, before the close of this book.

Another member of the said synod, whose sentence and award in the controversies there agitated is, I suppose, synodical, (justified I mean, and approved by the body of the synod; otherwise no man can tell by the printed acts of this synod what the judgment hereof was, but only what was the judgment of the particular members thereof, in petty consorts apart by themselves, and not in conjunction with the entire body) asserteth this position, that "there is a certain common philanthropy" or love of men "in God towards all mankind fallen, and he *seriously willeth*," or hath willed,"*the salvation of all men*."[97] Afterwards, speaking of the condemnation of those who believe not, he saith: "This event is not of itself intended by God, but follows by accident upon the default of man." Afterwards: "If this redemption be not supposed as *a common benefit bestowed on mankind*, that general and promiscuous preaching of the gospel committed unto the apostles to be performed among all nations, will" be found to "have no true foundation."

And again: "How shall any necessity lie upon me to believe that such a benefit belongs unto me, which though sufficient for me, yet was never truly intended for me?" Soon after he saith: "This redemption is the payment of a due" and valuable "price for us captives, not that we should come out of captivity after any manner," *i. e.* simply or absolutely, "but *that we might* and ought to come out of it,"[98] *i. e.* that we might come out upon our believing, as himself immediately explaineth.

It would be easy to produce many other assertions and positions from the Acts of this synod of like sense and import with these, and which are of a

97. Act. Syn. Dordr. par. ii. p. 103.
98. Vid. p. 117.

most notorious comportance with the sense and opinions of those men about the death of Christ, whose opinions, notwithstanding, they stigmatized as heterodox and erroneous, yea, and which stand at utter defiance with their own doctrines and sayings in other places. For if God "seriously willeth the salvation of all men;" if salvation be "a common benefit bestowed by God upon all men, and be truly intended for" or unto "all men;" if God "gave his Son a price of redemption for the sins of the whole world;" (all which, with much more, we have heard and seen delivered and asserted by this synod) how can it be true that "Christ died *adequately for all*, and only for *the elect*;" that Christ was "designed and given by the Father for a Mediator and head to a *certain number of men*;"[99] that the "Father loved only the elect, and gave only these unto his Son to be redeemed by him;"[100] that "the application of the benefits of Christ declares for whom the impetration of them was;"[101] that "God the Father ordained his Son Jesus Christ to be a Redeemer and propitiator for our sins, out of that love wherewith he particularly embraced his elect to eternal life?"[102] with ten times more alike loudly dissonant from those former sayings.

That notion of theirs which they oft repeat is, amongst many others, of very sad resentment, viz. that, "though some men be willing, or should be willing, to believe, or to partake of redemption by Christ, yet God is not willing they should;"[103] whereas the Scripture saith expressly, that "if there be first a willing mind, it is accepted according to that a man hath, and not according to that which he hath not." 2 Cor. viii. 12. That is, when a man is truly willing to do that which God requireth of him, but wanteth either strength, means, or opportunity for the doing of it, and upon this account only doth it not, God doth not reject him, or punish him for not doing the thing, but regards and rewards him for the uprightness of his heart, and the preparedness and readiness of his will to do it, in case means and opportunities were vouchsafed him.

So that, doubtless, if a man be truly willing to be redeemed or saved by Christ, no want of strength, means, or opportunities, in one kind or other, for his salvation, shall hinder him from being saved, because he is in this case accepted (*i. e.* measured and estimated) by God according to the ability vouchsafed unto him, which extended only to the enabling of him to work and bring his heart to a true willingness of being redeemed and saved by Christ, and which he hath with all faithfulness employed and improved accordingly; and not according to any greater or further abilities, which haply are given unto others, but have been denied unto him.

99. Act. Syn. Dordr. p. 100.   100. Ibid. p. 94.   101. Ibid.
102. Ibid. p. 84.   103. Ibid. p. 78, 103.

Now if God measures, judgeth, and esteemeth a man only "according to what he hath," *i. e.* according only to what power, means, or opportunities he hath for the performance of what is righteous and just, in case any man hath gone as far in or towards the performance hereof as such power, means, and opportunities do enable him to go, he must needs find grace and favourable acceptance with God, yea, the same grace and acceptance, proportionably, which he should or could have found with him in case, with more power, means, and opportunities, he had gone further, and done more. And besides, that God should not be willing that a man should be redeemed and saved by Christ, when as the man himself is truly willing in this kind, is a saying of a notorious inconsistency with truth, considering that the willingness of any man in this kind must of necessity proceed from a willingness in God semblable to it. For "it is God that worketh" in men as well "to will" as "to do;" and doubtless he worketh not in any man to will that which is contrary to his own will. But this by the way.

How scant and narrow that covering is which the synod casteth over the nakedness of the pre-mentioned contradictions to hide it from the eyes of men. Likewise, how the reasons and arguments of these inconsiderable and unworthy men professing the knowledge of God and the scriptures compares to the judgements of many during the Reformation will be examined in the following chapter.

CHAPTER IX
Declaring the sense and judgment of modern writers from the Reformation onward; and conclusions on the redemption of Christ for the world

LET us briefly consider what companions and friends we have, even amongst those of the reformed religion and Protestant party of men, in that great article of our faith which we have contended for hitherto, the gracious intentions of God towards all men without exception in the death of Christ and the redemption purchased thereby.

First, concerning those whose judgments and consciences rather consorted with Luther's doctrine than with Calvin's being upon this account distinguished by the name of Lutherans. These (more generally, and almost universally, at least as far as my inspection into their writings informeth me), teach the doctrine of general redemption by Christ as orthodox and sound. I shall only insist upon a few passages from the writings of two or three known authors of the Lutheran persuasion, leading men in their way.

Melancthon, Luther's great associate, teacheth, that "Every person of us apart ought to be firmly resolved of this, that we are pardoned and received by God; and that with this special" or particular "faith *every* particular *man* ought to apply the benefit of Christ to himself."[1] Elsewhere he saith, that the "counsel of God was, that *mankind* should be redeemed; and presently after asserteth the "love of God in his Son *towards mankind.*"[2] In another place he affirmeth that "God poured out his wrath against the *sins of mankind,*" not of a few particular men, "upon his Son." A little after, speaking of Christ, he saith, "He feels a greater burden, viz. the wrath of God against the *sins of mankind,* which he knoweth to be poured out upon him. He sorrowed also," and was troubled, "that a great part of mankind would perish through a contempt of this" great "benefit of God"[3] In another place he saith, "It is necessary to know that the gospel is a *universal promise, i. e.* that reconciliation" with God "is offered and promised to *all men.*" And "it is necessary to hold fast against" any "dangerous conceits about predestination, lest we fall to reason thus, that this promise belongeth to some few

1. Melancth. Loc. de Fide.
2. Idem, de Justificatione.
3. Idem. de Filio.

others, but doth not belong unto us. But let us be resolved of this, that the promise of the gospel is universal. For as the preaching of repentance is universal, so the preaching of remission of sins is universal also. But that all men do not obtain the promises of the gospel," *i. e.* the things here promised, "it ariseth from hence, that all men do not believe."[4] The writings of this author have in them a large and full eye of that doctrine which hath been protected hitherto.

Chemnitius, another learned champion of the Lutheran faith, riseth up in his might, from place to place, to maintain the same doctrine. "The whole transaction," saith he, "of the Mediator is considerable in this, whether" God "the Father be willing to accept that satisfaction and obedience for the *whole world.* Now, this he declared most signally in this, that he left not his Son, whom he smote for the sins of *the people,* in death, but raised him up from the dead, and placed him at the right hand of his Majesty."[5] Elsewhere he saith, "Lest therefore all mankind should perish for ever, that wonderful decree of the counsel of God concerning the incarnation of the Son of God was enacted, that he, being our Mediator in our nature assumed without sin, should be made subject to the law for us, and should bear sin, the guilt of sin, the wrath of God, and the punishments of the sins of the whole world, being derived" or cast "upon him."[6]

Again: "The Father did not pour out part of his wrath or of the curse, but his whole wrath, with all the dregs of the curse, into that cup which he gave unto his Son, the Mediator, to be drunk by him in his sufferings." And presently after: "Christ, upon the cross, being about to commend his spirit unto his Father, saith, 'It is finished;' whereby he testifieth that all those things which were necessary for the expiation of sins, and for redemption from the curse of the law, were fully, sufficiently, and super-abundantly consummated and discharged in" or by "his obedience and sufferings."[7]

And that he doth not speak this with particularity of respect to the sins or redemption of a few, or of the elect only, but simply and with reference to the sins and redemption of all men, appears, 1. From the clear drift and purport of the discourse in hand, which was to prove, against his Tridentine antagonists, that Christ, in and at his death, left nothing unperformed that was necessary or required, viz. by way of satisfaction, of any person whatsoever, for his redemption or for the expiation of his sins. The sense and doctrine of his adversaries being, that indulgencies or satisfactory performances by those yet living, were available, not only for the elect being in purgatory, (for they no where appropriate this element unto them) but for

---

4. Idem, de Prommisione Evangelii.   5. Chemn. Examen. part. i. de Justificatione.
6. Idem, ib. part. ii. de Satisfactione.   7. Idem, ib. part. iv. de Indulgentiis.

any or all without exception, which, according to the notion of their faith, were sent thither for want of a complete satisfaction made for their sins. 2. Soon after, in progress of the same discourse, he citeth this from the apostle, "Unus pro omnibus mortuus est– one died for *all men*," 2 Cor. v. 14; and from another apostle this, "Si quis peccaverit," &c., "If any man sin, we have an advocate with the Father, Jesus Christ the righteous: And he is the propitiation for our sins: and not for ours only, but for the sins of *the whole world*." 1 John ii. 1, 2.

3. There is not the least insinuation in the said passages of any limitation or restriction intended by him to the elect or their sins only. 4. Lastly, the general sense of the latter passages is fairly and fully comportant both with the express tenor of the former, and, indeed, with the judgment of the author in other parts of his writings, where he hath occasion to declare his sense in the point.

Luther himself led them into the way of the same doctrine, though, haply, he did not walk so uniformly or steadily in it as they did. "Christ," saith he, "is slain before," or in the sight of "the world, is condemned, goes down into hell," or into the grave. "But before God he is the salvation of *the whole world*, from the beginning to the end of it."[8] In another place, "The sins of the *whole world*, which are committed from the first man to the last day thereof, lie upon the back of that one man who was born of Mary."[9] Elsewhere, "We all fell in," or by, "the fall of Adam, our first parent, and this fall must be recovered by Christ, viz., by his ignominy, shame, reproach, and death," &c.[10] If Adam's fall, wherein all men without exception fell, be recovered or restored by Christ, all that fell thereby must needs be recovered or restored by him.

If only the elect, so called, be recovered, this is no recovery of Adam's fall, but only of a small or less considerable part of it, or rather of some few persons only who fell thereby. The same author in another place saith that Paul, in his Epistle to the Romans, writes, "That God promised by his prophets in the holy Scripture, the gospel concerning his Son Jesus Christ our Lord, namely, that all men should be saved by him, according to that which was said to Abraham, Gen. xxii. 'In thy seed shall all the nations of the earth be blessed. '" &c. And afterwards, "Christ, from the beginning of the world to the end thereof, remains the same, by whom all men are *together*," or alike "saved."[11] Elsewhere, this author affirms the grace of God to be "toti orbi communis,"[12] "common to the whole world;" and again he affirms that Christ is "Vita et lux omnium hominum," *i. e.* the life and

8. Luther. in Gen. c. 45, ver. 5.   9. Idem, Serm. I. de Passione, &c.   10. Idem. Postill. in Domin. Trinitatis.
11. Idem, Ibid. Prima Dominica in Adventu.   12. In Domin. 3. Advent.

light of all men,[13] to omit many other passages of like import that might readily be drawn together out of the writings of this noble champion of the Protestant faith. So that there is little question but that the Lutheran party of the Reformed religion do more generally, if not wholly and entirely, for I want the opportunity of books to inform me concerning the respective judgments of them all, accord with us in the generality of redemption purchased by Christ.

For the finishing of the chapter in hand, and, upon the matter, of this first part of our discourse, it remaineth only that I desire the impartial reader seriously, and as in the presence of God, to consider whether the testimonies and sayings which shall be presented unto him, in the remaining part of this chapter, out of the writings of Calvin, and some other principal men that are generally looked upon as followers of his doctrine, and, consequently, as adversaries to the great doctrine of universal redemption maintained in this discourse, whether, I say, these testimonies and sayings do not evince above and beyond all contradiction, that these men were not so thorough, uniform, settled, or consistent with themselves in their judgments about the doctrine of redemption as men had need be, whose authority and judgments are commonly taken for the standard of other men's faith, and judged little less than equal to the foundations of the prophets and apostles themselves, in matters of religion. Certain I am that the frequent and notorious inconsistencies that occur in their writings about the great article of the Christian faith, so much argued and debated in our present discourse, have ministered an unhappy advantage to some of our adversaries of the synagogue of Rome, to elevate and expose to contempt the credit, worth, learning, authority, of the principal supporters and defenders of the Protestant religion.[14]

I speak not those things, nor shall I speak any thing, God willing, at any time, to the undervaluing of the learning, parts, labour, faithfulness, signal serviceableness of these men to the Christian churches in their generations. I acknowledge that many of them equalized both in all intellectual and moral accomplishments and endowments, the best of the fathers, so called, of old. The only prize that we run for in the present race is, so far to reduce and temper their esteem and authority with us, that on the one hand, what was worthy, and of God, in them, may turn to a happy account unto us, and bless us. And on the other hand, that what was weak, and of men, in them, may not ensnare us, or balance the spiritual commodity accruing to us from what was honourable and beneficent in them, with loss and disadvantage.

13. Ad summam Missam in Natal. Domin.
14. Vid. Johan. Paul. Windeck. Controvers. de Mortis Christi efficacia, p. 47-49, &c.; and p. 258, 262, 267, &c.

I begin with Calvin himself, and humbly desire those that oppose his judgment and authority to obstruct the course of the doctrine avouched in this discourse, lest it should "run and be glorified" as truth ought to be, to consider whether these passages and sayings next ensuing be with it and for it, or against it. "Although," saith he, "there is nothing to be found in the world worthy the favour of God, yet he showeth himself propitious" or favourable "unto the whole world, in that he calls all men without exception to believe in Christ, which is nothing else but an entrance into life."[15] with more to like purpose transcribed Chap. I, of this discourse. Certainly if God's calling of all men without exception to believe in Christ be a sufficient argument or sign of his propitious and favourable inclination towards them, he must needs really intend the grace or good of salvation unto them; otherwise his calling of them to believe, as, namely, if it should be accompanied with a purpose or intent in him, either simply to destroy them, or to increase their destruction, would rather argue his hatred than any propitiousness of affection towards them. And if God intends the salvation of all men with out exception, certainly he hath provided salvation in Christ for them all. Elsewhere the same author saith, that "Although Christ suffered for the sins of the whole world, and be through the kindness" or good will "of God indifferently offered unto all men, yet all men do not receive" or take hold on "him."[16]

See this, and much more cited from him of like notion, Chap. II. In another place he discourseth thus: "Inasmuch as the utmost end of a blessed life standeth in the knowledge of God, that the entrance" or access "unto blessedness might not be shut up against any man, God hath not only implanted in the minds of men that which we call the seed of religion, but hath also manifested himself in the whole fabric" or workmanship "of the world after such a manner, and offers himself daily so plainly" or openly unto men "that they cannot open their eyes, but they must needs behold him."[17] If God provideth that the passage or way unto happiness may be open for every man, or, which is the same, obstructed or shut up against no man, doubtless there is happiness, and consequently salvation, provided in, or procured by Christ for every man. For there is no way or access for any man unto happiness but by Christ; no, nor yet by Christ himself except only for those whose sins are atoned by him. Of like import with the former is that saying also: "The fuller and more comprehensive sense is this, that God was in Christ; and then, that by his intercession he reconciled the world unto himself."[18] Questionless if an expositor of Scripture meets with

15. Calvin, in Joh. iii. 15, 16.   16. Calvin, ad Rom. v. 18.
17. Idem Institut. I.i. c. 5, section 1.   18. Idem, de 2 ad Cor, v. 19.

a figurative term or expression, I mean so apprehended by him, in the text which is before him, and which he is about to open, it is very improper for him to use the same word in the same figurative or improper sense in his exposition, especially without giving any notice of the figurativeness of it, or substituting a word of a more plain and ready signification for the explaining of it.

Therefore, if Calvin, by the word "world," 2 Cor. v. 19, understood the elect of God only, dispersed up and down the world, he would not in his exposition have used the same word to express them, especially without the help of some other, one or more, of a more plain and known signification in that kind. So that there is not the least question but that he, both in the text mentioned, as likewise in his Commentaries upon it, understood the word "world," in the ordinary and best known signification of it, *i. e.* for the generality or universality of men. Upon the same Scripture afterwards he demands, "For what purpose did God appear unto men in Christ?" He answereth and saith, "For reconciliation, that enmities being taken out of the way, *those that were extranged*" from him "might be adopted for sons." Now they that were estranged from God were not the elect only, but the whole universe of mankind with them. Therefore according to the express import of this piece of commentary, God designed in Christ the adoption of all men without exception for sons.

Nor doth he any whit less than confirm the same doctrine in saying, that "As by the offence of one Adam, judgment or guilt came upon all man to condemnation: so by the righteousness of one Jesus Christ, the gift or benefit of God abounded unto *all men to the justification of life*."[19] He speaketh likewise to the heart of the cause we plead, when he termeth that saying of the apostle, 1 Cor. viii. 11, "A memorable saying, whereby we are taught of how great an account the salvation of the brethren ought to be with us; and not only the salvation of them altogether, but of every one of them apart, inasmuch as the blood of Christ was shed for every one of them."[20] By "brethren," it is evident that he cannot mean only such who are elect, or predestinated unto salvation. 1. Because he speaks of all that profess Christianity, or that are members of any Christian church, amongst whom it is the known judgment of this author that there still are many hypocrites, and such who will not in fine be saved. 2. The elect, in his sense, I mean such who come at last to be actually saved, cannot be certainly known or discerned from others beforehand. Therefore this consideration, that Christ hath shed his blood for a man, can be no argument or motive at all unto me

19. Calvin. ad Rom. v. 18.
20 . Idem, in 1 Cor. viii. 11.

to regard his salvation the more, since it is impossible for me to know whether Christ hath shed his blood for him or no.

His meaning then, when he saith that the blood of Christ was shed for every particular person of the brethren, must needs be that it was shed as well for those who will not be saved by it as for those that will. See before upon this account, Chap. IV. And doth he not yet further plead the cause of the same doctrine with us when he saith, that "Since Christ will have the benefit of his death common unto all men, they do him wrong" or are injurious unto him "who by any opinion of theirs, restrain" or keep back "any man from the hope of salvation?"[21] Take this passage of his also into the account: "This is a marvelous love" of his "towards mankind, that he is willing to have all men saved, yea, and is ready to gather into salvation such as are perishing of their own accord. But the order here is to be observed, viz. that God is ready" or prepared "to receive all men unto" or upon "repentance, lest any man should perish."[22] In the heads of accord between him and the ministers of the Tigurine church, about the Sacrament, he saith, speaking of Christ, that "He is to be considered as a sacrifice of expiation, by which God is appeased" or pacified "towards *the world.*"[23]

In the Geneva Catechism, he teacheth all those that are to be catechised to look upon Christ as "salutem mundi," "the salvation of the world," yea, and to own him and believe in him, "as their surety, who hath undergone that judgment which they deserved, that he might reminder them free from guilt;"[24] with much more of like consideration. So that unless it be supposed, that Christ died for all such persons without exception, who should be persuaded and brought to learn and use this catechism, it will apparently follow, that the composer of it, and all parents and others that shall put their children or other persons upon the learning and pronouncing the words hereof, shall put them upon the speaking and professing those things, and that as matters of their Christian faith, of the truth whereof they have no sufficient ground or assurance; yea, and which are much more likely to be false than true. For if Christ died for the elect only, *i. e.* only for such who in the event will be saved, these being but few, in comparison of those who will perish, evident it is, that, speaking of particular persons before they believe savingly, or to justification, it is more likely they will perish than that they will be saved. Or, however, there is no sufficient ground to judge of them, or of any particular person of them by name, before they believe, that they are elected; or, consequently, that Christ was

21. Idem, in 1 Tim. ii. 5.   22.. Idem, in 2 Pet. iii. 9.
23. Idem, Opusc. p. 872.   24. Calvin. Opusc. p. 19.

their surety, or died to free them from the guilt of sin.

And if so, then they that are taught to say and profess, as an article of their Christian faith, that Christ died to save them, are put upon it, or tempted to profess that, as an article of their religion, which they have no rational or competent ground to believe to be so much as a truth. Yea, the clear truth is, that the opinion, which denieth the redemption of all men, without exception, by Christ, putteth all our ordinary catechisms to rebuke, as being snares and temptations upon all, or the greatest part of those who use them, to pretend a belief or confident persuasion of such a thing, which they have more cause to suspect for an error than to embrace as a truth.

This by the way. If the reader, to those passages lately insisted upon from the undoubted writings of Mr. Calvin, will please to add those other, from the same pen, formerly mentioned, (Chap. I, II and IV) which, though produced, haply, upon somewhat a more particular occasion respectively, yet speak, for substance, the same thing, he will, I presume, acknowledge, that which hath in effect been already said, that Calvin was not so far an enemy to general redemption, but that, without straining either his judgment or conscience, he did upon all occasions reconcile himself unto it, yea, and bottomed many carriages and passages of discourse upon it.

I was desirous to present the reader with the more variety, and greater number of testimonies from Calvin, wherein he plainly asserteth the doctrine of universal atonement, because he is generally notioned as a man clearest and most resolved in his judgment against it. I shall be more sparing in citations of a like import from others, who pass in common discourse as professed enemies, also, against the same doctrine. But whether they be so indeed, methinks these sayings following, with many more of a like inspiration, that might be added unto them, should put to a demurrer. "So God loved the world," &c. "By world," saith Musculus, "he understands universal mankind."[25] In another place: "After the same manner," he saith, "it is in this redemption of mankind, whereof we speak: that reprobates and men deplorably" or desperately "wicked, do not receive it, neither comes to pass through any defect of the grace of God, nor is it meet that for the sons of perdition's sake, that it should lose the glory and title of a universal redemption, inasmuch as it is prepared for all, and all are called unto it."[26]

Elsewhere he saith, "Christ died not for his friends alone, but for his enemies also: *not for some men only, but for all men.* This is the immense latitude" or compass "of the love of God."[27] I know not how a man can express his sense for universal redemption, though he should abound in it

25. Muscu. Loc. de Philanthropia.
26. Idem. Loc. de Redemptione. Gen. Human.
27. Idem, in 2 ad Cor. v. 14, 15.

never so much, in words more significant and distinct. These passages, with many others like unto them, have been formerly cited from this author.

Peter Martyr hath these sayings: "His will was," speaking of God, "that it should be well *with all men,* and that one only should in the mean time suffer."[28] Again, "It was meet that for our redemption some good thing should be offered unto God, which should equally, or rather more, please him, than all the sins of the world had displeased him."[29] In another place, he readily granteth, that God, with that will which is called his "antecedent will, willeth that all man should be saved;"[30] which is the express notion and sense wherein we declared our judgment in the point of universal redemption by Christ, noted in Chap. VI. Elsewhere he produceth this Scripture, "God will have all men to be saved," to prove that God is not the author of sin in the world, and upon this account argueth thus: "If God will have men saved, then he useth good means, and doth not stir them up to sin: for sin brings men to destruction."[31]

If his sense were, that God willeth only that the elect should be saved, then, notwithstanding this argument, God might be the author of all the sins in the world that are committed by far the greatest part of men, viz. by all those that are not elected; which, doubtless, was as far from his mind as it is from truth. For if God's will that men should be saved, be a reason to prove that he inclineth not men unto sin, the probatory force of it in this kind can extend no further, than to such men only whom he willeth should be saved.

Bucer, if there were any agreement between his judgment and his words, was as full and thorough for general redemption as any man. "Whereas," saith he, "the world was lost" or, undone "by one sin of Adam, the grace of Christ did not only abolish this sin, and that death which it brought" upon the world, "but likewise took away *an infinite number of other sins which we the rest of men have added* to that first sin."[32]

Afterwards, "If we consider that every particular man by his transgressions increaseth the misery of mankind, and that whosoever sinneth doth no less hurt his posterity than Adam did all men, it is a plain case, that the *grace of Christ hath removed more evils from men than the sin of Adam brought* upon them: for though there be no sin committed in all the world, which hath not its original from that first sin of Adam, yet all particular men who sin, as they sin voluntarily and freely, so do they make an addition to their own proper guilt and misery: *all which evils* since the alone *benefit of Christ hath taken away*, it must needs be that it hath taken away

28. P. Martyr, Loc. Com. Class. ii. cap. 17, s. 19.   29. Idem, ib.
30. Idem, Loc. Class. iii cap i. s. 45.   31. Loc. Com. Class. i. c. 14. s. 2.
32. Bucer. in Rom. v. 16.

the sins of many, and not of one only. Manifest therefore it is, that more evils have been removed by Christ than were brought in by Adam."[33] And yet further this author saith, "As by the fall of one sin prevailed over all, so as to make all liable unto condemnation: so, likewise, the righteousness of one so far took place on the behalf of all men, that all men may obtain the justification of life hereby."[34]

He that converseth much with the writings of other late Protestant authors, (such I mean to whom the lot is fallen of being esteemed orthodox) shall, upon a little observation, ever and anon find them borrowing this principle of their adversaries, that Christ died for all men, to support and strengthen their buildings, being, indeed, a principle so necessary that in many cases men can make no tolerable work without it. I may, I suppose, without prejudice or loss in the least to the cause we have undertaken, supersede the multiplication of instances from other authors of the same persuasion and repute with those last named, whereby it would appear as clear as the light at noon-day, that there are few of them, if any, but that now and then do homage within their pen to that great and sovereign truth of universal atonement by Christ. I shall therefore conclude with some single testimonies from several men, leaving the reader to pursue his satisfaction concerning the rest by his own reading.

Pareus, writing upon that of the author of Hebrews, "That he through the grace of God should taste of death for every man," saith, that "whereas he saith, 'for every man,' it respecteth the amplification" or extent "of the death of Christ. *He died not for some few; the efficacy*" or virtue "*of it appertains unto all*. Therefore there is life prepared in the death of Christ for all afflicted consciences."[35]

Gualter, preaching upon John iii. 16, and speaking of Christ, saith, that "he being to name those whom God so loved, doth not mention Abraham, Isaac, or Jacob, Moses, David, the prophets, the Virgin Mary, the apostles, or holy martyrs, but *the world, which* our evangelist affirmeth to *lie wholly in wickedness*, and *of which* Christ himself more than once affirmeth *the devil to be prince*."[36]

Hemmingius, in his book of Christian Institution, hath this saying, amongst many others of like import: "There is no reason why any man should think that the Son" of God "was sent into the world that he might" or should "redeem some certain select persons out of mankind, but rather that he should take away *the sins of the whole world*."[37]

Ursine, in his Catechetical Explications, discourseth thus: "As then

---

33. Idem, ad Rom. v. 17.   34. Idem, ad Rom. v. 18.   35. Pareus, ad Heb. ii. 9.
36. Gualter. Hom. xx. in Johan.   37. Hemming. de Institut. Christianâ.

Christ died for all men in respect of the sufficiency of his ransom, in respect of the efficiency of it only for those that believe, so also he was willing to die for *all men in common*, as to the sufficiency of his merit; that is, his will was to merit by his death," and this "most sufficiently," *i. e.* abundantly, "*grace, righteousness, life, for all men*, because he would have nothing wanting in him, or in his merit, that should render wicked men who perish inexcusable."[38] We formerly proved, that if Christ died sufficiently for all men, he died intentionally also for all; upon which account, amongst all our opposers, we found only Piscator and Beza true to their principles, who as well deny that Christ died sufficiently as efficaciously, or intentionally, for all men. (Chap. 1) But if Christ "merited, *i. e.* purchased or procured, "by his death, grace, righteousness, life, most sufficiently for all men," and this so or with such an intent, "that nothing might be wanting in his merit to make those that perish inexcusable," doubtless he merited as much for those who perish as for those that are saved, and consequently died as efficaciously for the one as for the other.

For what did he, or could he, merit more for those who come to be saved than "grace, righteousness, life," and this most sufficiently? Nor could he merit less for those who perish, to make them inexcusable, than such a sufficiency of grace, by the co-operation and assistance whereof they might have believed, as was sufficiently proved in the next preceding chapter.

Aretius, upon ver. 15 of the second chapter to the Hebrews, willeth us to "observe to whom the fruit" or benefit "of the death of Christ belongeth, and in what the deliverance which the apostle speaks of consists. This deliverance," saith he, "appertains unto all that were subject unto bondage in this life. Now we were all thus subject; therefore *the deliverance appertains unto all*. The deliverance is said to be general, or appertaining unto all men, because it *appertains unto all*" or whole "mankind, although all do not acknowledge the benefit, nor receive it with a thankful mind. Thus it comes to pass that the said deliverance comes to be" eventually "efficacious in believers only."[39]

J. Fox, our countryman, in his Meditations upon the Apocalypse, hath this passage, amongst many others of a concurrent sense and notion: "The Lord Christ then came into the world, being sent by his Father. And wherefore was he sent? That he might repair the losses which *nature*," he means the nature of man, "had sustained. For the Lord, seeing the miserable and lost condition of our infirmity, so prone unto evil by arm innate frailty, so loved *the world*, that of his own accord he bestowed his only begotten Son"

---

38. Ursin. Catech. par. ii. quæst. 11.
39. Aretius, ad Heb. ii.

upon it, "who might relieve the frailty" thereof, "change" or turn "death into salvation, pacify the wrath" conceived against it "in heaven," &c.[40]

The condition of the elect, or of believers, was not miserable, or however not the condition of these only. Therefore, this author, in saying that "the Lord so loved the world, that he voluntarily bestowed," &c., could not, by "the world," means such only, elect, or believers, but the generality of mankind, the condition of all which was equally "lost and miserable," and who are frequently signified and expressed by the word "world."

Lavater, preaching with his pen upon the prophet Ezekiel, teacheth the doctrine asserted by us in words to this effect: "Some say, I could willingly die, but that the greatness of my sins maketh me afraid of death. The minds" or consciences of these men "are to be raised with this consolation, that we know that God hath laid our sins upon Christ, so that he hath made satisfaction upon the cross for us all."[41] To a person troubled or dismayed with the fear of death through the greatness of his sins, it is a very faint consolation to understand or consider that God hath laid the sins of some few men upon Christ, or that he hath made satisfaction for the elect, or for those that believe, one main ground of his trouble or fear being whether he be of the number either of the one or the other. Therefore, doubtless, the author's sense in the passage was, that Christ hath made satisfaction upon the cross for all men without exception.

Chamier, as solemnly engaged an adversary against the opinion of general redemption as any, yet so far befriendeth the truth at unawares as to say that "the righteousness of Christ is common for the saving of *all men* unto eternal life."[42]

Mr. Perkins is known to have been also deeply baptized into the same spirit of opposition to us in the present controversy, yet I find these words cited from him, (for I have not, I confess, as yet found them in the tract itself out of which they are cited: "Every person in the church, by virtue of this command of God, 'Believe the gospel,' is bound to believe that he is redeemed by Christ, as well reprobates as elect, though in a different consideration," &c.) These words I so much believe are to be found in this author (though, as I now said, I have not yet met with them here) because I find the same words in effect, and not much differing in form, in other writers, partakers of the same apprehensions with him in the subject-matter in hand. For,

Zanchius expresseth himself to the same point thus: "As *every one* is commanded" by God "to believe, and this with a proper and singular faith,

40. Foxus, in Apoc. c. xiv. p. 538.
41. Lavater. In Ezek. Homil. xviii.
42. Chamier. Panstrat. t. iii. lib. xxi. cap. xxi. sect. 3, page 914.

that Christ died for him, and that his sins are expiated by the death and blood of Christ, that his sins are pardoned for Christ's sake,—that he is justified in" or by "Christ; so he is bound also to be fully persuaded" in himself "that he was long before, as viz. before the foundation of the world, chosen in Christ, and predestinated to the participation of these benefits."[43] Such sayings as these from men who professedly stand declared in their judgments for such a personal and particular redemption which excludeth the far greatest number of men from part or fellowship in it, are unto me, though no hard interpreter either of men's words or actions, of an interpretation of no good accord with the honour of their authors.

Bullinger, in his writings, frequently riseth up in confirmation of what his fellows sometimes affirm in the behalf of the doctrine of our present contest. Amongst other passages of this interest, I read words to this purpose: "It remains then an indubitable truth, that the Lord Christ is a full propitiation, satisfaction, offering and sacrifice for the sins, for the punishment, (I say) and for the fault" or delinquency *"of the whole world."*[44]

J. Jacobus Grynæus numbereth him amongst his "orthodoxgraphers," (*i. e.* his orthodox and sound writers) who reasoned thus against the Pelagian heretics, who denied that Christ died for all men: "If it were so, how could the apostle say, that as in Adam all die, so in Christ *all* shall be made alive?" yea, and saith withal, that "the catholic church utterly detests that opinion which denieth that Christ assumed the nature of man for all men, and that he died for all men."[45]

Dr. John Davenant, an eminent member of the Synod of Dort, instead of an answer to this argument of his adversaries against justification by the imputed righteousness of Christ, saith: "If the righteousness of Christ, which is the general price of the redemption of all men, be imputed to us, then we may truly be called the redeemers or saviours of the world," replieth thus: "The righteousness of Christ then is not imputed" for example "unto Peter, as" or as it is "the general *price of redemption for all men*, but as the price wherewith his soul is redeemed in particular."[46] In which words he plainly enough supposeth the said righteousness of Christ to be a general price for the redemption of all men.

Kimedontius, a great professor of the way and doctrine of Calvin in the present controversies, yet complains of those, as "injurious to him and his party, and no better than false witnesses, who clamour against them as if they denied that Christ died *for all men*, and was not the propitiation for the sins of the whole *world.*"[47]

43. Zanch. de Natura Dei. lib. v. cap. ii. qu. 1. thesi. 1.   44. Bullinger. de Justific. Fidei. Ser. vi.
45. Orthodoxographia, part. ii. p. 1503.   46. Joh. Davenantius, in Prælect. de Justitia Habit. p. 331.
47. Kimedont. Synops. de Redempt.

Because I would not overcharge the reader's patience above measure, I shall omit the Catechisms and Confessions of many Reformed churches, as of the Palatinate, Bern, Basil, Tigurum, Schaffhusen, with divers others, in which there are very plain and pregnant assertions of the doctrine of universal atonement by Christ. I shall conclude the demonstration of what we lately observed, (viz. that the doctrine of general redemption is a principle or notion of that sovereign use and necessity, that the professed enemies thereof cannot forbear it, or make any rational earnings in many their theological discourses without it) with a passage or testimony from no fewer than fifty-two ministers of the city of London, and these non de plebe virûm, which I find in a small pamphlet lately subscribed and published by them, and that for this very end, as themselves profess, to give testimony against errors and heresies.

In this their testimony, bewailing the prevailing of errors and heresies, so by them called, they bemoan the case of many of those, whom yet otherwhile they judge the happiest men in the world (those I mean for whom Christ died), thus: "Thousands and ten thousands of poor souls, which Christ hath ransomed with his blood, shall hereby be betrayed, seduced, and endangered to be undone to all eternity."[48] No sense, rationality, or truth can be made of this saying, but by the mediation of this hypothesis or ground, viz. that such persons who have "been ransomed with the blood of Christ" may be "undone" (*i. e.* perish) for ever. For whatsoever men may be brought into "danger" of suffering, doubtless there is a possibility, at least, that they may suffer, as we have reasoned the case further elsewhere,[49]. In that source also we put to rebuke that distinction of a possibility in respect of second causes, and in respect of the first cause or decree of God, evincing from express grounds of Scripture truth in this assertion, that "there is not the least danger of suffering inconvenience by any such means or causes, how likely or threatening soever, in themselves simply considered, to bring the inconvenience upon us, which we know to be throughly mated and over-balanced by means and causes of a contrary tendency and import."

I here add, that should the meaning of the authors of the said passage be, that those "ransomed with the blood of Christ" are "endangered" in respect of second causes or means only, but are in the meantime perfectly secured by God, or his decree, from suffering the danger, there had been no such cause of taking up that most solemn and pathetic lamentation over them which they do, but rather of rejoicing on their behalf, that being so "ran-

48. A Testimony to the Truth of Jesus Christ, &c. subscribed by fifty-two London ministers, p. 32.
49. Remedy of Unreasonableness, p. 13, 14.

somed," they are in no danger or possibility, through any "betraying" or "seduction" by any error or heresy whatsoever, of losing that grace or blessing of salvation which was purchased by the blood of Christ for them.

I shall not, I trust, need here to reinculcate that which hath been, and this more than once, so plainly expressed formerly, viz. that my intent in citing Calvin, with those other late Protestant writers which we have subjoined in the same suffrage of doctrine unto him, in favour of the doctrine of general redemption, is not to persuade the reader, that the habitual or standing judgment either of him, or of the greater part of the rest, was whole and entire for the said doctrine, or stood in any great propension hereunto, (though this I verily believe concerning sundry of them) much less to imply that they never, in other places of their writings, declared themselves against it. It was only to show, 1. That the truth of this doctrine is so near at hand; and, 2. That the influence of it is so benign and accommodatious unto many other truths and doctrines in Christian religion, that it is a hard matter for those that deal much in these affairs not to assume and assert it ever and anon, and to speak and argue many things upon the account of the authority of it; yea, though "extra casum necessitatis" on the one hand, and "incogitantiæ" on the other hand, they are wont to behold it, as God doth proud men, "afar off."

Let us draw up the sum total of these last two chapters, in a very few words, and so end the issue. First, we have seen the roots of that doctrine held forth in our present discourse, thoroughly watered with the fairest streams of the judgment, learning, approbation, and authority of the primitive times. Secondly, concerning times of a later date, we have found that the judgment and faith of that party of Protestant churches and writers which is known by the name of Lutheran, do more generally, if not universally, accord with the same doctrine. Thirdly, and lastly, that the other party of these churches and writers, viz. those who incline more to the sense and judgment of Calvin in matters of Christian concernment, together with Calvin himself, doth very frequently attest the same doctrine, yea, and cannot well want the service and assistance of it in the managing and carrying on many of their affairs.

The result of all is, that no considering or conscientious person whatsoever hath the least occasion to decline, or keep aloof off in judgment, from the said doctrine for want of company. There has been so great a number, as we have seen, of the best and most desirable, for companions in the way of faith, of those that have dwelt with flesh and blood since the apostles' days, having given the right hand of fellowship unto it in their respective generations.

Though Christ the Lord reigneth, whilst his enemies are yet unsubdued, and not put under his feet, yet he reigneth not so like unto himself, nor with that peaceableness and desirableness of government unto his subjects, as he shall and will reign, at least in the glorious result of his mediation, when all that which in any degree opposeth him in his government shall be wholly taken out of the way, or cause the least disquietment or discontent in all his kingdom. In like manner, though the judgment and conscience of a man may reign with much contentment and satisfaction, in the holding and professing of many a truth, by the demonstrative evidence and strength of such arguments and grounds upon which he clearly seeth it built. However, he may see it also encompassed and assaulted on every side with such objections and difficulties which are not at present subdued under him. Yet kingdom residents cannot be so well apayd, so full of peace and joy, as they may and will be when these objections shall be made to bow down before them and lick the dust at their feet, and all difficulties be perfectly reconciled with that truth which they hold and profess in this kind.

Upon this account, having in the procedure of our discourse settled this great doctrine, that "Christ gave himself a ransom for all men without exception," upon such pillars as scripture, reason, and authority, that no man that shall duly weigh the premises can reasonably question the truth thereof. I judged it necessary, nevertheless (God not laying my intentions in the dust by the hand of death or otherwise), to subjoin the vindication of the said doctrine, from all such objections, exceptions, or encumbrances, wherewith I find it on every side impugned, and the course of it much obstructed in the minds and judgments of some. So that they who are or shall be persuaded of the truth of it, may sit with so much the ease in their judgments, and reign in the happy contemplation and enjoyment of so blessed a truth, with so much the more peace and joy.

328

SCRIPTURE INDEX

Conversion information: i = 1, v = 5, x = 10, l = 50, c = 100

Made in the USA
Columbia, SC
04 March 2024

32669078R00183